Lecture Notes in Computer Sci

Commenced Publication in 1973
Founding and Former Series Editors:
Gerhard Goos, Juris Hartmanis, and Jan van Leeuwen

Klaus Havelund   Manuel Núñez
Grigore Roşu   Burkhart Wolff (Eds.)

Formal Approaches to Software Testing and Runtime Verification

First Combined International Workshops
FATES 2006 and RV 2006
Seattle, WA, USA, August 15-16, 2006
Revised Selected Papers

 Springer

Volume Editors

Klaus Havelund
Jet Propulsion Laboratory
Laboratory for Reliable Software
4800 Oak Grove Drive, M/S 301-285, Pasadena, CA 91109, USA
E-mail: mn@sip.ucm.es

Manuel Núñez
Universidad Complutense de Madrid
C/ Prof. José García Santesmases, s/n.
Dep. Sistemas Informáticos y Computación Facultad de Informática
28040 Madrid, Spain
E-mail: mn@sip.ucm.es

Grigore Roşu
University of Illinois at Urbana-Champaign
Department of Computer Science
201 N. Goodwin, Urbana, IL 61801, USA
E-mail: grosu@cs.uiuc.edu

Burkhart Wolff
Information Security, ETH Zürich
ETH Zentrum, CH-8092 Zürich, Switzerland
E-mail: bwolff@inf.ethz.ch

Library of Congress Control Number: 2006937542

CR Subject Classification (1998): D.2, D.3, F.3, K.6

LNCS Sublibrary: SL 2 – Programming and Software Engineering

ISSN   0302-9743
ISBN-10   3-540-49699-8 Springer Berlin Heidelberg New York
ISBN-13   978-3-540-49699-1 Springer Berlin Heidelberg New York

Springer is a part of Springer Science+Business Media

springer.com

© Springer-Verlag Berlin Heidelberg 2006

Typesetting: Camera-ready by author, data conversion by Scientific Publishing Services, Chennai, India
Printed on acid-free paper   SPIN: 11940197   06/3142   5 4 3 2 1 0

Preface

Software validation is one of the most cost-intensive tasks in modern software production processes. The objective of FATES/RV 2006 was to bring scientists from both academia and industry together to discuss formal approaches to test and analyze programs and monitor and guide their executions. Formal approaches to test may cover techniques from areas like theorem proving, model checking, constraint resolution, static program analysis, abstract interpretation, Markov chains, and various others. Formal approaches to runtime verification use formal techniques to improve traditional ad-hoc monitoring techniques used in testing, debugging, performance monitoring, fault protection, etc.

The FATES/RV 2006 workshop selected 14 high-quality papers out of 31 submissions. Each paper underwent at least three anonymous reviews by either PC members or external reviewers selected by them. In addition to the 14 regular papers, the proceedings contain two papers corresponding to the invited talks by Wolfgang Grieskamp (Microsoft Research, USA) and Oege de Moor (Oxford University, UK).

This was the first time that the two workshops, FATES and RV, were held together. The success of this joint edition shows that the integration of these two communities can be profitable for both of them. Previous editions of these two events were held in the following places: FATES 2001 was held in Aalborg (Denmark) and FATES 2002 in Brno (Czech Republic). In both cases, the workshop was affiliated with CONCUR. FATES 2003 and FATES 2004 were held in Montreal (Canada) and Vienna (Austria), respectively, in affiliation with ASE. FATES 2005 was co-located with CAV in Edinburgh (UK). Since 2003, the FATES workshop proceedings have been published by Springer (LNCS series). In parallel, RV 2001 was held in Paris (France), followed by RV 2002 in Copenhagen (Denmark), and RV 2003 in Boulder (USA). These first three editions were affiliated with CAV. RV 2004 was held in Barcelona (Spain), affiliated with TACAS 2004. Finally RV 2005 was held in Edinburgh (UK), co-located with CAV. All previous editions of RV were published in Elsevier's *Electronic Notes in Theoretical Computer Science*. In addition, selected papers from RV 2001 and RV 2002 were published in Springer's journal *Formal Methods in System Design*, in issues 24(2) (March 2004) and 27(3) (November 2005), respectively.

We would like to express our gratitude to all the authors and invited speakers for their valuable contributions. We would also like to thank all members of the FATES/RV 2006 Program Committee and the additional reviewers for their efforts to accurately review the papers on time. Wolfgang Grieskamp supported the organization of the workshop by providing a PC projector and the printouts of these preliminary proceedings. In addition, Microsoft Research gave financial support for the organization of the workshop. Finally, we would like to thank the local organization of FLoC 2006 for their help.

September 2006   Klaus Havelund
                                                        Manuel Núñez
                                                        Grigore Roşu
                                                        Burkhart Wolff

Table of Contents

Multi-paradigmatic Model-Based Testing

Wolfgang Grieskamp

Microsoft Research, Redmond, WA, USA
wrwg@microsoft.com

Abstract. For half a decade model-based testing has been applied at Microsoft in the internal development process. Though a success story compared to other formal quality assurance approaches like verification, a break-through of the technology on a broader scale is not in sight. What are the obstacles? Some lessons can be learned from the past and will be discussed. An approach to MBT is described which is based on *multi-paradigmatic* modeling, which gives users the freedom to choose among programmatic and diagrammatic notations, as well as state-based and scenario-based (interaction-based) styles, reflecting the different concerns in the process. The diverse model styles can be combined by model composition in order to achieve an integrated and collaborative model-based testing process. The approach is realized in the successor of Microsoft Research's MBT tool Spec Explorer, and has a formal foundation in the framework of action machines.

1 Introduction

Testing is one of the most cost-intensive activities in the industrial software development process. Yet, not only is current testing practice laborious and expensive but often also unsystematic, lacking engineering methodology and discipline, and adequate tool support.

Model-based testing (MBT) is one of the most promising approaches to address these problems. At Microsoft, MBT technology has been applied in the production cycle since 1999 [1,2,3,4,5]. One key for the relative success of MBT at Microsoft is its attraction for a certain class of well-educated, ambitious test engineers, to which it is one way to raise testing to a systematic engineering discipline.

However, at the larger picture, an estimate based on the number of subscriptions to internal mailing lists for MBT would count only about 5-10% of product teams which are using or have tried using MBT for their daily tasks. While these numbers can be considered a success compared to other formal quality assurance approaches like verification, they are certainly not indicating a break-through. So what are the obstacles in applying MBT, and how can a larger group of users be attracted to the technology?

This paper first makes an attempt to answer this question, based on feedback from the user base of the Spec Explorer tool [5], its predecessor AsmL-T [3], and other internal MBT tools at Microsoft. The major issues, apart of the ubiquitous problem in the industry that people do not have enough time to try out new technology and educate themselves, seem to be the steep learning curve for modeling notations together with the lack of state-of-the-art authoring environments, missing support for scenario-based (interaction-based) modeling, thus involving not only the test organization but also other

K. Havelund et al. (Eds.): FATES/RV 2006, LNCS 4262, pp. 1–19, 2006.

stakeholders in the process, poor documentation of the MBT tools, and last but not least technical problems like dealing with state explosion, fine-grained test selection, and integration with test management tools.

The paper then sketches a new model-based testing environment which is currently under development at Microsoft Research and attempts to overcome some of the obstacles. The environment, called "Spec Explorer for Visual Studio" (for short, SE$_{VS}$), tries to address the identified challenges by providing a full integration into the development environment of Visual Studio, using a *multi-paradigmatic* approach to modeling, allowing to describe models on different levels of abstraction, using scenario and state oriented paradigms as well as diagrammatic and programmatic notations, and enabling the combination of those diverse artifacts for a given modeling and testing problem.

SE$_{VS}$ is internally based on the framework of action machines [6,7], which allows for uniform encoding of models which can stem from a variety of notations, and to combine and relate them using various compositions. The action machine framework supports the representation of models with symbolic parts in states and actions, which gives rise to the expressive power of defining partial models on a higher level of abstraction and compose them with lower-level models.

This paper is organized as follows. Sect. 2 describes lessons learned in applying MBT at Microsoft and draws some conclusions. Sect. 3 gives a high-level overview on the approach of the SE$_{VS}$ tool using examples. Sect. 4 gives a summary of the formalization of the underlying concepts, and Sect. 5 concludes.

2   Model-Based Testing in Practice: Lessons Learned

MBT has a long application tradition at Microsoft, and various tools have been and are in use. The first tool, the Test Modeling Toolkit (TMT), was deployed in 1999, and is based on extended finite state machines (EFSM) [1]. Microsoft Research deployed two tools, AsmL-T in 2002 [3] and Spec Explorer in 2004 [5], both using executable specification languages based on the the abstract state machine paradigm (ASM) [8] as the modeling notation. Other internal tools which have not been published are also around. The general mailing alias used for internal discussion of MBT issues at Microsoft currently exceeds 700 members.

All these tools, though quite different in details and expressiveness, share some common principles. Models are described by *guarded-update rules* on a global data state. The rules describe transition between data states and are labeled with *actions* which correspond to invocations of methods in a test harness or in the actual system-under-test (SUT). Rules can be parameterized (and the parameters then usually also occur in the action labels). A user provides value domains for the parameters, using techniques like pairwise combination or partitioning. In the approach as realized by AsmL-T and Spec Explorer, the parameter domains are defined by expressions over the model state, such that for example they can enumerate the dynamically created instances of an object type in the state where the rule is applied.

A very simple example to demonstrate the basic concepts as they appear in Spec Explorer today is considered. The model describes the *publish-subscribe* design pattern which is commonly used in object-oriented software systems. According to this pattern,

```
class Publisher {
    Set<Subscriber> subscribers = Set{};
    [Action(ActionKind.Controllable)]
    Publisher(){}
    [Action(ActionKind.Controllable)]
    void Publish(object data)
    {
        foreach (Subscriber sub
                 in subscribers)
            sub.mbox += Seq{data};
    }
}
```

```
class Subscriber {
    Seq<object> mbox = Seq{};
    [Action(ActionKind.Controllable)]
    Subscriber(Publisher publisher)
    {
        publisher.subscribers += Set{this};
    }
    [Action(ActionKind.Observable)]
    void Handle(object data)
    requires mbox.Count > 0 &&
             mbox.Head.Equals(data);
    {
        mbox = mbox.Tail;
    }
}
```

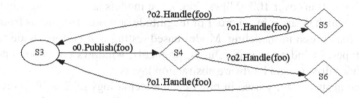

Fig. 1. Publisher-Subscriber Model

various subscriber objects are registered with a publisher object to receive asynchronous notification callbacks when information is published via the publisher object (in fact, the subscribers can dynamically register and unregister at a publisher, but this aspect is simplified here.) Thus this example includes dynamic object creation as well as reactive behavior.

The model is given in Fig. 1 (top). The state of the model consists of publisher and subscriber instances. A publisher has a field containing the set of registered subscribers, and a subscriber has a field representing the sequence of data it has received but not yet handled (its "mailbox"). The model simply describes how data is published by delivering it to the mailboxes of subscribers, and how it is consumed by a subscriber in the order it was published. The precondition of the handling method of the subscriber enables it only if the mailbox is not empty, and if the data parameter equals to the first value in the mailbox. Note that the Handle method is an *observable* action, which comes out as spontaneous output from the system under test (SUT).

Fig 1 (bottom) shows an excerpt from the state graph generated by Spec Explorer from this model. This kind of graph corresponds to an *interface automaton* [9]. In this fragment, one publisher and two subscribers are configured (the state graph omits the configuration phase). From state S3, a Publish invocation is fired, leading to state S4, which is an *observation* state where the outgoing transitions are observable actions. The meaning of an observation state is that the SUT has an internal choice to do *one* of the outgoing transitions, as opposed to a control state (S3) where it must accept *all* of the outgoing transitions. Thus, effectively, the model gives freedom to an implementation to process the subscribers of a publisher in any given order.

In order to generate the state graph, the model was augmented with further information: the parameters passed to the `Publish` method have been specified (here, `"foo"`), the number of publishers and subscribers to be created has been bounded, as well as the number of messages in the mailbox of a subscriber.

Such state graphs are then input to traversal algorithms to generate a test suite which can be executed offline, or are dynamically traversed using online/on-the-fly testing. For both cases, the test execution environment takes care of binding object values in the model to objects in the implementation, as well as queuing asynchronous observable action invocation events in the SUT for consumption by the model. For details, see [5].

In practice, models written with Spec Explorer are significantly larger than this simple example; yet they are rarely on the scale of real programs. In the applications at Microsoft, models typically introduce about 10 to 30 actions, with up to 2000 lines of model code, in exceptions over 10000 lines. Yet, these models are able to test features with a code-base which is larger by an order of magnitude or more. This stems from the level of abstraction chosen in modeling. Model-based testing is used for a wide range of application types, including user interfaces, protocols, windows core components, frameworks, device drivers, and hardware abstraction layers.

While in general successfully used in practice, the technology of Spec Explorer, as well of the other available tools at Microsoft, raises some challenges which hinder wider adoption. These will be discussed in the remainder of this section.

2.1 The Modeling Problem

Authoring. Computer folklore says: "every editor is better than a new editor". Though clearly this statement is sarcastic, one should not underestimate its wisdom. The author of this paper, for example, used to apply the `vi` editor (a great relict of very early Unix times) for his programming over many years, even though on the development platform Visual Studio was available, which provides automatic indentation, incremental compilation, context-sensitive completion, refactoring, and many more nice features.

When initially rolling out one approaches' favorite modeling notation to end users, the gravity of habits is even stronger: users are asked to use a new language in an authoring environment which usually does *not* provide the convenience features they are acquainted with from modern environments.

Notations have perhaps become less important today than the environments which support them. This at least applies to users which are heavily using these modern development environments – among which are most younger testers and developers. It might apply less to other stakeholders (like the author of this text, which is still using a `vi` emulation mode under Emacs to write this document in LaTeX).

The lesson learned is that if one comes up with a new notation, one should better be sure that either the users of that notation do not care about modern authoring support, or one should match this support. The later is unfortunately not trivial. The effort for decent authoring support for a language is probably an order of magnitude higher than providing its compiler.

Executable Specifications vs Programming Languages. The first generation of the Microsoft Research MBT tools was based on the Abstract State Machine Language

(AsmL), a high-level executable specification language, which integrates concepts from functional programming languages and specification languages like Z, B and VDM. Though the basic concepts of this language seem to be simple and intuitive (it uses a "pseudo-code" style notation and avoids any mathematical symbols), apart of some stellar exceptions, for most testers the learning curve was too steep (see [4] for a discussion).

Testers struggled with concepts like universal and existential quantification and set comprehensions. Under the assumption that the problem was not the concept itself but perhaps the unfamiliar way in which it was presented, the next generation, Spec Explorer, offered in addition to AsmL the Spec# notation, which disguised the high-level concepts in C# concrete syntax. Though this approach was more successful, the basic problems remained. Typically, beginners and even intermediate levels in Spec# prefer to write a loop where a comprehension would be much more natural and concise.

This phenomena is not just explained by the inability of users. It is more the *unwillingness* to learn many new concepts at the same time, in particular if they are not obviously coherent. Confronted with a new technology like MBT and the challenges to understand the difference between model and implementation and finding the right abstraction levels, having in *addition* the challenge to learn a new language, is mastered only by a minority.

Some people argue that a high-level notation which differs from the programming notations might support identifying different levels of abstractions, as they are essential for modeling. The AsmL and Spec# experiences do not confirm this, at least in the beginning of the adoption process. Rather, it seems that if the notation is mastered after some time, a misleading conceptualization takes place: abstraction is identified with notation, which after all is only syntactic sugar (in the case of executable specification languages). Someone who already masters the abstraction process will certainly benefit from a more concise way to write things down. But for others, the notation can be just a further roadblock in mastering the technology.

The conceptual distance between programming languages like C# and executable specification languages like Spec# is shrinking steadily. The new forthcoming C# version 3.0 will contain – in addition to the relatively declarative notational features C# has already now – support for comprehension notations (as part of the LINQ project [10]). When new language concepts are build into main-stream programming languages like C# or Java, a campaign is kicked off. Manufactures provide early technology previews, blogs and message boards are filled, books are written or newly edited, and so on. After some time, the concepts which might have appeared strange to the average programmer are familiar to many. Why trying to compete with this?

The lesson learned here is that it appears wiser not to mix evangelizing executable specification languages with the very core of model-based testing concepts. This should not mean that those notations do not have a place in MBT – they are indeed rather important. It just means that users should not be *forced* to use a new notation and environment in order to write their first models. Let them use existing programming notations and their authoring environments if they like. The core of a model-based testing approach and tool should be agnostic about this choice; it should be *multi-paradigmatic*.

Scaling Up to Model-Based Development. One of the promises of MBT is to be an entry door for model-based development. In course of applying MBT at Microsoft, several test teams have attempted to incorporate program managers, domain experts, business analysts, and the like into the modeling process. This has not been very successful so far, though some exceptions exist.

One interesting observation is that executable specification languages like AsmL, which provide a high-level pseudo-code style notation, are more attractive to those stakeholders than programming-oriented notations like Spec#. AsmL had more users authoring system models, compared to just models for test, whereas with the introduction of Spec# and Spec Explorer, these applications diminished. This is a strong argument to *continue* supporting high-level executable specification languages like AsmL for MBT (just do not make them the only choice).

However, it seems that the main obstacle here is not the language but the modeling style. AsmL, Spec#, or any of the other MBT approaches used at Microsoft are not attractive in the requirements phase since they are *state-based* instead of *scenario-based*. In this way they represent a design by itself – even if on an higher-level of abstraction. These high-level designs are well suited for analysis, but less well for understanding and communicating usage scenarios. Thus to incorporate stakeholders from the requirements league, scenario-based modeling must be supported.

Scenarios are also heavily used inside of the test organizations themselves. For example, *test plans* are commonly used at Microsoft to describe (in an informal way) what usage scenarios of a feature should be tested. These test plans, as well as the scenarios coming from the requirements phase, are intrinsically *partial*, omitting a lot of details, in particular oracles, parameter assignments, and so on. It is the job of the test engineers to "implement" these test plans.

The challenge for MBT to scale up to model-based development is the support of both the state-based and the scenario-based paradigm in one approach, where it is possible to *combine* (compose) models coming from those different sources. For example, a scenario might provide the control flow, and a state machine the oracle, and the composition of both produces an instantiated test suite.

How should scenario-based models be written down? In [11], a programmatic approach based on Spec# is suggested. While this approach is useful in some instances, diagrammatic approaches like activity charts or interaction charts look more promising, as far as stakeholders from the requirements phase should be involved. Because of the wealth of literature available, it seems wise to orient toward UML 2.0 when supporting diagrammatic notations, instead of inventing ones own. But again, the choice of the notation should *not* be part of the core of an MBT approach and tool.

Education and Documentation. For more than a decade, proponents of formal methods claim that the major problem in adoption is education. In particular universities are in charge of providing better preparation for those technologies. However, as long as there are no practical applications and tools around, only a minority of students will subscribe to this content.

Until then, the adoption problem must be solved in the field. To that end management support is the essence. At Microsoft, the most successful applications of MBT emerged in areas where the technology was pushed from management level by making time resources available for the adoption phase. This has to go in combination with introduction classes and seminars, and – most important – good documentation and samples. See [4] for a discussion.

2.2 The Technology Problems

State Explosion. MBT is known to easily generate a huge amount of tests from even small models. But this turns out to be more a problem in practice than an advantage, commonly referred to as the "state explosion problem". In fact, this is the main concern mentioned by users of MBT tools at Microsoft.

The state explosion problem has a number of facets. First, the time required to run a test-suite is a significant cost factor. For example, at Microsoft, developers need to run so-called "basic verification tests" (BVT) before they can submit sources to a shared depot. The time required to run the BVT is important for development productivity. If BVTs require hours to finish, developers tend to submit their changes in larger time intervals, which raises problems with the integration of their changes with other developers changes.

This is also a reason why stochastic on-the-fly/online testing is not the solution for the state explosion problem. It is not realistic to run millions of tests "over night" in the standard development process. Indeed, this kind of testing has its proper use in test deployments which run in test labs asynchronously with the development process and in larger time intervals.

Test Selection. The notion of *test selection* is generally used in the MBT community to name the process of selecting some representative set of tests from the model. Thus it should provide the tools to overcome the state explosion problem. Test selection traditionally covers graph traversal techniques which can be applied to models which are boiled down to some finite state machine representation, as well as techniques for generating parameters of tested actions, like pairwise combination, partitioning, and so on. In the context of models which have an unbounded state space, like Spec Explorer models, test selection can also include bounds, filters, state grouping, and other techniques to prune the state space.

While these techniques are mostly automated and well understood, it is a regular complain of MBT users at Microsoft that they have not enough *fine-grained* control over the test selection process. For example, a typical user problem is to choose the set of tests from the model where during some initialization phase an arbitrary path is sufficient, in the operation phase paths should be chosen such that all transitions are covered, and in the shutdown phase again an arbitrary path is good enough. MBT tools need to support this kind of fine-grained control over the test selection process.

Some tools support defining so-called *test purposes* which are combined with the model to slice some desired behavior, using special notations for that [12,13]. Instead of introducing a further notation for describing test purposes, it looks desirable to use models to express test purposes and view the test selection problem with test purposes as a model composition problem. Test purposes then fall together with test plans and requirement scenarios, as discussed previously. Even more than for those applications, models used as test purposes must allow to express partial behavior which omits many details.

Model Analysis. Another facet of the state explosion problem is the understanding of what the model actually does. Since models represent human abstractions they can be error-prone in missing some intended behaviors because of over-abstraction. Therefore, they require "debugging". Debugging a model for MBT effectively means exploring and analyzing the state space it spans, both by humans and automatically.

The Spec Explorer tool invests a great lot of detail to support human analysis by its viewing capabilities, which allow to visualize the state space directly or using projection techniques. These capabilities are one major cornerstone for the success of the tool, and need to be maintained and extended.

The Spec Explorer tool also supports model-checking with safety and liveness properties. However, this support is not very well developed in comparison to decent model-checking tools, and temporal property checking is not available. Model checking is a key feature that makes modeling more attractive for stakeholders outside of the test organization. Consequently, user requests for supporting model-checking in model-based testing tools come from this side.

Test Management. Test automation does not end with the generation of test cases. In particular, if it comes to testing of distributed systems and/or testing of software on heterogeneous hardware, *test management* is a significant effort of the overall process.

At Microsoft, a variety of test management tools are in use which allow distribution of test jobs on matching hardware and execution of orchestrated tests inclusive of logging for collecting the test results. Other tools support measuring coverage of test suites. The integration of this set of tools with model-based testing tools is only marginally developed, and an improvement here is an often requested feature. For example, users want end-to-end tracking of test case execution with the model source, test versioning, automatic bug filing, generation of repros for failed test runs, and so on.

Visual Studio Team Suite 2005 added support for test management, as well as for unit testing. It is desirable to leverage this support for an MBT solution integrated into Visual Studio. However, experiences show that requirements and tools for test management often differ from product unit to product unit. Thus a unified, single solution for test management might not be adequate. Therefore, the best strategy for an MBT tool seems be to have a well-defined abstraction layer over the test management support, which allows deployment of different tools underneath – very similar like development environments do today for source control and versioning. The definition of this layer is an open problem.

3   A Multi-paradigmatic Approach and Tool

Over the past year, Microsoft Research has developed a new tool for modeling and model-based testing, called "Spec Explorer for Visual Studio" (for short SE$_{VS}$), which strikes out to meet some of the challenges learned from the experiences with older tool generations. This tool provides a full integration of model-based testing and model-checking in the Visual Studio environment on base of a *multi-paradigmatic* approach to modeling as motivated in the previous section.

In its intended final stage of expansion, models can be written in SE$_{VS}$ using any .NET language (including AsmL), supporting whatever authoring environment is available for a given language. The tool also provides the use of UML 2.0 behavior diagrams, which are realized using Visual Studio's domain specific language support [14]. Models can be either state-based or scenario-based, in both textual and diagrammatic flavors.

A central feature of SE_{VS} is the ability to compose models stemming from different paradigms. For example, a scenario-based model (given in any notation) can be put in parallel composition with a state-based model (given in any notation), producing the combined behavior of both. As discussed in the previous section, the scenario model could e.g. be a test plan which describes a control flow on a high abstraction level, whereas the state-based model could represent the "implementation" of the omitted details of the test plan (and other test plans in the same domain).

Besides parallel composition, the tool supports various other compositions (for a complete description see [7]). SE_{VS} is based on the semantic and implementation framework of *action machines* [6]. The action machine framework supports the representation of models with symbolic, "omitted" parts in states and actions, which gives rise to the expressive power to define models on a higher level of abstraction and compose them with lower-level models. A synopsis of the formal background of action machines is given in Sect. 4.

This section provides a look-and-feel sample of the usage of SE_{VS}. Namely, it presents the well-known ATM (automatic teller machine) sample to illustrate the combination of different paradigms. The sample uses UML 2.0 activity charts to describe the behavior of the ATM in a scenario-based style. A state-based C# model is used to describe the sub-behavior of the "bank" actor in the overall model, which maintains a data-base of customers and their accounts.

3.1   The ATM Scenario Model

Fig. 2 shows a screen shot of Visual Studio displaying the activity chart for one depicted use case. The model is built from four use cases, which are hierarchicaly organized. The top-level use case "Session" describes an interaction of a customer with the bank via the ATM system, the use case "Transactions" describes an iteration of transactions a customer can perform, and the use cases "Inquiry" and "Withdrawal" describe the individual transaction types.

The activity diagram for the "Transactions" use case describes a loop where the user can enter a transaction type (variable `ttype`), and in dependency of that type the "Withdrawal" or the "Inquiry" use case is invoked, or processing further transactions is canceled.

Such scenario descriptions might result from the requirements phase or from modeling test plans. In course of concretizing them for an analysis or testing problem, the so-far abstract nodes of the activity are mapped to *action patterns*. In the screen shot, the tool tip underneath the activity "Input Transaction Type" shows such a mapping. Namely, this activity is mapped to the action invocation `console.InputTType (ttype)`, where `console` is a variable representing the customer console of the system, which has been declared elsewhere. This mapping has been performed manually based on an underlying object model for the ATM, but it can be also performed automatically by synthesizing actions from the activity node name and the variables in scope.

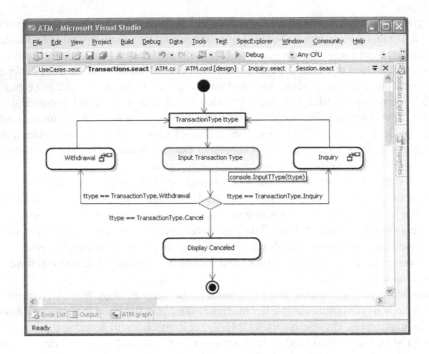

Fig. 2. ATM Use Case Diagram and the "Transactions" Use Case

Variables in activity charts play an important role for the expressiveness of the approach, since they bound inputs and outputs from different activities together. All variables are purely declarative (logical variables). Flows can add constraints over those variables. Variables may be scoped inside iterations, like here the `ttype` variable.

Action patterns might be more complex than just describing action invocations. They impose regular expression constructs plus all the composition operators available in the framework (see [7] for the action pattern language of SE$_{VS}$). The implementation of the activity chart shown in Fig. 2 is actually based on a translation into a single action pattern which looks as follows:

```
([TransactionType ttype]
 ( [. ttype == TransactionType.Withdrawal .] :
   Console.InputTType(ttype); Withdrawal(console,bank,cinfo)
 | [. ttype == TransactionType.Inquiry .] :
   console.InputTType(ttype); Inquiry(console,bank,cinfo)
 )
)*
([TransactionType ttype]
 [. ttype == TransactionType.Cancel .] :
 console.InputTType(ttype); console.DisplayCanceled()
)
```

Here, the notation `[T x]pat` introduces a variable scoped over action pattern `pat`, and `[.exp.]:pat` stands for a constraint expressed by an embedded host language expression `exp` (which can be C#); the other constructs come from regular expressions. The action pattern language is the only "new" language which is introduced by SE$_{VS}$. However, users do not need to know its full range of possibilities to use it.

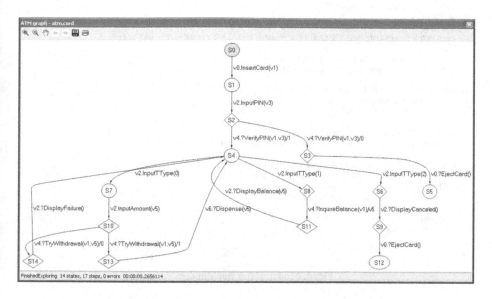

Fig. 3. Exploration Graph Resulting from ATM Model

Given a scenario model as above, users can *explore* it under SE$_{VS}$ to visualize its behavior. Exploration yields in a graph as shown in Fig. 3. This graph is similar to the one shown in Sect. 2 for the old Spec Explorer tool and basically depicts an *interface automaton* [9], where nodes of the graph represent states and transitions action invocations. Round nodes are control points where input is provided to the system and diamond nodes represent observation points where output is observed from the system. Note how variable v5 in the left part of the graph (which represents the amount a user want to withdraw) express causalities which go beyond pure control flow: the same given amount in v2.InputAmount(v5) must also be withdrawn from the bank (v4.?TryWithdrawal(v1,v5)). However, the model has also some partiality: the value of variable v5 is not fixed, and the model does not contain any information when the verification of a pin (state S2) or the withdrawal from the bank (state S10) is actually successful; it only states what the successive behavior is supposed to be in either of that cases.

3.2 Refining the Bank

The behavior generated from the ATM model, as shown in Fig. 3, is partial regarding the behavior of the bank. While such a model can already be used for testing (after providing some additional information for parameter domains and traversals, and then applying test selection), it may miss some important parts: If the bank is "trivial", that is always returns false on pin verification, no interesting tests are performed. Making the bank non-trivial can be either achieved in the manual setup for the test or can be modeled as well.

Fig. 4 gives a state-based model of the bank in C#. The model introduces four actions: In addition to VerifyPIN and TryWithdrawal, which already appeared in

```
class Bank {
  MapContainer<int,int> pins = new MapContainer<int,int>();
  MapContainer<int,int> balances = new MapContainer<int,int>();
  Bank(){
    pins = new MapContainer<int,int>();
    balances = new MapContainer<int,int>();
  }
  void AddCustomer(int id, int pin, int balance){
    Contracts.Requires(!pins.Contains(id));
    pins[id] = pin; balances[id] = balance;
  }
  bool VerifyPIN(int id, int pin){
    return pins.Contains(id) && pins[id] == pin;
  }
  bool TryWithdrawal(int id, int amount){
    Contracts.Requires(balances.Contains(id));
    if (balances[id] >= amount){
      balances[id] -= amount;
      return true;
    } else
      return false;
  }
}
```

Fig. 4. Model of the Bank in C#

the ATM scenario model, a constructor for the bank and an action `SetCustomer` is introduced which allows to add a customer with a given id, pin, and initial balance to the bank. The model uses library support to express pre-conditions (enabling conditions) of actions. `Contracts.Requires(!pins.Contains(id))`, for example, ensures that the action is only enabled if a customer with the given id is not yet added to the bank.

This model could be explored, analyzed and converted to a test suite by itself. Obviously, it would suffer from the problem of state explosion, since its state space is unbounded. In order to test the bank standalone, one could provide a scenario which prunes the behavior. However, the focus here is on combining it with the ATM model given before to not only prune the model, but also yield a composed model which is richer than each individual model.

A small piece of the action pattern language can be used for this purpose (in its intended final stage of expansion, SE$_{VS}$ will provide UI abstractions for defining such compositions). Let `BankModel` describe the model of the bank, and `Session` the model of the ATM, then the composition can be defined as follows:

(**new** `Bank();_.AddCustomer(1,1,10);Session())` |?| `Bank()`

Here a scenario is constructed which creates a new bank, adds one customer, and then runs the `Session` scenario; this scenario is composed in parallel with the bank model itself, where the |?| composition enforces synchronization of actions common to both operands, and allows interleaving of other actions. Note that since there is only one bank object ever created in this construction, an assignment to the bank receiver parameter can be left open, since there are no choices.

Fig. 5 shows the result of exploring the given composition. The parameter for `InputAmount` was fixed to 10 (in practice, one could use a larger domain, but the result would be harder to understand for the purpose of this paper). With an additional balance of 10 and a withdrawal amount of 10, there are two states in the composed

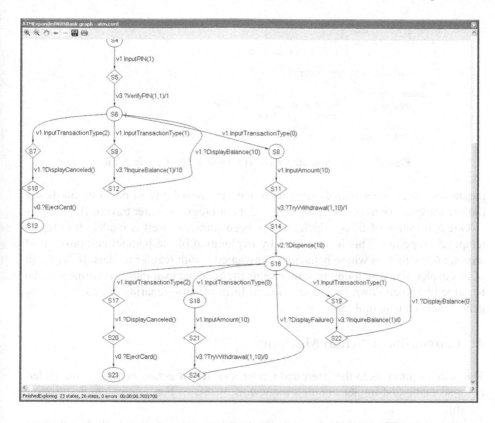

Fig. 5. Exploration Graph Resulting from ATM Model in Composition with Bank Model

model from which the customer can make transactions: in state S6 she has 10 dollars on the account, whereas in state S16, she has zero dollars on the account.

3.3 What Else?

The ATM sample showed only a fragment of the possibilities of the new tool. For example, the ATM scenario model could have been directly given in the action pattern language or defined *programmatically*. Fig. 6 gives an idea on how a programmed scenario looks like in AsmL (C# could have been used here as well). The SE$_{VS}$ implementation allows to create symbolic values in .NET programs. It is able to *abstract* the calls to actions over which a scenario program is defined. In other words, the action InputTType here is not really executed; instead, it will create a state transition in the generated behavior which is labeled with the action and its parameters. If an action is non-void the result will be represented by a free symbolic value.

In its final stage of expansion, SE$_{VS}$ will also allow to represent state-based models using diagrams, namely, by supporting Statecharts.

Other features which have been taken for granted here without deeper explanation are the possibility to explore symbolic state spaces, the traversal techniques and the

```
Transactions()
   var continue = true
   step while continue
      let ttype = Symbolic.Any<TransactionType>()
      step
         console.InputTType(ttype)
      step
         match ttype
            Cancel      : console.DisplayCanceled()
                          continue := false
            Inquiry     : Inquiry()
            Withdrawal  : Withdrawal()
```

Fig. 6. Scenario Program for the Transactions Use Case in AsmL

parameter selection techniques, and, moreover, the possibility to run tests on-the-fly (before traversal) or to persist test suites as data or programs (after traversal).

One application of SE_{VS} which has not been shown as well is model-checking of temporal properties. This is supported by exploration of the parallel composition of *anti-models* – models whose behavior is unwanted – with regular models. If the result of this exploration is non-empty, it represents the "counter examples". Anti-models can be directly written down by a user – in the form of anti-scenarios, for example – or generated from temporal formulas.

4   Foundations: Action Machines

This section provides to the interested reader a sketch of *action machines*, the under-lying semantic and implementation framework of SE_{VS}. For a complete description, see [6].

Action machines combine concepts from abstract state machines, finite automata, and labeled transition systems, and as such they constitute a novel hybrid. Their con-struction is motivated by the practical need to express *data* as well as *control* state, transitions which are labeled with actions, symbolic data and actions, and compositions of behavior, both in parallel and sequential style. In contrast to other approaches com-bining state and control based formalisms, action machines support full sharing of data state in compositions, which is essential for the application in SE_{VS}. The formalization of action machines uses natural semantics [15] and is very close to the actual imple-mentation. The implementation is based on the Exploring Runtime, a software-model checker for .NET [16].

Terms, Constraints, and Actions. An abstract universe of *terms* over a given signa-ture, $t \in \mathbb{T}$, is assumed. Terms capture values in the domain of the modeling and imple-mentation languages, constraints, as well as action labels. Terms also contain (logical) variables, $\mathbb{V} \subseteq \mathbb{T}$.

The class of terms which represent constraints is $\mathbb{C} \subseteq \mathbb{T}$. The actual structure of constraints does not matter. However, it is assumed that $\mathbb{C}$ contains at least the tautology true, equivalences between terms (denoted as $t_1 \equiv t_2$), and is closed under conjunction $(c_1 \wedge c_2)$.

Terms have an interpretation in a mathematical value domain, $\mathbb{D}$, which is described by a function $\xi_{\mathbb{T}} \in (\mathbb{V} \to \mathbb{D}) \times \mathbb{T} \to \mathbb{D}$. Given a value assignment to variable terms, the interpretation function delivers the value of the term in $\mathbb{D}$. For constraint terms, the truth value in the interpretation image is denoted as $\text{true}_\mathbb{D}$.

The further explicit structure of terms does not matter here. However, to aid intuition, and for use in examples, the structure of terms that represent *action labels* is described in an instance of the framework where actions stand for method invocations. $m(t_1, \ldots, t_n)/t$ denotes an action term representing a method invocation, where m is a symbol identifying the invoked method, t_i are input arguments, and t is the returned value. The symbol m behaves for the term language like a free constructor (self-interpreting function). Henceforth, two action labels are equivalent exactly when the action symbols are equal and the input and output terms are equivalent.

During the rest of this section an oracle for renaming of variables in terms is used: $\text{rename}(t)$ denotes the term t after renaming all variables to be distinct from other variables in use.

Environments. An *environment*, $e \in \mathbb{E}$, is a representation of a *(partial) global data state*. Let $\mathbb{L}$ be a countable set of *locations* (global state variables). An environment is syntactically represented by a pair (α, c), where $\alpha \in \mathbb{L} \rightarrowtail \mathbb{T}$ is a partial function from locations to terms, and $c \in \mathbb{C}$ is a constraint. A *model* of an environment is represented by a (total) function $\Gamma \in \mathbb{L} \to \mathbb{D}$; Γ is *valid* for e, denoted as $\Gamma \models e$, as follows:

$$\Gamma \models e \Leftrightarrow \exists v : \mathbb{V} \to \mathbb{D} \mid \xi_\mathbb{T}(v, c_e) = \text{true}_\mathbb{D} \wedge \forall l \in \text{dom}(\alpha_e) \cdot \Gamma(l) = \xi_\mathbb{T}(v, \alpha_e(l))$$

Note that locations not used by the environment can have arbitrary assignments in the model.

The interpretation of an environment is the set of models it has, denoted as $\xi_\mathbb{E}(e) = \{\Gamma \mid \Gamma \models e\}$. Environments are partially ordered by *subsumption* which directly maps to inclusion of environment model sets: $e_1 \sqsupseteq e_2 \Leftrightarrow \xi_\mathbb{E}(e_1) \supseteq \xi_\mathbb{E}(e_2)$. Subsumption $e_1 \sqsupseteq e_2$ indicates that e_1 is more general (contains less information) than e_2. This can be because e_1 fixes less locations than e_2, or because its constraint is weaker. Equivalence on environments, as derived from the subsumption ordering, is denoted as $e_1 \equiv e_2$, and coincides with model set equality.

With the ordering $\sqsubseteq = \sqsupseteq^{-1}$, environments build a *complete lattice* [17] with *meet* (least upper bound) $e_1 \sqcup e_2 = \xi_\mathbb{E}(e_1) \cup \xi_\mathbb{E}(e_2)$, *join* (greatest lower bound) $e_1 \sqcap e_2 = \xi_\mathbb{E}(e_1) \cap \xi_\mathbb{E}(e_2)$, and top and a bottom elements $\top_\mathbb{E}$ and $\bot_\mathbb{E}$, where $\top_\mathbb{E} = \mathbb{L} \to \mathbb{D}$ is the set of all environment interpretations and $\bot_\mathbb{E} = \varnothing$.

In the construction of action machine transitions the transition label is stored in the environment instead of representing it explicitly. This greatly simplifies the formalization of synchronization in composition, which is performed both on target environments and labels. Let $\nu \in \mathbb{L}$ denote a distinguished "scratch" location used for storing an action label. $e[t]$ denotes the environment where the term t is assigned to the location ν, and all other locations are mapped to the assignment in e. Henceforth, $\text{dom}(\alpha_{e[t]}) = \text{dom}(\alpha_e) \cup \{\nu\}$, $\alpha_{e[t]}(\nu) = t$ and $\forall l \in \text{dom}(\alpha_{e[t]}) \cdot l \neq \nu \Rightarrow \alpha_{e[t]}(l) = \alpha_e(l)$.

Computable Operations on Environments. Environment operations like joining are not computable in arbitrary term domains. The range of the computable part depends on the power of the underlying decision procedures (that is, a constraint solver or theorem prover), from which the formalization here intends to abstract.

To this end, is a *computable approximation to joining* is defined. One writes $(e_1 \sqcap_c e_2) \mapsto e_3$ to indicate that a join *may* result in an environment which has models. This operator is a relation on syntactic environment representations and is related to the model semantics as follows: $(e_1 \sqcap_c e_2) \mapsto e_3 \Rightarrow e_1 \sqcap e_2 \equiv e_3$, and $(\neg \exists e_3 \cdot (e_1 \sqcap_c e_2) \mapsto e_3) \Rightarrow e_1 \sqcap e_2 \equiv \bot_{\mathbb{E}}$. The incompleteness of an underlying decision procedure is reflected as follows: If an operational join proceeds, the resulting environment might be infeasible (has no models), but it respects the model semantics. If an operational join does not proceed, then also the model join is empty.

Similarly, a *computable approximation to extending an environment by a constraint* is required. Let c be a constraint. One writes $(e_1 \wedge_c c) \mapsto e_2$ to denote that e_2 is the extension of e_1 by c. The constraint c might share variables with e_1. Extension is explained as follows: let e'_2 be constructed as $(\alpha_{e_1}, [\![c_{e_1} \wedge c]\!])$, then $(e_1 \wedge_c c) \mapsto e_2 \Rightarrow e_2 \equiv e'_2$, and $\neg ((e_1 \wedge_c c) \mapsto e_2) \Rightarrow e'_2 \equiv \bot_{\mathbb{E}}$.

Machines. Let $\mathbb{E}$ denote an environment domain as described above. An action machine is given as a tuple $\mathbb{M} = (C, A, I, T)$. C is a set of so-called *control points*, and $A \subseteq C$ is a set of *accepting control points*. $I \subseteq \mathbb{E} \times \mathbb{E} \times C$ is the *initialization transition relation*, and $T \subseteq \mathbb{E} \times C \times \mathbb{E} \times C$ is the *(regular) transition relation*.

A pair of an environment and a control point is called a *(machine) state* and denoted as $e \cdot c \in \mathbb{E} \times C$. Initialization transitions from I relate an environment with an initial machine state. One writes $e_1 \longrightarrow_{\mathbb{M}} e_2 \cdot c_2$ for initialization transitions. Regular transitions from T lead from states to states; the action label is contained in the special location ν of the target environment. For readability, one writes $e_1 \cdot c_1 \overset{t}{\longrightarrow}_{\mathbb{M}} e_2 \cdot c_2$ for regular transitions, which is syntactic sugar for $(e_1, c_1, e_2[t], c_2) \in T$.

Initialization transitions are allowed to refine the environment, but not to change it. This is imposed by the following property which holds for every action machine $\mathbb{M}$: $\forall (e_1 \longrightarrow_{\mathbb{M}} e_2 \cdot c_2) \in I \cdot e_1 \sqsupseteq e_2$. Such a refinement could be, for example, the allocation of a new location, or the strengthening of the environment constraint.

Instances of Action Machines. Some instances of action machines are defined to illustrate the approach. The *guarded-update* machine shows the principal way how state-based notations, like AsmL or C#, are mapped into action machines. The guarded-update machine, $U_{I,R} = (C, A, I, T)$ is defined by a given initialization transition relation I and a set of rules R, $(t, p, u) \in R$, where $t \in \mathbb{T}$ is an action label term, $p \in \mathbb{C}$ is a constraint, and $u \in \mathbb{E} \to \mathbb{E} \times C$ is an update function which maps a given environment to a new machine state. One has $C = \{\diamond, \circ\}$ and $A = \{\circ\}$, that is the machine has exactly two control states, one of which is accepting and the other is not. The transition relation of the machine is defined by rule $U1$ in Fig. 7.

The *synchronized parallel composition* of two action machines results in a machine that steps both machines simultaneously. A transition is only possible if the action labels and the target environments can be joined. Let $\mathbb{M}_1 \parallel \mathbb{M}_2 = (C, A, I, T)$ denote the parallel machine, where $C = C_{\mathbb{M}_1} \times C_{\mathbb{M}_2}$ and $A = A_{\mathbb{M}_1} \times A_{\mathbb{M}_2}$. Rule $P1$ describes initialization transitions, while rule $P2$ describes regular transitions.

The *sequential composition* of two machines, $\mathbb{M}_1; \mathbb{M}_2 = (C, A, I, T)$, exhibits the behavior of $\mathbb{M}_1$, and when $\mathbb{M}_1$ is at an accepting control point, it also exhibits transitions into $\mathbb{M}_2$. One has $C = C_{\mathbb{M}_1} \uplus C_{\mathbb{M}_2}$ and $A = A_{\mathbb{M}_2}$. The regular transitions of $\mathbb{M}_2$ are

$$U1 \frac{(t_0, p_0, u) \in R \quad (t, p) = \mathrm{rename}(t_0, p_0) \quad (e[t] \wedge_c p) \mapsto e'[t'] \quad e''[t''] \cdot c' = u(e'[t'])}{e \cdot c \xrightarrow{t''}_{U_{I,R}} e'' \cdot c'}$$

$$P1 \frac{e \longrightarrow_{M_1} e_1 \cdot c_1 \quad e \longrightarrow_{M_2} e_2 \cdot c_2 \quad (e_1 \sqcap_c e_2) \mapsto e'}{e \longrightarrow_{M_1 \| M_2} e' \cdot (c_1, c_2)} \qquad P2 \frac{e \cdot c_1 \xrightarrow{t_1}_{M_1} e_1 \cdot c'_1 \quad e \cdot c_2 \xrightarrow{t_2}_{M_2} e_2 \cdot c'_2 \quad (e_1[t_1] \sqcap_c e_2[t_2]) \mapsto e'[t']}{e \cdot (c_1, c_2) \xrightarrow{t'}_{M_1 \| M_2} e' \cdot (c'_1, c'_2)}$$

$$S1 \frac{e \longrightarrow_{M_1} e' \cdot c_1}{e \longrightarrow_{M_1 ; M_2} e' \cdot c_1} \qquad S2 \frac{e \longrightarrow_{M_1} e_1 \cdot c_1 \quad c_1 \in A_{M_1} \quad e_1 \longrightarrow_{M_2} e_2 \cdot c_2}{e \longrightarrow_{M_1 ; M_2} e_2 \cdot c_2}$$

$$S3 \frac{e \cdot c \xrightarrow{t_1}_{M_1} e'_1 \cdot c'_1}{e \cdot c \xrightarrow{t_1}_{M_1 ; M_2} e'_1 \cdot c'_1} \qquad S4 \frac{e \cdot c \xrightarrow{t_1}_{M_1} e'_1 \cdot c'_1 \quad c'_1 \in A_{M_1} \quad e'_1 \longrightarrow_{M_2} e'_2 \cdot c'_2}{e \cdot c \xrightarrow{t_1}_{M_1 ; M_2} e'_2 \cdot c'_2}$$

Fig. 7. Guarded Update, Parallel, and Sequential Composition Rules

contained in T ($T_{M_2} \subseteq T$). Rule $S1$ and rule $S2$ describe initialization transitions of this machine; in the case that an initial control point of M_1 is accepting the machine offers also the initial control points of M_2. Rule $S3$ and $S4$ describe regular transitions; similar as with initialization, if an accepting control point is reached, the transition is duplicated to also reach an initial control point of the second machine. Note that in [6] a slightly more complex definition of sequential composition is provided which avoids duplication of transitions. The definition given here is sufficient for illustration but less practical.

The action machine framework provides many more composition operators, among the most interesting to mention are *alternating simulation*, *hiding*, and *hierarchical composition*. In order to formalize alternating simulation – the used testing conformance notion – in the presence of an incomplete decision procedure, [6] distinguishes between *may* and *must* transitions of action machines. May-transitions have been used in this paper. They represent an *over-approximation* and are thus safe (no false positives) when providing inputs to a system-under-test. However, for checking outputs of a system, must-transitions are required. The details can be found in [6].

Implementation. The implementation of action machines is based on the Exploring Runtime (XRT) [16], a software model-checker and virtual execution framework for .NET which is based on byte code interpretation. XRT provides symbolic state representation and exploration of full .NET code. Action machines are realized as a layer on top of XRT. This layer takes environments as provided by XRT's data state model and adds the constructs of action machines as a set of interfaces. Transition relations are described by lazy enumerations delivered by those interfaces. The interface abstraction is very close to the semantic model.

The action machine coordination language, Cord [7], is a declarative intermediate notation which realizes a textual frontend to action machines. Apart from providing action patterns, as used before in this paper, and composition between machines, it allows the definition of configurations for model-based testing and model-checking problems, like parameter generators, exploration bounds, traversals, and so on.

5 Conclusion

Model-based testing promises a significant contribution in raising software testing to a systematic engineering discipline, and providing an entry door to model-based development. Its application for internal development at Microsoft for half a decade is considered a success, though a break-through of the technology is not in sight. This paper attempted to identify some of the obstacles for wider adoption of MBT at Microsoft, which are typical at least for software development at enterprise level.

The conclusion drawn is that in order to address different concerns both inside the testing organizations as well as in the broader scope of model-based development, a model-based testing tool and approach should be multi-paradigmatic, supporting programmatic and diagrammatic notations, as well as state-based and scenario-based styles. Programmatic notations with decent authoring support should be provided for test engineers, best using mainstream programming languages, whereas diagrammatic, scenario-based notations as well as executable specification languages should be provided for test architects and stakeholders outside of the test organizations. Moreover, model-checking should be seen as an integral part of model-based testing tools. The paper sketched a new tool which is currently in development, "Spec Explorer for Visual Studio", which is designed from these goals, and proves that they are feasible. The semantic foundation of this tool, action machines, has been described as well. Whether the approach of this tool works in practice has to be validated once it has been rolled out to the internal Microsoft user community.

The general message of the paper does not come as a surprise: Multi-paradigmatic approaches are ubiquitous in model-based development, as for example reflected in UML. However, model-based testing requires that there are full programmatic notations, and not only diagrammatic ones, and puts strong demands on the semantic and tool-technical integration of the various behavioral notations, requiring them to be composable for a common testing goal. This demand is indeed also a long term goal for model-based development in general – yet the model-based testing application provides very concrete requirements, the implementation of which promises immediate payoff.

Acknowledgments. Many thanks go to my colleagues Colin Campbell, Yuri Gurevich, Lev Nachmanson, Kael Rowan, Wolfram Schulte, Nikolai Tillmann and Margus Veanes, and the numerous enthusiastic users of MBT at Microsoft which have made this work possible. Special thanks go to Nicolas Kicillof and the reviewers for reading an early draft of this paper.

References

1. Harry Robinson. Finite state model-based testing on a shoestring. In *STARWEST 99*. available online.
2. Wolfgang Grieskamp, Yuri Gurevich, Wolfram Schulte, and Margus Veanes. Generating finite state machines from abstract state machines. In *ISSTA'02*, volume 27 of *Software Engineering Notes*, pages 112–122. ACM, 2002.
3. Mike Barnett, Wolfgang Grieskamp, Lev Nachmanson, Wolfram Schulte, Nikolai Tillmann, and Margus Veanes. Towards a tool environment for model-based testing with AsmL. In Petrenko and Ulrich, editors, *Formal Approaches to Software Testing, FATES 2003*, volume 2931 of *LNCS*, pages 264–280. Springer, 2003.
4. Keith Stobie. Model based testing in practice at microsoft. In *Proceedings of the Workshop on Model Based Testing (MBT 2004)*, volume 111 of *Electronic Notes in Theoretical Computer Science*. Elsevier, 2004.
5. Colin Campbell, Wolfgang Grieskamp, Lev Nachmanson, Wolfram Schulte, Nikolai Tillmann, and Margus Veanes. Model-based testing of object-oriented reactive systems with Spec Explorer. Technical Report MSR-TR-2005-59, Microsoft Research, May 2005. to appear in *Formal Methods and Testing*, LNCS, Springer.
6. Wolfgang Grieskamp, Nicolas Kicillof, and Nikolai Tillmann. Action machines: a framework for encoding and composing partial behaviors. Technical Report MSR-TR-2006-11, Microsoft Research, February 2006. to appear in *International Journal of Software & Knowledge Engineering*.
7. Wolfgang Grieskamp and Nicolas Kicillof. A schema language for coordinating construction and composition of partial behaviors. In *Proceedings of the 28th International Conference on Software Engineering & Co-Located Workshops – 5th International Workshop on Scenarios and State Machines*. ACM, May 2006.
8. Y. Gurevich. Evolving Algebras 1993: Lipari Guide. In E. Börger, editor, *Specification and Validation Methods*, pages 9–36. Oxford University Press, 1995.
9. Luca de Alfaro and Thomas A. Henzinger. Interface automata. In *Proceedings of the 8th European Software Engineering Conference and the 9th ACM SIGSOFT Symposium on the Foundations of Software Engineering (ESEC/FSE)*, pages 109–120. ACM, 2001.
10. Microsoft. The LINQ project. http://msdn.microsoft.com/data/ref/linq, 2006.
11. Wolfgang Grieskamp, Nikolai Tillmann, and Margus Veanes. Instrumenting scenarios in a model-driven development environment. *Information and Software Technology*, 2004.
12. J.C. Fernandez, C. Jard, T. Jéron, and C. Viho. An experiment in automatic generation of test suites for protocols with verification technology. *Science of Computer Programming - Special Issue on COST247, Verification and Validation Methods for Formal Descriptions*, 29(1-2):123–146, 1997.
13. Jan Tretmans and Ed Brinksma. TorX: Automated model based testing. In *1st European Conference on Model Driven Software Engineering*, pages 31–43, Nuremberg, Germany, December 2003.
14. Microsoft. Domain specific language tools. http://msdn.microsoft.com/vstudio/dsltools, 2005.
15. G. Kahn. Natural semantics. In *Symposium on Theoretical Computer Science (STACS'97)*, volume 247 of *Lecture Notes in Computer Science*, 1987.
16. Wolfgang Grieskamp, Nikolai Tillmann, and Wolfram Schulte. XRT - Exploring Runtime for .NET - Architecture and Applications. In *SoftMC 2005: Workshop on Software Model Checking*, Electronic Notes in Theoretical Computer Science, July 2005.
17. B.A. Davey and H.A. Priestly, editors. *Introduction to Lattices and Order*. Cambridge University Press, 1990.

Aspects for Trace Monitoring

Pavel Avgustinov[1], Eric Bodden[2], Elnar Hajiyev[1], Laurie Hendren[2],
Ondřej Lhoták[3], Oege de Moor[1], Neil Ongkingco[1], Damien Sereni[1],
Ganesh Sittampalam[1], Julian Tibble[1], and Mathieu Verbaere[1]

[1] Programming Tools Group, Oxford University, United Kingdom
[2] Sable Research Group, McGill University, Montréal, Canada
[3] Programming Languages Group, University of Waterloo, Waterloo, Canada

Abstract. A *trace monitor* observes the sequence of events in a system, and takes appropriate action when a given pattern occurs in that sequence. Aspect-oriented programming provides a convenient framework for writing such trace monitors.

We provide a brief introduction to aspect-oriented programming in AspectJ. AspectJ only provides support for triggering extra code with single events, and we present a new language feature (named *tracematches*) that allows one to directly express patterns that range over the whole current trace. Implementing this feature efficiently is challenging, and we report on our work towards that goal.

Another drawback of AspectJ is the highly syntactic nature of the event patterns, often requiring the programmer to list all methods that have a certain property, rather than specifying that property itself. We argue that *Datalog* provides an appropriate notation for describing such properties. Furthermore, all of the existing patterns in AspectJ can be reduced to Datalog via simple rewrite rules.

This research is carried out with *abc*, an extensible optimising compiler for AspectJ, which is freely available for download.

1 Introduction

When checking temporal properties at runtime, it is convenient to use a special tool for instrumentation. Ideally we would like to give a clean, declarative specification of the property to be checked, and then leave it to a tool to insert the appropriate instrumentation, possibly applying optimisations to reduce the overheads inherent in checking properties at runtime.

Aspect-oriented programming shares many of these goals, and in fact its stated ambitions are even grander, namely to improve software modularity in general. Briefly, an aspect observes all events (method calls, field sets/gets, exceptions, ...) that occur in a system, and when certain events of interest happen, the aspect runs some extra code of its own. The events of interest are specified by the programmer via special patterns named *pointcuts*; the intercepted events are named *joinpoints*.

In this paper, we aim to assess the suitability of AspectJ (the most popular aspect-oriented programming language) for checking temporal properties. We do this via a familiar example, namely that of checking the safe use of enumerations (no updates to the underlying collection may happen while an enumeration is in progress).

In AspectJ one can specify only patterns that range over individual events, and we present a language extension where patterns can range over the whole computation

K. Havelund et al. (Eds.): FATES/RV 2006, LNCS 4262, pp. 20–39, 2006.

history instead. It is quite hard to implement such a feature efficiently, and we report on the success we have had in approaching the efficiency of hand-coded solutions.

Another difficulty with AspectJ is that the patterns are very syntactic. It is common, for instance, that one needs to intercept calls to 'any methods of a class *C* that may change the state of *C*'. In AspectJ the solution is to list all such methods by name. We propose to use *Datalog* instead to write queries that directly capture the property in question. Datalog is a little more verbose than the pattern language of AspectJ, but we show AspectJ patterns are merely syntactic sugar: they can all be translated into Datalog via a set of simple rewrite rules.

2   Aspect-Oriented Programming

In this section, we present aspect-oriented programming using fail-safe *Enumerations* as a motivating example. In subsequent sections, we will show how the aspect-oriented implementation of this example can be further improved using tracematches and Datalog pointcuts.

The *Enumeration* interface is an older version of the more well-known *Iterator* type: in particular it provides a *nextElement* method, and also *hasMoreElements*. An important difference is that implementations of *Iterator* are expected to be *fail-fast*: if the underlying collection is modified while iteration is in progress (through any method other than *Iterator.remove()*) an exception should be thrown. There is no such expectation for implementations of *Enumeration*.

To illustrate, suppose we have a vector *v* that is accessed by two concurrent threads. Thread 1 creates an enumeration (say *e*) over *v*, and does some enumeration steps. In the meantime, thread 2 modifies *v* by adding an element. When thread 1 does another enumeration step, its result is undefined. This situation is illustrated in Figure 1.

```
THREAD 1:                          THREAD 2:

...
Enumeration e = new MyEnum(v);
...
Elt a = (Elt) e.nextElement();      ...
...                                 v.add(b)
a = (Elt) e.nextElement();          ...
```

Fig. 1. Unsafe use of *Enumeration*

Of course there is an easy way to make implementations of *Enumeration* safe. First, add a *stamp* field of type *long* to both the *Vector* class, and to any class implementing *Enumeration*. One can think of this stamp as a version number: we use it to check whether the current version of a vector is the same as when the enumeration was created. Furthermore, every *Enumeration* should have a *source* field, which records the data source (a *Vector*) being enumerated.

Whenever a new enumeration *e* over a vector *v* is created, we make the following assignments:

```
e.stamp = v.stamp;
e.source = v;
```

The version of a vector *v* changes upon each modification, so whenever a change is made to *v*, we execute

```
v.stamp++;
```

Finally, whenever we do an enumeration step, it is checked that the version numbers are still in synch:

if (e.source != **null** && e.stamp != e.source.stamp)
   throw new ConcurrentModificationException();

We must make the check that the source is not null in case the enumeration *e* is in fact not over a vector, but instead over some other collection type.

2.1 Aspects

Aspect-oriented programming provides us with the means to implement the check outlined above in a nice, modular fashion. Intuitively, an aspect can inject new members into existing classes (the new *stamp* and *source* fields above). An aspect can also intercept events like the creation of an enumeration, and execute some extra code.

In AspectJ, aspects are implemented via a *weaver* that takes the original system and the aspect, and it instruments the original system as described in the aspect. As a consequence, aspects achieve the goal set out at the beginning of this paper: the instrumentation code is neatly separated from the system being observed.

An outline of the aspect for the example of fail-fast enumeration is shown in Figure 2. Note how we introduce the *stamp* field on *Vector* by the declaration on Line 3. It is declared *private* — that means it is visible only from the aspect that introduced it.

Similarly, we introduce the *stamp* and *source* fields on the *Enumeration* interface, along with appropriate accessor methods (Lines 6–12). This has the effect of introducing these new members on every *implementation* of *Enumeration* as well.

This mechanism of introducing new members onto existing classes is an admittedly rather crude form of *open classes*; we shall briefly mention some more disciplined alternatives below.

Now our task is to program the requisite updates to these newly introduced fields. In AspectJ, one does this through so-called *advice* declarations. A piece of advice consists of a pattern (the *pointcut*) describing the event we wish to intercept, some extra code to execute, and an instruction when to execute that code (before or after the event).

Figure 3 shows three pieces of advice. The first piece, on Lines 1-6, intercepts all constructor calls on implementations of the enumeration interface, where the constructor call has the data source *ds* of type *Vector* as its actual argument. We are assuming, therefore, that all enumerations over vectors are created via such constructor calls. As indicated earlier, here we have to set the version number (*stamp*) of the enumeration, as well as its *source* field.

The next piece of advice in Figure 3, on Lines 8-12, intercepts updates to the *Vector* class, and whenever they occur, the version number is incremented. Here we have

```
 1   public aspect SafeEnum {
 2
 3     private long Vector.stamp = 0;
 4
 5   // introduce new members on every implementation of Enumeration
 6     private long Enumeration.stamp;
 7     private void Enumeration.setStamp(long n) { stamp = n; }
 8     private long Enumeration.getStamp() { return stamp; }
 9
10     private Vector Enumeration.source;
11     private void Enumeration.setSource(Vector v) { vector = v;}
12     private Vector Enumeration.getSource() {return vector;}
13
14   // ... intercept creation, update and nextElement ...
15   }
```

Fig. 2. Making *Enumeration* safe

employed a named pointcut *vector_update* to describe all calls to methods that may change the state of *Vector*, and we shall look at its definition shortly.

The final piece of advice in Figure 3 occurs on Lines 14-19. This intercepts calls to *nextElement*, and it checks whether the version number on the enumeration agrees with that on the vector. If they do not coincide, an exception is thrown.

```
 1   synchronized after (Vector ds) returning (Enumeration e) :
 2       call (Enumeration+.new(..)) && args(ds)
 3   {
 4     e.setStamp(ds.stamp);
 5     e.setSource(ds);
 6   }
 7
 8   synchronized after (Vector ds) :
 9       vector_update() && target(ds)
10  {
11     ds.stamp++;
12  }
13
14  synchronized before(Enumeration e) :
15      call (Object Enumeration.nextElement()) && target(e)
16  {
17     if (e.getSource() != null && e.getStamp() != e.getSource().stamp)
18       throw new ConcurrentModificationException();
19  }
```

Fig. 3. Advice for safe enumeration

The final piece of code we must write to complete this aspect is the pointcut for intercepting calls that may change the state of the *Vector* class. The received way of doing that is to carefully examine each method in *Vector*, and list it in the pointcut. The result is shown in Figure 4. Note that to reduce the number of disjucts, we have used wildcards in the name patterns.

```
pointcut vector_update () :
    call  (* Vector.add* (..))  ||
    call  (* Vector. clear ())  ||
    call  (* Vector. insertElementAt (..))  ||
    call  (* Vector.remove* (..))  ||
    call  (* Vector. retainAll (..))  ||
    call  (* Vector. set* (..));
```

Fig. 4. Pointcut for updates on *Vector*

To use the aspect we have just written, one just includes it on the command line of the compiler, and the result is an instrumented version of the original program, now with the ability to catch unsafe uses of enumerations over vectors, whenever they occur.

2.2   Pros and Cons of Aspects

The advantages of using aspects are apparent. It allows easy, flexible instrumentation, while retaining the advantages (in particular good compiler error messages) of a high-level programming language. Experiments show that for the above example, the over-heads introduced by aspects (as compared to making the changes by hand in the original program) are negligible. Finally, AspectJ is a fairly mature programming language, with good tool support, and numerous textbooks for newcomers to get started.

Not all is rosy, however. Our purpose is to check a property of traces – that no updates occur during enumeration – and while that property is *encoded* in the above aspect, it would be much preferable to state the property directly, in an appropriate specification formalism. The compiler should then generate the checking code from the specification. Also the pointcut in Figure 4 leaves much to be desired: for a library class like *Vector* it might be acceptable, but what about a class that might change over time? Whenever a new method is introduced, we have to remember that the pointcut may need to be altered as well. Both of these problems (direct specification of trace properties and semantic pointcuts) will be addressed below.

There are some further disadvantages of aspects that we shall not discuss further, but it is still worthwhile to mention them here. For now, the semantics of aspects remain an area of active research. In particular, a crisp definition of the AspectJ language itself is still lacking. More generally, aspects introduce many problems with modular reasoning about programs, because they can interfere with existing code in unpredictable ways.

Finally, above we have made light of the problem of modifying library classes like *Vector* and *Enumeration*. Without support in the JVM, this is hard to achieve, and if we wish to use a compile-time weaver some trickery is needed to replace every *Vector* in an application by our own subclass *MyVector*. These changes, while somewhat akward, can be concisely expressed in AspectJ as well; a complete version of the above aspect, with these changes incorporated, is available on-line as part of a more general benchmark suite [2].

2.3 Further Reading

The AspectJ language was introduced by Kiczales *et al.* in [55]. It is now widely used in practice, and there is a wealth of textbooks available, for instance [19, 27, 41, 56, 57, 63]. We found especially Laddad's book [57] very helpful, because it discusses a wide variety of applications. It also identifies some common design patterns in aspect-oriented programming.

Method interception as found in aspect-oriented programming has its origins in previous work on meta-programming with objects, in particular [14, 54]. Of course there have been earlier systems that provided similar forms of method interception, for instance the POP-2 language [23] or even Cobol [59]. It was only with the advent of aspects, however, that this language feature was recognised as a structuring mechanism in its own right: before that, it was mostly used for debugging purposes.

The static features of aspects, namely the ability to inject new class members into existing classes also has a long history. Harrison and Ossher coined the term *subject-oriented programming* [48], but arguably their composition mechanisms are much more powerful than those offered by AspectJ, as their open classes can be symmetrically composed. Recent years have seen a lot of research on giving open classes a more disciplined basis, for instance [26]. Nested inheritance [64] and virtual classes [37, 65] have similar goals, while satisfying stronger formal properties.

While AspectJ is presently the most popular aspect-oriented programming language, it is certainly not the only language available. CaesarJ adds dynamic deployment of aspects, creating new instances of aspect classes and attaching them to computations at runtime; it also has a notion of virtual classes instead of AspectJ's member injections [7]. A long list of current aspect-oriented programming systems can be found at [6].

Following closely on the growing popularity of aspect-oriented programming, researchers have started to address the problem of defining its semantics. An early attempt was a definitional interpreter by Wand *et al.* [76]; this offered little help, however, in reasoning about aspect code. More refined models have since been proposed by Walker *et al.* [74], Bruns *et al.* [21], and Aldrich [4]. Aldrich's model is especially attractive because it gives a basis for modular reasoning about aspects. We have ourselves adapted his language design to a full extension of the AspectJ language [66].

Our own interest in AspectJ started with a study of the runtime overheads [36]. At the time, it was believed that such overheads are negligible, but it turns out that certain features (in particular the *cflow* pointcut and *around* advice) can lead to substantial costs at runtime. We therefore decided to implement our own extensible, optimising compiler, named the *AspectBench Compiler*, or *abc* for short [8]. Using its analysis infrastructure, we were able to eliminate most of the overheads we identified earlier [9] (one of the optimisations had been proposed earlier in [70], for a small toy language). *abc* is however not only intended for optimisation; it is also designed as a workbench for experiments in language design. The two major case studies we have undertaken so far are tracematches [5] (discussed in the next section), and open modules [66] (mentioned above). A detailed overview of all the work on *abc* to date, as well as a comparison with the other AspectJ compiler *ajc*, can be found in [10]. *abc* itself can be downloaded from [1].

3   Tracematches

Tracematches are a new feature that we have introduced into AspectJ. As mentioned earlier, normal advice in AspectJ is triggered by single events. Instead, in tracematches one can specify a regular pattern that is matched against the whole computation history so far.

We need to be a bit more precise about the nature of events at this point. In AspectJ, pointcuts intercept composite events like method calls, which have a duration. Instead, when we talk about a trace, we mean the sequence of before/after actions associated with such composite events: these are atomic.

To illustrate, an example tracematch is shown in Figure 5. It is intended to introduce an autosave feature into an existing editor system. A tracematch consists of three parts: the declaration of the symbols (events) of interest (Lines 3 and 4), a regular pattern (Line 6) and a piece of code (Line 8). Here there are two symbols: the end of a *save* operation, and the end of the execution of a command. The pattern specifies five consecutive occurrences of the *action* symbol. Because we have declared an interest in saves as well, that means the pattern only matches if five actions occur, with no intervening saves. When that happens, the extra code is run, and here that is just the *autosave* method.

```
1   tracematch() {
2
3      sym save after :     call ( * Application . save () )  ||  call ( * Application . autosave () );
4      sym action after :   call ( * Command.execute() );
5
6      action  [5]
7
8      { Application . autosave (); }
9   }
```

Fig. 5. An example tracematch

This is an important point: the symbol declarations determine what trace we match against. The original trace is *filtered*, leaving out all events that do not correspond to a declared symbol. The pattern is then matched against all suffixes of the filtered trace, and when it matches, the code in the body of the tracematch is executed. Note that we never filter out the very last event that happened: if we did, one could run the code some time after an actual match occurred, with some irrelevant events in between. This process of filtering and matching is illustrated in Figure 6.

The above tracematch is atypical because it does not bind any variables. Local tracematch variables may be declared in the header, and are bound by the matching process. In Figure 7, we have displayed a tracematch that is equivalent to the aspect for safe enumeration discussed earlier. This tracematch does bind two variables, namely the vector *ds* and the enumeration *e* (Line 1). Here there are three symbols of interest (Lines 3-5): creating an enumeration, doing a next step, and updating the source. We wish to catch unsafe uses of enumerations, and this is expressed by the pattern (Line 7). First we see an enumeration being created, then zero or more 'next' steps, one or more updates and finally an erroneous attempt to continue the enumeration.

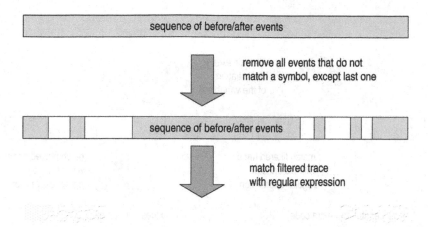

Fig. 6. Filtering of traces (no variables)

```
1   tracematch(Vector ds, Enumeration e) {
2
3       sym create_enum after returning(e) :  call (Enumeration+.new(..))  && args(ds);
4       sym call_next before :  call (Object Enumeration.nextElement())  && target(e);
5       sym update_source after :  vector_update()  && target(ds);
6
7       create_enum   call_next∗   update_source+   call_next
8
9       { throw new ConcurrentModificationException (); }
10
11  }
```

Fig. 7. Tracematch for safe enumeration

It might appear that there is no need to mention the intervening enumeration steps via *call_next* *. However, because of our definition of matching via filtering, that would be wrong. The pattern is matched against all suffixes of the filtered trace, and not to arbitrary subsequences.

The precise meaning of filtering in the presence of local tracematch variables is defined in the obvious manner: instantiate the free variables in all possible ways, and then match as we did before. This process is illustrated in Figure 8. As the figure suggests, if a match occurs with multiple variable bindings, the extra code is run for each of those bindings separately.

While it is nice to understand the semantics of tracematches in terms of all possible instantiations of its free variables, that does not provide a basis for implementation. We therefore also require an operational semantics. It is fairly obvious that this semantics will keep a finite state machine for the pattern. Each state of the machine is labelled with a *constraint* that describes the variable bindings made to arrive at that state. To wit, these constraints are equalities (variable = object), inequalities (variable ≠ object),

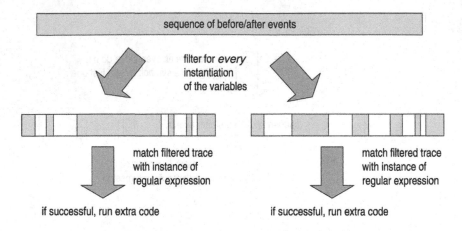

Fig. 8. Filtering of traces (with variables)

or combinations with conjunction and disjunction of these. A detailed definition of the operational semantics can be found in our original paper on tracematches [5].

Unfortunately a direct implementation of the operational semantics does not yield a practical system. The main problem is that of memory leaks, and there are two possible sources of these. First, we may hang on too long to existing objects, merely because they were bound to a tracematch variable. Second, partial matches may stay around forever, despite the fact that they can never be completed. In fact, we keep our constraints in disjunctive normal form, so 'partial matches' correspond to disjuncts in our representation of constraints.

To solve the problem of memory leaks, we have devised a static analysis of the tracematch, which classifies each variable v on each state s in one of three categories:

collectable when all paths in the automaton from s to all final states contain a transition that binds v. In that case we can use weak references for bindings of v. Furthermore, when the garbage collector nullifies that weak reference, we can discard all disjuncts that contain it.

weak not collectable, but the advice body does not mention v. We can still use weak references for bindings of v, but it would be incorrect to discard a disjunct upon nullification.

strong not collectable and not weak. A normal strong reference must be used to store bindings of v.

Note that this is a purely local analysis on the tracematch, involving no analysis of the instrumented system, so that it does not significantly affect compile times.

The technique appears to be highly effective in practice. As an example, we have applied this instrumentation to JHotDraw, the popular open source drawing program. It has a feature for animating a drawing; that in fact introduces an unsafe use of enumerations, because one can edit the drawing while the animation is in progress. The results of measuring memory usage over time are shown in Figure 9. We compared a number of different systems. First, we evaluated our tracematch implementation with leak detection and prevention disabled, using strong references for everything. This line (TMNoLeak) stops after a few steps because execution becomes infeasibly slow. PQL is a runtime trace property checking system created by Monica Lam and her students at Stanford [61]. We tried several version of this benchmark with PQL (PQL and PQL-Neg), and both show linear memory growth over time. Next the figure shows a naive aspect (AjNaive), that instead of using new fields associates time stamps via an identity hash map. The figure also shows a smarter aspect (AjNormal), that uses a weak identity hash map for the same purpose, and finally our optimised implementation of tracematches. The aspect shown at the beginning of this paper also has constant space usage. More details of these experiments can be found in a technical report [11].

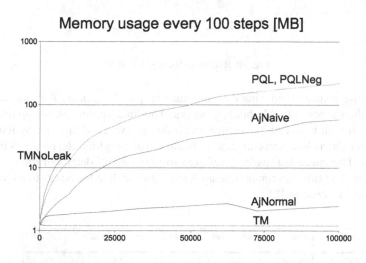

Fig. 9. Memory usage for SAFEENUM (moving average to show trends)

Timewise our implementation is still quite a lot behind the hand-coded aspect at the beginning of this paper. The time taken for 100,000 animation steps is shown in Figure 10. TM indicates our optimised implementation, whereas AjGold is the 'gold standard' aspect shown earlier. We believe that a static analysis of the instrumented program can bring one closer to the gold standard, but for now that remains future work. While this result may appear disappointing, we should mention the instrumented animation is still quite usable on a normal PC.

Figure 11 shows some further substantial applications of tracematches. It would take us too far afield to discuss each of these in detail, but a number of interesting trends can be identified. The first column shows the name of the tracematch being applied, the second the base program being instrumented, and the third column displays the size of that base program. Note that we have used some non-trivial applications. The column marked 'none' shows the execution time, in seconds, of the non-instrumented application. The 'AspectJ' column displays the execution time of a hand-coded version in AspectJ for each benchmark. The final three columns measure our own implementation. 'leak' refers to switching off the above analysis, whereas 'noidx' means that

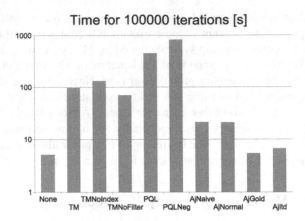

Fig. 10. Runtimes for SAFEENUM

we do not use a special indexing data structure to quickly identify the relevant partial matches when a new variable binding occurs. The final column is our optimised implementation with both leak prevention and indexing switched on. Clearly indexing is just as important as leak prevention, as indicated by the highlighted numbers in the top three rows. The interested reader is referred to [11] for full details of these and other experiments. The full experimental setup is available on-line for others to try with their own monitoring systems [2].

monitor	base	ksloc	none	aspectj	leak	noidx	TM
nulltrack	certrevsim	1.4	0.2	0.5	1.6	25.6	1.6
hashcode	aprove	438.7	345.0	458.9	>90m	>90m	845.1
observer	ajhotdraw	9.9	2.7	2.9	4.1	15.8	4.1
dbpooling	artificial	<0.1	70.0	4.5	5.0	4.8	4.9
luinmeth	jigsaw	100.9	13.6	18.0	21.9	20.9	22.4
lor	jigsaw	100.9	13.6	19.9	34.9	34.7	34.9
reweave	abc	51.2	4.5	5.4	9.1	9.0	8.7

Fig. 11. More tracematch benchmarks

3.1   Summary of Tracematches

The implementation of tracematches is surprisingly tricky to get right. Even ignoring the issue of space leaks, we found several bugs in our first prototype, which only came to light when we tried to prove the equivalence of the declarative and operational semantics. As shown by the above experiments, the implementation has now been thoroughly tested, and it is available in the standard distribution of the *AspectBench Compiler (abc)* for AspectJ.

The key to our efficient implementation consists of two parts: the prevention of memory leaks, and an efficient data structure for retrieving partial matches. Both of these only rely on local analysis of the tracematch itself, not of the instrumented program. We are currently investigating analyses of the instrumented program that may help to approach the efficiency of hand-coded solutions.

3.2 Further Reading

The idea of generating trace monitors from specifications is an old one, and there exists a very large amount of previous research on this topic, *e.g.* [5, 12, 16, 17, 25, 28, 31–35, 38, 40, 50, 61, 71, 72, 75]. These studies range from applications in medical image generation through business rules to theoretical investigations of the underlying calculus. The way the patterns are specified varies, and temporal logic, regular expressions and context-free languages all have been considered.

One theme shines through all of these previous works: trace monitors are an attractive, useful notion, worthy of integration into a mainstream programming language. This has not happened, however, because it turns out to be very difficult to generate efficient code when the trace monitor is phrased as a declarative specification.

Our own contributions have been to provide a solid semantic basis for trace monitors [5] (in particular a proof of equivalence between the declarative and operational semantics), and to devise optimisations that make trace monitors feasible in practice [11].

4   Datalog Pointcuts

We now turn to the way individual events are intercepted in AspectJ. Recall the definition of the *vector_update* pointcut in Figure 4: it was just a list of the relevant methods. It would be much nicer to express the desired semantic property directly, and leave it to the weaver to identify individual methods that satisfy the property.

So in this example, what is the property exactly? We are interested in methods that may change the behaviour of the *nextElement* method on the *Enumeration* interface. Therefore, we seek to identify those methods of *Vector* that write to a memory location that may be read by an implementation of *nextElement*. How do we express that intuition in a formal notation?

The key idea is that the program could be regarded as a relational database. Pointcuts are then just queries over that database, which are used to identify *shadows*. A shadow is a piece of code which at run-time gives rise to an event (a joinpoint) that can be intercepted by AspectJ.

Examples of the relations that make up a program are shown in Figure 12. The first three refer to declarations; the *implements* relation is not transitive. The shadow relations identify calls, method bodies, and field gets. Of course this list is not complete: there are shadows for all kinds of events that can be intercepted in AspectJ. Finally, there is the lexical containment relation *contains*. Again this is not assumed to be transitive.

We now have to decide on the query language for identifying shadows where the aspect weaver will insert some extra code. Many authors have suggested the use of logic

typeDecl (RefType T, String N, Boolean IsIntf, Package P)
  T has name N in package P, IsIntf indicates T interface or not
implements (Class C, Interface I)
  C implements interface I
methodDecl (Method M, String N, RefType C, Type T)
  M has name N, is declared in C, and has return type T
callShadow (Shadow S, Method M, RefType T)
  S is a call to M with static receiver type T
executionShadow (Shadow S, Method M)
  S is the body of M
getShadow (Shadow S, Field F, RefType T)
  S is get of F with static receiver type T
contains (Element P, Element C)
  C is lexically contained in P

Fig. 12. Program relations

programming for this purpose, in particular Prolog. There are numerous problems with that choice, however. First, it is notoriously hard to predict whether a Prolog query terminates. In the present setting, non-terminating queries yield uncompilable programs, which is undesirable. Second, to achieve acceptable efficiency, Prolog programs must be annotated with parameter modes, with the cut operation and with tabling instructions. Again, for this application that would not be acceptable. Yet, the arguments for using logic programming, in particular recursive queries, are quite compelling.

The appropriate choice is therefore 'safe, stratified *Datalog*' [39]. Datalog is similar to Prolog, but it does not allow the use of data structures; consequently its implementation is far simpler. The restriction to safe, stratified Datalog programs guarantees that all queries terminate. Yet, this restricted query language is powerful enough to express the properties we desire.

This is illustrated in Figure 13, which identifies the update methods M of the *Vector* class. It starts by finding the *Vector* class, and some implementation I of *Enumeration*; I contains a method N named *nextElement*. We check whether there exists a field F that may be read by N, while it may be written by M.

It remains to show how predicates like *mayRead(N,F)* can be defined. The key is that N does not need to directly read F; we must also cater for the situation where N calls another method, which in turn reads F. Similarly, the read shadow may not be directly lexically contained in the body of N, but perhaps in a method of a local class defined inside N. The relevant Datalog query is shown in Figure 14: M may transitively contain a shadow G which is a read of the field F.

4.1   An Alternative Surface Syntax

Datalog is powerful, but for really simple pointcuts (like identifying calls to a method with a specific signature) it is verbose and awkward. By contrast, the AspectJ pointcut language shines in such examples, not least because any valid method signature is also a valid AspectJ method pattern. This is one of the reasons newcomers find AspectJ easy to pick up: if you know Java, you know how to express simple pointcuts. Can we give Datalog a similarly attractive syntax?

```
vector_update_method(Method M) :-
    // M is a method in a class V named Vector
    typeDecl(V,'Vector',_,_),
    methodDecl(M,_,V,_,_),

    // N is a method named nextElement in an
    // implementation I of the Enumeration interface
    typeDecl(E,'Enumeration',_,_),
    implements(I,E),
    methodDecl(N,'nextElement',I,_),

    // N may read field F (possibly via a chain of calls)
    mayRead(N,F),

    // M may write field F
    mayWrite(M,F).
```

Fig. 13. Datalog for update methods

```
mayRead(Method M,Field F) :-
    callContains(M,G),
    getShadow(F,G).

callContains(Method M, Shadow G) :-
    mayCall*(M,M'),        // static call chain from M to M'
    executionShadow(E,M'),  // body of M' is E
    contains+(E,G),         // it contains a shadow G

mayCall*(Method X, Method Z) :- X=Z, method(X).
mayCall*(Method X, Method Z) :- mayCall(X,Y),mayCall*(Y,Z).

contains+(Element X, Element Z) :- contains(X,Z).
contains+(Element X, Element Z) :- contains(X,Y),contains+(Y,Z).
```

Fig. 14. Definition of *mayRead*

One might also be concerned about the formal expressive power of Datalog. When it comes to the finer points of AspectJ pointcuts, can they really be expressed as Datalog queries?

The answer to both of these questions is 'yes'. We have constructed a translation from AspectJ pointcuts to Datalog, which consists solely of simple rewrite rules. It is our intention to open up that implementation to advanced users, so they can define new query notations, along with rules for reducing them to Datalog.

Here is an example rule, used in the translation of *call* pointcuts.

$aj2dl$(call(methconstrpat),C,S)
$\rightarrow$
$\exists$ X, R : (*methconstrpat2dl*(methconstrpat,C,R,X), callShadow(S,X,R))

The constructor *aj2dl(PC,C,S)* is used to drive the translation: it takes a pointcut *PC*, the current aspect class *C*, and a shadow *S*. This will be reduced to a Datalog query containing just *C* and *S* as free variables. Our implementation uses *Stratego*, which allows one to record the rewrite rules in concrete syntax, almost exactly as shown above [73].

4.2 Further Reading

Various deficiencies of the AspectJ pointcut language are well-documented in the literature and on mailing lists [13, 18, 22, 49]. Such dissatisfaction has led to several proposals for adopting Prolog as an alternative pointcut language [30, 43, 45]. Indeed, examples of systems that have built on those ideas are Alpha, Aspicere, Carma, Compose*, LogicAJ, Sally, and Soul [3, 15, 20, 42, 44, 47, 69]. However, the complex operational behaviour of Prolog renders it, in our view, too strong for the purpose of a pointcut language. We believe that this is the principal reason that none of these research prototypes has found widespread usage.

The program understanding community has long advocated a view of software systems as a relational database [24, 60]. They also considered new query languages, including Prolog, with [53] being an early example. It was soon realised that at a minimum, the query language must be able to express transitive closure [67]. Jarzabek proposed a language named PQL [52] that added such operators to a variant of SQL (not to be confused with PQL of Lam *et al.*, discussed below). The SQL syntax makes it rather awkward to express graph traversals concisely, however. A modern system that uses a tabled variant of Prolog is JQuery [51, 62].

The program analysis community has also frequently revisited the use of logic programming for specifying analyses. An early example making the connection is a paper by Reps [68]. More recently [29] provided an overview of the advantages of using logic programming to specify complex dataflow analyses. Very recently Martin *et al.* proposed another PQL (not to be confused with Jarzabek's language discussed above), to find bugs in compiled programs [58, 61]. Interestingly, the underlying machinery is that of Datalog, but with a completely different implementation, using BDDs to represent solution sets [77].

All these developments led us to the conclusion that Datalog is an appropriate query language for applications in program understanding, for pointcuts in aspect-oriented programming, and for program analysis. We have implemented the CodeQuest system as a first prototype, and are now working towards its integration into our AspectJ compiler *abc* [46].

5 Conclusion

We have shown how aspects can be used for checking temporal properties at runtime. The design and implementation of new features for such property checking is an interesting new field, requiring the joint efforts of experts in specification formalisms, in aspect-orientation, in program analysis and in compiler construction. We believe we have only scratched the surface, and hopefully this paper will encourage others to join us in our exploration. It would be especially interesting to consider other logics for expressing trace properties. One of us (Bodden) has already implemented a similar system [17, 71] based on LTL in lieu of regular patterns, also on top of *abc*.

It is important that a system for runtime instrumentation allows the programmer to make a judicious choice between static properties and dynamic ones. Our use of Datalog to describe compile-time analysis, for the purpose of identifying instrumentation points, is a step in that direction.

It is unlikely that a perfect specification notation can be found to express all desirable properties. It seems that an extensible syntax, where programmers can introduce new notations that are reduced to existing notions, provides a good compromise.

Acknowledgments. We would like to thank Chris Allan, Aske Simon Christensen, Sascha Kuzins and Jennifer Lhoták for the collaboration that led up to this work. This research has been supported, in part, by EPSRC in the United Kingdom and by NSERC in Canada.

References

1. abc. The AspectBench Compiler. Home page with downloads, FAQ, documentation, support mailing lists, and bug database. http://aspectbench.org.
2. abc team.   Trace monitoring benchmarks.   http://abc.comlab.ox.ac.uk/packages/tmbenches.tar.gz, 2006.
3. Bram Adams. Aspicere. http://users.ugent.be/~badams/aspicere/, 2004.
4. Jonathan Aldrich. Open Modules: modular reasoning about advice. In Andrew P. Black, editor, *Proceedings of ECOOP 2005*, 2005.
5. Chris Allan, Pavel Avgustinov, Aske Simon Christensen, Laurie Hendren, Sascha Kuzins, Ondřej Lhoták, Oege de Moor, Damien Sereni, Ganesh Sittampalam, and Julian Tibble. Adding Trace Matching with Free Variables to AspectJ. In *Object-Oriented Programming, Systems, Languages and Applications*, pages 345–364. ACM Press, 2005.
6. AOSD.NET.   Tools for developers.   http://www.aosd.net/wiki/index.php?title=Tools_for_Developers, 2006.
7. Ivica Aracic, Vaidas Gasiunas, Mira Mezini, and Klaus Ostermann. An overview of AspectJ. In *Transactions on Aspect-Oriented Software Development*, volume 3880 of *Lecture Notes in Computer Science*, pages 135–173. Springer, 2006.
8. Pavel Avgustinov, Aske Simon Christensen, Laurie Hendren, Sascha Kuzins, Jennifer Lhoták, Ondřej Lhoták, Oege de Moor, Damien Sereni, Ganesh Sittampalam, and Julian Tibble. *abc*: An extensible AspectJ compiler. In *Aspect-Oriented Software Development (AOSD)*, pages 87–98. ACM Press, 2005.
9. Pavel Avgustinov, Aske Simon Christensen, Laurie Hendren, Sascha Kuzins, Jennifer Lhoták, Ondřej Lhoták, Oege de Moor, Damien Sereni, Ganesh Sittampalam, and Julian Tibble. Optimising aspectj. In *PLDI '05: Proceedings of the 2005 ACM SIGPLAN conference on Programming language design and implementation*, pages 117–128, New York, NY, USA, 2005. ACM Press.
10. Pavel Avgustinov, Aske Simon Christensen, Laurie Hendren, Sascha Kuzins, Jennifer Lhoták, Ondřej Lhoták, Oege de Moor, Damien Sereni, Ganesh Sittampalam, and Julian Tibble. *abc*: An extensible AspectJ compiler. In *Transactions on Aspect-Oriented Software Development*, volume 3880 of *Lecture Notes in Computer Science*, pages 293–334. Springer, 2006.

11. Pavel Avgustinov, Julian Tibble, Eric Bodden, Laurie Hendren, Ondřej Lhoták, Oege de Moor, Neil Ongkingco, and Ganesh Sittampalam. Efficient Trace Monitoring. Technical Report abc-2006-1, AspectBench Compiler Project, 2006. http://abc.comlab. ox.ac.uk/techreports#abc-2006-1.
12. Howard Barringer, Allen Goldberg, Klaus Havelund, and Koushik Sen. Rule-based runtime verification. In *Fifth International Conference on Verification, Model Checking and Abstract Interpretation (VMCAI 04)*, volume 2937 of *Lecture Notes in Computer Science*, pages 44–57. Springer, 2003.
13. Ohad Barzilay, Yishai A. Feldman, Shmuel Tyszberowicz, and Amiram Yehudai. Call and execution semantics in AspectJ. In *Foundations Of Aspect Languages (FOAL)*, pages 19–24, 2004. Technical report TR #04-04, Department of Computer Science, Iowa State University.
14. Daniel G. Bobrow, Kenneth Kahn, Gregor Kiczales, Larry Masinter, Mark Stefik, and Frank Zdybel. Commonloops: merging common lisp and object-oriented programming. In Norman K. Meyrowitz, editor, *ACM Conference on Object-Oriented Programming Systems, Languages and Applications (OOPSLA)*, volume 791, pages 152–184. ACM Press, 1986.
15. Christoph Bockisch. Alpha. http://www.st.informatik.tu-darmstadt.de/ static/pages/projects/alpha/index.html, 2005.
16. Christoph Bockisch, Mira Mezini, and Klaus Ostermann. Quantifying over dynamic properties of program execution. In *2nd Dynamic Aspects Workshop (DAW05)*, Technical Report 05.01, pages 71–75. Research Institute for Advanced Computer Science, 2005.
17. Eric Bodden. J-LO - A tool for runtime-checking temporal assertions. Master's thesis, RWTH Aachen University, 2005.
18. Ron Bodkin. Pointcuts need a long form. http://dev.eclipse.org/mhonarc/ lists/aspectj-users/msg05971.html, 2006.
19. Oliver Böhm. *Aspectorientierte Programmierung mit AspectJ 5*. Dpunkt.verlag, 2006.
20. Johan Brichau, Kim Mens, and Kris de Volder. SOUL/aop. http://prog.vub.ac.be/ research/aop/soulaop.html, 2002.
21. Glenn Bruns, Radha Jagadeesan, Alan Jeffrey, and James Riely. μABC: a minimal aspect calculus. In *Proceedings of CONCUR 2004*, volume 3170 of *Lecture Notes in Computer Science*, pages 209–224, 2004.
22. Bill Burke. *has* and *hasfield* pointcut expressions. http://aosd.net/pipermail/ discuss_aosd.net/2004-May/000958.html, 2004.
23. Rod M. Burstall and Robin J. Popplestone. POP-2 reference manual. In Bernard Meltzer and Donald Michie, editors, *Machine Intellingence*, volume 5, pages 207–246. Edinburgh University Press, 1968.
24. Yih Chen, Michael Nishimoto, and C. V. Ramamoorthy. The C information abstraction system. *IEEE Transactions on Software Engineering*, 16(3):325–334, 1990.
25. María Augustina Cibrán and Bart Verheecke. Dynamic business rules for web service composition. In *2nd Dynamic Aspects Workshop (DAW05)*, pages 13–18, 2005.
26. Curtis Clifton, Gary T. Leavens, Craig Chambers, and Todd Millstein. Multijava: modular open classes and symmetric multiple dispatch for java. In *OOPSLA '00: Proceedings of the 15th ACM SIGPLAN conference on Object-oriented programming, systems, languages, and applications*, pages 130–145, New York, NY, USA, 2000. ACM Press.
27. Adrian Colyer, Andy Clement, George Harley, and Matthew Webster. *Eclipse AspectJ: Aspect-Oriented Programming with AspectJ and the Eclipse AspectJ development tools*. Addison-Wesley, 2004.
28. Marcelo d'Amorim and Klaus Havelund. Event-based runtime verification of java programs. In *WODA '05: Proceedings of the third international workshop on Dynamic analysis*, pages 1–7. ACM Press, 2005.

29. Stephen Dawson, C. R. Ramakrishnan, and David Scott Warren. Practical program analysis using general purpose logic programming systems. In *ACM Symposium on Programming Language Design and Implementation*, pages 117–126. ACM Press, 1996.
30. Kris de Volder. Aspect-oriented logic meta-programming. In Pierre Cointe, editor, *2nd International Conference on Meta-level Architectures and Reflection*, volume 1616 of *Springer Lecture Notes in Computer Science*, pages 250–272, 1999.
31. Rémi Douence, Pascal Fradet, and Mario Südholt. A framework for the detection and resolution of aspect interactions. In *Proceedings of the ACM SIGPLAN/SIGSOFT Conference on Generative Programming and Component Engineering (GPCE'02)*, pages 173–188, 2002.
32. Rémi Douence, Pascal Fradet, and Mario Südholt. Composition, reuse and interaction analysis of stateful aspects. In Karl Lieberherr, editor, *3rd International Conference on Aspect-oriented Software Development*, pages 141–150, 2004.
33. Rémi Douence, Pascal Fradet, and Mario Südholt. Trace-based aspects. In *Aspect-oriented Software Development*, pages 141–150. Addison-Wesley, 2004.
34. Rémi Douence, Thomas Fritz, Nicolas Loriant, Jean-Marc Menaud, Marc Ségura, and Mario Südholt. An expressive aspect language for system applications with arachne. In *Aspect-Oriented Software Development*, pages 27–38, 2005.
35. Rémi Douence, Olivier Motelet, and Mario Südholt. A formal definition of crosscuts. In Akinori Yonezawa and Satoshi Matsuoka, editors, *Reflection 2001*, volume 2192 of *Lecture Notes in Computer Science*, pages 170–186. Springer, 2001.
36. Bruno Dufour, Christopher Goard, Laurie Hendren, Oege de Moor, Ganesh Sittampalam, and Clark Verbrugge. Measuring the dynamic behaviour of aspectj programs. In *OOPSLA '04: Proceedings of the 19th annual ACM SIGPLAN conference on Object-oriented programming, systems, languages, and applications*, pages 150–169, New York, NY, USA, 2004. ACM Press.
37. Erik Ernst, Klaus Ostermann, and William R. Cook. A virtual class calculus. In *POPL '06: Conference record of the 33rd ACM SIGPLAN-SIGACT symposium on Principles of programming languages*, pages 270–282, New York, NY, USA, 2006. ACM Press.
38. Thomas Fritz, Marc Ségura, Mario Südholt, Egon Wuchner, and Jean-Marc Menaud. An application of dynamic AOP to medical image generation. In *2nd Dynamic Aspects Workshop (DAW05)*, Technical Report 05.01, pages 5–12. Research Institute for Advanced Computer Science, 2005.
39. Hervé Gallaire and Jack Minker. *Logic and Databases*. Plenum Press, New York, 1978.
40. Simon Goldsmith, Robert O'Callahan, and Alex Aiken. Relational queries over program traces. In *Proceedings of the 20th Annual ACM SIGPLAN Conference on Object-Oriented Programming, Systems, Languages and Applications*, pages 385–402, 2005.
41. Joseph D. Gradecki and Nicholas Lesiecki. *Mastering AspectJ: Aspect-Oriented Programming in Java*. Wiley, 2003.
42. Trese group. Compose*. `http://janus.cs.utwente.nl:8000/twiki/bin/view/Composer/`, 2005.
43. Stefan Hanenberg Günter Kniesel, Tobias Rho. Evolvable pattern implementations need generic aspects. In *Proc. of ECOOP 2004 Workshop on Reflection, AOP and Meta-Data for Software Evolution*, pages 116–126. June 2004.
44. Kris Gybels. Carma. `http://prog.vub.ac.be/~kgybels/Research/AOP.html`, 2004.
45. Kris Gybels and Johan Brichau. Arranging language features for more robust pattern-based crosscuts. In *2nd International Conference on Aspect-oriented Software Development*, pages 60–69. ACM Press, 2003.
46. Elnar Hajiyev, Mathieu Verbaere, and Oege de Moor. Codequest: scalable source code queries with Datalog. In Dave Thomas, editor, *Proceedings of ECOOP 2006*, Lecture Notes in Computer Science. Springer, 2006.

47. Stefan Hanenberg and Rainer Unland. Sally. http://dawis.icb.uni-due.de/ ?id=200, 2003.
48. William Harrison and Harold Ossher. Subject-oriented programming (a critique of pure objects). In A. Paepcke, editor, *ACM Conference on Object-Oriented Programming Systems, Languages and Applications (OOPSLA)*, pages 411–428. ACM Press, 1993.
49. Jim Hugunin. Support for modifiers in typepatterns. http://dev.eclipse.org/ mhonarc/lists/aspectj-users/msg01578.html, 2003.
50. Peter Hui and James Riely. Temporal aspects as security automata. In *Foundations of Aspect-Oriented Languages (FOAL 2006), Workshop at AOSD 2006*, Technical Report #06-01, pages 19–28. Iowa State University, 2006.
51. Doug Janzen and Kris de Volder. Navigating and querying code without getting lost. In *2nd International Conference on Aspect-Oriented Software Development*, pages 178–187, 2003.
52. Stan Jarzabek. Design of flexible static program analyzers with PQL. *IEEE Transactions on Software Engineering*, 24(3):197–215, 1998.
53. Shahram Javey, Kin'ichi Mitsui, Hiroaki Nakamura, Tsuyoshi Ohira, Kazu Yasuda, Kazushi Kuse, Tsutomu Kamimura, and Richard Helm. Architecture of the XL C++ browser. In *CASCON '92: Proceedings of the 1992 conference of the Centre for Advanced Studies on Collaborative research*, pages 369–379. IBM Press, 1992.
54. Gregor Kiczales and Jim des Rivieres. *The Art of the Metaobject Protocol*. MIT Press, 1991.
55. Gregor Kiczales, John Lamping, Anurag Menhdekar, Chris Maeda, Cristina Lopes, Jean-Marc Loingtier, and John Irwin. Aspect-oriented programming. In Mehmet Aksit and Satoshi Matsuoka, editors, *European Conference on Object-oriented Programming*, volume 1241 of *Lecture Notes in Computer Science*, pages 220–242. Springer, 1997.
56. Ivan Kiselev. *Aspect-oriented programming with AspectJ*. SAMS, 2002.
57. Ramnivas Laddad. *AspectJ in Action*. Manning, 2003.
58. Monica S. Lam, John Whaley, V. Benjamin Livshits, Michael C. Martin, Dzintars Avots, Michael Carbin, and Christopher Unkel. Context-sensitive program analysis as database queries. In *PODS '05: Proceedings of the twenty-fourth ACM SIGMOD-SIGACT-SIGART symposium on Principles of database systems*, pages 1–12, New York, NY, USA, 2005. ACM Press.
59. Ralf Lämmel and Kris De Schutter. What does aspect-oriented programming mean to Cobol? In *AOSD '05: Proceedings of the 4th international conference on Aspect-oriented software development*, pages 99–110, New York, NY, USA, 2005. ACM Press.
60. Mark A. Linton. Implementing relational views of programs. In Peter B. Henderson, editor, *Software Development Environments (SDE)*, pages 132–140, 1984.
61. Michael Martin, Benjamin Livshits, and Monica S. Lam. Finding application errors using PQL: a program query language. In *Proceedings of the 20th Annual ACM SIGPLAN Conference on Object-Oriented Programming, Systems, Languages and Applications*, pages 365–383, 2005.
62. Edward McCormick and Kris De Volder. JQuery: finding your way through tangled code. In *OOPSLA '04: Companion to the 19th annual ACM SIGPLAN conference on Object-oriented programming systems, languages, and applications*, pages 9–10, New York, NY, USA, 2004. ACM Press.
63. Russell Miles. *AspectJ cookbook*. O'Reilly, 2004.
64. Nathaniel Nystrom, Stephen Chong, and Andrew C. Myers. Scalable extensibility via nested inheritance. In *OOPSLA '04: Proceedings of the 19th annual ACM SIGPLAN conference on Object-oriented programming, systems, languages, and applications*, pages 99–115, New York, NY, USA, 2004. ACM Press.
65. Martin Odersky and Matthias Zenger. Scalable component abstractions. In *OOPSLA '05: Proceedings of the 20th annual ACM SIGPLAN conference on Object oriented programming, systems, languages, and applications*, pages 41–57, New York, NY, USA, 2005. ACM Press.

66. Neil Ongkingco, Pavel Avgustinov, Julian Tibble, Laurie Hendren, Oege de Moor, and Ganesh Sittampalam. Adding open modules to AspectJ. In *AOSD '06: Proceedings of the 5th international conference on Aspect-oriented software development*, pages 39–50, New York, NY, USA, 2006. ACM Press.

67. Santanu Paul and Atul Prakash. Querying source code using an algebraic query language. *IEEE Transactions on Software Engineering*, 22(3):202–217, 1996.

68. Thomas W. Reps. Demand interprocedural program analysis using logic databases. In *Workshop on Programming with Logic Databases, ILPS*, pages 163–196, 1993.

69. Tobias Rho, Günter Kniesel, Malte Appeltauer, and Andreas Linder. LogicAJ. http://roots.iai.uni-bonn.de/research/logicaj/people, 2006.

70. Damien Sereni and Oege de Moor. Static analysis of aspects. In *Proceedings of the 2nd International Conference on Aspect-Oriented Software Development (AOSD)*, pages 30–39, 2003.

71. Volker Stolz and Eric Bodden. Temporal Assertions using AspectJ. In *RV'05 - Fifth Workshop on Runtime Verification*, volume 144(4) of *Electronic Notes in Theoretical Computer Science*, pages 109–124. Elsevier Science Publishers, 2005.

72. Wim Vanderperren, Davy Suvé, María Augustina Cibrán, and Bruno De Fraine. Stateful aspects in JAsCo. In *Software Composition: 4th International Workshop*, volume 3628 of *Lecture Notes in Computer Science*, pages 167–181. Springer, 2005.

73. Eelco Visser. Meta-programming with concrete object syntax. In *Generative programming and component engineering (GPCE)*, pages 299–315, 2002.

74. David Walker, Steve Zdancewic, and Jay Ligatti. A theory of aspects. In *ICFP '03: Proceedings of the eighth ACM SIGPLAN international conference on Functional programming*, pages 127–139, New York, NY, USA, 2003. ACM Press.

75. Robert Walker and Kevin Viggers. Implementing protocols via declarative event patterns. In *ACM Sigsoft International Symposium on Foundations of Software Engineering (FSE-12)*, pages 159–169, 2004.

76. Mitchell Wand, Gregor Kiczales, and Christopher Dutchyn. A semantics for advice and dynamic join points in aspect-oriented programming. *ACM Trans. Program. Lang. Syst.*, 26(5):890–910, 2004.

77. John Whaley, Dzintars Avots, Michael Carbin, and Monica S. Lam. Using datalog and binary decision diagrams for program analysis. In Kwangkeun Yi, editor, *Proceedings of the 3rd Asian Symposium on Programming Languages and Systems*, volume 3780 of *LNCS*, pages 97–118. Springer-Verlag, November 2005.

A Symbolic Framework for Model-Based Testing

L. Frantzen[1,2,*], J. Tretmans[2], and T.A.C. Willemse[2,**]

[1] Instituto di Scienza e Tecnologie della Informazione "Alessandro Faedo"
Consiglio Nazionale delle Ricerche, Pisa – Italy
`lars.frantzen@isti.cnr.it`
[2] Institute for Computing and Information Sciences
Radboud University Nijmegen – The Netherlands
{`lf, tretmans, timw`}`@cs.ru.nl`

Abstract. The starting point for Model-Based Testing is an implementation relation that formally defines when a formal model representing the System Under Test conforms to a formal model constituting its specification. An implementation relation for the formalism of Labelled Transition Systems is **ioco**. For **ioco** several test generation algorithms and test tools have been built. In this paper we define a framework for the symbolic implementation relation **sioco** which lifts **ioco** to Symbolic Transition Systems. These are transition systems with an explicit notion of data and data-dependent control flow. The introduction of symbolism avoids the state-space explosion during test generation, and it preserves the information present in data definitions and constraints for use during the test selection process. We show the soundness and completeness of the symbolic notions w.r.t. their underlying Labelled Transition Systems' counterparts.

1 Introduction

Model-Based Testing (MBT) is a form of black-box testing where a System Under Test (SUT) is tested for conformance against a formally described specification, or model, of the SUT. Test cases can be automatically generated from this model, and test results can be automatically evaluated.

The starting point for MBT is a precise definition of what it means that an SUT conforms to its specification. Such a definition is expressed by an *implementation relation*: a formal relation between the specification formalism and the implementation formalism. Although such a relation is formally expressed, it cannot be used to directly verify the relation between an SUT and its specification. Since an SUT is a physical system that we observe as a black-box, we can only perform tests on the black-box to check the relation to its specification.

* Lars Frantzen is supported by the Marie Curie Network TAROT (MRTN-CT-2004-505121) and by the Netherlands Organisation for Scientific Research (NWO) under project STRESS.
** Tim Willemse carried out this work as part of the TANGRAM project under the responsibility of the Embedded Systems Institute. Tangram is partially supported by the Netherlands Ministry of Economic Affairs under grant TSIT2026.

K. Havelund et al. (Eds.): FATES/RV 2006, LNCS 4262, pp. 40–54, 2006.
© Springer-Verlag Berlin Heidelberg 2006

Yet, it is assumed that the SUT exhibits a behavior which *could* be expressed in the implementation formalism, even if we do not know this behavior in detail. This assumption is commonly referred to as the *test hypothesis*. By so doing we can consider SUTs as formal systems, and we can formally reason about the soundness and completeness of the testing process.

Many different implementation relations have been proposed; see [3] for an overview of the state-of-the-art. A prominent example of an implementation relation is the implementation relation **ioco** [16], which is based on the formalism of *Labelled Transition Systems* (LTSs). Several testing tools implement it, e.g. TorX [1] and TGV [10]. The LTS formalism is a powerful semantic model to describe systems. However, it has some drawbacks which make its direct use for MBT cumbersome. In particular, the use of data values and variables is not possible. None the less all state-of-the-art modeling formalisms allow for such a symbolic treatment of data and often have underlying LTS-semantics, e.g. Statecharts [9] or the data-enriched process algebra LOTOS [2]. To use such a model for serving as the input to an LTS-based testing tool all data must be encoded in action names representing concrete values; there is no symbolic treatment of data. This mapping of data values leads to the infamous state space explosion problem, which limits the usability of test generation tools. A second disadvantage of this mapping is that all structure and information available in the data definitions and constraints is lost. This information can be very useful in the test selection process (see e.g. [4]).

To overcome these problems we introduced *Symbolic Transition Systems* (STS) in [6]. An STS is a transition system incorporating an explicit notion of data and data-dependent control flow, such as guarded transitions, founded on first order logic. The underlying first order structure gives formal means to define both the data part algebraically, and the control flow part logically. The emphasis in [6] was on presenting an on-the-fly algorithm for generating **ioco** test cases derived directly from STSs.

In this paper we go a fundamental step ahead by lifting the **ioco** relation to the level of STSs: we give a fully symbolic version of **ioco**, called **sioco**. Hence, **sioco** relates symbolic specifications to symbolically modeled implementations. The goal is to have a complete formal framework for symbolic testing. By being sound and complete for **ioco** the framework allows to reason about all conformance aspects, for instance repetitive quiescence. It serves as a foundation to define further symbolic aspects like symbolic test cases, coverage criteria based on symbolic reachability, etc., and to gain insight into the underlying symbolic mechanisms. Studying the implementation relation **sioco** and the concepts needed to define it, also provides a necessary and well-defined basis for the development of symbolic test generation tools.

Overview. In Sect. 2, we recall the first order concepts underlying the STS formalism. The **ioco** relation is summarized in Sect. 3. Section 4 introduces STSs and the symbolic framework. Section 5 defines the symbolic variant **sioco**. An outlook at applications of the presented theory is given in Sect. 6, followed by conclusions and related work in Sect. 7.

2   First Order Logic

We use basic concepts from first order logic as our framework for dealing with data. For a general introduction into logic we refer to [5]. Throughout this paper we use the following conventions: for sets A and B, the set of all total functions from A to B is denoted B^A. For functions $f:B{\rightarrow}C$ and $g:A{\rightarrow}B$, we denote the composition of f and g by $f \circ g$. We sometimes treat a tuple $\langle x_1, \ldots, x_n \rangle$ as the set $\{x_1, \ldots, x_n\}$ when the context allows this.

From hereon we assume a first order structure $(\mathfrak{S}, \mathfrak{M})$ as given. $\mathfrak{S} = (F, P)$ is a logical signature with F being a set of *function symbols*. Each $f{\in}F$ has a corresponding arity $n{\in}\mathbb{N}$. P is a set of *predicate symbols*. Each $p{\in}P$ has a corresponding arity $n{\in}\mathbb{N}^+$. The model $\mathfrak{M} = (\mathfrak{U}, (f_{\mathfrak{M}})_{f{\in}F}, (p_{\mathfrak{M}})_{p{\in}P})$ consists of $\mathfrak{U}$ being a non-empty set called *universe*, and for all $f{\in}F$ with arity n, $f_{\mathfrak{M}}$ is a function of type $\mathfrak{U}^n{\rightarrow}\mathfrak{U}$. For every $p{\in}P$ with arity n we have $p_{\mathfrak{M}} \subseteq \mathfrak{U}^n$. For simplicity, and without loss of generality, we restrict to one-sorted signatures.

Let $\mathfrak{X}$ be a set of *variables*; we assume sets $X, Y \subseteq \mathfrak{X}$. *Terms* over X, denoted $\mathfrak{T}(X)$, are built from variables $x{\in}X$ and function symbols $f{\in}F$. The set of variables appearing in a term t is denoted $\mathsf{var}(t)$. A *term-mapping* is a function $\sigma:\mathfrak{X} \rightarrow \mathfrak{T}(\mathfrak{X})$. For a given tuple of variables $\langle x_1, \ldots, x_n \rangle$ we set $\sigma(\langle x_1, \ldots, x_n \rangle) = \langle \sigma(x_1), \ldots, \sigma(x_n) \rangle$. The identity term-mapping id is defined as $\mathsf{id}(x) = x$ for all $x{\in}\mathfrak{X}$. By σ_X, we denote a restricted term-mapping σ that is only to be applied on variables from X, i.e., $\sigma_X(x) = \sigma(x)$ if $x{\in}X$, and x otherwise. The set of all term-mappings $\sigma{\in}\mathfrak{T}(\mathfrak{X})^{\mathfrak{X}}$ for which hold that $\sigma(x){\in}\mathfrak{T}(Y)$ for all $x{\in}X$, and $\sigma(x) = x$ for all $x \notin X$, is denoted $\mathfrak{T}(Y)^{\mathfrak{X}|X}$. We will omit the mentioning of $\mathfrak{X}$ and just write $\mathfrak{T}(Y)^X$ in the remainder.

The set of free variables of a first order formula φ is denoted $\mathsf{free}(\varphi)$. The set of all first order formulas φ satisfying $\mathsf{free}(\varphi) \subseteq X$ is denoted $\mathfrak{F}(X)$. A tautology is represented by $\top$; we set $\neg\top = \bot$. We write $\exists_X \varphi$ for the formula $\exists x_1 \exists x_2 \ldots \exists x_n : \varphi$, where $\{x_1, \ldots, x_n\} = X \cap \mathsf{free}(\varphi)$, referred to as the *existential closure* for X of φ. Analogously we define the *universal closure* $\forall_X \varphi$.

Let σ be a term-mapping. Given a formula φ, the *substitution* of $\sigma(x)$ for $x{\in}\mathsf{free}(\varphi)$ is denoted $\varphi[\sigma]$. Substitutions are side-effect free, i.e. they do not add bound variables. This is achieved using an implicit proper renaming of bound variables. Likewise, for a term t, the *substitution* of $\sigma(x)$ for $x{\in} \mathsf{var}(t)$ is denoted $t[\sigma]$. Together we get $[\sigma] : \mathfrak{F}(\mathfrak{X}) \cup \mathfrak{T}(\mathfrak{X}) \rightarrow \mathfrak{F}(\mathfrak{X}) \cup \mathfrak{T}(\mathfrak{X})$.

A *valuation* is a function $\vartheta{\in}\mathfrak{U}^{\mathfrak{X}}$. For a given tuple of variables $\langle x_1, \ldots, x_n \rangle$ we set $\vartheta(\langle x_1, \ldots, x_n \rangle) = \langle \vartheta(x_1), \ldots, \vartheta(x_n) \rangle$. Let $*$ denote an arbitrary element of the set $\mathfrak{U}$. A *partial valuation* is a function $\vartheta_X{\in}\mathfrak{U}^X$; ϑ_X can be extended to a valuation ϑ as follows: $\vartheta(x) = \vartheta_X(x)$ if $x{\in}X$, and $\vartheta(x) = *$ when $x{\in}\mathfrak{X} \setminus X$. Having two partial valuations $\vartheta{\in}\mathfrak{U}^X$ and $\varsigma{\in}\mathfrak{U}^Y$, with $X \cap Y = \emptyset$, their union $(\vartheta \cup \varsigma){\in}\mathfrak{U}^{X \cup Y}$ is defined as $(\vartheta \cup \varsigma)(x) = \vartheta(x)$ if $x{\in}X$, and $(\vartheta \cup \varsigma)(x) = \varsigma(x)$ if $x{\in}Y$. The *satisfaction* of a formula φ w.r.t. a given valuation ϑ is denoted $\vartheta \models \varphi$. The extension to evaluate terms based on a valuation ϑ is called a *term-evaluation* and denoted $\vartheta_{\mathsf{eval}}:\mathfrak{T}(\mathfrak{X}) \rightarrow \mathfrak{U}$.

3   A Testing Relation for Labelled Transition Systems

We assume the reader has some basic familiarity with (**ioco**-based) model-based testing techniques as described in e.g. [16], and recall only those concepts and conventions relevant to this paper.

Definition 1. *A Labelled Transition System (LTS) is a tuple* $\mathcal{L} = \langle S, s_0, \Sigma, \rightarrow \rangle$, *where S is a set of* states *and $s_0 \in S$ is the* initial state. *The set Σ is a set of* observable action labels. *The action label $\tau \notin \Sigma$ denotes an* unobservable *action;* Σ_τ *abbreviates the set $\Sigma \cup \{\tau\}$. The relation $\rightarrow \subseteq S \times \Sigma_\tau \times S$ is the* transition relation; $s \xrightarrow{\mu} s'$ *abbreviates $(s, \mu, s') \in \rightarrow$.*

Let $\mathcal{L} = \langle S, s_0, \Sigma, \rightarrow \rangle$ be an LTS. The generalized transition relation $\Longrightarrow \subseteq S \times \Sigma^* \times S$ of $\mathcal{L}$ is obtained in the standard way, i.e. it is the smallest relation satisfying:

(Tϵ) $s \overset{\epsilon}{\Longrightarrow} s$, with $s \in S$,
(Tτ) $s \overset{\sigma}{\Longrightarrow} s'$ if $s \overset{\sigma}{\Longrightarrow} s''$ and $s'' \xrightarrow{\tau} s'$, with $s, s', s'' \in S$ and $\sigma \in \Sigma^*$,
(Tμ) $s \overset{\sigma \cdot \mu}{\Longrightarrow} s'$ if $s \overset{\sigma}{\Longrightarrow} s''$ and $s'' \xrightarrow{\mu} s'$, with $s, s', s'' \in S$, $\sigma \in \Sigma^*$ and $\mu \in \Sigma$.

We use the following shorthand notations and functions:

1. $s \xrightarrow{\mu}$ abbreviates $\exists s' \in S : s \xrightarrow{\mu} s'$, with $s \in S$ and $\mu \in \Sigma_\tau$,
2. $s \overset{\sigma}{\Longrightarrow}$ abbreviates $\exists s' \in S : s \overset{\sigma}{\Longrightarrow} s'$, with $s \in S$ and $\sigma \in \Sigma^*$,
3. $traces(s) =_{def} \{ \sigma \in \Sigma^* \mid s \overset{\sigma}{\Longrightarrow} \}$, with $s \in S$,
4. $der(s) =_{def} \{s' \mid \exists \sigma \in \Sigma^* : s \overset{\sigma}{\Longrightarrow} s'\}$, with $s \in S$.

A specialization of the model of LTSs is the model of *Input-Output Labelled Transition Systems* (IOLTSs), which captures the notion of initiative of actions (i.e. whether the action is an input or an output).

Definition 2. *An IOLTS is a tuple* $\langle S, s_0, \Sigma_I, \Sigma_U, \rightarrow \rangle$, *such that* $\langle S, s_0, \Sigma_I \cup \Sigma_U, \rightarrow \rangle$ *is an LTS and $\Sigma_I \cap \Sigma_U = \emptyset$; Σ_I is the set of* inputs *and Σ_U is the set of* outputs.

Let $\mathcal{L} = \langle S, s_0, \Sigma_I, \Sigma_U, \rightarrow \rangle$ be an IOLTS. An *observation* from $\mathcal{L}$ is an output action $\mu \in \Sigma_U$ or the refusal of all outputs; we refer to such a refusal as *quiescence*. A state $s \in S$ in $\mathcal{L}$ is *quiescent*, denoted $\delta(s)$, iff $\forall \mu \in \Sigma_U \cup \{\tau\} : s \xrightarrow{\mu}$. Let δ be a constant not part of any action label set; Σ_δ abbreviates $\Sigma_I \cup \Sigma_U \cup \{\delta\}$, and Σ_δ^* is referred to as the set of *extended traces*. We define the *suspension transition relation* $\Longrightarrow_\delta \subseteq S \times \Sigma_\delta^* \times S$ as the smallest relation satisfying rules Tϵ, Tτ, Tμ (with $\Longrightarrow_\delta$ replacing $\Longrightarrow$) and Tδ, where Tδ is given as:

(Tδ) $s \overset{\sigma \cdot \delta}{\Longrightarrow}_\delta s'$ if $s \overset{\sigma}{\Longrightarrow}_\delta s'$ and $\delta(s')$, with $s, s' \in S$ and $\sigma \in \Sigma_\delta^*$.

We define the following functions for arbitrary $s \in S$, $C \subseteq S$ and $\sigma \in \Sigma_\delta^*$:

1. $Straces(s) =_{def} \{\sigma \in \Sigma_\delta^* \mid s \overset{\sigma}{\Longrightarrow}_\delta \}$, is the set of *suspension traces*,
2. C **after** $\sigma =_{def} \bigcup_{s \in C} s$ **after** σ, where s **after** $\sigma =_{def} \{s' \in S \mid s \overset{\sigma}{\Longrightarrow}_\delta s'\}$,

3. $out(C) =_{def} \bigcup_{s \in C} out(s)$, where $out(s) =_{def} \{\mu \in \Sigma_U \mid s \xrightarrow{\mu}\} \cup \{\delta \mid \delta(s)\}$.

The *testing hypothesis* [16] states that implementations can be modeled as *input-enabled* IOLTSs, where an IOLTS $\langle S, s_0, \Sigma_I, \Sigma_U, \rightarrow \rangle$ is input-enabled if and only if:

$$\forall s \in der(s_0) \forall \mu \in \Sigma_I : \ s \text{ after } \mu \neq \emptyset.$$

The conformance testing relation **ioco** is defined as follows:

Definition 3. *Let* $\mathcal{S} = \langle S, s_0, \Sigma_I, \Sigma_U, \rightarrow_{\mathcal{S}} \rangle$ *be a specification IOLTS, and let* $\mathcal{F} \subseteq Straces(s_0)$. *An input-enabled IOLTS* $\mathcal{P} = \langle P, p_0, \Sigma_I, \Sigma_U, \rightarrow_{\mathcal{P}} \rangle$ *is* **ioco**$_{\mathcal{F}}$-*conform to* $\mathcal{S}$, *denoted by* $\mathcal{P}$ **ioco**$_{\mathcal{F}}$ $\mathcal{S}$, *iff*

$$\forall \sigma \in \mathcal{F} : out(p_0 \text{ after } \sigma) \subseteq out(s_0 \text{ after } \sigma)$$

4   The Symbolic Framework

In practical situations, LTSs lack the required level of abstraction for modeling complex, data-intensive systems. This problem is solved by the model of *Symbolic Transition Systems* (see e.g. [15,6]), which we introduce in this section.

4.1   Syntax and Semantics for Symbolic Transition Systems

The STS model extends the model of LTSs by incorporating an explicit notion of data and data-dependent control flow (such as guarded transitions), founded on first order logic.

Definition 4. *An STS is a tuple* $\mathcal{S} = \langle L, l_0, \mathcal{V}, \mathcal{I}, \Lambda, \rightarrow \rangle$, *where* L *is a set of locations and* $l_0 \in L$ *is the* initial location. $\mathcal{V}$ *is a set of* location variables *and* $\mathcal{I}$ *is a set of* interaction variables; $\mathcal{V} \cap \mathcal{I} = \emptyset$, *and we set* $Var =_{def} \mathcal{V} \cup \mathcal{I}$. Λ *is the set of* gates; *constant* $\tau \notin \Lambda$ *denotes an* unobservable gate; Λ_τ *abbreviates* $\Lambda \cup \{\tau\}$. *The relation* $\rightarrow \subseteq L \times \Lambda_\tau \times \mathfrak{F}(Var) \times \mathfrak{T}(Var)^{\mathcal{V}} \times L$ *is the* switch relation; $l \xrightarrow{\lambda, \varphi, \rho} l'$ *abbreviates* $(l, \lambda, \varphi, \rho, l') \in \rightarrow$, *where* φ *is the* switch restriction *and* ρ *is the* update mapping. *We use the following functions and vocabulary:*

1. **arity** $: \Lambda_\tau \rightarrow \mathbb{N}$ *is the* arity function,
2. **type**(λ) *yields a tuple of size* **arity**(λ) *of interaction variables for gate* λ,
3. $\mathcal{S}$ *is* well-defined *iff* **arity**$(\tau) = 0$, **type**(λ) *yields a tuple of distinct interaction variables, and* $l \xrightarrow{\lambda, \varphi, \rho} l'$ *implies* free$(\varphi) \subseteq \mathcal{V} \cup$ **type**(λ) *and* $\rho \in \mathfrak{T}(\mathcal{V} \cup \text{\textbf{type}}(\lambda))^{\mathcal{V}}$,
4. $\mathcal{S}(\iota)$ *is an* initialized *STS, where* $\iota \in \mathfrak{U}^{\mathcal{V}}$ *initializes all variables from* $\mathcal{V}$ *in* l_0.

We only consider well-defined STSs in this paper.

Example 1. The STS $\langle \{l_i \mid 0 \leq i \leq 5\}, l_0, \{\text{rp}, \text{q}, \text{r}\}, \{\text{prod}, \text{quant}, \text{ref}\}, \Lambda, \rightarrow \rangle$, with $\Lambda = \{?\text{rq}, !\text{gq}, ?\text{ord}, !\text{confirm}, !\text{cancel}\}$ is depicted in Fig. 1; $\rightarrow$ is given by the directed edges linking the locations. We have e.g. **arity**$(?\text{rq}) = 2$ and **type**$(?\text{rq}) =$ <prod,quant>. The underlying first order structure is based on a natural number universe with the common "less-than" predicate $<$. The STS specifies a simplified supplier system which can be requested for a quote for a given product **prod** and

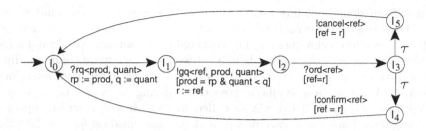

Fig. 1. An STS specifying a simplified *Supplier*

quantity quant via gate ?rq located on the switch from l_0 to l_1. The requested product and quantity are stored in the location variables rp and q, respectively. Next a quote is returned via gate !gq which must deal with the same product and with a quantity less than the requested one. Subsequently, the quote can be ordered via gate ?ord by giving the correct reference number from the received quote. Finally the supplier nondeterministically communicates a cancellation of the order via the !cancel gate, or confirms the order via the !confirm gate. As a convention, switch constraints ⊤ and update-mappings id are not explicitly drawn. We will refer to this STS in the following examples as the Supplier STS.   □

The interpretation of an STS is defined in terms of LTSs.

Definition 5. *Let* $\mathcal{S} = \langle L, l_0, \mathcal{V}, \mathcal{I}, \Lambda, \rightarrow \rangle$ *be an STS. Its interpretation* $[\![\mathcal{S}]\!]_\iota$ *in the context of* $\iota \in \mathfrak{U}^{\mathcal{V}}$, *is defined as* $[\![\mathcal{S}]\!]_\iota = \langle L \times \mathfrak{U}^{\mathcal{V}}, (l_0, \iota), \Sigma, \rightarrow \rangle$ *for all* $\iota \in \mathfrak{U}^{\mathcal{V}}$, *where*

- $\Sigma = \bigcup_{\lambda \in \Lambda}(\{\lambda\} \times \mathfrak{U}^{\text{arity}(\lambda)})$, *is the set of actions.*
- $\rightarrow \subseteq (L \times \mathfrak{U}^{\mathcal{V}}) \times (\Sigma \cup \{\tau\}) \times (L \times \mathfrak{U}^{\mathcal{V}})$ *is defined by the following rule:*

$$\frac{l \xrightarrow{\lambda, \varphi, \rho} l' \quad \varsigma \in \mathfrak{U}^{\text{type}(\lambda)} \quad \vartheta \cup \varsigma \models \varphi \quad \vartheta' = (\vartheta \cup \varsigma)_{\text{eval}} \circ \rho}{(l, \vartheta) \xrightarrow{(\lambda, \varsigma(\text{type}(\lambda)))} (l', \vartheta')}$$

The semantics of an initialized STS $\mathcal{S}(\iota)$ *is given by the LTS* $[\![\mathcal{S}]\!]_\iota$.

4.2   Symbolic Executions and Symbolic States

The notion of a trace of an STS can be defined by appealing to the semantics of an initialized STS. This, however, suffers from the disadvantage that all high-level information and structure about the data that is communicated over gates is lost. Therefore, we choose to define a notion of traces on the level of *symbolic executions*.

Symbolic execution as a technique was initially developed to symbolically execute imperative programs with the aim of proving correctness. This can be a hard task since the symbolic execution tree can for instance be of infinite size due to loops in the program. For this reason already early approaches suggested to just partially generate the execution tree for testing the program against a given specification, see e.g. [12].

Even if our domain of interest, i.e. reactive systems, has some fundamental originalities like nondeterminism, non-termination, etc., many of the classical symbolic execution techniques can be recovered in our setting. We do not adopt the symbolic tree representation, though, instead we use a more compact, linear representation which fits better to the standard notions we have introduced in Sect. 3. Whereas in a symbolic tree the ordering of events is encoded in its depth, we do so explicitly via so called *history variables*, which represent possible interactions. These variables provide a representation for the data that could have been communicated over a particular gate appearing at some point in a symbolic execution.

Example 2. Starting in location l_0 we can let the Supplier symbolically move to location l_1. Here the gate ?rq requests a product prod and a quantity quant. These values are stored in the location variables rp and q, respectively. All we know after executing this switch symbolically is that rp equals the value of prod, and q equals the value of quant. Proceeding symbolically we may encounter again the interaction variables prod or quant, hence it is necessary to make explicit that we are referring to the first occurrence of these variables within the symbolic execution. We do so by introducing the history variables $prod_1$ and $quant_1$. Hence we can, after moving from l_0 to l_1, formally record that rp $\mapsto prod_1$ and q $\mapsto quant_1$. Proceeding now from l_1 to l_2 the gate !gq returns a quote which also consists of a quantity, represented again by the interaction variable quant. This variable is now constrained by quant $<$ q. In our symbolic context this equals quant $< quant_1$. Also here we have to refer to the correct occurrence of the interaction variable, so we introduce another history variable $quant_2$ and record here $quant_2 < quant_1$. Analogously we get $prod_2 = prod_1$ and r $\mapsto ref_2$. □

For the remainder of this section we assume an STS $\mathcal{S} = \langle L, l_0, \mathcal{V}, \mathcal{I}, \Lambda, \rightarrow \rangle$. Henceforth, we assume to have *history variable sets* $\mathcal{I}_1, \mathcal{I}_2, \dots$ which are disjoint from each-other and from the set Var of $\mathcal{S}$. We set $\widehat{\mathcal{I}} =_{def} \bigcup_j \mathcal{I}_j$, and $\widehat{Var} =_{def} \mathcal{V} \cup \widehat{\mathcal{I}}$. In addition, we assume to have bijective *variable-renamings* $r_n \in \mathcal{I}_n^{\mathcal{I}}$.

The generalized switch relation $\Longrightarrow \subseteq L \times \Lambda^* \times \mathfrak{F}(\widehat{Var}) \times \mathfrak{T}(\widehat{Var})^{\mathcal{V}} \times L$, is defined as the smallest relation satisfying the following three rules:

(Sϵ) $l \xrightarrow{\epsilon, \ \top, \ id} l$,

(Sτ) $l \xrightarrow{\sigma, \ \varphi \wedge \psi[\rho], \ [\rho] \circ \pi} l'$ if $l \xrightarrow{\sigma, \ \varphi, \ \rho} l''$ and $l'' \xrightarrow{\tau, \ \psi, \ \pi} l'$,

(Sλ) $l \xrightarrow{\sigma \cdot \lambda, \ \varphi \wedge (\psi[r_n])[\rho], \ ([\rho] \circ ((r_n] \circ \pi))_{\mathcal{V}}} l'$ if $l \xrightarrow{\sigma, \ \varphi, \ \rho} l''$ and $l'' \xrightarrow{\lambda, \psi, \pi} l'$ and $n = length(\sigma)+1$.

Analogously to the generalized transition relation $\Longrightarrow$ for LTSs, the generalized switch relation hides unobservable events without affecting the observable events that can follow it. The intuition behind a generalized switch $l \xrightarrow{\sigma, \varphi, \rho} l'$ is that location l' can be reached from location l via a series of interactions over gates, the sequence of which is dictated by σ, and the values that are passed over these gates satisfy the conditions collected in φ (called *attainment constraint*[1]); the values for the location variables $\mathcal{V}$ are specified by *update-mapping* ρ.

Using a *variable-shifting* for the involved attainment constraints and term-mappings, generalized switches can be composed to yield larger generalized switches. A variable-shifting function re-indexes sets of history variables: having renamings $r_{(j,k)} \in \mathcal{I}_k^{\mathcal{I}_j}$ between all pairs $\mathcal{I}_j$ and $\mathcal{I}_k$, defined as $r_{(j,k)} =_{def} r_k \circ r_j^{-1}$, for all $i, j, k \in \mathbb{N}^+$ (where $r_k \in \mathcal{I}_k^{\mathcal{I}}$ is a bijective renaming function for history variables), we define a *variable-shifting* function $s^{\gg i} \in \widehat{\mathcal{I}}^{\widehat{\mathcal{I}}}$ for all $i \in \mathbb{N}$ as follows:

$$s^{\gg i}(x) =_{def} \begin{cases} r_{(j,j+i)}(x) & \text{if } x \in \mathcal{I}_j \text{ for some } j, \\ x & \text{otherwise} \end{cases}$$

Proposition 1. *If* $l \xrightarrow{\sigma_1, \, \varphi_1, \, \rho_1} l''$ *and* $l'' \xrightarrow{\sigma_2, \, \varphi_2, \, \rho_2} l'$ *and* $n = length(\sigma_1)$, *then also* $l \xrightarrow{\sigma_1 \cdot \sigma_2, \, \varphi_1 \wedge (\varphi_2[s^{\gg n}])[\rho_1], \, ([\rho_1] \circ ([s^{\gg n}] \circ \rho_2))_{\mathcal{V}}} l'$.

Note that there may be a large number of different executions (generalized switches) to get from l to l'. Each of these may have different effects on the values for the location variables at location l'. Therefore, given a location, we have no means to deduce what the possible values for the location variables are. These values are required to compute the semantical states of an STS, which in turn is required for defining the implementation relation **ioco**. To solve this issue, we introduce the concept of *symbolic states*. Symbolic states provide a finite characterization of (possibly infinite) sets of semantical states of an STS.

Definition 6. *A symbolic state is a tuple* $(l, \varphi, \rho) \in L \times \mathfrak{F}(\widehat{Var}) \times \mathfrak{T}(\widehat{Var})^{\mathcal{V}}$. *When the history variables referenced by attainment constraint* φ *and update-mapping* ρ *are from a set not above some* $i \in \mathbb{N}$, *we may add an* index *to the symbolic state* (l, φ, ρ) *and refer to it as an* indexed symbolic state, *denoted* $(l, \varphi, \rho)_i$. *We require that* $(l, \varphi, \rho)_i$ *satisfies:*

1. $\varphi \in \mathfrak{F}(\mathcal{V} \cup \bigcup_{j \leq i} \mathcal{I}_j)$, *and*
2. $\rho \in \mathfrak{T}(\mathcal{V} \cup \bigcup_{j \leq i} \mathcal{I}_j)^{\mathcal{V}}$.

The interpretation of a symbolic state in the context of location variable valuation ι and history variable valuation υ is a set of states of $[\![\mathcal{S}]\!]_\iota$.

Definition 7. *Let* $\iota \in \mathfrak{U}^{\mathcal{V}}$ *and let* $\upsilon \in \mathfrak{U}^{\widehat{\mathcal{I}}}$. *The interpretation of a symbolic state* (l, φ, ρ) *with respect to* ι *and* υ *is defined by:*

$$[\![(l, \varphi, \rho)]\!]_{\iota, \upsilon} =_{def} \{(l, \ (\iota \cup \upsilon)_{\text{eval}} \circ \rho) \mid \iota \cup \upsilon \models \varphi\}$$

Remark that $|[\![(l, \varphi, \rho)]\!]_{\iota, \upsilon}| \leq 1$; as a convention we identify the singleton set with its only element, omitting the set notation at our convenience. For sets of symbolic states $\mathcal{C} \subseteq L \times \mathfrak{F}(\widehat{Var}) \times \mathfrak{T}(\widehat{Var})^{\mathcal{V}}$, we define the following shorthands:

---

[1] The attainment constraint φ corresponds to what is called a *path condition* in the literature for symbolic execution of programs.

1. $[\![\mathcal{C}]\!]_{\iota,\upsilon} =_{def} \bigcup_{(l,\varphi,\rho)\in\mathcal{C}} [\![(l,\varphi,\rho)]\!]_{\iota,\upsilon}$,
2. $[\![\mathcal{C}]\!]_{\iota} =_{def} \bigcup_{\upsilon\in\mathfrak{U}^{\hat{\mathcal{I}}}} [\![\mathcal{C}]\!]_{\iota,\upsilon}$.

Example 3. The history variables for the Supplier are $\mathcal{I}_j = \{\mathsf{prod}_j, \mathsf{quant}_j, \mathsf{ref}_j\}$ with $j\in\mathbb{N}^+$. A generalized switch is $l_0 \xrightarrow{\text{?rq·!gq·?ord·!cancel, } \varphi, \ \rho} l_0$ with $\varphi = (\mathsf{prod}_2 = \mathsf{prod}_1)\wedge(\mathsf{quant}_2 < \mathsf{quant}_1)\wedge(\mathsf{ref}_3 = \mathsf{ref}_2)\wedge(\mathsf{ref}_4 = \mathsf{ref}_2)$ and $\rho = \{\mathsf{rp} \mapsto \mathsf{prod}_1, \mathsf{q} \mapsto \mathsf{quant}_1, \mathsf{r} \mapsto \mathsf{ref}_2\}$. The symbolic state (l_0, φ, ρ) can be indexed by 4 or greater, and $[\![\{(l_0, \varphi, \rho)\}]\!]_{\iota} = \{(l_0, \{\mathsf{rp} \mapsto x, \mathsf{q} \mapsto y, \mathsf{r} \mapsto z\}) \mid x, z\in\mathbb{N}, y\in\mathbb{N}^+\}$ for all $\iota\in\mathfrak{U}^{\mathcal{V}}$. □

5 A Symbolic Implementation Relation for STSs

In this section, we introduce the necessary concepts to define the implementation relation **sioco** on the level of STSs, which we prove to be equivalent to **ioco** on LTSs. We specialism the model of STSs by recognizing input-gates and output-gates. The resulting model is called *Input-Output Symbolic Transition Systems* (IOSTSs).

Definition 8. *An IOSTS is a tuple* $\langle L, l_0, \mathcal{V}, \mathcal{I}, \Lambda_I, \Lambda_U, \rightarrow\rangle$ *with* $\langle L, l_0, \mathcal{V}, \mathcal{I}, \Lambda_I \cup \Lambda_U, \rightarrow\rangle$ *being an STS and* $\Lambda_I \cap \Lambda_U = \emptyset$; Λ_I *is the set of* input gates *and* Λ_U *is the set of* output gates.

Throughout this section we assume a given IOSTS $\mathcal{S} = \langle L, l_0, \mathcal{V}, \mathcal{I}, \Lambda_I, \Lambda_U, \rightarrow\rangle$. The interpretation of $\mathcal{S}$ is a function from initialization functions to IOLTSs; it is a straightforward adaptation of Def. 5, in which Σ_I is the set of actions $(\lambda, \_)$ with $\lambda\in\Lambda_I$, and Σ_U is the set of actions $(\lambda, \_)$ with $\lambda\in\Lambda_U$. Distinguishing between input- and output interactions at the symbolic level allows us to define a symbolic analogue to quiescence. Since quiescence of a location $l\in L$ depends on the values for the location variables and the existence of proper values for interaction variables, we are primarily interested in the condition under which location l is quiescent. This symbolic quiescence condition is denoted $\Delta(l)\in\mathfrak{F}(\mathcal{V})$, and is defined as follows:

$$\Delta(l) =_{def} \bigwedge\{\neg\exists_{\mathsf{type}(\lambda)}\psi \mid \exists l', \pi \ : \ l \xrightarrow{\lambda,\psi,\pi} l' \text{ with } \lambda\in\Lambda_U \cup \{\tau\}\}$$

Example 4. To transform the Supplier STS into an IOSTS we set $\Lambda_I = \{\text{?rq, ?ord}\}$ and $\Lambda_U = \{\text{!gq, !confirm, !cancel}\}$. We get $\Delta(l_1) = \neg(\exists\mathsf{ref}\exists\mathsf{prod}\exists\mathsf{quant} \ : \ \mathsf{prod} = \mathsf{rp} \wedge \mathsf{quant} < \mathsf{q})$ for the Supplier. In the underlying natural numbers model the satisfiability of this formula boils down to $\mathsf{q} = 0$, i.e. l_1 is quiescent given that the requested quote has a zero quantity. The switch restriction from l_1 to l_2 is unsolvable, resulting in deadlock. □

Communications over output gates $\lambda\in\Lambda_U$, or the refusals δ of any output communication are the observables of an IOSTS. In contrast to the semantic framework of LTSs, these communications may depend on values that were communicated at an earlier stage, meaning that the observations are conditional. The combination of such conditions and the communications over a gate is referred to as a *symbolic observation*. Let the set of symbolic observations $\mathcal{O}$ for a given IOSTS $\mathcal{S}$ be defined as the set $\mathcal{O} =_{def} (\Lambda_U \cup \{\delta\}) \times \mathfrak{F}(\widehat{Var}) \times \mathfrak{F}(\widehat{Var \cup \mathcal{I}})$ with $\mathsf{free}(\psi) \subseteq \mathsf{type}(\lambda_\delta) \cup \widehat{Var}$ for all $(\lambda_\delta, \varphi, \psi) \in \mathcal{O}$ (assuming $\mathsf{type}(\delta) = \emptyset$). We interpret a symbolic observation in terms of semantic actions:

Definition 9. *Let $(\lambda_\delta, \varphi, \psi)$ be a symbolic observation. The interpretation* $[\![(\lambda_\delta, \varphi, \psi)]\!]_{\iota,\upsilon}$ *of $(\lambda_\delta, \varphi, \psi)$ is given in the context of $\iota \in \mathfrak{U}^{\mathcal{V}}$ and $\upsilon \in \mathfrak{U}^{\widehat{\mathcal{I}}}$:*

$$[\![(\delta, \varphi, \psi)]\!]_{\iota,\upsilon} = \{\delta \mid \iota \cup \upsilon \models \varphi \wedge \psi\}$$

$$[\![(\lambda, \varphi, \psi)]\!]_{\iota,\upsilon} = \{(\lambda, \varsigma(\mathsf{type}(\lambda))) \mid \iota \cup \upsilon \cup \varsigma \models \varphi \wedge \psi \text{ with } \varsigma \in \mathfrak{U}^{\mathsf{type}(\lambda)}\}$$

The interpretation of a set $O \subseteq \mathcal{O}$ in the context of $\iota \in \mathfrak{U}^{\mathcal{V}}$ and $\upsilon \in \mathfrak{U}^{\widehat{\mathcal{I}}}$ is defined as follows: $[\![O]\!]_{\iota,\upsilon} =_{def} \bigcup_{(\lambda_\delta, \varphi, \psi) \in O} [\![(\lambda_\delta, \varphi, \psi)]\!]_{\iota,\upsilon}$

The function $\mathbf{out}_s$ is defined on symbolic states, yielding a set of observations.

Definition 10. *Let (l, φ, ρ) be a symbolic state. We define:*

$$\mathbf{out}_s((l, \varphi, \rho)) =_{def} \{(\lambda, \varphi, \psi[\rho]) \in \mathcal{O} \mid \exists l', \pi : l \xrightarrow{\lambda, \psi, \pi} l'\} \cup \{(\delta, \varphi, \Delta(l)[\rho])\}$$

Let $\mathcal{C}$ be a set of symbolic states. Here we set:

$$\mathbf{out}_s(\mathcal{C}) =_{def} \bigcup_{(l, \varphi, \rho) \in \mathcal{C}} \mathbf{out}_s((l, \varphi, \rho))$$

Lemma 1. *For all $\iota \in \mathfrak{U}^{\mathcal{V}}$, $\upsilon \in \mathfrak{U}^{\widehat{\mathcal{I}}}$ and sets $\mathcal{C}$ of symbolic states we have:*

$$[\![\mathbf{out}_s(\mathcal{C})]\!]_{\iota,\upsilon} = \mathbf{out}([\![\mathcal{C}]\!]_{\iota,\upsilon})$$

From hereon, we set $\Lambda_\delta =_{def} \Lambda_I \cup \Lambda_U \cup \{\delta\}$. We define the *symbolic suspension switch relation* $\Longrightarrow_\delta \subseteq L \times \Lambda_\delta^* \times \mathfrak{F}(\widehat{Var}) \times \mathfrak{T}(\widehat{Var})^{\mathcal{V}} \times L$ as the smallest relation satisfying rules $S\epsilon$, $S\tau$, $S\lambda$ (with $\Longrightarrow_\delta$ replacing $\Longrightarrow$) and $S\delta$, given as:

(Sδ) $l \xrightarrow{\sigma \cdot \delta, \ \varphi \wedge \Delta(l')[\rho], \ \rho} _\delta l'$ if $l \xrightarrow{\sigma, \varphi, \rho} _\delta l'$.

The rule $S\delta$ reveals the fact that quiescence is an intrinsic semantical property. During a symbolic execution we can at any step just *hypothesize* that the system is quiescent and add a corresponding logical statement to the attainment constraint (that is what rule $S\delta$ does). Solving the constraint semantically means to compute the conditions under which quiescence really occurs (i.e. the traces which lead to a quiescent state).

The history variables that are allowed to be addressed in a sequence $\sigma \in \Lambda_\delta^*$ are given by $\mathsf{var}(\sigma)$, where $\mathsf{var} : \Lambda_\delta^* \to 2^{\widehat{\mathcal{I}}}$ is defined inductively as:

$$\begin{cases} \mathsf{var}(\epsilon) & = \emptyset \\ \mathsf{var}(\sigma \cdot \delta) = \mathsf{var}(\sigma) \\ \mathsf{var}(\sigma \cdot \lambda) = \mathsf{var}(\sigma) \cup \{r_{length(\sigma)+1}(\nu) \mid \nu \in \mathsf{type}(\lambda)\} \end{cases}$$

Lemma 2. *If* $l \overset{\sigma,\,\varphi,\,\rho}{=\!=\!=\!\Longrightarrow}_\delta l'$ *then we have* $\varphi \in \mathfrak{F}(\mathcal{V} \cup \mathrm{var}(\sigma))$ *and* $\rho \in \mathfrak{T}(\mathcal{V} \cup \mathrm{var}(\sigma))^{\mathcal{V}}$ *and* $(l', \varphi, \rho)_{length(\sigma)}$ *is an indexed symbolic state.*

Let $\mathcal{E}$ denote the set of *symbolic extended traces* $\{(\sigma, \varphi) \in \Lambda_\delta^* \times \mathfrak{F}(\widehat{Var}) \mid \mathrm{free}(\varphi) \subseteq \mathcal{V} \cup \mathrm{var}(\sigma)\}$. The interpretation of symbolic extended traces is given below:

Definition 11. *Let* $\iota \in \mathfrak{U}^{\mathcal{V}}$ *and let* $\upsilon \in \mathfrak{U}^{\widehat{\mathcal{I}}}$. *The interpretation of a symbolic extended trace* (σ, φ) *with respect to* ι *and* υ *is an extended trace, defined by:*

$$[\![(\sigma, \varphi)]\!]_{\iota,\upsilon} =_{def} \{\mathbf{etrace}_\upsilon(\sigma) \mid \iota \cup \upsilon \models \varphi\}$$

where $\mathbf{etrace}_\upsilon(\sigma)$ *is inductively defined as follows:*

$$\begin{cases} \mathbf{etrace}_\upsilon(\epsilon) & = \epsilon \\ \mathbf{etrace}_\upsilon(\sigma \cdot \delta) = \mathbf{etrace}_\upsilon(\sigma) \cdot \delta \\ \mathbf{etrace}_\upsilon(\sigma \cdot \lambda) = \mathbf{etrace}_\upsilon(\sigma) \cdot (\lambda, \upsilon(r_n(\mathrm{type}(\lambda)))) & \text{with } n = length(\sigma) + 1 \end{cases}$$

Note that $|[\![(\sigma, \varphi)]\!]_{\iota,\upsilon}| \leq 1$; as a convention, we identify the singleton set with its only element. For sets $E \subseteq \mathcal{E}$, we define the following shorthands:

1. $[\![E]\!]_{\iota,\upsilon} =_{def} \bigcup_{(\sigma,\varphi) \in E} [\![(\sigma, \varphi)]\!]_{\iota,\upsilon}$,
2. $[\![E]\!]_{\iota} =_{def} \bigcup_{\upsilon \in \mathfrak{U}^{\widehat{\mathcal{I}}}} [\![E]\!]_{\iota,\upsilon}$.

To complete the set of symbolic counterparts for the relevant semantical notions we define a symbolic $\mathbf{after}_s$ function, mapping pairs of indexed symbolic states and symbolic extended traces to new indexed symbolic states.

Definition 12. *Let* $(l, \varphi, \rho)_i$ *be an indexed symbolic state and let* $(\sigma, \chi) \in \mathcal{E}$ *be a symbolic extended trace. We define the binary function* $\mathbf{after}_s$ *as follows:*

$$(l, \varphi, \rho)_i \,\mathbf{after}_s(\sigma, \chi)$$
$$=_{def} \{(l', \varphi \wedge ((\psi \wedge \chi)[s^{\gg i}])[\rho], ([\rho] \circ ([s^{\gg i}] \circ \pi))\upsilon)_{i+length(\sigma)} \mid l \overset{\sigma,\psi,\pi}{=\!=\!=\!\Longrightarrow}_\delta l'\}$$

Let $\mathcal{C}$ be a set of indexed symbolic states. Here we set
$$\mathcal{C} \,\mathbf{after}_s(\sigma, \chi) =_{def} \bigcup_{(l,\varphi,\rho)_i \in \mathcal{C}} (l, \varphi, \rho)_i \,\mathbf{after}_s(\sigma, \chi).$$

Lemma 3. *Let* $(l, \varphi, \rho)_i$ *be an indexed symbolic state and let* $(\sigma, \chi) \in \mathcal{E}$ *be a symbolic extended trace. Then for all* $\iota \in \mathfrak{U}^{\mathcal{V}}$ *and* $\upsilon \in \mathfrak{U}^{\widehat{\mathcal{I}}}$, *we have:*

$$[\![(l, \varphi, \rho)_i \,\mathbf{after}_s(\sigma, \chi)]\!]_{\iota,\upsilon} = [\![(l, \varphi, \rho)_i]\!]_{\iota,\upsilon} \,\mathbf{after}\, [\![(\sigma, \chi)]\!]_{(\iota \cup \upsilon)_{eval} \circ \rho,\, \upsilon \circ s^{\gg i}}$$

Example 5. For the Supplier we get $(l_2, \mathsf{r} > \mathsf{prod}_3, \mathsf{id})_3 \,\mathbf{after}_s(?\mathsf{ord}, \mathsf{ref}_1 < 42) = \{(l_i, \xi, \mathsf{id})_4 \mid i = 3, 4, 5\}$ with $\xi = \mathsf{r} > \mathsf{prod}_3 \wedge \mathsf{ref}_4 = \mathsf{r} \wedge \mathsf{ref}_4 < 42$. If we call the latter set M and apply common first order equalities we get $\mathbf{out}_s(M) = \{(\delta, \xi, \perp), (!\mathsf{confirm}, \xi, \mathsf{ref} = \mathsf{r}), ((!\mathsf{cancel}, \xi, \mathsf{ref} = \mathsf{r}))\}$. □

The symbolic concepts that have been introduced so far provide a characterization of the semantically relevant concepts that were introduced in Section 3. The precise connection is established in the following two theorems.

Theorem 1 (Soundness). *Let* $\mathcal{S} = \langle L, l_0, \mathcal{V}, \mathcal{I}, \Lambda_I, \Lambda_U, \rightarrow \rangle$ *be an IOSTS. Then for all* $\iota \in \mathfrak{U}^{\mathcal{V}}$ *and all* $v \in \mathfrak{U}^{\widehat{\mathcal{I}}}$ *we have: if both* $l \xrightarrow{\sigma, \varphi, \rho}_\delta l'$ *and* $\iota \cup v \models \varphi$ *then also*

$$[\![(l, \top, \mathrm{id})]\!]_{\iota, v} \xrightarrow{[\![(\sigma, \varphi)]\!]_{\iota, v}}_\delta [\![(l', \varphi, \rho)]\!]_{\iota, v}.$$

Theorem 2 (Completeness). *Let* $\mathcal{S} = \langle L, l_0, \mathcal{V}, \mathcal{I}, \Lambda_I, \Lambda_U, \rightarrow \rangle$ *be an IOSTS. For all states* $(l, \iota), (l', \iota')$ *we have:* $(l, \iota) \xrightarrow{\overline{\sigma}}_\delta (l', \iota')$ *implies there is a valuation* $v \in \mathfrak{U}^{\widehat{\mathcal{I}}}$ *and a suspension switch* $l \xrightarrow{\sigma, \varphi, \rho}_\delta l'$ *satisfying* $\iota \cup v \models \varphi$, $\overline{\sigma} = [\![(\sigma, \varphi)]\!]_{\iota, v}$ *and* $(l', \iota') = [\![(l', \varphi, \rho)]\!]_{\iota, v}.$

The set of *symbolic suspension traces* of a location l of an IOSTS $\mathcal{S}$ is denoted $Straces_s(l)$, which is defined as $Straces_s(l) =_{def} \{(\sigma, \varphi) \in \mathcal{E} \mid \exists l', \rho : l \xrightarrow{\sigma, \varphi, \rho}_\delta l'\}$.

Corollary 1. *Let* $\mathcal{S}(\iota) = \langle L, l_0, \mathcal{V}, \mathcal{I}, \Lambda_I, \Lambda_U, \rightarrow \rangle$ *be an initialized IOSTS. Then we have* $[\![Straces_s(l_0)]\!]_\iota = Straces((l_0, \iota))$.

Definition 13. *Let* $\mathcal{S}(\iota)$ *be an initialized IOSTS. We set:* $\mathcal{S}(\iota)$ *is input enabled* $\Leftrightarrow_{def} [\![\mathcal{S}]\!]_\iota$ *is an input-enabled IOLTS.*

Now we are in the position to give the symbolic **sioco** variant of the **ioco** relation, based on the notions introduced so far.

Definition 14 (sioco). *Let* $\mathcal{F}_s$ *be a set of symbolic extended traces for an initialized specification IOSTS* $\mathcal{S}(\iota_S) = \langle L_S, l_S, \mathcal{V}_S, \mathcal{I}, \Lambda, \rightarrow_S \rangle$, *satisfying* $[\![\mathcal{F}_s]\!]_{\iota_S} \subseteq Straces((l_0, \iota_S))$. *An implementation, given as an input-enabled IOSTS* $\mathcal{P}(\iota_P) = \langle L_P, l_P, \mathcal{V}_P, \mathcal{I}, \Lambda, \rightarrow_P \rangle$, *with* $\mathcal{V}_S \cap \mathcal{V}_P = \emptyset$, *is* $\mathbf{sioco}_{\mathcal{F}_s}$-*conform to* $\mathcal{S}(\iota_S)$ *(written* $\mathcal{P}(\iota_P) \, \mathbf{sioco}_{\mathcal{F}_s} \, \mathcal{S}(\iota_S))$ *iff*

$$\forall (\sigma, \chi) \in \mathcal{F}_s \; \forall \lambda_\delta \in \Lambda_U \cup \{\delta\} : \iota_P \cup \iota_S \models \overline{\forall}_{\widehat{\mathcal{I}} \cup \mathcal{I}} \big(\Phi(l_P, \lambda_\delta, \sigma) \wedge \chi \rightarrow \Phi(l_S, \lambda_\delta, \sigma) \big)$$

where $\Phi(\varkappa, \lambda_\delta, \sigma) = \bigvee \{\varphi \wedge \psi \mid (\lambda_\delta, \varphi, \psi) \in \mathbf{out}_s((\varkappa, \top, \mathrm{id})_0 \, \mathbf{after}_s(\sigma, \top))\}$

The following theorem expresses that **sioco** coincides with **ioco**.

Theorem 3. *Let* $\mathcal{S}(\iota_S) = \langle L, l_0, \mathcal{V}, \mathcal{I}, \Lambda_I, \Lambda_U, \rightarrow \rangle$ *be an initialized IOSTS and let* $\mathcal{P}(\iota_P)$ *be an input-enabled IOSTS. Let* $\mathcal{F}_s$ *be a set of symbolic extended traces for* $\mathcal{S}$, *satisfying* $[\![\mathcal{F}_s]\!]_{\iota_S} \subseteq Straces((l_0, \iota_S))$. *Then*

$$\mathcal{P}(\iota_P) \, \mathbf{sioco}_{\mathcal{F}_s} \, \mathcal{S}(\iota_S) \text{ iff } [\![\mathcal{P}]\!]_{\iota_P} \, \mathbf{ioco}_{[\![\mathcal{F}_s]\!]_{\iota_S}} \, [\![\mathcal{S}]\!]_{\iota_S}$$

6 Application

The concepts that we have defined can be employed to define relations such as *symbolic state inclusion*, which allow one to efficiently prune symbolic executions (see e.g. [7]). Another example of how our theory contributes in improving and studying practically relevant testing problems is given in this section. We first define a naive (but often used) coverage measure that is based on reachability of states, and show that in the presence of data and control, coverage measures that are based on the concepts of locations and symbolic states are much more appropriate. In practice, a coverage measure can be used to fuel the test selection process; such a test selection process could e.g. be combined with the on-the-fly test derivation algorithm we presented in [6]. Note that the coverage measures described in this section are defined on the basis of the specification, rather than on the implementation (which is considered to be a black box). The underlying assumption is that a higher coverage value is an indication of a higher test quality; as such, one would always aim at a coverage value of 1 (i.e. full coverage).

We assume that the execution of a set of *test cases* (see e.g. [16] for a definition) on an implementation has resulted in a number of *test runs*, which we assume can be represented by a prefix-closed set of extended traces. Let $\mathcal{L} = \langle S, s_0, \Sigma_I, \Sigma_U, \to \rangle$ be an LTS-specification; a state-coverage measure $P_s(R)$ of a set of executed test runs $R \subseteq \Sigma_\delta^*$ can be defined as the ratio between states that have potentially been covered by test runs from R, and the total number of reachable states:

$$P_s(R) =_{def} \frac{\mid \bigcup_{\rho \in R} \ s_0 \ \textbf{after} \ \rho \mid}{\mid der(s_0) \mid}$$

State-coverage quickly becomes impractical when data plays a role, since the set of reachable states becomes extremely large or even infinite. This is exemplified by the Supplier STS: there is an infinite number of initial transitions leading to an infinite number of reachable states, since the underlying LTS model of the Supplier STS is infinitely branching in its initial state, effectively giving $P_s(R) = 0$ for all sets of test runs R. Note that this problem persists, even when we consider an alternative definition of P_s which relies on the total number of states that can be reached within a finite (known) number of steps.

A coverage measure that side-steps this problem is *location-coverage* for STSs. Let $\mathcal{S}(\iota) = \langle L, l_0, \mathcal{V}, \mathcal{I}, \Lambda_I, \Lambda_U, \to \rangle$ be an STS-specification (we assume it has semantics $\langle S, s_0, \Sigma_I, \Sigma_U, \to \rangle$); a location-coverage $P_l(R)$ of a set of executed test runs $R \subseteq \Sigma_\delta^*$ is defined as the ratio between locations that have potentially been covered by test runs from R, and the total set of reachable locations of $\mathcal{S}$:

$$P_l(R) =_{def} \frac{\mid \{l' \in L \mid \exists \rho \in R : \ \exists \iota' \in \mathfrak{U}^\mathcal{V} : \ (l', \iota') \in s_0 \ \textbf{after} \ \rho\} \mid}{\mid \{l' \in L \mid \exists \iota' \in \mathfrak{U}^\mathcal{V} : \ (l', \iota') \in der(s_0))\} \mid}$$

While the (in)finiteness of a state space is irrelevant for the location-coverage (in the usual case that L is finite), a major drawback of location-coverage is that e.g. a full coverage largely relies on control-flow; data is not considered on equal footing. In the Supplier STS, this means that $P_l(R) = 1$ does not imply that R has a test run $?\mathsf{rq}\langle p, 0\rangle$ (where $p \in \mathbb{N}$ is some instantiation), leading to a data-dependent quiescence observation.

A refinement of location-coverage that *does* treat data and control on equal footing is *symbolic state-coverage*. Let $n \in \mathbb{N}$ be the maximal length of a test run. The symbolic state-coverage $P_{ss}(R, n)$ of a set of executed test runs $R \subseteq \Sigma_\delta^*$ of length at most n is defined as the ratio between the symbolic states that have been covered by test runs from R, and the total set of (semantically) reachable symbolic states of $\mathcal{S}$ (using experiments of length n at most):

$$P_{ss}(R,n) =_{def} \frac{\mid \{(l,\varphi,\rho) \mid \exists\sigma\in\Lambda_\delta^{\leq n} : l_0 \xrightarrow{\sigma,\varphi,\rho}_\delta l \text{ and } [\![\{(\sigma,\varphi)\}]\!]_\iota \cap R \neq \emptyset\} \mid}{\mid \{(l,\varphi,\rho) \mid \exists\sigma\in\Lambda_\delta^{\leq n} : l_0 \xrightarrow{\sigma,\varphi,\rho}_\delta l \text{ and } [\![\{(\sigma,\varphi)\}]\!]_\iota \neq \emptyset\} \mid}$$

We leave it to the reader to check that in order to achieve $P_{ss}(R,n) = 1$, with $n > 1$ for the Supplier STS, the set R must also contain a test run $?rq\langle p,0\rangle$ (for some $p\in\mathbb{N}$). A test selection process aiming at a particular coverage using coverage measure P_{ss} could employ (subsets of) the set appearing in the denominator of P_{ss} to select test cases that reach symbolic states in this set.

7   Conclusions and Related Work

We have presented a symbolic implementation relation **sioco**, and proven its soundness and completeness w.r.t. the semantical **ioco** relation. The symbolic concepts that were needed to define **sioco** are not mere artefacts of the definition of **sioco**, but they have their own merits. We illustrated this by defining a test coverage measure that is based on symbolic states, which has advantages over coverage measures based on locations or semantic states. Similar advantages were found when investigating symbolic test case generation (not discussed in this paper), and, we expect to be able to reuse these concepts in e.g. test data selection.

To the best of our knowledge, this is the first approach that gives a fully symbolic implementation relation including quiescence. A closely related approach is described in [15], that uses a variant of a symbolic transition system and a weaker relation, e.g. they do not deal with quiescence. In [11] the problem of symbolic reachability analysis is approached with over-approximation techniques.

Also [7] presents a symbolic variation of the theme which is more focused on implementation issues. Their models are syntactically less expressive, e.g. inputs cannot directly be constrained, and the underlying implementation relation is not fully **ioco** (repetitive quiescence is missing). By having a simpler model without dedicated interaction variables, some computational tasks are easier to solve, for instance symbolic quiescence becomes quantifier-free.

Symbolic transitions systems are somewhat similar to *Statecharts* [9], and to their UML-variant called *State Machines* [14]. State Machines, though, tend to be applied in a synchronous setting, where inputs and outputs appear together on a single transition. This has consequences for compositionality issues, nondeterminism, etc., and corresponds to the semantical model of a *Mealy Machine* (also called *Finite State Machine* (FSM)). There is an important branch of formal testing which is based on Mealy Machines and their symbolic variant called *Extended Finite State Machine*, see [13] for a survey. Also the approach to testing in general differs, see e.g. [8] for a comparison. The testing approaches which are based on LTSs have instead an asynchronous nature, inputs and outputs appear here isolated on transitions. We hope that the presented framework can aid in embedding and reasoning about the many variations of LTS-based testing approaches which have been defined.

It is one of our main current research directions to investigate efficient implementations of the presented framework. One concrete instance is a Java-based test system for testing web services implementing the on-the-fly algorithm of [6] together with the symbolic coverage criteria as being indicated in Sect. 6.

References

1. A. Belinfante, J. Feenstra, R.G. de Vries, J. Tretmans, N. Goga, L. Feijs, S. Mauw, and L. Heerink. Formal test automation: A simple experiment. In G. Csopaki, S. Dibuz, and K. Tarnay, editors, *IWTCS'99*, pages 179–196. Kluwer Academic Publishers, 1999.
2. T. Bolognesi and E. Brinksma. Introduction to the ISO specification language LOTOS. *Computer Networks*, 14(1):25–59, January 1988.
3. M. Broy, B. Jonsson, J.P. Katoen, M. Leucker, and A. Pretschner, editors. *Model-based Testing of Reactive Systems: Advanced Lectures*, volume 3472 of *LNCS*. Springer, 2005.
4. A.D. Brucker and B. Wolff. Symbolic test case generation for primitive recursive functions. In *FATES 2004*, volume 3395 of *LNCS*, pages 16–32. Springer-Verlag, 2005.
5. H. Ehrig, B. Mahr, F. Cornelius, M. Große-Rhode, and P. Zeitz. *Mathematisch-strukturelle Grundlagen der Informatik*. Springer, 2nd edition, 2001.
6. L. Frantzen, J. Tretmans, and T.A.C. Willemse. Test generation based on symbolic specifications. In *FATES 2004*, volume 3395 of *LNCS*, pages 1–15. Springer-Verlag, 2005.
7. C. Gaston, P. Le Gall, N. Rapin, and A. Touil. Symbolic execution techniques for test purpose definition. In M. Ü. Uyar, A. Y. Duale, and M. A. Fecko, editors, *TestCom 2006*, volume 3964 of *LNCS*, pages 1–18. Springer, 2006.
8. N. Goga. Comparing torx, autolink, tgv and uio test algorithms. In *SDL '01: Proceedings of the 10th International SDL Forum Copenhagen on Meeting UML*, pages 379–402, London, UK, 2001. Springer-Verlag.
9. D. Harel. Statecharts: A visual formalism for complex systems. *Science of Computer Programming*, 8(3):231–274, 1987.
10. C. Jard and T. Jéron. TGV: theory, principles and algorithms. In *IDPT '02*. Society for Design and Process Science, 2002.
11. B. Jeannet, T. Jéron, V. Rusu, and E. Zinovieva. Symbolic test selection based on approximate analysis. In *TACAS*, pages 349–364, 2005.
12. J. C. King. A new approach to program testing. In *Proceedings of the international conference on Reliable software*, pages 228–233, New York, NY, USA, 1975. ACM Press.
13. D. Lee and M. Yannakakis. Principles and methods of testing finite state machines - A survey. In *Proceedings of the IEEE*, volume 84, pages 1090–1126, 1996.
14. Object Management Group. *UML 2.0 Superstructure Specification*, ptc/03-08-02 edition. Adopted Specification.
15. V. Rusu, L. du Bousquet, and T. Jéron. An Approach to Symbolic Test Generation. In W. Grieskamp, T. Santen, and B. Stoddart, editors, *IFM'00*, volume 1945 of *LNCS*, pages 338–357. Springer-Verlag, 2000.
16. J. Tretmans. Test generation with inputs, outputs and repetitive quiescence. *Software—Concepts and Tools*, 17(3):103–120, 1996.

A Test Calculus Framework Applied to Network Security Policies

Yliès Falcone[1], Jean-Claude Fernandez[1], Laurent Mounier[1],
and Jean-Luc Richier[2]

[1] Vérimag Laboratory, Gières, France
[2] LSR-IMAG Laboratory, St Martin d'Hères, France
{Ylies.Falcone, Jean-Claude.Fernandez, Laurent.Mounier,
Jean-Luc.Richier}@imag.fr

Abstract. We propose a syntax-driven test generation technique to au-
tomaticaly derive abstract test cases from a set of requirements expressed
in a linear temporal logic. Assuming that an elementary test case (called
a "tile") is associated to each basic predicate of the formula, we show how
to generate a set of test controlers associated to each logical operator,
and able to coordinate the whole test execution. The test cases produced
are expressed in a process algebraic style, allowing to take into account
the test environment constraints. We illustrate this approach in the context of network security testing, for which more classical model-based
techniques are not always suitable.

1 Introduction

Testing is a very popular validation technique, used in various application domains, and for which several formalizations have been proposed. In particular, a
well-defined theory is the one commonly used in the telecommunication area for
conformance testing of communication protocols [1]. This approach, sometimes
called "model-based" approach, consists in defining a conformance relation [2,3]
between a specification of the system under test and a formal model of its actual
implementation. The purpose of the test is then to decide if this relation holds or
not. A practical interest is that test cases can be automatically produced from
this specification. Several tools implement this automatic generation technique,
e.g. [4,5,6,7].

However, this model-based approach requires a rather complete *operational
specification* of the system under test, defined on a precise interface level. If
this constraint can be usually fulfilled for specific pieces of software (e.g., a
communication protocol), it may be difficult to achieve for large systems. A
typical example of such situation is testing the compliance of a network to a
given security policy. Indeed, security rules are usually enforced by combining
several mechanisms, operating at different architectural levels (fire-walls, antivirus softwares, cryptographic protocols, etc.). Clearly, all these levels can be
hardly encompassed in a single operational model of the network behaviour.

In a previous work [8], we have proposed an alternative approach for testing
system requirements expressed as a set of (temporal) logic formulae. For each

K. Havelund et al. (Eds.): FATES/RV 2006, LNCS 4262, pp. 55–69, 2006.
© Springer-Verlag Berlin Heidelberg 2006

formula ϕ, an abstract test case t_ϕ is produced following a syntax-driven technique: assuming that an elementary test case t_i (called hereafter a "tile") has been associated to each literal p_i of formula ϕ, the whole test case t_i is obtained by combining the tiles using test operators corresponding to the logical operators appearing in formula ϕ. This provides a structural correspondence between formulae and tests and it is easy to prove that the test obtained are sound with respect to the semantics of the formulae (in other words we give a "test based" semantics of the logic which is compatible with the initial one). The originality of this approach is then that a part of the system specification is encoded into the tiles, that can be provided by the system designer or a by a test expert. We claim that it is easier to obtain that a global operational specification.

This paper extends this previous work from the test execution point of view. In [8], abstract test cases were directly expressed by labelled transition systems, independently of the test architecture. We propose here to better take into account the test execution and to express the test cases in a higher level formalism. In particular we show how to produce well structured test cases consisting of a set of test drivers (one test driver for each elementary tile), coordinated by a set of test controllers (corresponding to the logical operators appearing in the formula). Thus, independent parts of the formula can be tested in parallel (either to speed up the test execution, or due to test environment constraints), each local verdicts being combined in a consistent way by the test controllers. Formally, test cases are expressed in a classical process algebra (called a "test calculus"), using basic control operators (parallel composition and interruption) and data types to handle test parameters and verdicts.

This paper is organized as follows: section 2 introduces our "test calculus" process algebra, and section 3 defines the notions of test execution and test verdicts. We propose in section 4 a simple temporal logic allowing to express network security requirements, and we show how to produce test cases from this logic in section 5. Finally, section 6 provides some examples in the context of network security policies.

2   Test Process Algebra

To model processes, we define a rather classic term algebra with typed variables, inspired from CCS [9], CSP [10] and Lotos. We suppose a set of predefined actions Act, a set of types $\mathcal{T}$, and a set of variables Var. Actions are either modifications of variables or communications through channels which are also typed. In the following, we do not address the problem of verifying that communications and assignments are well-typed. We denote by $expr_\tau$ (resp. x_τ) any expression (resp. variable) of type τ. Thus, when we write $x_\tau := expr_\tau$, we consider that this assignment is well typed.

A test is described as a term of our process algebra. We distinguish between elementary test cases, which are elements of a basic process algebra and compound test cases. We give the syntax and an operational semantics of this test process algebra.

2.1   Basic Processes

Our basic process algebra allows to describe sequences of atomic actions, communication and iteration. A term of this algebra is called a tile, which are the elementary test components and we note $TILE$ the set of all tiles.

The syntax of tiles and actions is given by the following grammar:

$$e ::= \alpha \circ e \mid e + e \mid nil \mid recX \; e \mid X$$
$$\alpha ::= [b]\gamma$$
$$\gamma ::= x_\tau := expr_\tau \mid !c(expr_\tau) \mid ?c(x_\tau)$$
$$b ::= true \mid false \mid b \vee b \mid b \wedge b \mid \neg b \mid expr_\tau = expr_\tau$$

where $e \in TILE$ is a tile, b a boolean expression, c a channel name, γ an action, $\circ$ is the *prefixing* operator ($\circ : Act \times TILE \rightarrow TILE$), $+$ the *choice* operator, X a term variable, and $recX : TILE \rightarrow TILE$ allows *recursive* tile definition (with X a term variable) [1]. When the condition b is true, we abbreviate $[true]\gamma$ by γ. The special tile nil does nothing.

There are two kinds of actions ($\gamma \in Act$). The first ones are the internal actions (modification of variables). The second ones are the communication actions. Two kinds of communications exist: $?c(x_\tau)$ denotes value reception on a channel c which is stored in variable x_τ; $!c(expr_\tau)$ denotes the emission of a value $expr_\tau$ on a channel c. Communication is done by "rendez-vous".

2.2   Composing Processes

Processes are compositions of tiles. Choices we made about composition operators came from needs appearing in our case studies in network security policies [8]. Composing tests in sequence is quite natural; however, for independent actions, and in order to speed-up test executions, one might want to parallelize some tests executions, for example, if one wants to scan several computers on a network. The parallel composition is also used to model the execution and communication between the test processes and the rest of the system. We assume a set $\mathcal{C}$ of channels used by tiles to communicate. We distinguish internal channels (set $\mathcal{C}_{in}$) and external channels (set $\mathcal{C}_{out}$), and we have $\mathcal{C} = \mathcal{C}_{in} \cup \mathcal{C}_{out}$.

In case of several processes executing in parallel, one might want to interrupt them. We choose to add an operator providing an exception mechanism: it permits to replace a process by an other one on the reception of a communication signal.

So, we define a set of operators, $\{\|_{\mathcal{L}}, \ltimes^{\mathcal{I}}\}$, respectively the parallel (with communication through a channel list $\mathcal{L} \subseteq \mathcal{C}$), and exception (with an action list $\mathcal{I}$) compositions.

The grammar for term processes ($TERM$) is:

$$t ::= e \mid t \|_{\mathcal{L}} t \mid t \ltimes^{\mathcal{I}} t$$

---

[1] we will only consider *ground* terms: each occurence of X is binded to $recX$.

The parallel operator $\|_{\mathcal{L}}$ is associative and commutative. It expresses either the interleaving of independant action or the emission $!c(expr_\tau)$ of the value of an expression $expr_\tau$ on a channel c. When the value is received by a process $?c(x_\tau)$, the communication is denoted at the syntactic level by $c(expr_\tau/x_\tau)$. The independent and parallel execution $\|_\emptyset$ is noted $\|$.

The Join-Exception operator $\ltimes^{\mathcal{I}}$ is used to interrupt a process and replace it with an other when a synchronization/global/communication action belonging to its synchronization list $\mathcal{I}$ occurs. Intuitively, considering two processes t, t' and a communication action α, $t \ltimes^{\{\alpha\}} t'$ means that if α is possible, t is replaced by t', else t continues normally.

2.3   Semantics

$$
\frac{\alpha \in Act}{\alpha \circ t \xrightarrow{\alpha} t} \, (\circ)
\qquad
\frac{t[recX \circ t/X] \xrightarrow{\alpha} t' \qquad \alpha \in Act}{recX \circ t \xrightarrow{\alpha} t'} \, (rec)
$$

$$
\frac{\alpha \in Act \qquad t_2 \xrightarrow{\alpha} t_2'}{t_1 + t_2 \xrightarrow{\alpha} t_2'} \, (+)
$$

$$
\frac{\alpha \notin \{[b]!c(expr_\tau), [b]?c(x_\tau) | c \in \mathcal{L}, b \in \mathbb{B}_{exp}\} \qquad t_1 \xrightarrow{\alpha} t_1'}{t_1 \|_{\mathcal{L}} t_2 \xrightarrow{\alpha} t_1' \|_{\mathcal{L}} t_2} \, (\|_{\neg\mathcal{L}})
$$

$$
\frac{c \in \mathcal{C}_{in} \wedge c \in \mathcal{L} \qquad t_1 \xrightarrow{[b]!c(expr_\tau)} t_1' \qquad t_2 \xrightarrow{[b]?c(x_\tau)} t_2'}{t_1 \|_{\mathcal{L}} t_2 \xrightarrow{[b]c(expr_\tau/x_\tau)} t_1' \|_{\mathcal{L}} t_2'} \, (\|_{\mathcal{C}_{in}})
$$

$$
\frac{c \in \mathcal{C}_{out} \wedge c \in \mathcal{L} \qquad t_1 \xrightarrow{[b]!c(expr_\tau)} t_1'}{t_1 \|_{\mathcal{L}} t_2 \xrightarrow{[b]!c(expr_\tau)} t_1' \|_{\mathcal{L}} t_2} \, (! \, \|_{\mathcal{C}_{out}})
$$

$$
\frac{c \in \mathcal{C}_{out} \wedge c \in \mathcal{L} \qquad t_1 \xrightarrow{[b]?c(x_\tau)} t_1'}{t_1 \|_{\mathcal{L}} t_2 \xrightarrow{[b]?c(x_\tau)} t_1' \|_{\mathcal{L}} t_2} \, (? \, \|_{\mathcal{C}_{out}})
$$

$$
\frac{\alpha \in \mathcal{I} \qquad t_2 \xrightarrow{\alpha} t_2'}{t_1 \ltimes^{\mathcal{I}} t_2 \xrightarrow{\alpha} t_2'} \, (\ltimes_\alpha^{\mathcal{I}})
\qquad
\frac{\alpha \notin \mathcal{I} \qquad t_1 \xrightarrow{\alpha} t_1'}{t_1 \ltimes^{\mathcal{I}} t_2 \xrightarrow{\alpha} t_1' \ltimes^{\mathcal{I}} t_2} \, (\ltimes_{\neg\alpha}^{\mathcal{I}})
$$

Fig. 1. Rules for term rewriting

Let $Dom(\tau)$ be the domain of the value s of type τ. A runtime environment ρ maps the set of variables to the set of values. We note $\mathcal{E}$ the set of all environments. Actions modify environments in a classical way; we note $\rho \xrightarrow{\gamma} \rho'$ the modification of environment ρ into ρ' by action γ. For example, $\rho \xrightarrow{x_\tau := expr_\tau} \rho[\rho(exp_\tau)/x_\tau]$, where $\rho[\rho(exp_\tau)/x_\tau]$ is the environment ρ in which variable x_τ is associated the value $\rho(exp_\tau)$. In the following, environments are extended to any typed expression.

A *labelled transition system* (LTS, for short) is a quadruplet (Q, A, T, q^0) where Q is a set of states, A a set of labels, T the transition relation ($T \subseteq Q \times A \times Q$)

and q^0 the initial state ($q^0 \in Q$). We will use the following definitions and notations: $(p, a, q) \in T$ is noted $p \xrightarrow{a}_T q$ (or simply $p \xrightarrow{a} q$). An *execution sequence* λ is a composition of transitions: $q^0 \xrightarrow{a_1} q_1 \xrightarrow{a_2} q_2 \cdots \xrightarrow{a_n} q_n$. We denote by σ^λ (resp. α^λ) the sequence of states (resp. observable actions) associated with λ. The sequence of actions α^λ is called a *trace*. We note by Σ_S, the set of finite execution sequences starting from the initial state q^0 of S. For any sequence λ of length n, λ_i or $\lambda(i)$ denotes the i-th element and $\lambda_{[i \cdots n]}$ denotes the suffix $\lambda_i \cdots \lambda_n$.

The semantics of a process is based on a LTS where states are "configurations", pairs (t, ρ), t being a term of the process algebra, ρ an environment, and transitions are given by definition 2. Configurations are used to represent process evolutions. We note $\mathcal{C}_{term} \stackrel{\text{def}}{=} TERM \times \mathcal{E}$ the set of configurations.

Definition 1 (Term-transition). *A term rewriting transition $\rightarrow$ is an element of $TERM \times Act \times TERM$. We say that the term t is rewritten in t' by action α. We note: $t \xrightarrow{\alpha} t'$. This semantics is similar with the CCS one [9].*

Term-transitions are defined in Figure 1 (using the fact that $\|$ and $+$ are commutative and associative).

Definition 2 (Transitions). *A transition is an element of $\mathcal{C}_{term} \times Act \times \mathcal{C}_{term}$. We say that the term t in the environment ρ is rewritten in t' modifying the environment ρ in ρ'.*

We have four transition rules, one for an assignment, and three for communication exchange. They are defined in Figure 2.

$$\frac{\rho(b) = true \qquad \rho(expr_\tau) = v \qquad t \xrightarrow{[b]x_\tau := expr_\tau} t'}{(t, \rho) \xrightarrow{x_\tau := v} (t', \rho[v/x_\tau])} \; (:=)$$

$$\frac{\rho(expr_\tau) = v \qquad t \xrightarrow{[b]!c(expr_\tau)} t' \qquad \rho(b) = true}{(t, \rho) \xrightarrow{!c(v)} (t', \rho)} \; (!)$$

$$\frac{v \in Dom(\tau) \qquad t \xrightarrow{[b]?c(x_\tau)} t' \qquad \rho(b) = true}{(t, \rho) \xrightarrow{?c(v)} (t, \rho[v/x_\tau])} \; (?)$$

$$\frac{\rho(expr_\tau) = v \qquad t \xrightarrow{[b]c(expr_\tau/x_\tau)} t' \qquad \rho(b) = true}{(t, \rho) \xrightarrow{c(v)} (t, \rho[v/x_\tau])} \; (c(expr_\tau/x_\tau))$$

Fig. 2. Rules for environment modification

3   Test Execution and Test Verdicts

As seen in the previous section, the semantics of a test case represented by a $TERM$ process t is expressed by a LTS $S_t = (Q^t, A^t, T^t, q_0^t)$. From a practical point of view the System Under Test (SUT) is not a formal model (it is a black-box implementation interacting with a tester). However, and similarly to the classical conformance testing theory, we consider here that its underlying execution model can be expressed by a LTS $I = (Q^I, A^I, T^I, q_0^I)$. A *test execution* is then a sequence of interactions between t and the SUT to deliver a *verdict* indicating whether the test succeeded or not. We first explain how verdicts are computed in our context, and then we give a formal definition of a test execution.

3.1   Tiles Verdicts

We assume in the following that any elementary tile t_i owns at least one variable used to store its *local verdict*, namely a value of enumerated type $Verdict = \{pass, fail, inc\}$. This variable is supposed to be set to one of these values when tile execution terminates. The intuitive meaning we associate to each of these values is similar to the one used in conformance testing:

- *pass* means that the test execution of t_i did not reveal any violation of the requirement expressed by t_i;
- *fail* means that the test execution of t_i did reveal a violation of the requirement expressed by t_i;
- *inc* means that the test execution of t_i did not allow to conclude about the validity of the requirement expressed by t_i.

We now have to address the issue of combing the different verdicts obtained by each tile execution of a whole test case.

3.2   Verdict Management

The solution we adopt is to include in the test special processes (called *test controlers*) for managing tile verdicts. When tiles end their execution, i.e. have computed a verdict, they emit it toward a designated test controler which captures it. Depending on verdicts received, the controller emits a final verdict – and may halt the executions of some tests if they are not needed anymore. The "main" controler then owns a variable v_g to store the final verdict.

Test controllers can easily be written in our process algebra with communication operations as shown on the following example. The whole test case is then expressed as a term of our process algebra (with parallel composition and interuptions between processes).

An example of test controller. Let us consider a test controller waiting to receive two pass verdicts in order to decide a global *pass* verdict (in other cases, it emits the last verdict received). Let c_v, be the channel on which verdicts are waited. The environment of this controller contains three variables, v for the verdicts received, v_g for the global verdict, and N to count numbers of verdicts remaining. An LTS representation is shown in Figure 3 and a corresponding algebraic expression is:

$$C \stackrel{\text{def}}{=} (recX \ ?c\_v_i(v_i) \circ [v_i = pass] \ N\text{--} \circ X) \ +$$
$$([v_i \in \{inc, fail\}] \ v_g := v_i \circ !c\_v_g(v_g) \circ !Stop \circ nil) \ +$$
$$([N = 0] \ v_g := pass \circ !c\_v_g(v_g) \circ !Stop \circ nil)$$

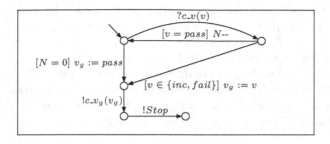

Fig. 3. Verdict controller combining pass verdicts

3.3   Test Execution

An execution of a test t (modelled by an LTS S_t) on a SUT (modelled by a LTS I), noted $\text{Exec}(t, I)$, is simply expressed as a set of common execution sequences of S_t and I, defined by a composition operator $\otimes$.

Let $\lambda_I = q_0^I \xrightarrow{a_1} q_1^I \xrightarrow{a_2} q_2^I \cdots \xrightarrow{a_n} q_n^I \cdots \in \Sigma_I$ and $\lambda_{S_t} = q^{0,t} \xrightarrow{a_1} q_1^t \xrightarrow{a_2} q_2^t \cdots \xrightarrow{a_n} q_n^t \in \Sigma_{S_t}$, then $\lambda_{S_t} \otimes \lambda_I = (q^{0,t}, q_0^I) \xrightarrow{a_1} (q_1^t, q_1^I) \cdots \xrightarrow{a_n} (q_n^t, q_n^I) \in \text{Exec}(t, I)$.

Let $\Sigma_{S_t}^{\text{pass}}$ (resp. $\Sigma_{S_t}^{\text{fail}}, \Sigma_{S_t}^{\text{inconc}}$) be the sets of states of S_t where variable v_g is set to $pass$ (resp. $fail, inc$):

$$\Sigma_{S_t}^{\text{pass}} = \{(r, \rho) \mid \rho(v_g) = pass\}$$
$$\Sigma_{S_t}^{\text{fail}} = \{(r, \rho) \mid \rho(v_g) = fail\}$$
$$\Sigma_{S_t}^{\text{inc}} = \{(r, \rho) \mid \rho(v_g) = inc\}$$

For $\lambda \in \text{Exec}(t, I)$, we define the verdict function: $\text{VExec}(\lambda) = pass$ (resp. $fail, inconc$) iff there is $\lambda_{S_t} \in \Sigma_{S_t}^{\text{pass}}$ (resp. $\Sigma_{S_t}^{\text{fail}}, \Sigma_{S_t}^{\text{inconc}}$) and $\lambda_I \in \Sigma_I$ such that $\lambda_{S_t} \otimes \lambda_I = \lambda$.

4   Security Rules Formalization

This work was initiated by a case study those objectives was to test the compliance of the IMAG network (which connects the IMAG's laboratories) to a security policy. This security policy is expressed as a set of informal rules describing (conditional) *obligations* and *interdictions* that have to be fulfilled by the network administrators. We focussed our attention to a subset of rules dedicated to electronic mail and users account management. As a mater of fact, it happened that most of these rules could be formalized using a simple logic where interdiction, obligation and permission are expressed by means of temporal modalities. We give here the syntax and semantics of this logic.

4.1   Syntax

A security policy rule is expressed by a logical *formula* (φ), built upon *literals*. Each literal can be either a *condition literal* ($p_c \in P_c$), or an *event literal*

($p_e \in P_e$). A condition literal is a (static) predicate on the network configuration (e.g., $extRelay(h)$ holds iff machine h is configured as an external mail relay), and an event literal corresponds to the occurrence of a transition in the network behavior (e.g., $enterNetwork(m)$ holds if message m is received by the network). A conjunction of condition literals is simply called a *condition* (C), whereas a conjunction of a single event literal and a condition is called a *(guarded) event* (E). The abstract syntax of a formula is given in Table 1. The intuitive meaning of these formulae is the following:

- An $\mathcal{O}$-Rule expresses a *conditional obligation*: when a particular condition holds, then another condition should also hold (logical implication).
- An $\mathcal{O}_T$-Rule expresses a *triggered obligation*: when a given event happens, then another condition should hold (or some event should occurs) before expiration of a given amount of time.
- An $\mathcal{F}$-Rule expresses an *interdiction*: when a given condition holds, or when a given event happens, then a given event is always prohibited.

Table 1. Syntax of logic formulae

$$
\begin{array}{lll}
\varphi ::= & C \Rightarrow \mathcal{O}\,C & \text{($\mathcal{O}$-Rule)} \\
& | \quad E \Rightarrow \mathcal{O}_T\,C \mid E \Rightarrow \mathcal{O}_T\,E & \text{($\mathcal{O}_T$-Rule)} \\
& | \quad C \Rightarrow \mathcal{F}\,C \mid C \Rightarrow \mathcal{F}\,E & \text{($\mathcal{F}$-Rule)} \\
E ::= & p_e[C] \mid p_e & \text{(Event)} \\
C ::= & \bigwedge_{i=1}^{n} p_{c_i} & \text{(Condition)}
\end{array}
$$

4.2 Semantics

Formulas are interpreted over LTS. Intuitively, a LTS S satisfies a formula φ iff *all* its execution sequences λ do, where condition literals are interpreted over *states*, event literals are interpreted over *labels*. We first introduce two interpretation functions for condition and event literals:

$f_c : P_c \to 2^Q$, associates to p_c the set of states on which p_c holds;

$f_e : P_e \to 2^A$, associates to p_e the set of labels on which p_e holds.

The satisfaction relation of a formula φ on an execution sequence λ ($\lambda \models \varphi$) is then (inductively) defined as follows:

- $\lambda \models C$ for $C = p_c^1 \wedge \cdots \wedge p_c^n$ iff $\forall i.\ \sigma^\lambda(1) \in f_c(p_c^i)$
- $\lambda \models p_e$ iff $\alpha^\lambda(1) \in f_e(p_e)$
- $\lambda \models p_e[C]$ iff $(\alpha^\lambda(1) \in f_e(p_e) \wedge \lambda(2) \models C)$
- $\lambda \models \varphi_1 \Rightarrow \mathcal{O}\,\varphi_2$ iff $((\lambda \models \varphi_1) \Rightarrow (\lambda \models \varphi_2))$
- $\lambda \models \varphi_1 \Rightarrow \mathcal{O}_T\varphi_2$ iff $((\lambda \models \varphi_1) \Rightarrow (\exists j \in [1, |\lambda|].\ \lambda(j) \models \varphi_2))$
- $\lambda \models \varphi_1 \Rightarrow \mathcal{F}\varphi_2$ iff $((\lambda \models \varphi_1) \Rightarrow (\forall j \in [1, |\lambda|].\ \lambda(j) \not\models \varphi_2))$

Finally, $S \models \varphi$ iff $\forall \lambda \in \Sigma_S.\ \lambda \models \varphi$.

5   Test Generation

We define a structural generation function *GenTest* to convert a rule into the desired combination of elementary tiles with controllers. It associates controllers in such a way that the final verdict is *pass* iff the rule is satisfied by the SUT. Each controller emits its verdict on a channel, and may uses variables. In the following, new variables and channels will be silently created whenever necessary.

GenTest generates parallel and architecturally independent sub-tests. Formula semantics is ensured by the controller verdict combinations. Suitable scheduling of sub-tests is supplied by the controllers through channels used to start and stop sub-tests (given below by *Test* function).

5.1   Test Generation Function *GenTest*

Transformation of tiles. Given a tile t_p (computing its verdict in the variable ver) associated to an elementary predicate p, the *Test* function transforms it. Intuitively, $Test(t_p, \mathcal{L})$, where $\mathcal{L}$ is a channel list, is t_p modified in order to be controlled through the channel list $\mathcal{L}$. More formally:

$$Test(t_p, \{c\_start, c\_stop, c\_loop, c\_ver\}) \stackrel{def}{=}$$
$$recX \,(?c\_start() \circ t_p \circ (?c\_loop() \circ X + !c\_ver(ver) \circ nil)) \ltimes^{\{?c\_stop()\}} ?c\_stop() \circ nil$$

A representation on a LTS is shown in Figure 4.

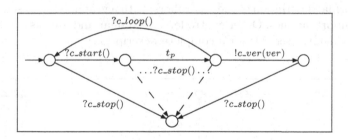

Fig. 4. Extension of tile t_p in a testing form

GenTest definition. The rule general form is: $P_l \Rightarrow \mathcal{M} P_r$ where $P_l, P_r \in \{E, C\}$ are predicates and $\mathcal{M} \in \{\mathcal{O}, \mathcal{O}_T, \mathcal{F}\}$ a modality.

The *GenTest* function is defined on the rule structure, giving an expression to be instantiated according to the different modalities. We suppose that the final verdict is emitted on the *main* channel, and t_{c_i}, t_{p_e} are the tiles respectively associated to elementary predicates c_i, p_e.

$$GenTest(P_l \Rightarrow \mathcal{M} P_r) \stackrel{def}{=} \quad (GenTest_P(P_l, \mathcal{L}_l) \parallel GenTest_P(P_r, \mathcal{L}_r)) \parallel_{\mathcal{L}} \mathbb{C}_{\mathcal{M}}(\mathcal{L}_l, \mathcal{L}_r)$$
$$\text{with } \mathcal{L} = \mathcal{L}_l \cup \mathcal{L}_r,$$
$$\mathcal{L}_l = \{c\_start_l, c\_stop_l, c\_loop_l, c\_ver_l\}, \ \mathcal{L}_r = \{c\_start_r, c\_stop_r, c\_loop_r, c\_ver_r\}$$

$GenTest_P(p_e[C], \{c\_start, c\_stop, c\_loop, c\_ver\}) \overset{\text{def}}{=}$
$\quad (Test(t_{p_e}, \mathcal{L}_e) \parallel GenTest_C(C, \mathcal{L}_c)) \parallel_{\mathcal{L}} \mathsf{C}_E(\{c\_start, c\_stop, c\_loop, c\_ver\}, \mathcal{L}_e, \mathcal{L}_c)$
$\quad \text{with } \mathcal{L} \overset{\text{def}}{=} \mathcal{L}_e \cup \mathcal{L}_c$
$\quad \mathcal{L}_e = \{c\_start_e, c\_stop_e, c\_loop_e, c\_ver_e\}, \quad \mathcal{L}_c = \{c\_start_c, c\_stop_c, c\_loop_c, c\_ver_c\}$
$GenTest_P(p_e, \{c\_start, c\_stop, c\_loop, c\_ver\}) \overset{\text{def}}{=} Test(t_{p_e}, \{c\_start, c\_stop, c\_loop, c\_ver\})$

$GenTest_P(C, \mathcal{L}) \overset{\text{def}}{=} GenTest_C(C, \mathcal{L})$

$GenTest_C(\wedge_{i=1}^n c_i, \{c\_start, c\_stop, c\_loop, c\_ver\}) \overset{\text{def}}{=}$
$\quad \text{if } n = 1, \quad Test(t_{c_1}, \{c\_start, c\_stop, c\_loop, c\_ver\})$
$\quad \text{else } /* \ n > 1 \ */$
$\quad\quad \parallel_{i=1}^n Test(t_{c_i}, \mathcal{L}_i) \parallel_{\mathcal{L}} \mathsf{C}_\wedge(\{c\_start, c\_stop, c\_loop, c\_ver\}, (\mathcal{L}_i)_{i=1\ldots n}, n)$
$\quad\quad \text{with } \mathcal{L} = \cup_{i=1}^n \mathcal{L}_i; \forall i \in \{1\ldots n\}, \mathcal{L}_i = \{c\_start, c\_stop, c\_loop, c\_ver_i\}$

5.2   Verdict Controllers

Several verdict controllers are used in the *GenTest* definition. Controllers have different purposes. They are first used to manage the execution of sub-tests corresponding to the components of the rule. For example, for a $\mathcal{O}_T$ formula, we have to wait for the left-side subtest before starting the right-side subtest. Controllers are also used to "implement" the formula semantics by combining verdicts from sub-tests.

Controllers definitions are parameterized with channel parameters. We give here an informal description of the controllers, with a graphical representation for the more important ones. Other controllers are similar and are easy to formalize in our test calculus (see [11] for a complete description).

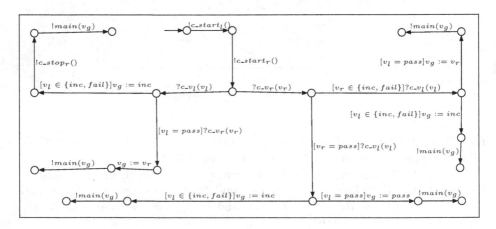

Fig. 5. An instantiated LTS representation of the $\mathsf{C}_\mathcal{O}$ controller

Formula level controllers. They emit their verdict on the channel *main*.

1. $\mathcal{C}_{\mathcal{O}}(channel\_list, channel\_list)$. This controller is used to manage the execution of tiles corresponding to the left and right part of a static implication. The controller starts the two tests corresponding to the two sides of the implication. Then it waits for the reception of a verdict (verdicts can arrive in any order). According to the semantics of implication and the first verdict received, it decides either to wait for the second verdict or to emit a verdict immediately. The controller takes two channel lists as parameters for managing the execution and verdict of each side of the implication. The associated environment contains three variables. A LTS representation of $\mathcal{C}_{\mathcal{O}}(\{c\_start_l, c\_stop_l, c\_v_l, c\_loop_l\}, \{c\_start_r, c\_stop_r, c\_v_r, c\_loop_r\})$ is shown in Figure 5.

2. $\mathcal{C}_{\mathcal{O}_T}(channel\_list, channel\_list)$. This controller is used to manage the execution of tiles corresponding to the sides of an implication with a triggered obligation. The controller starts the test corresponding to the left side of the implication. If this test is inconclusive or fails, a *inc* verdict is decided. Otherwise, the timer and the second test are started. If the test emits *pass*, the final verdict is *pass*. As long as the timer is not expired, (that is, the boolean variable t_out is false), if the second test ends with *fail* or *inc*, the test is started again. When the the timer expires, a stop signal ($!c\_stop_r$) is sent to the right side test. In that case, the final verdict is *inc* if an *inc* verdict occurred, *fail* otherwise. A LTS representation of $\mathcal{C}_{\mathcal{O}_T}(\{c\_start_l, c\_stop_l, c\_loop_l, c\_ver_l\}, \{c\_start_r, c\_stop_r, c\_loop_r, c\_ver_r\})$ is shown in Figure 6.

3. $\mathcal{C}_{\mathcal{F}}(channel\_list, channel\_list)$. This controller is similar to the $\mathcal{C}_{\mathcal{O}}$ controller. It waits for a fail verdict for the right-side subtest in order to conclude on a *pass* verdict.

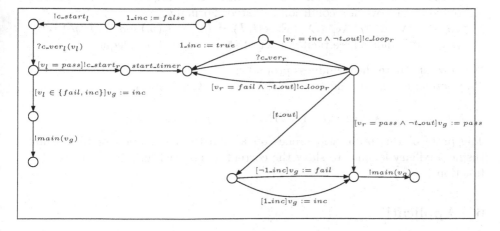

Fig. 6. An instantiated LTS representation of the $\mathcal{C}_{\mathcal{O}_T}$ controller

Predicate Level Controllers

1. $C_E(channel\_list, channel\_list, channel\_list)$. This controller is used to manage executions and verdicts around an event. The controller starts the execution of the event, and then, depending on the verdict received, it starts the sub-tests associated to the condition predicates in E. These conditions have to be tested after the event.
2. $C_\wedge(channel\_lists, integer)$. Informally this controller starts different tests and waits for verdicts. Like the other controllers it controls sub-tests with a channel. If all tests succeed, the controller emits a *pass* verdict. If some tests do not respond *pass* the controller emits the last verdict received and stops the other potentially executing sub-tests. This controller is a generalization of the one presented in 3.1.

5.3   Soundness Proposition

We now express that an abstract test case produced by function *GenTest* is always *sound*, i.e. it delivers a *fail* verdict when executed on a network behavior I only if formula ϕ does not hold on I. To do this, we follow a very similar approach than in [8]. Two hypotheses are required in order to prove this soundness property:

H1. First, for any formula φ, we assume that each elementary test case t_i provided for the (event or condition) literals p_i appearing in φ is *strongly sound* in the following sense:
Execution of t_i on SUT I always terminate, and
$\forall \lambda \in \text{Exec}(t_i, I) \cdot \text{VExec}(\lambda) = Pass \Rightarrow \lambda \models p_i \wedge (\text{VExec}(\lambda) = Fail \Rightarrow \lambda \not\models p_i)$.
H2. Second, we assume that the whole execution of a (provided or generated) test case t associated to a condition C is *stable* with respect to condition literals: the valuation of these literal does not change during the test execution. This simply means that the network configuration is supposed to remain stable when a condition is tested. Formally:
$\forall p_i \in P_c. \forall \lambda \in \Sigma_I \cdot \lambda_{S_t} \otimes \lambda \in \text{Exec}(t, I) \Rightarrow (\sigma^\lambda \subseteq f_c(p_i) \vee \sigma^\lambda \cap f_c(p_i) = \emptyset)$
where σ^λ denotes here tacitly a set of states instead of a sequence.

We now formulate the soundness property:
Proposition: Let φ a formula, I an LTS and $t = \text{GenTest}(\varphi)$. Then:

$$\lambda \in \text{Exec}(t, I) \wedge \text{VExec}(\lambda) = fail \implies I \not\models \varphi$$

The proof of this proposition relies on a structural induction of the formula (using auxiliary lemmas to show the correctness of each intermediate *GenTest* function).

6   Application

In this section we apply the *GenTest* function to two rule patterns taken from the case study presented in [8].

6.1 $\mathcal{O}$-Rule

Consider the requirement *"External relays shall be in the DMZ [2]"*, this could be reasonably understood as *"If a host is an external relay, it has to be in the DMZ"*. A possible modelisation is:

$$extRelay(h) \Rightarrow \mathcal{O}\,(inDMZ(h))$$

The goal of this test is to verify that each external relay h is in the DMZ. The *GenTest* function can be applied on this formula, leading to the following test:

$GenTest(extRelay(h) \Rightarrow \mathcal{O}\,(inDMZ(h)))$
$\quad = \Big(GenTest_P(extRelay(h), \mathcal{L}_l) \parallel GenTest_P(inDMZ(h), \mathcal{L}_r)\Big) \parallel_{\mathcal{L}} \mathsf{C}_{\mathcal{O}}(\mathcal{L}_l, \mathcal{L}_r)$
$\quad = \Big(Test(t_{extRelay(h)}, \mathcal{L}_l) \parallel Test(t_{inDMZ(h)}, \mathcal{L}_r)\Big) \parallel_{\mathcal{L}} \mathsf{C}_{\mathcal{O}}(\mathcal{L}_l, \mathcal{L}_r)$
where $\mathcal{L} = \mathcal{L}_l \cup \mathcal{L}_r$
$\qquad \mathcal{L}_l = \{c\_start_l, c\_stop_l, c\_v_l, c\_loop_l\}$ and $\mathcal{L}_r = \{c\_start_r, c\_stop_r, c\_v_r, c\_loop_r\}$

For a given machine h, predicates $extRelay(h)$ and $inDMZ(h)$ can be checked either by analyzing the configuration of devices in the network and/or administrators' databases (if this information can be trusted), or rather by testing the actual behaviour of this machine (does it act as an external relay?). In this last case, we need some tiles for these two predicates.

A possible tile for $t_{extRelay(h)}$ consists in attempting to send a mail m from an external machine he to an internal machine hi by first opening a connection from he to h (!$connect(he, h)$), and then asking for mail transfers from he to h (!$transfer(he, h, m)$) and from h to hi (!$transfer(h, hi, m)$). If these operation succeed the verdict is *pass*, otherwise it is *fail* (h does not act as an external relay). Not that if the connection from he to h fails for external reasons (e.g, network overloading) then the verdict is *inc* (inconclusive). This tile can be formalized as follows:

$t_{extRelay(h)} \overset{\text{def}}{=}$
$\quad !connect(he, h)\circ$
$\qquad (?ok\circ !transfer(he, h, m)\circ$
$\qquad\qquad [?ok\circ !tranfer(h, hi, m) \circ (ver := pass)\circ nil + ?ko\circ(ver := fail)\circ nil]$
$\qquad + (?ko \circ (ver := inc) \circ nil))$

6.2 $\mathcal{O}_T$-Rule

Security policies may also express availability requirements. Consider *"When there is a request to open an account, user privileges and resources must be activated within one hour"*. We formalize this requirement as:

$$request\_open\_account(c)[\neg ex\_account(c)] \Rightarrow \mathcal{O}_{1H}(open\_account(c)[allocate\_disk(c)])$$

---

[2] for *demilitarized zone*, a strongly controlled buffer zone between the inside and outside of the network.

Supposing that there exists a tile for each predicate and that all tiles are independent. One could generate a test from appropriate derivation:

$$GenTest(req\_acc(c)[\neg ex\_acc(c)] \Rightarrow \mathcal{O}_{1H}(op\_acc(c)[alloc(c)]))$$
$$= \Big((Test(t_{req\_acc(c)}, \mathcal{L}_{le}) \parallel Test(ex\_acc(c), \mathcal{L}_{lc})) \parallel_{\mathcal{L}_{le} \cup \mathcal{L}_{lc}} \mathsf{C}_E(\mathcal{L}_l, \mathcal{L}_{le}, \mathcal{L}_{lc})\Big)$$
$$\parallel \Big((Test(t_{op\_acc(c)}, \mathcal{L}_{re}) \parallel Test(t_{alloc\_disk(c)}, \mathcal{L}_{rc})) \parallel_{\mathcal{L}_{re} \cup \mathcal{L}_{rc}} \mathsf{C}_E(\mathcal{L}_r, \mathcal{L}_{re}, \mathcal{L}_{rc})\Big)$$
$$\parallel_{\mathcal{L}} \mathsf{C}_{\mathcal{O}_{1H}}(\mathcal{L}_l, \mathcal{L}_r)$$
with: $\mathcal{L} = \mathcal{L}_l \cup \mathcal{L}_r$, $\mathcal{L}_x = \{c\_start_x, c\_stop_x, c\_loop_x, c\_ver_x\}_x, x \in \{l, r, le, lc, re, rc\}$

7   Conclusion

We have proposed a test generation technique for testing the validity of a temporal logical formula on a system under test. The originality of this approach is to produce the tests by combinations of elementary test cases (called tiles), associated to each atomic predicates of the formula. These tiles are supposed to be provided by the system designer or a test expert, and, assuming they are correct, it can be proved that the whole test case obtained is sound. The practical interest of this approach is that it can be applied even if a formal specification of the system under test is not available, or if the test execution needs to mix several interface levels. A concrete example of such a situation is network security testing, where the security policy is usually expressed as a set of logical requirements, encompassing many network elements (communication protocols, firewalls, antivirus softwares, etc.) and those behavior would be hard to describe on a single formal specification. The abstract test cases we obtain are expressed in a process algebraic style, and they are structured into test drivers (the tiles), and test controllers (encoding the logical operators). This approach makes them close to executable test cases, and easy to map on a concrete (and distributed) test architecture. Independent parts of the tests can then be executed concurrently.

This work could be continued in several directions. First, the logic we proposed here could be extended. So far, the kind of formulae we considered was guided by a concrete application, but, staying in the context of network security, other deontic/temporal modalities could be foreseen, like "interdiction within a delay", or "permission". We also believe that this approach would be flexible enough to be used in other application domains, with other kinds of logical formulae (for instance with nested temporal modalities, which were not considered here). A second improvement would be to produce a clear diagnostic when a test execution fails. So far, test controllers only propagate "fail" verdicts, but it could be useful to better indicate to the user why a test execution failed (which sub-formula was unsuccessfully tested, and what is the incorrect execution sequence we obtained). Finally, we are currently implementing this test generation technique, and we expect that practical experimentations will help us to extend it towards the generation of *concrete* test cases, that could be directly executable.

References

1. ISO/IEC 9946-1: OSI-Open Systems Interconnection, Information Technology - Open Systems Interconnection Conformance Testing Methodology and Framework. International Standard ISO/IEC 9646-1/2/3 (1992)
2. Brinksma, E., Alderden, R., Langerak, R. Van de Lagemaat, J., Tretmans, J.: A Formal Approach to Conformance Testing. In De Meer, J., Mackert, L., Effelsberg, W., eds.: Second International Workshop on Protocol Test Systems, North Holland (1990) 349–363
3. Tretmans, J.: Test Generation with Inputs, Outputs, and Quiescence. In Margaria, T., Steffen, B., eds.: Second Int. Workshop on Tools and Algorithms for the Construction and Analysis of Systems (TACAS'96). Volume 1055 of Lecture Notes in Computer Science., Springer-Verlag (1996) 127–146
4. Jard, C., Jéron, T.: TGV: theory, principles and algorithms. In: The Sixth World Conference on Integrated Design & Process Technology (IDPT'02), Pasadena, California, USA (2002)
5. Belinfante, A., Feenstra, J., de Vries, R., Tretmans, J., Goga, N., Feijs, L., Mauw, S., Heerink, L.: Formal Test Automation : a Simple Experiment. In: 12th International Workshop on Testing of Communicating Systems, G. Csopaki et S. Dibuz et K. Tarnay, Kluwer Academic Publishers (1999)
6. Schmitt, M., Koch, B., Grabowski, J., Hogrefe, D.: Autolink - A Tool for Automatic and Semi-Automatic Test Generation from SDL Specifications. Technical Report A-98-05, Medical University of Lübeck (1998)
7. Groz, R., Jéron, T., Kerbrat, A.: Automated test generation from SDL specifications. In Dssouli, R., von Bochmann, G., Lahav, Y., eds.: SDL'99 The Next Millenium, 9th SDL Forum, Montreal, Quebec, Elsevier (1999) 135–152
8. Darmaillacq, V., Fernandez, J.C., Groz, R., Mounier, L., Richier, J.L.: Test Generation for Network Security Rules. In: 18th IFIP International Conference, TestCom 2006, New York, LNCS 3964, Springer (2006)
9. Milner, R.: A Calculus of Communicating Systems. Volume 92 of Lecture Notes in Computer Science. Springer-Verlag, Berlin (1980)
10. Hoare, C.A.R.: Communicating Sequential Processes. Prentice-Hall (1985)
11. Falcone, Y.: Un cadre formel pour le test de politiques de sécurité. Master's thesis, Université Joseph Fourier, Grenoble, France (2006)

Hybrid Input-Output Conformance and Test Generation*

Michiel van Osch

Technische Universiteit Eindhoven
Department of Mathematics and Computer Science
5600 MB, Eindhoven, The Netherlands
m.p.w.j.van.osch@tue.nl

Abstract. Input-output conformance test theory for discrete systems
has established itself in research and industry already. A couple of years
ago also input-output conformance test theories for timed systems were
defined. The next step is to develop conformance test theory for hybrid
systems as well. In this paper we present a conformance relation for
model-based testing of hybrid systems and we formalize tests for hybrid
systems.

1   Introduction

A hybrid system is a system with both discrete behavior and continuous behavior. It has discrete controllers or computers, running discrete software, with
discrete input and discrete output; it receives continuous input through the observations of sensors; and it generates continuous output through actuators (e.g.
motors, hydraulics, heaters). A hybrid system can be very complex and testing
it thoroughly can be of critical importance. This is the case when the safety of
people is involved or when an unreliable machine may cause a huge loss of profit
for a manufacturer.

The main purpose of model-based conformance testing is to develop a test
tool that uses a formal specification to generate tests. These tests describe the
input with which the system under test should be stimulated, and the output
that is expected from it. Model-based test generation is preferably supported
by a mathematical input-output conformance theory that formally defines when
an implementation is to be considered conform a specification. With respect to
this theory, the set of tests generated from a specification by the algorithm can
then be proved to be sound (meaning that only faulty implementations can fail a
generated test) and exhaustive (meaning that every faulty implementation fails
at least one generated test). Some of the main advantages of model-based testing
are that, since tests are automatically generated and executed, many more tests
can be performed in less time, and tests can be easily repeated. Moreover, the
specifications can also be used to formally verify the design of a system.

---

* This work has been carried out as part of the TANGRAM project under the responsibility of the Embedded Systems Institute. This project is partially supported by
  the Netherlands Ministry of Economic Affairs under grant TSIT2026.

K. Havelund et al. (Eds.): FATES/RV 2006, LNCS 4262, pp. 70–84, 2006.

Tretmans [8] proposed an input-output conformance test theory for discrete event systems; it led to the test tool TorX [10], which has been successfully applied in several industrial settings. Recently, extensions for real-time systems were proposed [2, 5, 6]. In this paper we present an input-output conformance test theory for hybrid systems.

We start from the assumption that the specification is a hybrid transition system, which has a discrete transition relation labelled with actions and a continuous transition relation labelled with trajectories (flows of variables). With every hybrid transition relation we associate a set of tests, which are themselves a special kind of hybrid transition systems. Roughly, tests are generated from the specification by a recursive algorithm that chooses to either select an input action or an input trajectory from the specification, or to evaluate the observed output (actions and trajectories). If the observed output action or trajectory is allowed according to the specification, test case generation may continue or end with the verdict **pass**, whereas if the output action or trajectory is not allowed according to the specification, then the test aborts with the verdict **fail**.

For the purpose of validating the test generation algorithm, we also develop a mathematical input-output conformance theory for hybrid transition systems. In this theory it is assumed that also the implementation is a hybrid transition system, which is moreover assumed to be input enabled (at all times it should be able to accept any input from its environment). We propose an input-output conformance relation that formalizes the idea that, in every reachable state, a correct implementation should only perform output actions or output flows that are allowed according to the specification.

This paper is organized as follows. In Section 2 we informally discuss some of the issues that play a rôle in a theory of model-based input-output conformance testing for hybrid systems. In Section 3 we introduce hybrid transition systems. In Section 4 we formalize when an implementation (an input enabled hybrid transition system) should be considered conform a specification (also a hybrid transition system). In Section 5 we inductively associate with every specification a set of tests. In Section 6 we discuss some issues that will still need to be solved before our theory can be implemented. The paper ends with some conclusions in Section 7.

2   Hybrid Model-Based Testing by an Example

In this section we informally introduce the main concepts of model-based testing for hybrid systems. Consider a simple brake control system of a car. The system allows a car to stay behind another car. The system continuously measures the distance with the car in front. If the car comes too close to the car in front it starts braking. The brake system can be turned ON or turned OFF. If the system is turned OFF, then a warning light is turned ON to notify the driver. If the system detects a new car in front, the driver is also notified.

Testing a system means stimulating it with input behavior and observing the output behavior. For instance, the brake system is stimulated by turning it ON

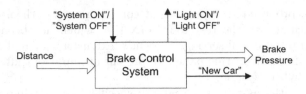

Fig. 1. A Braking System of a Car

and it is observed whether the warning light is turned OFF. Or, the sensor which is measuring the distance with the car in front is stimulated with distance measurement and the change of brake pressure is observed.

What makes testing hybrid systems difficult is that continuous input and continuous output always occur, that they occur in synchrony and that they depend on each other. If the brake system is stimulated with a steadily decreasing distance, then the brake pressure should increases steadily. It is even possible that the continuous input depends on the continuous output. For instance, if the car brakes, the amount of brake pressure influences how rapidly the distance with the car in front decreases (or increases). Furthermore, discrete output behavior also depends on continuous input behavior and discrete output behavior may have time constraints. For instance, if the distance measurement with the car in front makes a jump (which means a new car is detected), then a "New Car" output has to occur within 0.5 seconds. A test is passed if only expected output is observed (given the input applied) and it fails if an unexpected output is observed. If the brake pressure does not increase while the distance with the car in front decreases (as expected), then the test fails.

The goal of model-based testing, in the form we consider it, is to automate test generation and execution. The behavior of the system is specified by a formal model and tests are automatically generated from this specification. The specification can be a transition system, an automaton, a process algebra term, or a (formal) specification language. Tests are generated by selecting discrete or continuous input from the specification and enumerating the possible observations. A verdict pass or fail is attached to each possible observation in accordance with the specification. Tests are executed by automatically stimulating the implementation with the input described by the test and simultaneously observing the output from the implementation.

It is usually assumed that the implementation is input enabled. It is possible to stimulate the system under test (which is the system that is tested) with every conceivable behavior at any moment in time.This assumption simplifies automated test generation and execution because the test tool does not need to check whether the implementation accepts the input. In most cases it is also a natural assumption on the implementation. Stimulating the brake system with "Hello World" instead of "System ON" affects the system and it should be possible to test this. It is not required that the specification is input enabled. This makes it possible to steer the test process as only the behavior is tested for which the specification provides the input. For example it is possible to only specify gradual distance change and test the system using this input, or it is possible to specify a jump in distance change and test the system using this input.

The conformance relation formally defines if an implementation conforms to the specification. The test generation procedure defines how tests are generated from a specification. With a formal definition of how a test is constructed and a formal conformance relation it is possible to prove whether our tests are sound and exhaustive with respect to the conformance relation. That is, if the implementation conforms to the specification then the implementation will pass all tests that can be generated from the specification and if the implementation is not conform the specification then it is possible to generate a test which fails.

In this paper we define a formal conformance relation and formal tests for hybrid systems.

3   Hybrid Transition Systems

We define our hybrid input-output conformance relation on the semantic model of hybrid transition systems [3]. We only introduce the definitions necessary for our theory. We only use symbolic states and we leave open the initial valuation of variables (which can be defined by the initial state). Before we can formally define hybrid transition systems, we first need to define trajectories. In order to define trajectories we need some mathematical preliminaries.

1. An interval over $\mathbb{R}$ is called *left-closed* if it has a minimum, *right-closed* if it has a maximum, and *closed* if it has both a minimum and a maximum.
2. Let $f : A \to B$ be a function; for $A' \subseteq A$ we define f restricted to A', denoted by $f \lceil A'$, as the function $f \lceil A' : A' \to B$ defined by $f \lceil A'(a) = f(a)$ for $a \in A'$.
3. Let $f : A \to B$ with $A \subseteq \mathbb{R}$ be a function and let $A + t = \{a + t | a \in A\}$; for $t \in \mathbb{R}$ we define $f + t : A + t \to B$ by $(f + t)(t') = f(t' - t)$, with $t' \in A + t$.

A trajectory is defined as a function from a interval to a vector of valuations of variables. A trajectory is defined over a right-closed interval of $\mathbb{R}$, starting at 0.

Definition 1

1. *Let V be a set of (continuous) variables. A valuation for V, denoted by val(V), is a function that associates with each variable $v \in V$ a value of the type of v. We write val(V) for the set of all valuations for V.*
2. *Let $t \in \mathbb{R}^{>0}$ be a positive real number and let V be a set of variables. A trajectory σ is a function $\sigma : (0, t] \to val(V)$ that associates with each element in the domain $(0, t]$ a valuation. We write trajs(V) for the set of all trajectories with respect to V.*
3. *Let σ be a trajectory. We write dom(σ) for the domain of σ, $\sigma.fval$ for the first valuation of σ, $\sigma.lval$ for the last valuation of σ, and $\sigma.ltime$ for the maximum of the domain of σ. Note that $\sigma(\sigma.ltime) = \sigma.lval$.*

4. Let σ and σ' be trajectories. The concatenation of σ and σ' (denoted by $\sigma \frown \sigma'$) is defined as:

$$\sigma \frown \sigma' = \sigma \cup (\sigma' + \sigma.ltime).$$

5. Let σ be a trajectory on variables V; for $V' \subseteq V$ we define σ restricted to V', denoted by $\sigma \downarrow V'$ as the function $\sigma \downarrow V' : J \to (V' \to val(V'))$ defined by $\sigma \downarrow V'(t) = \sigma(t) \lceil V'$ with $t \in J$.

6. Let σ be a trajectory defined over an interval $(0, t]$, with $t > 0$ and let $t' \in \mathbb{R}^{>0}$ with $t' \leq t$; then:

$$\sigma \trianglelefteq t' = \sigma \lceil (0, t'];$$
$$\sigma \trianglerighteq t' = (\sigma \lceil (t', t]) - t'.$$

7. Let σ and σ' be two trajectories; then σ is a prefix of σ', denoted by $\sigma \leq \sigma'$, if there exists a $t \in \mathbb{R}^{>0}$ such that $\sigma = \sigma' \trianglelefteq t$. We write $\sigma < \sigma'$ if $\sigma \leq \sigma'$ and $\sigma.ltime < \sigma'.ltime$.

A hybrid transition system is a tuple consisting of a set of states, an initial state, a set of discrete transitions, and a set of continuous transitions. Every transition has a label. A label is either an action or a trajectory. The set of actions A is partitioned into disjunct sets of input actions A_I and output actions A_O and internal action τ, i.e. $A = A_I \uplus A_O \uplus \{\tau\}$. Every trajectory is defined on a set of variables V. V is partitioned into disjunct sets of input variables V_I and output variables V_O, i.e. $V = V_I \uplus V_O$.

A trajectory also models time. The interval over which the trajectory is defined is the time in which the flow takes place.

Definition 2. A hybrid transition system (HTS) is a tuple $\mathcal{H} = (S, s_0, \to, \rightsquigarrow)$, where

- S is a (possibly infinite) set of states;
- $s_0 \in S$ is the initial state;
- $\to \subseteq S \times A \times S$ is the set of discrete transitions for a set of actions A; and
- $\rightsquigarrow \subseteq S \times \Sigma \times S$ is the set of continuous transitions for a set of trajectories Σ.

From now on, $\mathcal{H}$ always is a HTS $\mathcal{H} = (S, s_0, \to, \rightsquigarrow)$. We write $s \xrightarrow{a} s'$ instead of $(s, a, s') \in \to$. We write $s \xrightarrow{\sigma} s'$ instead of $(s, \sigma, s') \in \rightsquigarrow$. We also write $s \xrightarrow{a}$ instead of $\exists_{s' \in S} : s \xrightarrow{a} s'$. and we write $s \xrightarrow{\sigma}$ instead of $\exists_{s' \in S} : s \xrightarrow{\sigma} s'$.

For our theory we need to assume three conditions on every HTS $\mathcal{H}$. The first condition we call trajectory interpolation, the second condition we call trajectory additivity, and the third condition we call trajectory determinism.

- **A1:** If $s \xrightarrow{\sigma' \frown \sigma''} s''$, then there exists a $s' \in S$ such that $s \xrightarrow{\sigma'} s'$ and $s' \xrightarrow{\sigma''} s''$.
- **A2:** If $s \xrightarrow{\sigma'} s'$ and $s' \xrightarrow{\sigma''} s''$ then $s \xrightarrow{\sigma' \frown \sigma''} s''$.
- **A3:** If $s, s', s'' \in S$ such that $s \xrightarrow{\sigma} s'$ and $s \xrightarrow{\sigma} s''$ then $s' = s''$.

We use the standard definition of input action enabling. A HTS accepts any input action in every state. Our definition of input trajectory enabling is that a HTS accepts any input trajectory in every state, possibly interrupted by an output action or τ, with the exception of states in which no trajectories are possible. Observe that in this definition, after a trajectory is interrupted, the trajectory can still be completed. The reason is that, since the system accepts any input trajectory, it also accepts the suffix of the interrupted trajectory after the output action or τ.

Definition 3. *Let $\mathcal{H}$ be a HTS.*

- *$\mathcal{H}$ is input action enabled if for every $s \in S$ and $i \in A_I$: $s \xrightarrow{i}$.*
- *$\mathcal{H}$ is input trajectory enabled if for every $s \in S$:*
  1. *there exists an action $a \in A_O \cup \{\tau\}$ such that $s \xrightarrow{a}$ and there does not exist a $\sigma \in \Sigma$ such that $s \overset{\sigma}{\rightsquigarrow}$; or*
  2. *for every $u \in trajs(V_I)$ there exists a $\sigma \in \Sigma$ with $\sigma \downarrow V_I \leq u$ and:*
     (a) *$\sigma \downarrow V_I = u$ and there exists an $s' \in S$: $s \overset{\sigma}{\rightsquigarrow} s'$; or*
     (b) *$\sigma \downarrow V_I < u$ and there exists an action $a \in A_O \cup \{\tau\}$ and $s' \in S$ such that: $s \overset{\sigma}{\rightsquigarrow} s' \xrightarrow{a}$.*
- *$\mathcal{H}$ is input enabled if it is both input action enabled and input trajectory enabled.*

The execution of a hybrid transition system is described by a sequence of observable actions and trajectories. A transition with an action or a trajectory leads to a state from which another transition can be taken. A sequence of which the start state is the initial state of the HTS is called a trace. Note that in our definition the internal action τ does not occur in a sequence or a trace.

Definition 4. *Let $\mathcal{H}$ be a HTS.*

1. *We inductively define the generalized transition relation $\Rightarrow \subseteq S \times (A \cup \Sigma)^* \times S$ as the least relation that satisfies for all $s, s', s'' \in S$:*
   - *$s \overset{\epsilon}{\Rightarrow} s$;*
   - *if $s \xrightarrow{\tau} s'$, then $s \overset{\epsilon}{\Rightarrow} s'$;*
   - *if $s \xrightarrow{a} s'$, then $s \overset{a}{\Rightarrow} s'$;*
   - *if $s \overset{\sigma}{\rightsquigarrow} s'$, then $s \overset{\sigma}{\Rightarrow} s'$; and*
   - *if $s \overset{\alpha}{\Rightarrow} s'$ and $s' \overset{\beta}{\Rightarrow} s''$, then $s \overset{\alpha\beta}{\Rightarrow} s''$.*
2. *If $s \in S$ is a state of S, then a trace of HTS $\mathcal{H}$ is a sequence $\alpha \in (A \cup \Sigma)^*$ such that $s_0 \overset{\alpha}{\Rightarrow} s$. The set of all traces of $\mathcal{H}$ is denoted by $traces(\mathcal{H})$.*

For a state s and a sequence α we also write $s \overset{\alpha}{\Rightarrow}$ instead of $\exists_{s' \in S} : s \overset{\alpha}{\Rightarrow} s'$.

We denote by s **after** α the set of reachable states from s after a trace α.

Definition 5. *Let $\mathcal{H}$ be a HTS, $s \in S$ and $\alpha \in (A \cup \Sigma)^*$; then:*

$$s \text{ after } \alpha = \{s' | s \overset{\alpha}{\Rightarrow} s'\}.$$

For a set of states $C \subseteq S$ we define:

$$C \text{ after } \alpha = \bigcup_{c \in C} c \text{ after } \alpha.$$

We sometimes write $\mathcal{H}$ **after** α instead of s_0 **after** α.

4   The Hybrid Input-Output Conformance Relation

In this section we define the conformance relation for hybrid systems. This conformance relation tells us whether a hybrid implementation conforms to a hybrid specification. This is the case if, in every reachable state, the implementation only contains specified discrete and continuous output behavior. The implementation is not conform a specification if, in some reachable state, the implementation performs an output action or a trajectory that is not specified.

We define our conformance relation on the class of systems that can be described by a hybrid transition system. Both the implementation and the specification are defined as hybrid transition systems. An implementation is input enabled and a specification does not need to be input enabled.

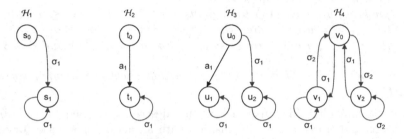

Fig. 2. Example Hybrid Transition Systems

Figure 2 shows four hybrid transition system examples. In these examples σ_1 and σ_2 with input variables V_I and output variables V_O, and a_1 is an output action. We assume that conditions **A1** to **A3** hold, even though we cannot depict this (as this means we need to draw infinitely many states and transitions). These examples are not input enabled either. Still, we will use them to illustrate our theory.

Intuitively, $\mathcal{H}_3$ is not conform $\mathcal{H}_1$ because $\mathcal{H}_3$ can perform an output action (in state u_0), while $\mathcal{H}_1$ cannot. On the other hand, $\mathcal{H}_1$ conforms to $\mathcal{H}_3$ because $\mathcal{H}_3$ allows all the behavior that $\mathcal{H}_1$ can display. $\mathcal{H}_3$ is not conform $\mathcal{H}_2$ because when according to $\mathcal{H}_2$ an output action has to happen, according to $\mathcal{H}_3$ it may not happen. On the other hand, $\mathcal{H}_2$ conforms to $\mathcal{H}_3$ because when the output action a_1 occurs, it can also occur according to $\mathcal{H}_3$. If the flow of input variables in trajectory σ_1 is different from the flow of input variables in trajectory σ_2 (i.e., $\sigma_1 \downarrow V_I \neq \sigma_2 \downarrow V_I$), then $\mathcal{H}_4$ conforms to $\mathcal{H}_1$. The reason is that with respect to the input trajectory $\mathcal{H}_4$ displays the same output behavior as $\mathcal{H}_1$. However, if the flow of input variables is the same for σ_1 and σ_2 (or there are no input variables) and the flow of output variables is not the same for σ_1 and σ_2, then $\mathcal{H}_4$ is not conform $\mathcal{H}_1$ because $\mathcal{H}_4$ can display output behavior that is not allowed according to $\mathcal{H}_1$. For our conformance relation we first define the set of trajectories allowed in a state s by $\mathbf{traj}(s)$ and we define the trajectories allowed in a set of states C by $\mathbf{traj}(C)$.

Definition 6. *Let $\mathcal{H}$ be a HTS and let $s \in S$ be a state of $\mathcal{H}$; then:*

$$\mathbf{traj}(s) = \{\sigma \in \Sigma | s \overset{\sigma}{\leadsto}\}.$$

For a set of states $C \subseteq S$ we define:

$$\mathbf{traj}(C) = \bigcup_{c \in C} \mathbf{traj}(c).$$

For instance, $\mathbf{traj}(s_0)$ of $\mathcal{H}_1$ is $\{\sigma_1\}$ and $\mathbf{traj}(u_0)$ of $\mathcal{H}_4$ is $\{\sigma_1, \sigma_2\}$.

Since an implementation is input enabled and a specification does not have to be input enabled, the specification determines which trajectories are relevant in our relation. Namely, those trajectories for which an input trajectory exists in the specification. For instance, in case we determine whether $\mathcal{H}_4$ conforms to $\mathcal{H}_3$: if $\sigma_1 \downarrow V_I \neq \sigma_2 \downarrow V_I$, then we only want to take into account σ_1 ; and if $\sigma_1 \downarrow V_I = \sigma_2 \downarrow V_I$, then we want to take into account σ_1 and σ_2.

Definition 7. *Let Σ_I and Σ_S be two sets of trajectories on a set of variables V with input variables $V_I \subseteq V$; then:*

$$\mathbf{infilter}(\Sigma_I, \Sigma_S) = \{\sigma \in \Sigma_I | \exists_{\sigma' \in \Sigma_S} : \sigma \downarrow V_I = \sigma' \downarrow V_I\}.$$

For instance, if $\sigma_1 \downarrow V_I \neq \sigma_2 \downarrow V_I$, then $\mathbf{infilter}(\mathbf{traj}(v_0), \mathbf{traj}(s_0)) = \{\sigma_1\}$.

As described earlier, in a hybrid transition system time progresses through trajectories. Actions are instantaneous. It is possible to specify that time cannot progress unless an action happens first. It allows us for instance to specify urgent actions, by states from which exactly one action is possible and no trajectories are possible. However, because we want to restrict conformance of the implementation to the set of possible input trajectories we do not know whether according to implementation an (output) action had to happen. For instance, if we apply the **infilter** with $\mathcal{H}_3$ as implementation and $\mathcal{H}_2$ as specification; then, in the initial states u_0 and t_0 respectively, the resulting set of trajectories turns out to be empty ($\mathbf{infilter}(\mathbf{traj}(u_0), \mathbf{traj}(s_0)) = \emptyset$). The information that a_1 did not have to happen is lost. To solve this problem we use a symbol ξ which indicates that, in a state, besides output actions also trajectories are allowed.

Definition 8. *Let $\mathcal{H}$ be a HTS and let $s \in S$ be a state of $\mathcal{H}$; then:*

$$\mathbf{out}(s) = \begin{cases} \{o \in A_O | \exists_{s' \in S} : s \overset{o}{\to} s'\} \cup \{\xi\}, & \text{if } \exists_{\sigma \in \Sigma, s' \in S} : (s \overset{\sigma}{\leadsto} s'); \\ \{o \in A_O | \exists_{s' \in S} : s \overset{o}{\to} s'\} & , \text{otherwise.} \end{cases}$$

For a set of states $C \subseteq S$ we define:

$$\mathbf{out}(C) = \bigcup_{c \in C} \mathbf{out}(c).$$

For instance, $\mathbf{out}(s_0)$ of $\mathcal{H}_1$ is $\{\xi\}$ and $\mathbf{out}(u_0)$ of $\mathcal{H}_3$ is $\{a_1, \xi\}$.

Finally we can define our conformance relation for hybrid systems called **hioco**. Informally, in every reachable state the set of output actions and the set of trajectories performed by the implementation, filtered on input allowed by the specification, should be a subset of the set of output actions and the set of trajectories in the specification.

Definition 9. *Let $\mathcal{S}$ be a HTS and let $\mathcal{I}$ be an input enabled HTS. We say that $\mathcal{I}$ is input-output conform $\mathcal{S}$ (notation: $\mathcal{I}$ **hioco** $\mathcal{S}$) iff:*

$$\forall_{\alpha \in traces(\mathcal{S})} : \mathbf{out}(\mathcal{I} \textbf{ after } \alpha) \subseteq \mathbf{out}(\mathcal{S} \textbf{ after } \alpha) \wedge$$

$$\mathbf{infilter}(\mathbf{traj}(\mathcal{I} \textbf{ after } \alpha), \mathbf{traj}(\mathcal{S} \textbf{ after } \alpha)) \subseteq \mathbf{traj}(\mathcal{S} \textbf{ after } \alpha).$$

Checking the conformance using our relation for our example systems with respect to some of the others has the following results.

- $\mathcal{H}_1$ is input-output conform $\mathcal{H}_3$.
- $\mathcal{H}_2$ is input-output conform $\mathcal{H}_3$.
- $\mathcal{H}_3$ is not input-output conform $\mathcal{H}_2$ because after the trace ϵ, $\mathbf{out}(t_0) = \{a_1, \xi\}$ and $\mathbf{out}(s_0) = \{\xi\}$ and therefore $\mathbf{out}(t_0) \nsubseteq \mathbf{out}(s_0)$.
- If we assume that $\sigma_1 \neq \sigma_2$ and $\sigma_1 \downarrow V_I \neq \sigma_2 \downarrow V_I$, then $\mathcal{H}_4$ is input-output conform $\mathcal{H}_1$ and $\mathcal{H}_4$ is input-output conform $\mathcal{H}_3$.
- If we assume that $\sigma_1 \neq \sigma_2$ and $\sigma_1 \downarrow V_I = \sigma_2 \downarrow V_I$, then $\mathcal{H}_4$ is not input-output conform $\mathcal{H}_1$ because $\mathbf{infilter}(\{\sigma_1, \sigma_2\}, \{\sigma_1\}) = \{\sigma_1, \sigma_2\}$ and therefore $\{\sigma_1, \sigma_2\} \nsubseteq \mathbf{traj}(t_0)$.

These results comply with our intuition about when these examples should be conform each other or not.

5   Tests for Hybrid Systems

In the rest of this paper, HTS $\mathcal{S} = (S_{\mathcal{S}}, s_{0\mathcal{S}}, \rightarrow_{\mathcal{S}}, \rightsquigarrow_{\mathcal{S}})$ always is a specification and HTS $\mathcal{I} = (S_{\mathcal{I}}, s_{0\mathcal{I}}, \rightarrow_{\mathcal{I}}, \rightsquigarrow_{\mathcal{I}})$ always is an implementation. For testing the conformance between a hybrid implementation and a hybrid specification we associate a set of tests with the specification. A hybrid test is a hybrid transition system $\mathcal{TC} = (T \cup \{\mathbf{pass}, \mathbf{fail}\}, t_0, \rightarrow_{\mathcal{TC}}, \rightsquigarrow_{\mathcal{TC}})$ with a tree like structure and two terminal states **pass** or **fail** as leaves. Besides being deterministic for trajectories, a test is also deterministic with respect to actions. A hybrid test has the following properties.

- The states **pass** and **fail** are terminal states of the test. That is, there does not exist $a \in A \cup \Sigma_{\mathcal{TC}}$ such that $\mathbf{pass} \xrightarrow{a}$ or $\mathbf{fail} \xrightarrow{a}$.
- A test is deterministic with respect to actions. That is, for all $t, t', t'' \in T$ and $a \in A$, if $t \xrightarrow{a}_{\mathcal{TC}} t'$ and $t \xrightarrow{a}_{\mathcal{TC}} t''$, then $t' = t''$.
- The conditions **A1**, **A2**, and **A3** hold for tests as well.

A test is associated to a specification as follows. If according to the specification some input actions are allowed, the test can allow one of these input actions. If according to the specification some output actions are allowed but no trajectories, the allowed output actions may lead to the verdict **pass** or continuation of the test. The other output actions and all trajectories lead to the verdict **fail**. If according to the specification trajectories are allowed, a particular input trajectory is chosen. If the complete trajectory (including output variables) is allowed according to the specification, then the test may lead to the verdict **pass** or testing may be continued. All other trajectories lead to the verdict **fail**. It may be that applying the selected input trajectory and observing the output trajectory is interrupted by an output action. If this interruption is allowed according to the specification, then the test may be continued or the verdict **pass** may be given. If the output action was not allowed the verdict **fail** is given.

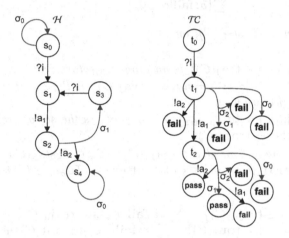

Fig. 3. Example Hybrid Test

Figure 3 depicts an illustrative (but not complete) test $\mathcal{TC}$ generated from a hybrid system $\mathcal{H}$. In our displayed system the transition with output action $!a_2$ means that trajectory σ_1 is interrupted. Note that also for this example we did not depict all the transitions and states such that **A1** to **A3** hold.

The example test $\mathcal{TC}$ says first to apply the input action $?i$ to the implementation, and immediately observe the output action $!a_1$. The observation of all other behavior (output actions or trajectories) leads to the verdict **fail**. After that, either the complete trajectory σ_1 or the prefix of this trajectory followed by output action $!a_2$ is correct behavior and leads to a verdict **pass**. All other behavior leads to the verdict **fail**.

Tests are described by a process algebra like notation for action prefixing or trajectory prefixing, and alternative composition. I.e., $a; \mathcal{TC}$ denotes a test prefixed by an action a, $\sigma; \mathcal{TC}$ denotes a test prefixed by a trajectory σ, $\sum \mathcal{TS}$ denotes the alternative composition of a set of tests $\mathcal{TS}$. We write $\mathcal{TC} + \mathcal{TC}'$ instead of $\sum\{TC, TC'\}$. For the formal definition of this notation we refer to the report version of this paper [12]. We also write **pass** for the HTS $(\{\mathbf{pass}\}, \mathbf{pass}, \emptyset, \emptyset)$ and we write **fail** for the HTS $(\{\mathbf{fail}\}, \mathbf{fail}, \emptyset, \emptyset)$.

Definition 10. *Let S be a specification and let $C \subseteq S$ be a non-empty set of states; then the set of tests $Tests_S(C)$ is inductively defined as follows:*

1. ***pass** is an element of $Tests_S(C)$;*
2. *if $i \in A_I$ and C **after** $i \neq \emptyset$ and $TC' \in Tests_S(C$ **after** $i)$, then $i; TC'$ is an element of $Tests_S(C)$;*
3. *if $\mathbf{traj}(C) = \emptyset$ and, for all $o \in A_O$ with $o \in \mathbf{out}(C)$, $TC_o \in Tests_S(C$ **after** $o)$, then*

$$\sum\{o; TC_o | o \in A_O \cap \mathbf{out}(C)\}+$$
$$\sum\{o; \mathbf{fail} | o \in A_O \setminus \mathbf{out}(C)\}+$$
$$\sum\{\sigma; \mathbf{fail} | \sigma \in \Sigma\}$$

is an element of $Tests_S(C)$; or
4. *if*
   - *$u \in \{\sigma \downarrow V_I | \sigma \in \mathbf{traj}(C)\}$ is an input trajectory and*
   - *$\mathbf{traj}_u(C) = \{\sigma | \sigma \downarrow V_I = u \wedge \sigma \in \mathbf{traj}(C)\}$ is the set of trajectories with input trajectory u and*
   - *$\mathbf{subtraj}_u(C) = \{\sigma | \exists_{\sigma' \in \mathbf{traj}_u(C)} : \sigma \leq \sigma'\}$ is the set of prefixes of the set of trajectories $\mathbf{traj}_u(C)$,*

   *and $j = u.ltime$ and for all $\sigma \in \mathbf{traj}_u(C)$, $TC_\sigma \in Tests_S(C$ **after** $\sigma)$ and for all $\sigma' \in \mathbf{subtraj}_u(C)$ and $o \in \mathbf{out}(C$ **after** $\sigma')$, $TC_{\sigma'o} \in Tests(C$ **after** $\sigma'o)$, then*

$$\sum\{\sigma; TC_\sigma | \sigma \in \mathbf{traj}_u(C)\} + \sum\{\sigma; \mathbf{fail} | \sigma \notin \mathbf{subtraj}_u(C)\} +$$
$$\sum\{o; TC_o | o \in A_O \cap \mathbf{out}(C)\} + \sum\{o; \mathbf{fail} | o \in A_O \setminus \mathbf{out}(C)\}+$$
$$\sum\{\sigma'; o; TC_{\sigma'o} | \sigma' \in \mathbf{subtraj}_u(C) \wedge \sigma'.ltime < j \wedge o \in \mathbf{out}(C$ **after** $\sigma')\} +$$
$$\sum\{\sigma'; o; \mathbf{fail} | \sigma' \in \mathbf{subtraj}_u(C) \wedge \sigma'.ltime < j \wedge o \notin \mathbf{out}(C$ **after** $\sigma')\}$$

is an element of $Tests_S(C)$.

Note that in a test we do not need a special action to observe the symbol ξ that we used in our conformance relation because ξ can be observed by applying and observing a trajectory.

The execution of a test is defined by the synchronous composition of the test and the implementation.

Definition 11. *Let TC be a test and $\mathcal{I}$ be an implementation. The synchronous composition of TC is defined as $TC \parallel \mathcal{I} = (S, (t_0, s_0), \to, \rightsquigarrow)$ with:*

- *$S = T \times S_\mathcal{I}$;*
- *$\to = \{(t, s) \xrightarrow{a} (t', s') | t \xrightarrow{a}_{TC} t' \wedge s \xrightarrow{a}_\mathcal{I} s' \wedge a \in A\} \cup \{(t, s) \xrightarrow{\tau} (t, s') | s \xrightarrow{\tau}_\mathcal{I} s'\}$;*
- *$\rightsquigarrow = \{(t, s) \xrightarrow{\sigma} (t', s') | t \xrightarrow{\sigma}_{TC} t' \wedge s \xrightarrow{\sigma}_\mathcal{I} s' \wedge \sigma \in \Sigma\}$.*

Definition 12. *Let $\mathcal{TC}$ be a test and $\mathcal{I}$ be an implementation. The set of test runs, defined by $testruns(\mathcal{TC} \parallel \mathcal{I})$, is the set of all traces that lead to a state* **pass** *or* **fail**.

$$testruns(\mathcal{TC} \parallel \mathcal{I}) = \{\alpha | \exists_{s \in S_{\mathcal{I}}} : (t_0, s_0) \overset{\alpha}{\Rightarrow} (\textbf{pass}, s) \ \lor \ (t_0, s_0) \overset{\alpha}{\Rightarrow} (\textbf{fail}, s)\}$$

We say a hybrid implementation passes a hybrid test if only the verdict **pass** is reachable in the execution of the test.

Definition 13. *If $\mathcal{TC}$ is a test and $\mathcal{I}$ is an implementation, then $\mathcal{I}$* **passes** $\mathcal{TC}$ *is defined as*

$$\mathcal{I} \ \textbf{passes} \ \mathcal{TC} \iff \forall_{\alpha \in testruns(\mathcal{TC} \parallel \mathcal{I})} : \exists_{s' \in S} : (t_0, s_0) \overset{\alpha}{\Rightarrow} (\textbf{pass}, s').$$

If $\mathcal{TCS}$ is a set of tests, then

$$\mathcal{I} \ \textbf{passes} \ \mathcal{TCS} \iff \forall_{\mathcal{TC} \in \mathcal{TCS}} : \mathcal{I} \ \textbf{passes} \ \mathcal{TC}.$$

6   Towards Hybrid Model-Based Testing in Practice

The next step in our research will be to develop tooling based on our hybrid test theory. As a first step we reformulate the inductive definition of tests in section 4 as a recursive test generation algorithm. Let $\mathcal{S}$ be a specification and let C be a set of initial states of $\mathcal{S}$; then tests are generated by the following algorithm.

algorithm $\textbf{tcg}(\mathcal{S}, C) =$
   select non-deterministically
      1. $\mathcal{TC} := \textbf{pass}$
      2. *select an* $i \in \{a | a \in A_I \wedge C \ \textbf{after} \ a \neq \emptyset\}$
         $\mathcal{TC} := i; \textbf{tcg}(\mathcal{S}, C \ \textbf{after} \ i)$
      3. *if* $\textbf{traj}(C) = \emptyset$ *and there exists an* $o \in A_O$ *such that* $C \ \textbf{after} \ o \neq \emptyset$, *then*

$$\begin{aligned}
\mathcal{TC} := &\sum\{o; \textbf{tcg}(\mathcal{S}, C \ \textbf{after} \ o) | o \in A_o \cap \textbf{out}(C)\} + \\
&\sum\{o; \textbf{fail} | o \in A_o \backslash \textbf{out}(C)\} + \\
&\sum\{\sigma; \textbf{fail} | \sigma \in \Sigma\}
\end{aligned}$$

      4. *if* $\textbf{traj}(C) \neq \emptyset$ *then*
         select an $u \in \{\sigma \downarrow V_I | \sigma \in \textbf{traj}(C)\}$
         let $\textbf{traj}_u(C) = \{\sigma | \sigma \downarrow V_I = u \wedge \sigma \in \textbf{traj}(C)\}$
         let $\textbf{subtraj}_u(C) = \{\sigma | \exists_{\sigma' \in \textbf{traj}_u(C)} : \sigma \leq \sigma'\}$

$$\mathcal{TC} := \quad \sum\{\sigma; \mathbf{tcg}(\mathcal{S}, C \text{ after } \sigma) | \sigma \in \mathbf{traj_u}(C)\} +$$
$$\sum\{\sigma; \mathbf{fail} | \sigma \notin \mathbf{subtraj_u}(C)\} +$$
$$\sum\{o; \mathcal{TC}_o | o \in A_O \cap \mathbf{out}(C)\} + \sum\{o; \mathbf{fail} | o \in A_O \backslash \mathbf{out}(C)\} +$$
$$\sum\{\sigma'; o; \mathbf{tcg}(\mathcal{S}, C \text{ after } \sigma'o) | \sigma' \in \mathbf{subtraj_u}(C) \wedge$$
$$\sigma'.ltime < u.ltime \wedge o \in \mathbf{out}(C \text{ after } \sigma')\} +$$
$$\sum\{\sigma'; o; \mathbf{fail} | \sigma' \in \mathbf{subtraj_u}(C) \wedge$$
$$\sigma'.ltime < u.ltime \wedge o \notin \mathbf{out}(C \text{ after } \sigma')\}$$

     return $\mathcal{TC}$

This algorithm is not directly implementable. Below we discuss several implementation issues that need to be resolved.

In our theory and our algorithm a test has uncountable many states and trajectories and summations over infinite domains. In practice we can of course only deal with finite representations for tests: e.g. trajectories specified as differential equations or algebraic equations, or only by specifying on valuations of variables, and sets of states represented symbolically: e.g. by zones.

In our algorithm we did not define how we select input actions and input trajectories. In practice we need to select and generate possible input trajectories in some way. A first way is to let the test generator choose input actions and trajectories at random. A second way is to have the user of the test tool manually select input and construct tests interactively with the tool. A third way is to do guided input selection based on coverage criteria or based on the (physical) behavior of the environment of the system under test.

In our theory continuous behavior is defined over a dense real time domain. In practice tests can only be executed by stimulating the implementation with samples of input, and by observing samples of output in small time steps. In this case selecting a trajectory is selecting a sequence of samples. We can only conclude a verdict with respect to the samples we observe. If according to our specification we need to observe a constant flow of 0, then it is theoretically possible that we observe value 0 in all samples, while in between samples the value fluctuates. Furthermore, samples will be rounded and therefore we can only conclude a verdict with respect to rounded observations.

In our theory the behavior of a test with respect to an implementation is defined by the synchronous composition of a test and an implementation. In practice we need to stimulate the implementation with input generated from the test and we need to observe the output from the implementation. The first option is to generate executable code from a test. This program provides input for an implementation and observes the output of the implementation. An infrastructure is needed to connect implementation and test. The second option is on the fly test generation. In this case a test tool selects one input (action or trajectory), computes which verdict to attach to the output, and then provides the input to the implementation. It observes the output from the implementation simultaneously, after which a new input (action or trajectory) is selected and applied (in case the test did not lead to verdict fail). An infrastructure is needed to connect the test tool with the implementation under test. On the fly test generation seems more practical. However it might not be possible to the select input and apply the input and observe the output and give a verdict, all in real-time. We need to investigate which method works (best).

For the implementation of a tester we want to use an existing specification language and reuse algorithms of existing hybrid system tools (e.g. Charon [1], HyTech [4], or hybrid χ [11]).

7 Conclusions

In this paper we presented the hybrid input-output conformance relation **hioco** for hybrid systems. This relation defines in which cases we consider an hybrid implementation correct with respect to a hybrid specification. We presented an inductive definition of tests that is sound and exhaustive. For the formal proofs of soundness and exhaustiveness of our tests we refer to the report version of this paper [12].

Our hybrid conformance relation and test definition are based on the discrete conformance relation of Tretmans [8, 9] and his test generation procedure for discrete systems. The differences are, besides including trajectories, that we do not have the quiescence action δ and that we introduce the symbol ξ to indicate the presence of urgent actions. In our tests we observe this ξ implicitly when an urgent output action did not occur but a trajectory is applied and observed instead.

The real-time conformance relation developed by Brandan [2] is also based the discrete conformance theory of Tretmans. However, we believe that our hybrid conformance relation is closer related to the real-time conformance relation of Krichen [5] because in that relation time is viewed as (continuous) output of the implementation. We do not find it necessary to restrict our theory to non Zeno systems, unlike Brandan. However, in practice we only consider non Zeno systems because in practice time cannot stop.

The next step in our research is to take our hybrid test theory into practice and develop tooling. We acknowledge that in our theory we allow uncountable many actions, trajectories, states, and uncountable many tests. We also acknowledge that in our theory we allow dense real-time and trajectories are selected, applied and observed in synchrony with each other and without delay. We need to fit our theory to what is possible in practice but we can still relate a practical implementation to the theory.

The only research in hybrid model based testing before our hybrid test theory was a proof of concept tester [7] developed at the University of Pennsylvania. No theory was formed for this test tool. The idea of this tool is that a tester is generated from an environment model (that provides the input) and check temporal properties at run time. This is different from our theory in which we generate tests, containing both input and possible output. The advantage of our theory is that we also specifies the relation between input and output. With the Charon tester it is only possible to test whether the continuous output of the implementation stays within certain bounds. In our theory we test whether the continuous output variables behave according to the specified flow of variables.

Acknowledgments

Hereby I would like to thank Bas Luttik and Jos Baeten from the Computer Science department of the Technische Universiteit Eindhoven for their help in forming this theory and reviewing this paper. Furthermore I would like to thank Jan Tretmans, Tim Willemse and René de Vries of the Radboud Universiteit Nijmegen for their good advices as well.

References

1. R. Alur, T. Dang, J. Esposito, R. Fierro, Y. Hur, F. Ivancic, V. Kumar amd I. Lee, P. Mishra, G. Pappas, and O. Sokolsky. Hierarchical Hybrid Modeling of Embedded Systems. In *EMSOFT'01: First Workshop on Embedded Software*, 2001.
2. L. Brandán Briones and Ed Brinksma. A test generation framework for quiescent real-time systems. In J. Grabowski and B. Nielsen, editors, *FATES04. Formal Approaches to Testing of Software (4th International Workshop)*, 2004.
3. P.J.L. Cuijpers, M.A. Reniers, and W.P.M.H. Heemels. Hybrid transition systems. Computer Science Reports 02-12, TU/e Department of Computer Science, December 2002.
4. T.A. Henzinger, P.-H. Ho, and H. Wong-Toi. Hytech: A model checker for hybrid systems. In *Software Tools for Technology*, volume Transfer 1, 1997.
5. M. Kirchen and S. Tripakis. Black-box Conformance Testing for Real-time Systems. In *SPIN 2004*, pages 109–126. Springer-Verlag, 2004.
6. K. Larsen, M. Mikucionis, and B. Nielsen. Online Testing of Real-time Systems. In J. Grabowski and B. Nielsen, editors, *FATES04. Formal Approaches to Testing of Software (4th International Workshop)*, 2004.
7. L. Tan, O. Sokolsky, , and I. Lee. Specification-based Testing with Linear Temporal Logic. In *IEEE Internation Conference on Information Reuse and Integration (IRI'04)*, 2004.
8. J. Tretmans. Test Generation with Inputs, Outputs and Repetitive Quiescence. *Software—Concepts and Tools*, 17(3):103–120, 1996.
9. J. Tretmans. Testing concurrent systems: A formal approach. In J.C.M Baeten and S. Mauw, editors, *CONCUR'99 – 10th Int. Conference on Concurrency Theory*, volume 1664 of *Lecture Notes in Computer Science*, pages 46–65. Springer-Verlag, 1999.
10. J. Tretmans and E. Brinksma. TorX: Automated Model Based Testing. In A. Hartman and K. Dussa-Ziegler, editors, *Proceedings of the 1st European Conference on Model-Driven Software Engineering*, 2003.
11. D.A. van Beek, K.L. Man, M.A. Reniers, J.E. Rooda, and R.R.H. Schiffelers. Syntax and Consistent Equation Semantics of Hybrid Chi. *Journal of Logic and Algebraic Programming, special issue on hybrid systems*, to appear.
12. M. van Osch. Hybrid input-output conformance and test generation. Technical report, Technische Universiteit Eindhoven, 2006.

Generating Tests from EFSM Models Using Guided Model Checking and Iterated Search Refinement

Juhan-P. Ernits[1,3], Andres Kull[2], Kullo Raiend[2], and Jüri Vain[1,3]

[1] Dept. of Comp. Sci. Tallinn Univ. of Technology, Raja 15, 12618 Tallinn, Estonia
vain@ioc.ee
[2] Elvior, Mustamäe tee 44, Tallinn 10621, Estonia
{andres.kull, kullo.raiend}@elvior.ee
[3] Inst. of Cybernetics, Akadeemia 21, 12618 Tallinn, Estonia
juhan@cc.ioc.ee

Abstract. We present a way to generate test sequences from EFSM models using a guided model checker: Uppaal Cora. The approach allows to specify various structural test coverage criteria of EFSMs, for example, selected states/transitions, all transitions, all transition pairs, etc. We describe a method to construct Uppaal models to achieve test sequences satisfying these criteria and experiment with the search options of Uppaal to achieve test sequences that are suboptimal in terms of length. We apply a bitstate hashing space reduction based iterated search refinement method to shorten the length of test sequences with respect to the length gained using depth first search. The test generation method and different search strategies are compared by applying them on a stopwatch and INRES protocol based case study. The outcome shows the feasibility of applying guided model checking in conjunction with iterated search refinement for generating suboptimal test sequences.

1 Introduction

In this paper we target test generation for software systems from specifications in the form of extended finite state machines (EFSMs). We propose a method of test generation that combines techniques of model construction with bitstate hashing based iterated search refinement in model checking.

One possible motivation for working with EFSMs is that specifications provided in terms of, for example, suitably restricted UML statecharts can be converted into EFSMs. Converting UML statecharts to EFSMs is not the topic of the current paper and thus we use EFSMs as the starting point for the reason that they provide a semantically well-defined model representation that can be applied for test generation. The problem of generating test sequences is formulated as a bounded reachability problem and solved by model checking.

The procedure of searching for a suitable test sequence is simple if the software is modeled as a finite state machine that has neither variables nor guard conditions. Introducing variables and guard conditions, as in EFSMs, makes the search much more complex.

K. Havelund et al. (Eds.): FATES/RV 2006, LNCS 4262, pp. 85–99, 2006.

The complexity arises from the large number of combinations of values that the variables can be assigned and from the need to satisfy guard conditions for taking transitions. One well known option for generating tests for EFSMs is to use the search machinery provided out-of-the-box by model checkers.

If a model checker solves a reachability task, it generates a witness trace that corresponds to an abstract test sequence.

The most critical factor of space exploration based methods is scalability, i.e., the ability to handle the exponential growth of the search space.

One example of problems where scalability quickly becomes acute, is targeting some structural test coverage criteria that result in long traces. For example *all transitions* of the Implementation Under Test (IUT) model or *all possible subsequences of transitions of some length* $k > 1$ of the IUT. Our goal is to generate preset tests for models of deterministic IUT models.

We compare different search strategies and iterated search refinement on the well-known benchmark examples of stopwatch and the INRES protocol [1].

We show how guiding the search with a cost variable influences the lengths and required amounts of memory of test generation. In fact, we merge guiding together with iterated search refinement to reduce the lengths of generated test sequences and to improve the scalability of applying explicit state model checking for test generation.

We use the model checker Uppaal and its guided counterpart Uppaal Cora [2] because it enables us to demonstrate both, the influence of guiding, and iterated search refinement, in the presented context of test generation.

2   Related Work

The most common coverage criteria in the context of model-based testing are structural coverage criteria, such as state coverage and transition coverage [3]. Test generation according to structural coverage criteria is often treated as a reachability problem and solved either by symbolic or explicit state model checking [4].

An automated test generation tool SAL-ATG based on SAL2 symbolic model checker is proposed in [5]. An alternative approach to test case generation by explicit state model checking is studied extensively on the basis of the Uppaal family of tools[1]. Special testing environments Uppaal Tron [7] and Uppaal CoVer [8], [9] have been built upon the main search engine of Uppaal.

Cost automata based Uppaal Cora [2] is designed for solving cost guided reachability problems and can be used also for introducing context information to guide test case generation. One important problem in using model checking for test case generation is encoding test coverage criteria. In [10] the structural coverage criteria are represented by a set of CTL formulae. Similarly, temporal logics LTL and CTL are used respectively in [11] and in [8] for specifying path conditions that are transformed to property automata. In SAL-ATG the test

---

[1] The representation of time in Uppaal is symbolic. The representation of locations and integer and boolean variables is explicit state [6].

purpose is stated directly as an observer state machine. Finding a minimal-cost or time optimal witness for a formula is combinatorially hard. Existing model checkers search minimal-cost witnesses typically by breadth-first search (enhanced with some heuristic) of state space that is known to be a NP-hard problem [10].

The search options of model checking tools have a significant influence on the performance of reachability search when the whole state space need not be traversed. For instance, traversal options such as depth first, breath first, random first etc are supported by the majority of model checkers. Optimization techniques used in model checking include also preprocessing of the model, for example, cone of influence reduction [5]. Instrumenting the model with trap variables is a standard technique used in prioritized traversal [8]. One step further is combining model checking with other methods using scriptable model checkers as reported in [5]. It is shown that combining different methods by scripting allows even a bounded model checker to reach deep states at low resource footprint.

The work presented in the current paper takes a different approach by combining guiding of Uppaal Cora with iterated search refinement.

3   Case Studies

We use the following two case studies in the paper: stopwatch [5] and a modified INRES protocol [1].

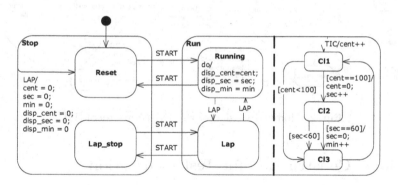

Fig. 1. Stopwatch as UML state machine

Stopwatch. In [5] it was claimed that explicit state model checkers are not suitable for finding test cases from models that have deep counter-dependent loops. Such a counter (in the range 0..6000) is present in the stopwatch example. Referring to our experiments with Uppaal Cora we show how guiding and iterated search refinement improve test generation using explicit state model checking.

The stopwatch in [5] is modeled using Stateflow notation. In Fig. 1 there is an equivalent UML state machine. For our experiments we used a flattened representation in Uppaal.

Modified INRES protocol. INRES protocol is a well-known example in the model verification and test generation community. The protocol is simple but not trivial and provides a good reference for studying performance and scalability issues of competing methods. We use it to demonstrate the scalability of our test generation method. The case study shows that the generation of test sequences for "all transition triples" test coverage results in very long test sequences. The protocol was introduced in [1] and was modified in [12] and is depicted in Fig. 2 as an EFSM. We chose this particular model because it has several loops, for example, a self loop (at the `Sending` state) and a (minimally) two-step loop (`Sending`, `Blocked`, `Sending`), the depths of which depend on the input parameters `datarequest.n` and `datarequest.b` respectively.

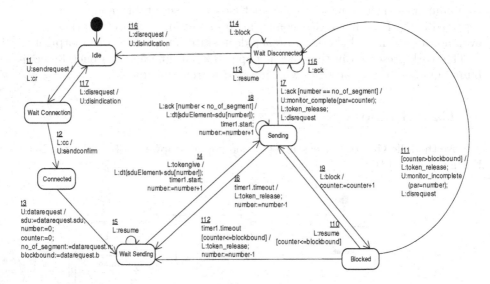

Fig. 2. Modified version of the INRES protocol [12]

4 Model Construction for Test Generation

An Extended Finite State Machine (EFSM) is a FSM extended with variables with finite domains, for example, Booleans and bounded integers. In addition to input and output, every transition may have a guard condition and assignments to variables. We assume that the EFSM of the initial IUT is deterministic and strongly connected.

The source EFSM that is given as a UML state machine is transformed into a Uppaal automaton in three steps. In the first step, the UML state machine is flattened and parallel states are sequentialized. The result is transformed to a Uppaal automaton in the second step. We are interested in finding a sequence of transitions that satisfies the selected structural coverage criterion in the model, thus the inputs and outputs of the model are abstracted away, so that only the information influencing the control flow of the Uppaal model is kept. Thus we reduce the search space in a way that makes trace generation by model checking feasible. In the last step the model is annotated with auxiliary variables to mark passing certain states or transitions. Such trap variable declarations, trap variable assignments and, additionally, cost functions are added to each transition according to the selected coverage criterion. After the generation of test sequence the inputs and outputs associated with each transition in the test sequence are reintroduced in the tester code generation step, which is beyond the scope of the current paper.

As in [5], [10], [13], and [14], we encode the coverage criterion as a reachability problem using trap variables. For example, in the case of all transitions criterion, an initially false boolean trap variable t_i is added to the model for each transition and an assignment $t_i = true$ is added to each transition. A witness trace that passes all transitions at least once is generated by the model checker by checking reachability of the property $E\Diamond(t_1 \wedge t_2 \wedge ... \wedge t_n)$, where n is the number of transitions in the model. We extend this approach for k-switch [15] coverage criterion.

1-switch criterion requires that all pairs of consecutive transitions are covered by a test sequence at least once. For the construction of a reachability property corresponding to the 1-switch criterion we add trap variables $t_i t_j$ for each feasible transition pair (t_i, t_j). Trap variables $t_i t_j$ are initially set to false. To remember the previously visited transition an auxilary variable $prev$ is declared. On each transition t_j a case statement is added for assigning 1-switch trap variables to true depending on the previously passed transition, in Fig. 3 (left), where $t_{i1}, ..., t_{il}$ are incoming transitions to the source state of transition t_j. The property to be checked involves a conjunction of all feasible 1-switch trap variables $t_i t_j$: $E\Diamond \bigwedge_{i,j}(t_i t_j)$.

```
select (prev) {
    case (prev==ti1) ti1tj=true;
    ...
    case (prev==til) tiltj=true;
}
```

```
select (prev) {
    case (prev==i1)
        select (befprev) {
            case (befprev==tj1) tj1ti1tk=true;
            ...
            case (befprev==tjm) tjmti1tk=true;
        }
    ...
    case (prev==til)
        select (befprev) {
            case (befprev==tj1) tj1tiltk=true;
            ...
            case (befprev==tjm) tjmtiltk=true;
        }
}
```

Fig. 3. Trap variable assignments for 1-switch for t_j (left) and 2-switch for t_k (right)

2-switch is a triple of consecutive transitions and a test satisfying *all 2-switches coverage* criterion passes all feasible transition triples. For transforming all 2-switches criterion to a reachability problem we add a trap variable $t_i t_j t_k$ for each feasible triple and auxilary variables `prev` and `befprev` to remember the previous and before-the-previous traversed transition, respectively. In Fig. 3 (right) there is an example of a nested case statement that is added to each transition t_k for assigning 2-switch trap variables where $t_{j1}, ..., t_{jm}$ are incoming transitions to the source state of transition t_j. The property to be checked contains a conjunction of all feasible 2-switch trap variables $t_i t_j t_k$: $E\Diamond \bigwedge_{i,j,k}(t_i t_j t_k)$.

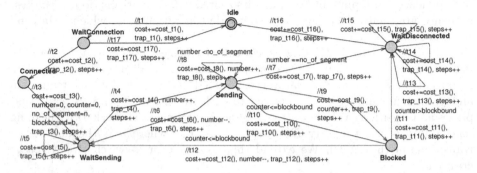

Fig. 4. Uppaal model of the modified INRES protocol with traps and cost functions

In Fig. 4 there is a Uppaal representation of the INRES model in Fig. 2 for generating all 2-switch test sequence. In Fig. 5 (left) there is an example of the relevant trap variable assignment function, where case statements are implemented in terms of if-then-else.

```
// 2-switch trap variable assignments
// procedure on the transition t1

void trap_t1() {
    if (prev==16) {
        if (befprev==7) t7t16t1=true;
        else if (befprev==11) t11t16t1=true;
        else if (befprev==13) t13t16t1=true;
        else if (befprev==14) t14t16t1=true;
        else if (befprev==15) t15t16t1=true;
    }
    else if (prev==17)
            if (befprev==1) t1t17t1=true;
    befprev=prev; prev=1;
}
```

```
//2-switch cost function on the transition t1

int cost_t1() {
    if (prev==16 and (
        (befprev==7 and t7t16t1) or
        (befprev==11 and t11t16t1) or
        (befprev==13 and t13t16t1) or
        (befprev==14 and t14t16t1) or
        (befprev==15 and t15t16t1)
        )) return PENALTY;
    if (prev==17 and (
        (befprev==1 and t1t17t1)
        )) return PENALTY;
    return 0;
}
```

Fig. 5. Implementations of the trap assignment function (left) and cost assignment function (right)

Uppaal Cora has support for guiding the reachability search with a built-in cost variable which can be used to minimise the lengths of generated test sequences. We define the cost variable assignment on each transition so that the cost increment is zero while the switch has not been passed (the trap variable of the switch is false) and increases the cost by a fixed penalty after it is set to true. In Fig. 5 (right) there is an example of a cost function used in the experiments.

5   Iterated Search Refinement for Test Generation

Model checking in general involves searching possibly very large state spaces to prove or disprove a query — a formula typically in some temporal logic. We make use of the feature of model checking to generate witness traces. We specify one test coverage criterion at a time as a reachability query.

We chose to use Uppaal Cora version 060206 because it enabled us to demonstrate the behaviour of regular search options and in addition the influence of guiding and iterated search refinement in the presented context of test generation using a single model format and thus avoiding influences to results that may be introduced by converting a model to several modelling formalisms.

5.1   Standard Search and Trace Generation Options of Model Checking

Standard search strategies typically used to traverse the state space are *depth first* and *breadth first*. The standard version of Uppaal implements both [16] and additionally also a *random depth first* search strategy. Breadth first search looks for all reachable states at current search depth before proceeding deeper while depth first search takes one path and goes along it deeper until the property is satisfied or it needs to backtrack to look at alternative paths. Reachability queries considered in the current context do not in practice require full traversal of the state space if the property is satisfiable.

Trace generation options that Uppaal provides [16] are for generating *some*, *shortest*, and *fastest* trace. Since we have currently omitted the use of clocks in our models, we do not use the latter option in the experiments.

Additional search strategies of guided model checking provided by Uppaal Cora are *best first*, *random best depth first*, and *smallest heur first* [2]. As we use only the *cost* variable for guiding, the latter search option is not used in the experiments.

An additional trace generation option of guided model checking provided by Uppaal Cora is *best* trace. This means that the trace generated has the lowest aggregate value of cost in the context of the search strategy used.

5.2   Iterated Search Refinement Using Bitstate Hashing

Bitstate hashing, also known as supertrace, is a well known method applied for model checking and thoroughly analysed in [17] for reducing memory consumption of the whole state space search by storing only a single bit for each seen state at the address calculated by a hash function. The drawback of the method is the possibility of hash collisions that will result in unexplored parts of the search space, rendering the method sound but incomplete. Still, fast reachability checks that yield a valid trace can be quite useful for applying model checking, for example, for test sequence generation from an EFSM model.

In general, the bigger the hash table, the lower the probability of hash collisions. But big hash tables may still require unavailable amounts of memory. Iterated search refinement is briefly mentioned in [18] and is based on the idea of iteratively increasing the size of the hash table and thus search thoroughness. We make use of the property of a division remainder based hash function to distribute hash collisions pseudorandomly as the divisor (the hash table size) is changed. Thus, the states considered similar by collisions change too. Since Uppaal uses a modulus based hash function [6] for bitstate hashing, we use unmodified Uppaal Cora to compare the influences of different search options.

Basic Iterated Search Refinement, ISR, works as follows. There is a model M and a reachability query q. The bitstate hash table is initially set very small (for example 1 bit). The reachability of the query q is checked on model M. If a trace to the reachable state is not found then the bitstate hash table size is increased by 1. The hash table size is increased by small steps for some configurable number of times and then it is increased by some factor, for example 2. The small steps are necessary to try several different paths at each thoroughness level and big steps are to speed up finding the appropriate hash table size for the particular task. The minimal size of the bitstate hash table yielding a trace may differ by many orders of magnitude for different tasks. The bigger the hash table, the longer each iteration step takes.

Improvement of the first result gained in the basic approach is possible for some specific types of models. Let us assume that we look for a trace that is as short as possible and exhaustive search is not possible due to memory and/or processor time limits. Then we can iteratively constrain the reachability query by the trace length bound found in the previous step. In such an approach there is no clear criterion when to stop, as we cannot be sure if the result gained at some iteration step is actually the shortest possible. The most important criterion is the amount of time we have to wait for an improved result.

Combining ISR with guiding is a very important aspect in the current approach. Namely, the shape of the reachable search space of a model given a bitstate hash table size is dependent on search strategy, as the state hashing to some address in the bitstate hash table is traversed only during the first visit and the next states hashing to the same value are already considered seen.

6   Comparison of Search Strategies for Test Generation

In this section we present a comparison of different search strategies and trace generation options that can be used in model checking for test sequence derivation. The experiments are run on an EFSM represented as a Uppaal model of the stopwatch example described in Section 3. All experiments described in this paper were run on a 2.4 GHz Xeon processor with 512 kB of cache, 533 MHz FSB and 6 GB of 266 MHz DDR memory.

The Uppaal model of the stopwatch is presented in Fig. 6. The model is decorated with trap variables that are used for finding a trace that passes through all transitions. The transitions are labelled by the names of trap variables, for example //t0. To make the comparison of all available search options possible, the model is optimised by declaring variables min, disp_cent, disp_sec, disp_min, and steps as *hidden* (*meta*), meaning that the states where only the

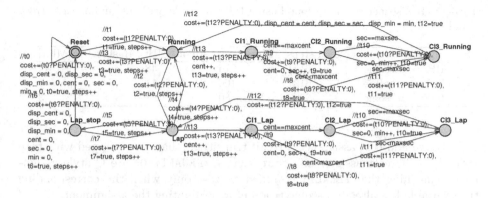

Fig. 6. Uppaal model of the stopwatch with trap variables and cost assignments

values of such *hidden* variables are different are considered equivalent by the model checker. The `steps` variable is used for capturing the length of the trace.

The model is also decorated with assignments to a special purpose built-in `cost` variable which is used for guiding the model checker.

Table 1. Test sequence lengths found using different search options for the model without guiding

Search order	Trace	No. of steps	Time [sec]	Memory [MB]
BF	some	6012	21	146
DF	some	30009	52	45
RDF	some	8988	12	12

In Table 1 there are experimental results of applying Breadth First (BF), Depth First (DF) and Random Depth First (RDF) search strategies on the model in Fig. 6 with the goal of covering all transitions (equivalent to all trap variables t0...t13 becoming true). The trace generation option is set to *some* because setting it to *best* caused the model checker to run out of memory (3GB per process due to 32 bit architecture). Breadth first search did not yield an answer without declaring some of the integer variables to be *hidden*. We can see that depth first search yielded an answer quickly but the trace is 5 times longer than the minimal, which is 6011 steps in length. Random depth first search yielded a better answer than regular depth first.

In Table 2 there are results for applying the iterated search refinement with the same search strategies. The figures show that using breadth first search consumes considerably more memory and requires considerably more time to find an answer than depth first and random depth first search. By comparing the results in Table 1 and in Table 2, we can see that the result obtained by depth first search using ISR is considerably shorter.

But can we improve these results? Intuitively, if we could guide the search, we should find a shorter trace sooner.

Table 2. Test sequence lengths found using ISR and model without guiding (first trace found)

Search order	Trace	No. of steps	Time [sec]	Mem. [MB]	Hash table [Mbit]
BF	some	6141	276	48	44
DF	some	6137	106	11	1
RDF	some	9000	80	11	3

First, we add cost assignments to all transitions that are equipped with trap variables. The cost assignments `cost+=(trap?PENALTY:0)` are C style assignments, meaning that `PENALTY` is added to cost only when the corresponding trap variable has already become true before evaluating the assignment.

Table 3. Test sequence lengths found using guiding with cost variable definition

Search order	Trace	No. of steps	Time [sec]	Memory [MB]
BeF	best	6011	22	147
RBDF	best	N/A	2230	out of memory

Table 3 summarizes the results of applying Uppaal Cora with Best First (BeF) and Random Best Depth First (RBDF) search. One can see that best first strategy yields the optimal answer but requires a considerable amount of memory for this rather small example. In fact, the result is very close to breadth first search in the model without guiding. Random best depth first did not yield an answer at all due to running out of memory.

Table 4. Test sequence lengths found using ISR and a model with cost assignments on all transitions (first trace found)

Search order	Trace	No. of steps	Time [sec]	Mem. [MB]	Hash table [Mbit]
BeF	some	6302	6063	622	1408
BeF	best	6155	5837	628	1408
RBDF	some	8508	138	17	3
RBDF	best	8505	138	21	3

Next we combine guiding and ISR. The results of running ISR with cost assignments on every transition are presented in Table 4. The results show that using the best first search strategy combined with ISR produces considerably worse results than breadth first search. Random best depth first search gives interesting results that are comparable to random depth first search in the uniterated case (Table 1) and to depth first and random depth first in the iterated case without guiding (Table 2).

The results are not significantly improved. Can we tune guiding for better results?

We tune the model by removing the cost of taking entry transitions to loops where counters are incremented, for example transition t13 in Fig. 6. In this way we relieve multiple entries to loops from penalties and thus make the model checker choose such transitions more often. This requires an extra analysis of the model which is currently not automated.

Table 5. Test sequence lengths found by Uppaal Cora using ISR and model with guiding and loop entry optimisations

Search order	Trace	No. of steps	Time [sec]	Mem. [MB]	Hash table [Mbit]
		First trace found			
BeF	some	6226	5745	625	1408
BeF	best	6254	5485	599	1408
RBDF	some	7279	259	12	5
RBDF	best	6714	286	27	5
	Shortest trace found before system memory or hash table overflow				
BeF	some	6151	7431	628	1408
BeF	best	6133	8059	599	1408
RBDF	some	6011	3810	265	176
RBDF	best	6011	3515	310	176

The results of running the ISR on the tuned guided model are presented in Table 5. The first results obtained by the ISR algorithm by random best depth first search with either some or best trace generation option are significantly better than in the previous case. Additionally, if the iteration is continued, the actual optimum is also reachable by ISR (the lower half of Table 5.). The drawback of ISR is that there is no indication how far the current result is from the optimal value.

We presented a comparison of different search strategies on a relatively small and optimised example. In the next section we look at how depth first search without iteration, depth first search with iteration and random best depth first with best trace generation option behave on a larger example. These options are chosen because these have low memory footprint and yield relatively good results and thus have the potential to be scalable.

7 Scalability of ISR and Guiding for Test Generation

The modified INRES protocol in Fig. 2 contains a self-loop where a variable is incremented (transition t8) and several cycles of two or more transitions (for example, a variable is incremented in the cycle containing t9 and t10). The test sequence length depends on the parameters n and b defining the upper limits of loop counters. A manually obtained estimation of the shortest length of all 2-switch test sequence can be given as $352 + 15n + 26b$, when $n \geq 5$ and $b \geq 3$.

Table 6. Combinations of search options used for the INRES case study

Abbreviation	ISR	Search order	Trace	Guiding
DF	-	depth first	some	-
IterDF	first result	depth first	some	-
IterRBDF	first result	random best depth first	best	uniform
IterRBDF tuned	first result	random best depth first	best	tuned

Next we present the results of searching for all 2-switch test sequences in the model in Fig. 2 using options listed in Table 6. The results that are obtained using random best depth first search and ISR are average values of 3 runs. While the first value found can vary considerably in different runs, the value obtained by refining the initial result for some proportional amount of time converges fast. *Uniform* guiding means that all trap variables are associated with similar cost and *tuned* guiding means that the cost functions have been modified not to penalize for entering the loops where counters are incremented, i.e. consequent incrementations of the counters is favoured.

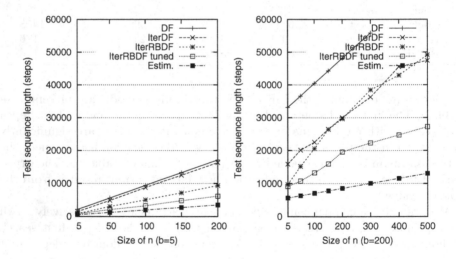

Fig. 7. Lengths of sequences in the INRES model for the 2-switch coverage criterion

The trace lengths of all 2-switch test sequences generated with different search options are given in Fig. 7. *Estim.* stands for the estimated value. The line representing DF search ends at $n = 300$ on the rightmost diagram because the model checker ran out of memory. We see that the iterated approach scales with all selected combinations of options for larger models than the depth first search. Tuned guiding yields traces that are quite close to the estimated shortest.

The maximum amount of memory that was required to generate the traces is given in Fig. 8. We can see that DF search takes little memory in the case where counters are shallow (the diagram on the left) but the amount of required

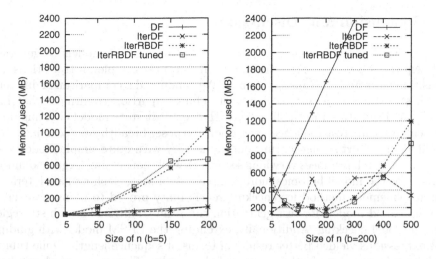

Fig. 8. Memory required to find sequences for the 2-switch coverage criterion

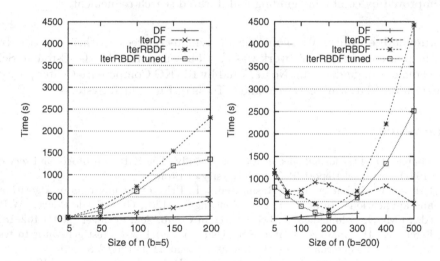

Fig. 9. Time spent for finding sequences for the 2-switch coverage criterion

memory increases rapidly when the counters become deeper (the diagram on the right). The iterated approach requires much less memory than plain DF search.

The time it took to generate the traces is given in Fig. 9. We can see that the gain in memory and shorter trace lengths is paid for with processor time. The iterative approach takes generally much longer than depth first search. This problem can be relieved by running the iterations on multiple processors in parallel as each iteration is independent. In addition, in most cases, it is OK to wait for more than just a few seconds for a test sequence satisfying some stronger structural coverage criterion.

8   Conclusion and Discussion

We presented a way to build Uppaal models from EFSM models to generate test sequences covering some structural criteria, for example all transitions, all transition pairs and all transition triples. We conducted a comparison of different search strategies on a stopwatch model. The comparison confirmed what has previously been stated in the literature, that explicit state model checking does not scale well for test sequence generation purpose: breadth first search, which would yield a short sequence, runs out of memory with quite simple models and depth first search produces very long sequences while consuming large amounts of memory as the model becomes more complex. A bitstate hashing based iterated search refinement method for checking reachability proved to be more scalable on unmodified models for test generation than the traditional search strategies used in model checking. Additionally, extending the EFSM model with guiding cost expressions yielded better results in terms of sequence length. Some tuning of the cost expressions further improved the results. Thus, we have shown how the lengths of test sequences generated using explicit state model checking can be improved by combining guiding and iterated search refinement.

Acknowledgements. We thank the anonymous referees for their constructive and helpful comments. This work was partially supported by the Estonian Science Foundation under grant No 5775 and by ELIKO Competence Center project "Integration Platform for Development Tools of Embedded Systems".

References

1. Hogrefe, D.: OSI-formal specification case study: The INRES protocol and service (1991) Technical Report 91-012, University of Bern.
2. Behrmann, G., Larsen, K.G., Rasmussen, J.I.: Priced timed automata: Algorithms and applications. In de Boer, F.S., Bonsangue, M.M., Graf, S., de Roever, W.P., eds.: FMCO. Volume 3657 of Lect. Notes in Comp. Sci., Springer (2004) 162–182
3. Farchi, E., Hartman, A., Pinter, S.S.: Using a model-based test generator to test for standard conformance. IBM Systems Journal **41**(1) (2002) 89–110
4. Edmund M. Clarke, J., Grumberg, O., Peled, D.A.: Model checking. MIT Press, Cambridge, MA, USA (1999)
5. Hamon, G., de Moura, L., Rushby, J.: Generating efficient test sets with a model checker. In: 2nd International Conference on Software Engineering and Formal Methods, Beijing, China, IEEE Computer Society (2004) 261–270
6. Bengtsson, J.: Clocks, DBMs and states in timed systems. PhD thesis (2002)
7. Larsen, K.G., Mikucionis, M., Nielsen, B., Skou, A.: Testing real-time embedded software using UPPAAL-TRON: an industrial case study. In: EMSOFT '05: Proc. of the 5th ACM International Conference on Embedded Software, New York, NY, USA, ACM Press (2005) 299–306
8. Blom, J., Hessel, A., Jonsson, B., Petterson, P.: Specifying and Generating Test Cases Using Observer Automata. In Gabowski, J., Nielsen, B., eds.: Proc. of the 4th International Workshop on Formal Approaches to Testing of Software (FATES 2004). Number 3395 in Lect. Notes in Comp. Sci., Springer (2005) 125–139

9. Hessel, A., Larsen, K.G., Nielsen, B., Petterson, P., Skou, A.: Time-optimal Real-Time Test Case Generation using UPPAAL. In Petrenko, A., Ulrich, A., eds.: Proc. of the 3rd International Workshop on Formal Approaches to Testing of Software (FATES 2003). Number 2931 in Lect. Notes in Comp. Sci., Springer (2004) 136–151

10. Hong, H.S., Lee, I., Sokolsky, O., Ural, H.: A temporal logic based theory of test coverage and generation. In: TACAS '02: Proceedings of the 8th International Conference on Tools and Algorithms for the Construction and Analysis of Systems, London, UK, Springer-Verlag (2002) 327–341

11. Gunter, E.L., Peled, D.: Model checking, testing and verification working together. Formal Asp. Comput. **17**(2) (2005) 201–221

12. Bourhfir, C., Dssouli, R., Aboulhamid, E., Rico, N.: Automatic executable test case generation for extended finite state machine protocols. In: Proceedings of the 10th International IFIP Workshop on Testing of Communicating Systems (IWTCS'97), Cheju Islands, Korea, Chapman & Hall (1997) 75–90

13. Mücke, T., Huhn, M.: Generation of optimized testsuites for UML statecharts with time. In Groz, R., Hierons, R.M., eds.: TestCom. Volume 2978 of Lecture Notes in Computer Science., Springer (2004) 128–143

14. Hessel, A., Larsen, K., Nielsen, B., Pettersson, P., Skou, A.: Time-optimal realtime test case generation using UPPAAL. In: FATES'03, Montreal (2003)

15. Chow, T.S.: Testing software design modeled by finite-state machines. IEEE Trans. Software Eng. **4**(3) (1978) 178–187

16. Behrmann, G., David, A., Larsen, K.G.: A tutorial on Uppaal. In Bernardo, M., Corradini, F., eds.: SFM. Volume 3185 of Lecture Notes in Computer Science., Springer (2004) 200–236 (updated version available from http://www.uppaal.com).

17. Holzmann, G.J.: An analysis of bitstate hashing. Form. Methods Syst. Des. **13**(3) (1998) 289–307

18. Holzmann, G.J., Smith, M.H.: Automating software feature verification. Bell Labs Technical Journal **5**(2) (2000) 72–87

Decompositional Algorithms for Safety Verification and Testing of Aspect-Oriented Systems*

Cheng Li and Zhe Dang**

School of Electrical Engineering and Computer Science
Washington State University, Pullman, WA 99164, USA
zdang@eecs.wsu.edu

Abstract. To efficiently solve safety verification and testing problems for an aspect-oriented system, we use multitape automata to model aspects and propose algorithms for the aspect-oriented system specified by a number of primary labeled transition systems (some of them are black-boxes) and aspects. Our algorithms combine automata manipulations over the aspects and primary systems with black-box testing over each individual black-box, but without generating the woven system.

1 Introduction

Aspect-oriented Programming (AOP) [1] has been considered among "ten emerging areas of technology that will soon have a profound impact on the economy and on how we live and work" [14]. In a software system, a concern is understood as a property of interest. Separation of concerns has long been regarded as a main principle in software engineering. A concern can be implemented as a *component* (if it can be cleanly encapsulated in a generalized procedure or object) or as a cross-cutting *aspect* (if otherwise; e.g., a security aspect interleaved with several components) [1]. In AOP, *primary systems* can be *woven* with aspects into *woven systems* – final executables – by aspect *weavers*. This process is called *weaving*, which has provided a new way to compose a complex system, whose reusability, extensibility and adaptability may also be increased. The successes of AOP at the code level (e.g., AspectJ [2]) have also inspired researchers to study methodologies in aspect-oriented design that bring in cross-cutting concerns even at earlier software development stages [9,10,8,12,3,4].

Despite its convenience in addressing cross-cutting concerns, introducing aspects into a system on the other hand raises a quality assurance issue in the woven system: how to assure that a collection of aspects really add the functionality they are supposed to, and moreover, do not invalidate desirable properties of the primary system to which the aspects are woven? That is, we would like to assure that aspects perform their intended behavioral modifications over the primary system without producing any undesirable side effects. Theoretically, it is clear that, once a primary system is given, a well-specified aspect (we assume that the aspect "knows" how to weave) will give us a construction on the woven system. Therefore, the quality assurance problem is essentially a verification

---

* The work was supported in part by NSF Grant CCF-0430531.
** Corresponding author.

K. Havelund et al. (Eds.): FATES/RV 2006, LNCS 4262, pp. 100–114, 2006.

problem and verification techniques like model checking [5] can be applied on the woven system directly. However, this direct approach has serious issues:

- Before the model-checking starts on the woven system, one *has to* wait till the woven system is constructed. But when the model-checking actually starts, the state space in the woven system may have already exploded, in particular when nested weaving is involved.
- When the primary system contains components that are black-boxes (such as a COTS component, whose source code or design details are unavailable), a woven system may not even be available.

To address the issues, in this paper, we study fundamental algorithms that are possible to verify/test an aspect-oriented system or design, but without weaving (i.e., without constructing the woven system).

In our study, a system or design is modeled as a labeled transition system. An aspect is a multitape automaton, or more precisely, the tuple language accepted by the automaton. It characterizes how behaviors of several primary systems can be woven into a behavior of the woven system. We then define an aspect-oriented system $\mathcal{A}$ as a tree whose leaves are primary systems and nonterminal nodes are aspects. As defined in the paper, the woven system, also denoted by $\mathcal{A}$, can be constructed through automata manipulations (assuming that the automata for the aspects as well as the primary systems are of finite-state). We study the safety verification problem as follows: Given a regular set Bad (of event sequences), whether the woven system has a behavior in Bad. Our safety verification algorithm is a top-down and then bottom-up process that explores the structure of the tree $\mathcal{A}$ (using automata manipulations), during which a regular $badSet$ is calculated and updated for each node. Once any one of these $badSet$s becomes empty, the algorithm halts. Our algorithm makes it possible to obtain the answer to the safety verification problem before the entire tree is explored. We also study the safety testing problem which is exactly the same as the safety verification problem, except that one or more of the primary systems are black-boxes. Our safety testing algorithm explores the structure of the tree $\mathcal{A}$ and makes use of the white-box primary systems as well as the *test results* of those black-boxes that have been tested in the algorithm. Then, the algorithm computes, through automata manipulations, a $badSet$ for the black-box that is about to test. This $badSet$ has the following property: a behavior of the black-box that is not in the $badSet$ can not cause the woven system $\mathcal{A}$ to have a behavior in the given Bad. Hence, this $badSet$ can be used to further eliminate the *unnecessary tests* that would otherwise be tested on the black-box. The algorithm selects and performs tests for each of the black-boxes in this way. The algorithm halts when one of these $badSet$s becomes empty. Therefore, essentially, our safety testing algorithm is decompositional and dynamic: tests run on a black-box are tailored to the specific safety testing problem instance of $\mathcal{A}$. Furthermore, tests performed over a black-box will be used later in the algorithm to further trim away unnecessary tests performed over other black-boxes.

2   Related Work

Recently, a significant amount of papers have been published to address the modeling and verification problems of aspect-oriented systems.

In [18,16], model-checking has been used to verify aspect-oriented systems at the source code level by extracting finite-state designs. Unfortunately, such an approach may cause false negatives on the verification results. References [9,10,8,12,3] extend the UML (Unified Modeling Language) to support aspect-oriented design, where the primary system and aspects can be woven at the design level. However, since the semantics of UML is not formal in general, the woven design can not be faithfully verified. To address the issue, some researchers seek to translate a subclass of aspect-oriented UML to a formal specification language associated with a formal analysis tool. For instance, in [4], performance is modeled as an aspect using aspect-oriented UML which is translated into Rapide ADL [15] to evaluate if the woven system satisfies a time-response requirement. Reference [17] adapts a role-based aspect-oriented modeling method for aspect-oriented UML design and uses Alloy, a lightweight formal specification language and analysis tool, to verify the woven system. However, as pointed out by authors, the translation from UML to Alloy was done manually and only worked for some special cases.

Our approach is totally different from all approaches we mentioned above. Our safety verification and testing algorithms verify and test aspect-oriented systems without constructing the actual woven systems. We also believe that our formal approach of using multitape automata and their manipulations in studying verification problems of aspect-oriented systems is also new: this approach will also make research results that are already established in automata theory be available in analyzing aspects and aspect-oriented systems, e.g., aspects that are of infinite-state.

Our algorithms are also related to our decompositional testing algorithms [6] for concurrent systems containing black-box components. In these latter algorithms which are inspired by the decompositional verification ideas by Giannakopoulou et. al.[7], test sequences are generated and run on a concurrent component that are customized to its specific deployment environment. Since blackbox testing (instead of verification) is used in [6], unlike the framework in [7], the testing algorithms in [6] does not require a complete specification about a component to be incorporated into the concurrent system. On the other hand, we study decompositional testing algorithms for aspect-oriented systems in this paper instead of concurrent systems in [6].

3   Systems, Transactions, and Aspects

In this paper, a system M is a (nondeterministic) labeled transition system, where its labels, called (external) events, are drawn from a given finite alphabet Σ. Formally, $M = (Q, q_0, \Sigma, \delta)$, where Q is a (not necessarily finite) set of states (with $q_0 \in Q$ being the initial state) and $\delta \subseteq Q \times (\Sigma \cup \{\epsilon\}) \times Q$ defines transitions, each of which is in the form of (q, a, q'), for some $q, q' \in S$ and $a \in \Sigma \cup \{\epsilon\}$, indicating that state q transits to state q' while event a is observed (when $a = \epsilon$ (i.e., a is *silent*), nothing is observed). Therefore, when M runs by following the state transitions, one observes a sequence of events, i.e., a word w in Σ^*. Formally, an *execution* of M is, for some n, a sequence $(q_0, a_1, q_1)(q_1, a_2, q_2), \cdots, (q_{n-1}, a_n, q_n)$ of transitions in δ, which starts from the initial state q_0. A word w is a *behavior* of M if, for some execution of M shown above, w is $a_1 \cdots a_n$ (after ignoring all the silent events in $a_1 \cdots a_n$). In particular, when the word ends with a special event $\heartsuit \in \Sigma$, its is called a valid *transaction* of M. Notice that the special symbol is an indication of the end of a transaction and, moreover, there could be multiple appearances of $\heartsuit$'s before the last appearance of $\heartsuit$ in the transaction. As usual, we use $L(M)$ to denote the set of all transactions of M.

The events in Σ serves as the interface of M. Even though M can be an infinite-state system (i.e., the state set Q is infinite), its behaviors over the interface could be simple; e.g., $L(M)$ forms a regular language (such a view of *interface automata* is studied in [11]). Clearly, when M is a finite-state system (i.e., the state set Q is finite), $L(M)$ has to be a regular language.

Labeled transition systems M are a popular abstract representation of a software system and its design. In case when the transition graph δ of M is unknown (but its interface Σ is known), M is considered as a black-box. In this paper, we assume that the black-box can be tested. That is, there is a procedure $\mathbf{BTest}(M, w)$ that returns a definite (yes/no) answer on whether w is a transaction of M. In automata theory, this is called membership testing; i.e., whether $w \in L(M)$. Clearly, in order for one to implement the procedure $\mathbf{BTest}$, a number of requirements of M must be met (e.g., one needs to distinguish input events and output events in M, one might want to assume that M is input deterministic, M has an implementation to run, etc.; see [13] for a comprehensive survey on black-box testing). For ease of presentation, we simply assume that the black-box M has already met all the necessary requirements such that the black-box testing procedure $\mathbf{BTest}$ does exist and is given. As we all know, black-box testing can even run on infinite-state systems.

An important class of verification queries, called the *safety verification problem*, is as follows:

Given: a system M and a set $Bad \subseteq \Sigma^*$,
Question: $L(M) \cap Bad = \emptyset$?

In above, $Bad \subseteq \Sigma^*$ specifies a set of *bad* transactions that are not supposed to be the transactions of M. Clearly, a negative answer to the **Question** indicates an error in the system with respect to its requirement specified as "no Bad transactions". Automata-theoretic model-checking techniques can be used to solve the safety verification problem when both M and Bad are in certain restricted forms. In particular, when M is a finite-state system and Bad is a regular set, the problem can be solved.

When M is a black-box, the safety verification problem can not be solved in general. In this case, black-box testing can be used to obtain an inconclusive answer as follows. We assume that a procedure $\mathbf{GenTests}(M, \Sigma)$ is given which returns a set of words. Each word w that is in the set and in Bad is then run on the testing procedure $\mathbf{BTest}(M, w)$. If one of such w is *successful* (i.e., $\mathbf{BTest}(M, w)$ returns "yes"), then a negative answer to the **Question** in the safety verification problem is identified. Otherwise, the answer is inconclusive. The set of tests that $\mathbf{GenTests}$ generates has to be finite (patience of a test engineer is practically bounded). In practice, it is still an ongoing research issue in Software Engineering on how to define an "adequate" $\mathbf{GenTests}$, in particular when M is a grey-box (with partial information on its transition graph known). Nevertheless, in this paper, we assume that such a $\mathbf{GenTests}$ exists and given (e.g., a straightforward version of **GenTests** is to return the set of all words in Σ^* whose length are not longer than 40).

Before we proceed further, we present a simple banking system (modified from [12]) shown in Figure 1, which will be used throughout this paper. With this simple banking system, a customer can open and close a bank account. With a bank account, the customer can login to the system and perform a number of *atomic* accesses on the bank account, then logout the system. An atomic access can be any one of withdraw, deposit or getBlance on the account. According to Figure 1,

$$open, deposit, getBlance, logout, \heartsuit$$

is a valid transaction: the customer opens an account and deposits some money on the account, then getBlance of the new created account before logout. However,

$$open, withdraw, getBlance, logout, \heartsuit$$

is not valid transaction: the figure specifies that any costumer should deposit some cash to the account first, before withdrawing from the account.

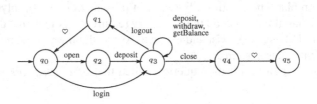

Fig. 1. A simple banking system

In aspect-oriented software development, an aspect can be understood as a structural transformer (e.g., a program transformer in AspectJ) or a behavioral transformer (a relation between event sequences). We use the latter understanding in this paper and thus an aspect is called a *behavioral aspect*. The semantics of the aspect, which is specified by the relation, is independent of the syntax (i.e., the transition graph) and the semantics (i.e., the behaviors) of a primary system M. Therefore, even without the primary system M, one can still design an aspect. Also, it guarantees that the semantics of the woven system does not change whenever the semantics of the primary system does not change. In the following, we will present a formal definition of an aspect, which can be applied to several primary systems (e.g., "interleaving" can be considered as an aspect that weaves two systems into one where the two systems run concurrently).

Formally, a k-ary *behavioral aspect* A is a relation $A \subseteq (\Sigma^*)^k \times \Sigma^*$, which specifies how to weave k primary behaviors into a woven behavior. Let $M_1, \cdots, M_k$ be labeled transition systems over events Σ. The set of *woven transactions*, written $A(L(M_1), \cdots, L(M_k))$, is the set of all words $w\heartsuit$ such that there are transactions $w_1\heartsuit, \cdots, w_k\heartsuit$ in $L(M_1), \cdots, L(M_k)$, respectively, satisfying $(w_1\heartsuit, \cdots, w_k\heartsuit, w\heartsuit) \in A$. To further abuse the notation, we simply use $A(M_1, \cdots, M_k)$ to denote the set. For a given behavioral aspect A, a *weaving function* is a function $W_A(M_1, \cdots, M_k)$ that maps from

$M_1, \cdots, M_k$ (called primary systems) to some system M, called a woven system, such that $L(M) = A(M_1, \cdots, M_k)$. Notice that, even though a behavioral aspect is independent of the transition graphs of the primary systems, as an exercise in computability theory, one can show that a computable weaving function always exists and can be constructed for a given recursively enumerable behavioral aspect, when the primary systems are given as Turing machines (or any other universal computing devices). That is, the existence of such a computable weaving function tells us that, in the most general sense, a woven system can be constructed automatically from primary systems using a behavioral aspect.

4   Finite-State Behavioral Aspects and Weaving

We now study finite-state behavioral aspects that are tuple languages accepted by multi-tape finite automata. A (nondeterministic) multitape finite automaton consists of a finite control and n (for some n) input tapes. Each tape has a one-way and read-only head. The automaton starts in its initial state with all the heads on the leftmost cells of their tapes. Each transition is of the form $(q, a_1, \cdots, a_n, p)$ where q and p are states and $a_1, \cdots, a_n$ are symbols (in $\Sigma \cup \{\epsilon\}$). On firing the transition, the automaton can, when in state q, for each i, read a_i from the i-th tape, and enter state p. The automaton accepts the tuple of n input strings if each head reaches the right end of its tape while entering a designated final state. It is known that multitape finite automata are essentially different from (one-tape) NFA; e.g., the equivalence problem (whether two automata accept the same language) is undecidable for multitape finite automata.

A k-ary behavioral aspect A is of *finite-state* if there is a $(k+1)$-tape finite automaton M such that A equals the $(k + 1)$-tuple language accepted by M. In this case, we sometimes abuse the A as the M.

Now let us go back to the simple banking system example. As the simple banking system evolves, the requirement changes. Developers might be asked to add a new feature to the system: Every atomic access to an account should be logged by recording the name of the accessing customer and the type of the access in a log file. This logging feature is a typical example of a crosscutting concern, which can not be easily represented in an object-oriented design as it interleaves the same feature into every atomic access in the original simple banking system. Adding such a feature is best supported by aspect-oriented software development. In this example, we use a `logging` aspect to implement this feature.

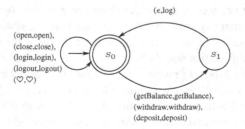

Fig. 2. The `logging` aspect modeled as a two-tape finite automaton

The logging aspect is quite simple. Figure 2 shows how the logging aspect can be modeled as a deterministic two-tape automaton A. A has two states S_0 and S_1 and two transitions between them. For transition from S_0 to S_1, the two tapes of A read same input; for the transition from S_1 to S_0, the first tape reads nothing and the second tape reads log as input. As a result, whenever there is an atomic access in primary behavior, there is a same atomic access appended by a log event in woven behavior. It should be noticed that our logging aspect does not log the events open, close, login, logout since they are not atomic accesses. Therefore, the aforementioned primary behavior open, deposit, getBlance, logout, $\heartsuit$ becomes the following woven behavior after weaving the logging aspect and the simple banking system: open, deposit, log, getBlance, log, logout, $\heartsuit$. Indeed, the logging aspect defines a relationship between the behavior of a primary system and the behavior of a woven system.

Let A be a k-ary finite-state behavioral aspect and $M_1, \cdots, M_k$ be finite-state systems. In this case, a woven system $M = W_A(M_1, \cdots, M_k)$ can be constructed as follows (sketch). M is a finite automaton that simulates the multitape automaton A. During the simulation, the tape contents of the first k tapes in A are guessed and also run over the systems $M_1, \cdots, M_k$, respectively. The content of the last tape in A is fed by the input tape content of M itself. M accepts when A accepts. It can be shown that, in worst case, the size (state number) of the woven system is $O(|A| \cdot |M_1| \cdots |M_k|)$. Apply the weaving process to the simple banking system in Figure 1 and the logging aspect in Figure 2, the woven system is shown in Figure 3.

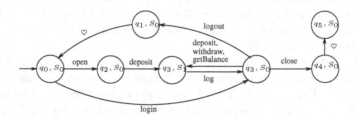

Fig. 3. The simple banking system woven with the logging aspect

5   Safety Verification and Testing of Aspect-Oriented Systems

At the heart of aspect-oriented software development methodology, aspects are used along with multiple primary systems to construct a final woven system through (nested) weaving. One can raise the same safety verification problem for the woven system. However, one of the difficulties now is how to deal with the case when some of the primary systems are black-boxes (a white-box can also be marked as a black-box when its behaviors are hard to analyze; e.g., some infinite-state systems.). Our solution is a decompositional algorithm that combines model-checking with black-box testing. Before we proceed further, we first formally define aspect-oriented systems. To simplify our presentation (but WLOG), we assume that a behavioral aspect is 2-ary.

Let $M_1, \cdots, M_n$ be some given primary systems, and $A_1, \cdots, A_m$ be some given (2-ary) behavioral aspects. An *aspect-oriented system* $\mathcal{A}$ is a binary tree T where each node is either a leaf or a nonterminal node (with two children). There are n leaves in T, which are labeled with $M_1, \cdots, M_n$, respectively. Each nonterminal node is labeled with an aspect A_i for some $1 \leq i \leq m$. Notice that distinct nonterminal nodes could have the same label. For a nonterminal node u, we use $u.left$ and $u.right$ to indicate its left and right children, respectively. The semantics of the aspect-oriented system $\mathcal{A}$ is defined recursively as follows. We associate a system M_u to each node u in T. When u is a leaf, M_u is simply the system M_i originally labeled on u. Then, recursively, when u is a nonterminal node, M_u is the woven system $W_A(M_{u.left}, M_{u.right})$, where A is the behavioral aspect originally labeled on u. The final woven system of $\mathcal{A}$ is then specified by the woven system associated with the root node $root$; i.e., M_{root}. Sometimes, we simply use $\mathcal{A}$ itself to indicate the M_{root}. Figure 4 (a) shows an $\mathcal{A}$ with four primary systems and three aspects.

5.1 Safety Verification Algorithm for Aspect-Oriented Systems

The *safety verification problem for aspect-oriented systems* is to decide whether an aspect-oriented system $\mathcal{A}$ has a bad transaction in a given regular set Bad; i.e., $L(\mathcal{A}) \cap Bad = \emptyset$?. Suppose that all the primary systems $M_1, \cdots, M_n$ as well as all the behavioral aspects $A_1, \cdots, A_m$ in $\mathcal{A}$ are of finite-state. To solve the problem, a naive approach would be to construct the final woven system $\mathcal{A}$ (which is still a finite-state system) directly and then use this $\mathcal{A}$ to check against the emptiness of $L(\mathcal{A}) \cap Bad$. However, there is an issue with this approach. Calculating the final woven system $\mathcal{A}$ is expensive: in worst case, the size of the woven system is $O(N^n \alpha^n)$ where N is a state number bound for the primary systems $M_1, \cdots, M_n$, and α is a state number bound for the aspects $A_1, \cdots, A_m$. But the real issue is that one has to perform such an expensive calculation before the verification result on the emptiness of $L(\mathcal{A}) \cap Bad$ could be obtained (whose time complexity is $O(N^n \alpha^n |M_{Bad}|)$) where $|M_{Bad}|$ is the size of a finite automaton accepting Bad). Therefore, it is desirable to design a verification algorithm where the verification result can be established earlier (e.g., before the entire woven system $\mathcal{A}$ is calculated) whenever it is possible. To this end, we present a safety verification algorithm **verifyAOS**($\mathcal{A}$, Bad). For each node u in the tree $\mathcal{A}$, the algorithm

---

Algorithm 1. verifyAOS($\mathcal{A}$, Bad)

1: initialize($\mathcal{A}$, Bad)
2: checkNode($root$)
3: return "no"   //$\mathcal{A}$ does have Bad transactions

---

maintains and updates a set, denoted by $u.badSet$, which is always a regular set in Σ^*. Initially (line 1), only the set in the root node, $root.badSet$, is set to be the given Bad; the sets in other nodes are all Σ^*. Then (line 2), the algorithm updates all the $badSets$ in the tree starting from the root, during which the main algorithm **verifyAOS**($\mathcal{A}$, Bad) could halt with "yes" (i.e., $\mathcal{A}$ does not have Bad transactions) returned (otherwise, as in line 3, "no" is returned).

We now explain the procedure checkNode($root$) in line 2 in a little more detail. For each node u starting from the root, it "projects" its current $u.badSet$ down to its left child; i.e., $(u.left).badSet$ is set to be $\text{Project}_A(\downarrow, \Sigma^*, u.badSet)$, where A is the aspect that u is labeled with. [1] Similarly, u also projects $u.badSet$ down to its right child. In case when u is a leaf, it intersects its current $u.badSet$ with the transaction set of the system M that u is labeled with and obtains a new $u.badSet$. Then, for each nonterminal node u (from the lowest level up to the root), the procedure will project the new $badSets$ of u's children up to u itself; i.e.,

$$u.badSet := \text{Project}_A((u.left).badSet, (u.right).badSet, \downarrow)$$

It shall be noticed that, during the procedure, once a $badSet$ becomes empty (this could happen at an earlier stage of the execution), we can conclude that A does not have Bad transactions – no further execution of the algorithm is necessary. In the following, we present the recursive procedure checkNode(NODE u):

Procedure 2. checkNode (NODE u)

```
1:  if u is a leaf then
2:      M be the primary system that u is labeled with
3:      u.badSet := u.badSet ∩ L(M)
4:      if u.badSet is empty then
5:          return "yes"    // A does not have Bad transactions
6:          exit    // the main algorithm verifyAOS halts
7:      end if
8:  else
9:      let A be the aspect that u is labeled with
10:     (u.left).badSet := Project_A(↓, Σ*, u.badSet)
11:     (u.right).badSet := Project_A(Σ*, ↓, u.badSet)
12:     checkNode(u.left)
13:     checkNode(u.right)
14:     u.badSet := Project_A((u.left).badSet, (u.right).badSet, ↓)
15:     if u.badSet is empty then
16:         return "yes" and exit
17:     end if
18: end if
```

Due to space limitation, we omit the correctness proof of the algorithm. Notice that, in our algorithm presentation, set operations, such as emptiness testing, intersection, and Project_A, are used. In fact, one can use finite automata to represent $badSets$ and multitape finite automata to represent aspects A. It should be straightforward that all these set operations can be implemented using the corresponding automata manipulations. One can also prove that, in worst case, the time complexity of our algorithm is $O(|M_{Bad}| \cdot N^n \cdot \alpha^n \cdot |M_{Bad}|^n \cdot \alpha^{n \log n})$, comparing to the naive algorithm's time complexity $O(|M_{Bad}| \cdot N^n \cdot \alpha^n)$ mentioned earlier. Notice that N (the state number

---

[1] For a 2-ary aspect A, and sets X and Y, we define $\text{Project}_A(\downarrow, X, Y)$ to be the set of all $w\heartsuit$ such that there are $x\heartsuit \in X$ and $y\heartsuit \in Y$ satisfying $x\heartsuit$ and $y\heartsuit$ can be woven into $w\heartsuit$ using A; i.e., $(w\heartsuit, x\heartsuit, y\heartsuit) \in A$. Accordingly, $\text{Project}_A(X, \downarrow, Y)$ and $\text{Project}_A(X, Y, \downarrow)$ can be defined.

in primary systems) is the dominate parameter which is usually $\gg$ all the other parameters (specifications for Bad and for aspects are typically simple and n is also small). So, as long as $N \gg$ the slow down factor $|M_{Bad}|^n \cdot \alpha^{n \log n}$, our algorithm's worst-case time complexity is the same as the naive one, not to mention the additional benefit of possible earlier termination when worst-cases do not happen.

5.2 Safety Testing Algorithm for Aspect-Oriented Systems

When some of the primary systems are black-boxes (whose state number could be infinite), the *safety testing problem* for $\mathcal{A}$ is exactly the safety verification problem for $\mathcal{A}$ in which each black-boxes M is replaced with a finite-state system M' whose transactions are exactly those in $\mathbf{GenTests}(M, \Sigma)$. We shall emphasize that, even though $\mathbf{GenTests}(M, \Sigma)$ could return a huge set of tests (such as strings on Σ not longer than 40), the safety testing problem is to seek a *definite* yes/no answer. In this case, one would follow the naive approach by first testing each black-box M using the tests generated from $\mathbf{GenTests}(M, \Sigma)$ and then replacing the M with a system whose behavior is exactly those successful tests. However, exhaustive testing of the entire test set $\mathbf{GenTests}(M, \Sigma)$ is not feasible. It is desirable to have an algorithm using the tree $\mathcal{A}$ as well as the set Bad to trim the test set $\mathbf{GenTests}(M, \Sigma)$ before actual tests are run on the M (i.e., tests on a black-box are tailored to the specific safety testing problem of $\mathcal{A}$). Furthermore, successful tests themselves are valuable information on the actual behavior of M. This information should be used to further trim away unnecessary tests performed over other black-boxes. To this end, we propose a safety testing algorithm **testAOS**($\mathcal{A}$,Bad) as follows:

Algorithm 3. testAOS($\mathcal{A}$, Bad)

1: initialize($\mathcal{A}$, Bad)
2: trim($root$)
3: **for** each leaf node u labeled with a black box **do**
4:     propagate($root$)
5:     test(u)
6:     trim($root$)
7: **end for**
8: return "no"

Each node u in $\mathcal{A}$ is associated with $u.badSet$, $u.flag$ (which is *white* or *black*), and Boolean value $u.updated$. Initially (line 1), only the set in the root node, $root.badSet$, is set to be the given Bad; the sets in other nodes are all Σ^*. Also, for each leaf node u, if it is labeled by a black-box then its flag is *black* else the flag is *white*. The rest of initialize($\mathcal{A}$,Bad) in line 1 is to run init($root$), which is defined recursively in Procedure 4.

Roughly speaking, init($root$) recursively "projects down" the Bad set to the $badSet$ of each nonterminal node and leaf, much the same as checkNode($root$) does in **verifyAOS**. When a leaf is a *white* primary system M, an updated $badSet$ is calculated by intersecting it with $L(M)$. Additionally, for a *black* node, all its ancestors are also flagged *black*.

Procedure 4. init(Node u)

1: **if** $u.badSet$ is empty **then**
2:      return "yes" and exit   //the main algorithm **testAOS** halts
3: **end if**
4: **if** u is a leaf with a $white$ flag **then**
5:      let M be the primary system that u is labeled with
6:      $u.badSet := u.badSet \cap L(M)$
7:      **if** $u.badSet$ is empty **then**
8:          return "yes" and exit
9:      **end if**
10:     set $u.updated$ to be $True$
11: **else**
12:     let A be the aspect that u is labeled with
13:     $(u.left).badSet := \text{Project}_A(\downarrow, \Sigma^*, u.badSet)$
14:     $(u.right).badSet := \text{Project}_A(\Sigma^*, \downarrow, u.badSet)$
15:     init($u.left$)
16:     init($u.right$)
17:     set $u.updated$ to be $False$
18:     **if** each of u's two children has a $white$ flag **then**
19:         set the flag of u to be $white$
20:     **else**
21:         set the flag of u to be $black$
22:     **end if**
23: **end if**

Procedure 5. trim(Node u)

1: **if** u is not a leaf **then**
2:     trim($u.left$)
3:     trim($u.right$)
4: **end if**
5: **if** u has at least a child whose $updated$ is $True$ **then**
6:     let A be the aspect that u is labeled with
7:     $u.badSet := \text{Project}_A((u.left).badSet, (u.right).badSet, \downarrow)$
8:     **if** $u.badSet$ is empty **then**
9:         return "yes" and exit
10:     **end if**
11:     set $u.updated$ to be $True$
12:     **if** each of u's two children has a $white$ flag **then**
13:         delete these two children (so u is a leaf now)
14:     **end if**
15: **end if**

In line 2 of **testAOS**, trim($root$) "projects up" all the "updated" $badSet$s at leaf nodes to all their ancestors by updating the ancestors' $badSet$s. In the mean time, a $white$ node becomes a $white$ leaf (i.e., children are trimmed away) whenever the children are also $white$ nodes. The procedure is presented in Procedure 5.

Now, the for-loop of **testAOS** (lines 4,5,6) is to test each black-box primary system one by one. Suppose that we are currently processing black-box M that is labeled on some leaf node u. We first use propagate($root$) in line 4 to "project down" the updated $badSet$ of the root all the way to every black-box which then obtains a new (and smaller) $badSet$. Later in line 5, the black-box M at node u is tested using tests that are in both **GenTests**(M, Σ) and the new $u.badSet$. All the successful tests are collected and form the "updated" $u.badSet$ now. At this time, the black-box node u is flagged $white$ (the black-box M is finished processing). Finally in line 6, this newly added $white$ node u and the test results (recorded in the "updated" $u.badSet$) are used to "trim" the tree (as well as update all the $badSets$ of its ancestors). When the for-loop continues, the next black-box picked will again first "propagate" the root's updated $badSet$ (as a result of the previous black-box's test results), and so on. Details of propagate($root$) and test(u) are shown in Procedures 6 and 7.

Procedure 6. propagate(Node u)

1: **if** $u.badSet$ is empty **then**
2:    return "yes" and exit
3: **end if**
4: set $u.updated$ to be $False$
5: **if** u is not a leaf and $u.left$ has a $black$ flag **then**
6:    $(u.left).badSet := \text{Project}_A(\downarrow, \Sigma^*, u.badSet) \cap (u.left).badSet$
7:    propagate($u.left$)
8: **end if**
9: **if** u is not a leaf and $u.right$ has a $black$ flag **then**
10:    $(u.right).badSet := \text{Project}_A(\Sigma^*, \downarrow, u.badSet) \cap (u.right).badSet$
11:    propagate($u.right$)
12: **end if**

Procedure 7. test(Node u)

1: let M be the black-box primary system labeled on leaf u
2: **for** each test $w\heartsuit$ in **GenTests**(M, Σ)$\cap u.badSet$ **do**
3:    run black-box testing **BTest**($M, w\heartsuit$)
4: **end for**
5: set $u.badSet$ to be the set all successful tests $w\heartsuit$
6: set the flag of u to be $white$
7: set $u.updated$ to be $True$

Figure 4 shows an example execution of the safety testing algorithm **testAOS** over the aspect-oriented system $\mathcal{A}$ shown in Figure 4 (a), where M_1, M_2, M_3, M_4 are primary systems (in which M_2 and M_4 are black-boxes), and A_1, A_2, A_3 are behavioral aspects.

At any time when the algorithm **testAOS** runs, if the $badSet$ at some node becomes empty, then the algorithm halts and return a "yes" answer to the safety testing problem. When this happens before any black-box primary system is tested, we simply do not need test any black-box at all for the safety testing problem. When this happens

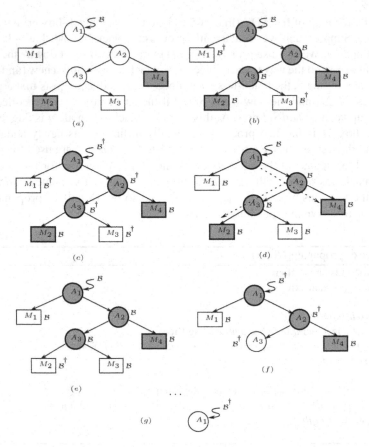

Fig. 4. An example run of safety testing algorithm **testAOS** over the aspect-oriented system in (a). The black boxes M_2 and M_4 are lightly shaded and (the root node labeled with aspect) A_1 is associated with a *badSet* initially being the regular set *Bad*. In the sequel, each *badSet* at a node is simply denoted by a special symbol $\mathcal{B}$ in the figure. (b) the result of running init(A_1) at line 1 of **testAOS**. Each non-root node is associated with a $\mathcal{B}$ using Project operations. When the node is a white-box node, i.e. M_1 or M_3, its $\mathcal{B}$ is further *updated* by $\mathcal{B} \cap M$, which is denoted as $\mathcal{B}^\dagger$. The flag (i.e., in the figure, a shaded/clear circle corresponds to a *black/white* flag) of each nonterminal node is set according to the flags of the two children. (c) The result of running trim(A_1) at line 2 of **testAOS**. The $\mathcal{B}$ of each node is updated to $\mathcal{B}^\dagger$ using Project operations if one of the children is associated with $\mathcal{B}^\dagger$. In our example, since M_3 was associated with $\mathcal{B}^\dagger$ in (b), the $\mathcal{B}$ of the parent A_3 is therefore updated to $\mathcal{B}^\dagger$. Similarly, the $\mathcal{B}$ of A_2 as well as A_1 is also updated to $\mathcal{B}^\dagger$. (d) The result of running propagate(A_1) at line 4 of **testAOS**. From (c), a new $\mathcal{B}$ is associated with the root A_1, then all shaded nodes (flagged with *black*) are associated with new $\mathcal{B}$'s recursively using Project operations starting from the root A_1. In this step, *updated* is reset to *False* in all nodes; i.e., all updated $\mathcal{B}^\dagger$ is renamed as un-updated $\mathcal{B}$. (e) The result of running test(M_2) at line 5 of **testAOS**. Through testing, the black-box M_2 is associated with an updated $\mathcal{B}^\dagger$ and its flag is set to *white* (M_2, after testing, is a white-box now). (f) trim(A_1) again at line 6 of **testAOS**. Notice that the flags of A_3's children (M_2 and M_3) are both *white* now. In this case, both children are deleted from the tree after $\mathcal{B}$ of A_3 is updated. (g) Repeat procedures from d to f (i.e., the for-loop in **testAOS**) until all the black-boxes are tested.

after some black-boxes have already been tested, all the remaining black-boxes are not needed to test. Also in the algorithm, procedures trim($root$) and propagate($root$) work together to make sure that, after a black-box is tested, the test results (the successful tests) are used to create a smaller test set for each of the remaining black-boxes yet to be tested.

Again, due to space limitation, the correctness prove of the algorithm is omitted. Similarly, in the algorithm, all the set operations can be implemented through automata manipulations. It is hard to conduct a precise complexity analysis for the safety testing algorithm, since the test results for a black-box affect the test sets that will be run over the other black-boxes. At least when there is no black-box, **testAOS** does not perform worse than **verifyAOS**. It is reasonable to assume that black-box testing is expensive, in particular when one exhaustively runs every test from a huge (e.g., 10^{24} in [6]) test set generated from **GenTests**. The saved testing time resulted from eliminating a large number of unnecessary tests from the test set would well make up the overhead of calculating the unnecessary tests using our algorithm **testAOS**. For instance, concurrent composition (through interleaving) can be considered as a concurrency aspect (though it is very special). The case-study performed in [6] is a very special case of our safety testing algorithm that runs over one white-box and three black-boxes and with only one 4-ary concurrency aspect (which is the root). The case-study shows that a huge test set with 10^{24} tests is reduced into a set with 10^5 tests after removing all unnecessary tests. On the other hand, state-space explosion seems unavoidable when a even larger test set is selected. In that case-study, automata manipulations (for the concurrency aspect and tests results) failed to complete. We would anticipate similar experimental results for our safety testing algorithm **testAOS**.

6   Conclusions

In this paper, we use multitape automata to model aspects and study verification and testing algorithms for an aspect-oriented system specified by a number of primary labeled transition systems (some of them are black-boxes) and aspects. Our algorithms combine automata manipulations with black-box testing over each individual black-box, but without generating the woven system.

In a forthcoming paper, we are going to implement the algorithms and perform case-studies in order to justify the real-world efficiency of the algorithms. The authors thank Anneliese Andrews and Curtis Dyreson for discussions.

References

1. G. Kiczales, J. Lamping, A. Mendhekar, C. Maeda, C. Lopes, J.-M. Loingtier, and J. Irwin. Aspect-oriented Programming. In *ECOOP'97*, LNCS 1241, pages 220–242, Springer, 1997.
2. R. Laddad. *AspectJ in Action: Practical Aspect-Oriented Programming*. Manning Publications Co., 2003.
3. E. Barra, G. Gnova, and J. Llorens. An Approach to Aspect Modeling with UML 2.0. In *5th AOSD Modeling With UML Workshop*, San Francisco, California, USA, October 2004.

4. K. Cooper, L. Dai and Y. Deng. Modeling Performance as an Aspect: a UML Based Approach. In *4th AOSD Modeling With UML Workshop*, San Francisco, California, USA, October 2003.
5. E. M. Clarke, O. Grumberg, and D. A. Peled. *Model Checking*. The MIT Press, 1999.
6. G. Xie and Z. Dang. Testing Systems of Concurrent Black-boxes: a Decompositional Approach. In *FATES'05*, LNCS 3997, pages 170–189, Springer, 2006.
7. D. Giannakopoulou, C. Pasareanu, and H. Barringer. Assumption Generation for Software Component Verification. In *ASE'02*, IEEE Computer Society, 2002.
8. M. E. Fayad and A. Ranganath. Modeling Aspects using Software Stability and UML. In *4th AOSD Modeling With UML Workshop*, San Francisco, California, USA, October 2003.
9. R. France, I. Ray, G. Georg, and S. Ghosh. An Aspect-Oriented Approach to Early Design Modeling. *IEE Proceedings - Software*, 151(4):173–185, 2004.
10. I. Hammouda, M. Pussinen, M. Katara, and T. Mikkonen. UML-based Approach for Documenting and Specializing Frameworks Using Patterns and Concern Architectures, In *4th AOSD Modeling With UML Workshop*, San Francisco, California, USA, October 2003.
11. L. Alfaro and T. A. Henzinger. Interface Automata. In *FSE'01*, pages 109–120, ACM Press, 2001.
12. M. M. Kande, J. Kienzle, and A. Strohmeier. *From AOP to UML - a Bottom-up Approach*. In *3rd AOSD Modeling With UML Workshop*, San Francisco, California, USA, October 2002.
13. D. Lee, M. Yannakakis. Principles and Methods of Testing Finite State Machines - a Survey. *Proceedings of the IEEE* 84(8):1090-1126, 1996.
14. http://www.globalfuture.com/mit-trends2001.htm
15. http://pavg.stanford.edu/rapide/rapide-pubs.html
16. M. Sihman and S. Katz. Model Checking Applications of Aspects and Superimpositions. In *FOAL'03*, Boston, Massachusetts, USA, March 2003.
17. S. Nakajima and T. Tamai. Lightweight Formal Analysis of Aspect-Oriented Models. In *5th AOSD Modeling With UML Workshop*, San Francisco, California, USA, October 2004.
18. N. Ubayashi and T. Tamai. Aspect-oriented Programming with Model Checking. In *AOSD'02*, Enschede, The Netherlands, April 2002.

Model-Based Testing of Thin-Client Web Applications

Pieter Koopman, Rinus Plasmeijer, and Peter Achten

Software Technology, Nijmegen Institute for Computing and Information Sciences,
Radboud University Nijmegen
{pieter, rinus, P.Achten}@cs.ru.nl

Abstract. In this paper we present a novel automated, on-line, model-based testing system for on-the-fly testing of thin-client web applications. Web applications are specified by means of Extended State Machines. To handle dynamic web applications, arbitrarily large and complex state input and output types, and the transport of information from the web-page to the state of the specification, we define a new, ioco like, conformance relation. In this conformance relation a specification is a function from state and input to functions from output to the new states. The implementation builds on the G∀ST test tool and spots errors in real web applications.

1 Introduction

Web-applications have rapidly become popular. Web-interfaces are defined for many ordinary applications. Just like any other software system these web-applications and interfaces tend to contain mistakes. In order to determine the quality of software with a web-based interface it needs to be tested. Testing such software can be done most thoroughly and cost effectively by using an automatic model based test system. Such a system automatically generates test sequences based on a formal specification of the desired behavior of the system, executes the associated tests, and makes a verdict based on the observed behavior of the implementation under test, the iut.

In this paper we present a novel testing system that performs automated, on-line, model-based testing of thin-client (no processing on the client) web applications. Systems are specified using non-deterministic Extended State Machines (ESMs) with arbitrarily rich states, inputs, and outputs. Additionally, the transitions in these state machines are specified by defining them as functions over the output domain to the reachable states. This allows us to concisely express highly dynamic systems with states that depend on the output and eliminates the need to specify and enumerate all possible HTML outputs. For these systems we define a conformance relation that is closely related to the well-known *ioco* relation [20,19]. The system performs on-line testing, as propagated by e.g. Larsen *et al.*[10]. We identify the same advantages: we can employ potentially long test runs, we can limit the state space to a finite portion, and use non-deterministic specifications.

K. Havelund et al. (Eds.): FATES/RV 2006, LNCS 4262, pp. 115–132, 2006.
© Springer-Verlag Berlin Heidelberg 2006

We intend to perform a black box test and look only at the input and output of the web application. For a web application this implies that the test system performs an input from the current page, e.g. press a button or edit a text field, and receives a new page in HTML. We restrict ourselves to testing the web application based on the HTML input elements available in the page. Hence, we do not consider navigating by back/forward browser buttons, window cloning and history caches. Furthermore, we restrict ourselves to thin clients. The behavior of the web-interface should be determined by exchanging HTML code with the server instead of things like Java(scripts) embedded in the web-page. This restriction enables us to investigate the response to an input just by looking at the HTML code.

We show how a web application can be specified by an ESM. Since there is always a strict relation between selecting an input from the current page and obtaining a new page, we prefer a state machine based specification rather than a specification by a Labeled Transition System (LTS). The web application itself can have an arbitrary complex state, and can contact any system it needs, e.g. a database. As mentioned above, in our black box approach we restrict ourselves to the input to the web-application and the associated new page (in sharp contrast with the approach by Margaria *et al.*[15]) This may appear to be very restrictive, but that is not the case. The test engineer can incorporate any knowledge of the back-end of the system in the ESM specification.

The specification of the web-application can be nondeterministic, either because the iut is not deterministic, or because the specification has only partial knowledge of the world. One of the case studies in this paper tests a web-shop. If it is not known whether an item is available in the web-shop, the specification should handle the situation that the item is available and that it is unavailable. The output of a web-application is typically large, containing a lot of HTML code that is sent to the browser. We do not want to specify each and every detail of this HTML code, nor do we wish to enumerate all allowed responses. Special about our approach is that instead of explicitly describing the allowed outputs in the specification, we use a function that has the actual output as argument and yields the allowed target states. This function can be a predicate that checks aspects of the HTML code. Typical examples are the presence of buttons and key texts. The function can also extract information from the HTML code and store it in the target state. An example of information that we want to store in the state of the specification is the result of queries executed by the web-application. The results can determine future behavior, and should be consistent with later responses of the web-application. In this way we can test the contents of the HTML code produced by very dynamical web-applications, like web-shops.

We define a conformance relation that incorporates parameterized data types for state input and output (infinite number of states), nondeterministic systems, and functions from the output to the target state. The conformance relation is based on the well-known *ioco* relation. As a host language, we use the pure functional programming language Clean [18]. Clean is a state-of-art programming language with support for Algebraic Data Types (ADTs), generic programming

[1], and features the generic test tool G∀ST [6] that is used in this work to implement the testing framework.

The remainder of this paper is structured as follows: we present the formal definitions and the conformance relation in Sect. 2. In Sect. 3 we introduce the test tool G∀ST and explain how it is used to implement the test system based on the formal definitions. Two case studies are presented in Sect. 4: one of a small number guessing game, and one of a dedicated web-shop. Related work is discussed in Sect. 5. Finally, we conclude in Sect. 6.

2   Specification

The test tool G∀ST can handle two kinds of properties. It can test properties stated in logic about (combinations of) functions and it can test the behavior of reactive systems based on an Extended State Machine (ESM). Web applications are reactive systems.

An ESM consists of states with labeled transitions between them. A transition is of the form $s \xrightarrow{i/o} t$, where s, t are states, i is an input which triggers the transition, and o is a, possibly empty, sequence of outputs. The domains of the states, S, inputs, I, and outputs, O, are given by arbitrarily complex, recursive ADTs. These types can be used to model parameterized states, inputs and outputs. None of these types is required to be finite. The model of the system can be nondeterministic, it is possible to define several transitions for one combination of state and input. The conformance relation defined in Sect. 2.2 states that the tested system is free to choose one of these transitions. This constitutes the main difference with traditional testing with state machines where the testing algorithms can only handle finite domains and deterministic systems [12].

A transition $s \xrightarrow{i/o} t$ is represented by the tuple (s, i, o, t). A relation based specification δ_r is a set of these tuples: $\delta_r \subseteq S \times I \times O^* \times S$. Since none of these types is finite, there can be infinitely many transitions. Our specification describes synchronous systems. As reaction on input i the system produces a list of outputs. We assume that we are able to detect the end of this list of outputs. This is similar to detecting *quiescence* in many *ioco* based approaches [19].

For instance, a system that has natural numbers as state, input and output can have transitions of the form: $\forall s, i : \mathbb{N} \cdot s \xrightarrow{i/[s,s+i]} i$ which is equivalent to the set $\{(s, i, [s, s+i], i) | s \in \mathbb{N}, i \in \mathbb{N}\}$. The output of this system consists of the previous input and the sum of the previous input and the current input. The new state is the current input. This rule describes obviously infinitely many individual transitions. Usually we omit the universal quantifiers and write $s \xrightarrow{i/[s,s+i]} i$.

Such an infinite set of transitions is fine for a mathematical specification, but unsuited as a specification for model based testing. Listing all transitions in a table, as is often done for FSM based testing, is impossible. For our ESMs this would yield an infinite table. A predicate that given the source state, input, output and target state tells whether the transition is allowed is also not suited for several reasons. First of all, we want an easy way to determine for which inputs a transition is defined given the current state s. Secondly, we want to compute the target state, t, from a known source state, the supplied input and the observed output.

2.1 Transition Functions

In [7,23] we defined a transition function that meets the requirements that were mentioned in the previous section. The transition function δ_f is defined by $\delta_f(s,i) = \{(o,t)|(s,i,o,t) \in \delta_r\}$. Hence, $s \xrightarrow{i/o} t$ is equivalent to $(o,t) \in \delta_f(s,i)$. The type of δ_f is $s \times i \rightarrow \mathbb{P}(o^* \times s)$, with $\mathbb{P}\, x$ powerset of x. The system containing only the transition $s \xrightarrow{i/[s,s+i]} i$ can be specified by $\delta_f(s,i) = \{([s,s+i],i)\}$.

The transition function δ_f works very well as specification in model based testing if the number of output-target state tuples, (o,t) in the specification is small. In a number of situations the number of output-target state tuples can become very large. A typical example is an authentication protocol. On the input get-challenge, the protected system should produce a number from a large set, say a 64-bit number. This would require 2^{64} output-target state tuples. For web based specifications the situation is even worse. We do not want to specify each and every detail of the HTML code obtained from the server. We only require some details like the title of the web page and the availability of certain buttons. This would require an unbounded number of output-target state tuples.

In order to cope with these requirements we replace [1] the output-target state tuples by a function from output to the allowed target states. This yield a new kind of transition function called $\delta_F(s,i)$ of type $s \times i \rightarrow (o^* \rightarrow (\mathbb{P}\, s))$:

$$\exists f \in \delta_F(s,i) \wedge (o \mapsto T) \in f \Leftrightarrow \forall t \in T : (s,i,o,t) \in \delta_r.$$

or in other words $s \xrightarrow{i/o} t \Leftrightarrow \exists f \in \delta_F(s,i) : t \in f(o)$.

For our example $s \xrightarrow{i/[s,s+i]} i$ we can use the transition function

$$\delta_F(s,i) = \{f\} \textbf{ where } f\, o = \textbf{if } (o == [s,s+i]) \textbf{ then } \{i\} \textbf{ else } \emptyset$$

If we require that the output is a value between the current state and current input we have: $\delta_F(s,i) = \{\, o \rightarrow \textbf{if } (s \leq o \wedge o \leq i \vee i \leq o \wedge o \leq s)\, \{i\}\, \emptyset\}$ This system is much harder to describe by a function yielding a set of tuples, the number of tuples and their contents depends on s and i. Enumerating all possibilities is cumbersome and can yield a very large set of tuples. Hence, the specification by transition functions that yield a function instead of a set of output-target state pairs really adds descriptive power.

A specification is *partial* if for some state s and input i we have $\delta_F(s,i) = \emptyset$. A specification is *deterministic* if for all states and inputs all functions from the corresponding set of functions contain at most one function and there is at most one target state for each output. Formally: $\forall s\, \forall i, \forall o : \#\bigcup f(o)|f \in \delta_F(s,i) \leq 1$.

---

[1] The test tool G∀ST allows that the transition function yields tuples or functions. This gives maximum freedom in the specification of the system. For simplicity we assume here that the new transition function always yields a function.

A *trace* σ is a sequence of inputs and associated outputs from a given state. Traces are defined inductively: the empty trace connects a state to itself: $s \overset{\epsilon}{\Rightarrow} s$. We combine a trace $s \overset{\sigma}{\Rightarrow} t$ and a transition $t \overset{i/o}{\longrightarrow} u$ from the target state t, to trace $s \overset{\sigma;i/o}{\Longrightarrow} u$. We define $s \overset{i/o}{\longrightarrow} \equiv \exists t.s \overset{i/o}{\longrightarrow} t$ and $s \overset{\sigma}{\Rightarrow} \equiv \exists t.s \overset{\sigma}{\Rightarrow} t$. All traces from state s are: $traces(s) = \{\sigma | s \overset{\sigma}{\Rightarrow}\}$. The inputs allowed in a state are given by $init(s) = \{i | \exists o : s \overset{i/o}{\Longrightarrow}\}$. The states after trace σ in state s are given by s after $\sigma \equiv \{t | s \overset{\sigma}{\Rightarrow} t\}$. We overload *traces*, *init*, and after for sets of states instead of a single state by taking the union of the individual results. When the transition function, δ_F, is not clear from the context, we add it as subscript.

2.2 Conformance

The basic assumption for testing is that the iut has the same input/output behavior as a state machine: all output is initiated by an input. This implies that it is possible to obtain a trace from the iut. Since we do black box testing, the state of the iut is invisible. It is assumed that the iut accepts any trace of the specification. This is a weaker requirement than *total* or *input enabled* which is often assumed in similar conformance relations. These traces only contain inputs/output pairs covered by the specification. This means for instance that if the specification allows to push a button on a web-page after a sequence of transitions, that the iut should accept this input as well.

Conformance of the iut to the specification spec is defined as (s_0 is the initial state of spec, and t_0 the initial state of iut):

$$\text{iut } conf \text{ spec} \equiv \forall \sigma \in traces_{\text{spec}}(s_0), \forall i \in init(s_0 \text{ after}_{\text{spec}} \sigma), \forall o \in O^*.$$

$$(t_0 \text{ after}_{\text{iut}} \sigma) \overset{i/o}{\longrightarrow} \Rightarrow (s_0 \text{ after}_{\text{spec}} \sigma) \overset{i/o}{\longrightarrow}$$

Intuitively: if the specification allows input i after trace σ, then the observed output of the iut should be allowed by the specification. If spec does not specify a transition for the current state and input, anything is allowed. This notion of conformance is very similar to the *ioco* relation [20,19] for LTSs. In a LTS each input and output is modeled by a separate transition. In our approach an input and all induced outputs up to *quiescence* are modeled by a single transition.

2.3 Testing Conformance

The conformance relation *conf* tells when an implementation iut conforms to a specification spec. In practice it is usually impossible to determine conformance by testing. Both the number of traces of the specification, $traces_{\text{spec}}(s_0)$, and the length of individual traces can be infinite. This implies that determining conformance by experimentation generally requires the execution of infinitely many transitions, and hence takes infinitely long. Instead of determining the conformance of all transitions from all possible traces, we determine the correctness of a limited amount of transitions in a limited number of traces. As usual, testing approximates the conformance relation. If we find an error during testing the conformance relation does not hold. When no errors are found we gain confidence in the conformance of the iut to the specification, but errors may remain.

For the implementation of a test system it is very inconvenient to record all traces of the specification corresponding to the observed trace of the implementation. There can be a huge number, in fact even infinitely many, of these traces of the specification. Instead of keeping track of all traces of the specification that conform to the observed trace, our test algorithm records all states in the **after** set of the specification given the observed trace. By a well engineered specification, this set can always be sufficiently small.

In the test algorithm we assume that the iut is available as a function of type $(S_{iut} \times I) \to (O^* \times S_{iut})$. In this function S_{iut} is the abstract state of the iut that is carried around as a black box. The test algorithm for a single trace is:

$$\mathsf{testConf}_F : \mathbb{N} \times (\,I\!P\,S) \times S_{iut} \to \mathsf{Verdict}$$

$$\mathsf{testConf}_F\,(n, s, u) = \mathbf{if}\ s = \emptyset$$

$$\mathbf{then}\ \mathsf{Fail}$$

$$\mathbf{else\ if}\ init\,(s) = \emptyset \vee n = 0$$

$$\mathbf{then}\ \mathsf{Pass}$$

$$\mathbf{else}\ \mathsf{testConf}_F\,(n - 1, t, v)$$

$$\mathbf{where}\ i \in init(s);\ (o, v) = \mathsf{iut}\,(u, i);\ s \xrightarrow{i/o} t$$

Since the transition function yields a function, the new set of possible states is actually computed as $t = \bigcup \{f(o)\,|\,\forall f \in \delta_f(s_i, i), \forall s_i \in s\}$. Due to the overloading of the transition notation we can write it concisely as $s \xrightarrow{i/o} t$.

Testing of a single trace is initiated by $\mathsf{testConf}\,(N, \{s_0\}, S_{iut}^0)$, where N is the maximum length of this trace, s_0 the initial state of the specification, and S_{iut}^0 the initial abstract state of the iut. The input i used in each step can be chosen arbitrarily from the set $init(s)$. In the actual implementation it is possible to control this choice. In a complete test the nondeterministic computation $\mathsf{testConf}\,(N, \{s_0\}, S_{iut})$ is repeated M times. Before each of these test runs, the iut is brought to its initial state by applying the function $reset : S_{iut} \to S_{iut}$ to the state of the iut. If one of these test runs yields Fail, the iut is known to be not conforming to the specification, otherwise it passes the conformance test.

Due to the dynamic choice of the input to be used in the next transition the testing is called *on-the-fly*. This means that input generation, test execution, and result analysis are performed in lock-step, so that only the inputs actually needed are generated.

2.4   Testing Consistency of Outputs

For large and rich outputs, like HTML code, the internal consistency of the output as well as the consistency of the output with the target state requires some attention. For instance, if one goes to the next page in a series of pages in a web-shop, it is required that the items displayed in the HTML code are indeed the items on the desired page.

In principle it is possible to handle this in the transition function. If the output does not correspond to the intended target state, the transition function can simply yield an empty set of states. If there are no other transitions specified, there will be no target state and hence our test algorithm will determine an error. However, it can be pretty hard to spot the error in the given trace. We can improve this by introducing a separate predicate over the observed output and the set of target states of the specification. If the predicate holds, testing continues as usual. Otherwise, we have found an error and testing terminates [2]. To capture this notion we define a new transition function δ_P that is very similar to δ_F. The extension is that a transition $s \xrightarrow{i/o;p(o,t)} t$ implies $s \xrightarrow{i/o} t \wedge p(o,t)$. Written in terms of the transition function this is: $s \xrightarrow{i/o;p(o,t)} t \Leftrightarrow \exists f \in \delta_F(s,i) :$ $t \in f(o) \wedge p(o,t)$. The corresponding testing algorithm makes clear why it is more convenient to have a predicate of type $O^* \times \mathbb{P}\,S \rightarrow \mathsf{Bool}$ than $O^* \times S \rightarrow \mathsf{Bool}$:

$$\mathsf{testConf}_P : \mathbb{N} \times (\mathbb{P}\,S) \times S_{iut} \rightarrow \mathsf{Verdict}$$
$$\mathsf{testConf}_P\,(n,s,u) = \mathbf{if}\ s = \emptyset$$

$$\quad \mathbf{then}\ \mathsf{Fail}$$
$$\quad \mathbf{else\ if}\ init\,(s) = \emptyset \vee n = 0$$
$$\quad \mathbf{then}\ \mathsf{Pass}$$
$$\quad \mathbf{else\ if}\ P_{\mathrm{consistent}}(o,t)$$
$$\quad \mathbf{then}\ \mathsf{testConf}_P\,(n-1,t,v)$$
$$\quad \mathbf{else}\ \mathsf{Fail}$$
$$\quad \mathbf{where}\ i \in init(s);\ (o,v) = \mathsf{iut}\,(u,i);\ s \xrightarrow{i/o} t$$

G∀ST implements this algorithm extended with the collection of data indicating the trace and the error if testing yields Fail. Moreover, the test engineer is able to influence testing details like the choice of the input i from $init(s)$.

3   G∀ST

The test tool G∀ST executes conformance tests according to the conformance relation in Sect. 2. In order to execute such a conformance test we use: **(1)** a specification in some executable form; **(2)** an implementation of the conformance test algorithm; and **(3)** an interface to the iut. We discuss these topics briefly.

In Sect. 2 we have shown that specifications are represented by functions over user defined, and problem dependent, ADTs for state, input and output. Instead of defining a new language for this purpose, we use the high level functional programming language Clean as carrier for these specifications. Modern functional programming languages are known for their high expressive power and concise function definitions. We consider it much better to reuse decades of language design and compiler technology than to define a new language.

---

[2] In the actual implementation of G∀ST, this predicate is replaced by a function yielding success or a list of error messages.

For the implementation of the test system we also use Clean. This prevents a language border between the specification and its use. Moreover, Clean provides polymorphism, overloading and generic programming. These techniques enable us to use functions over various types in a very convenient way. This is particulary useful for the functions used as specification. The types used in these functions for state, input and output are tailor-made for the system at hand. Using generic programming the generation of input elements [8], the printing and comparing of elements of all types needed can be generated automatically.

The test tool G∀ST implements the test algorithm presented above with a few additional bells and whistles. For instance, the system records the trace leading to an error. Most importantly, it controls the choice of the input to be applied to the iut. By default G∀ST generates a list of elements and pseudo randomly selects an input element, i, that is accepted by the specification. That is, there is a state s_i in the set of possible states of the system such that $\delta_f(s_i, i) \neq \emptyset$. The test engineer can provide a user defined selection algorithm. A default algorithm is provided to select all traces needed to fully test a FSM. The test engineer can provide an algorithm to guide the test to specific targets.

In order to apply an input to the iut and to obtain the answer, the test system needs an interface to the iut. G∀ST assumes that there are two functions in this interface. The first function takes the input to the iut as argument and yields the corresponding output from the iut to G∀ST. In the case of testing web applications typical inputs are pushing buttons and editing text boxes. The output is the HTML code that corresponds with the new web page. The second function, reset, brings the iut to its initial state at the start of a new trace.

4   Testing Web Applications

We test web applications from the viewpoint of a user. The user enters a URL in a browser and obtains an initial web-page. In such a page there can be various ways to give input, like buttons, edit fields, and dropdown menus. If the user supplies such an input, the browser sends the current page and information about the input to the web application. In response the web application sends a new web-page in HTML to the browser.

For automatic model based testing, our test system G∀ST provides the input and checks the HTML code received as response. We use a data structure representing the HTML code instead of a textual representation. The data structures for HTML from the iData approach [16,17] are reused. Without restricting the general approach in any way we test web applications constructed with iData. Compared with testing an arbitrary web application it has as advantage that it enables us to make a shortcut that increases the speed of testing. Instead of transforming the data structures generated by the web-application to HTML text, transmitting this text over the web, parsing the text, and converting it to a suitable data structure to inspect the code in a structural way, we directly pass the HTML data structure to the web-interface of G∀ST. Also the input is sent directly as data structure from G∀ST to the web-application under test.

Within the HTML data structure all viewable information is stored in a list of body-tags. The recursive ADT for body-tags contains separate cases for items like strings, tables, buttons, and edit fields. To retrieve information from these data structures easily we have created functions to select strings, tables and table contents from HTML or body-tags. The function findBodyTags finds the named list of body-tags in a specification.

In the examples below we assume that we have limited information of the iut. In the number guessing game the specification does not know the number to be found, and in the CD-shop the specification does not know the content of the CD database at the back-end of the application. Nevertheless, we are able to do useful tests and to spot errors in both cases. Including the CD database in the specification allows us to check more details of the obtained web-pages.

4.1   Example 1: A Number Guessing Game

The first example is a number guessing game that randomly selects a number between integer bounds *low* and *up*. After each guess, the game provides feedback: if the number is too low (high), the guess count is incremented, and the player is told that the number to guess is larger (smaller); if the number matches, then the player's name and used number of guesses are entered and displayed in the Hall of Fame. At any time, a different player name can be entered.

Although this is a small example, there are many aspects that can be tested. To mention just a few of them: **(1)** the game should give consistent answers to guesses; **(2)** the Hall of Fame should add the player with the given name and number of guesses; **(3)** the Hall of Fame should be persistent and not alter existing entries; **(4)** entering a different player name should not change the state. Here we test aspect **(1)** and **(4)**.

The specification is a state transition function written in Clean [18] is given in figure 1. The function spec is the heart of the specification. The state used in this specification consists only of the integer to be guessed. The transition from initial state to running state (line 2) is a standard idiom for web applications. In this line Init is some integer value outside the range of valid numbers to be guessed. Line 3 captures every switch to a new name. Lines 4-7 are concerned with numerical input. Lines 5 and 6 handle incorrect inputs. Line 5 states that if the input i is smaller than the goal g only the transitions described by the function tooLow are allowed. Line 6 states that only the transition described by tooHigh is allowed when i>g. If i is neither smaller nor larger than g, it will be equal to g. This is handled in line 7. In this situation the guess should be correct. This is handled by the function correct.

The functions tooLow, tooHigh, and correct are the functions that compute the reachable states from the associated input and output page. They are very similar. They inspect the HTML text elements that are tagged with labels "Hint" and "Answer". For instance, correct demands that the text line labeled with "Answer" has content "Congratulations" and resets to a new guess state. Note that each function alternative yields a list of functions of type [Html] → [Int]. This is the instance of $O^* \rightarrow I\!\!P\,S$ for this test.

```
spec :: Int In → [[Html] → [Int]]                                       1
spec Init input = [ FTrans (λhtml = newGuess)]                          2
spec r (StringTextBox s) = [λhtml = [r]]                                3
spec g (IntTextBox i)                                                    4
    | i<g      = [(tooLow [g])]                                          5
    | i>g      = [(tooHigh [g])]                                         6
    | otherwise = [(correct newGuess)]                                   7

tooLow r [html]                                                          8
    | htmlTexts (findBodyTags "Answer" html) == ["Sorry"] ∧             9
      htmlTexts (findBodyTags "Hint" html) == ["larger"] = r            10
    | otherwise = []                                                     11
tooHigh r [html]                                                         12
    | htmlTexts (findBodyTags "Answer" html) == ["Sorry"] ∧             13
      htmlTexts (findBodyTags "Hint" html) == ["smaller"] = r           14
    | otherwise = []                                                     15
correct r [html]                                                         16
    | htmlTexts (findBodyTags "Answer" html) == ["Congratulations"] = r 17
    | otherwise = []                                                     18
```

Fig. 1. The specification of the number guessing game

The function newGuess yields the list of states for a new game. Since we assumed that the specification has no knowledge about the choice of numbers to be guessed, it yields the list of all numbers from the lower bound up to the upper bound: newGuess = [low..up].

The states of numbers, g, that appear to be incorrect will be eliminated as soon as the iut gives a reply that is not consistent with the behavior of spec for that g. Suppose that low is 1, up is 10. This implies that all number from 1 to 10 are allowed states in the specification after initialization. Assume that we supply the input 5 and the iut replies Sorry, larger. This will eliminate states 1 to 5. When the next input is 4 and the iut would answer Sorry, smaller this is clearly inconsistent behavior. The specification will notice this since there is no transition matching this HTML-output on input 4 for states 6 to 10. As a result the set of allowed states in the specification becomes empty. Hence, the iut did a transition that is not covered by the specification, i.e. an error occurred.

Input Generation. The inputs for this web-application are either a new name in the string text box, or a new guess in the integer text box. This is modeled by the algebraic data type In.

```
:: In = StringTextBox String | IntTextBox Int
```

During testing instances of this type are needed in order to determine the next input. G∀ST is able to derive all possible inputs values from the type definition for In automatically. However, the generic generation algorithm used for this has no notion of the intended use of these values and will produce many values that are not very sensible for testing this web-application. Instead of deriving values for the type In, we specify to use only the name Tester and the integer values from low-1 to up+1.

ggen{|In|} = [StringTextBox "tester": [IntTextBox i \\ i ← [low-1..up+1]]]

The border values low-1 and up+1 are added to include some invalid numbers in the tests. A single name appears to be sufficient in the tests. Using different names would be very simple. G∀ST tries these values in a pseudo random order. In each state G∀ST applies the first input element that is accepted by one of the current states of the specification (e.a. is an element of $init(s)$). Since all inputs of type In are accepted by the given specification, the sequence of inputs used in the tests is a pseudo random choice of elements from the values defined above.

Test Results. We have run the test against an iut that interprets the switching of player names differently than the specification does: whenever a new player name is entered, the iut starts with a new number to guess. This violates the behavior specified at line 3 of the test specification: nothing should change. After entering a new name the iut gives answers that are not consistent to previous guesses. G∀ST spots that there are no transitions according to the reactions observed from the iut for the remaining states. Hence an issue is reported. When testing against a maximum trace length of 100 transitions, the system requires on average 3 paths to reveal the error (more precisely, 325 transitions). The average testing time was 0.80 sec per detected error. Testing was done on an AMD Athlon XP 2200+, 1.80GHz PC, 512MB RAM, running Microsoft Windows XP.

This very simple example shows that G∀ST is able to find real errors in web-applications. In order to find this inconsistent behavior, the test system has to gather information from the HTML-page generated by the iut and compare it with information from previous responses.

Efficient State Representation in the Specification. The specification in Fig. 1 uses one state for each value that is still a possible number to be guessed. For ranges up to hundreds of allowed numbers this is no problem. When the range of numbers would be extended to many thousands of values, handling all these individual numbers in the test system states takes a noticeable amount of time. Fortunately, it easy to change the specification such that also a huge range of numbers to be guessed can be handled. The numbers that might be correct is always the entire sequence of numbers from the largest guess that was too low, up to the smallest guess that was to high. Instead of storing all possible numbers, we can better store the bounds of this sequence. The corresponding specification is given in Fig. 2. The type SpecState defined in line 1 stores the bounds of the correct numbers in the arguments of the constructor RunningS. Line 2 states that the bounds of the possible correct numbers are initial the bounds given in the game. Line 3 and 4 handles the initial game and entering a new name, these are direct mirrors of line 2 and 3 of spec in figure 1. Line 7 and 8 state that for a guess outside the bounds only the corresponding output with Sorry is allowed. When the input is equal to both bounds, it has to be correct

```
:: SpecState = InitS | RunningS Int Int                                    1
newGame = RunningS low up                                                  2

spec2 :: SpecState In → [[Html]↦[SpecState]]                               3
spec2 InitS input          = [λhtml = [newGame]]                          4
spec2 r (StringTextBox s) = [λhtml = [r]]                                 5
spec2 (RunningS l u) (IntTextBox i)                                       6
    | i < l = [tooLow [RunningS l u]]                                     7
    | i > u = [tooHigh [RunningS l u]]                                    8
    | i ⩵ l ∧ i ⩵ u = [correct [newGame]]                                9
    | l⩽i ∧ i⩽u = [tooLow [RunningS (i+1) u], tooHigh [RunningS l (i-1)]] 10
                ,correct [newGame]]                                       11
```

Fig. 2. The specification of the number guessing game using one single state

(line 9). Otherwise the guess might be too low, too high or correct. The state is adapted correspondingly in line 10 and 11.

Testing with this specification produces the same issue as the tests with the previous specification. Since the number to be guessed in in the range from 1 to 10, choice of the seed for the pseudo random numbers in G∀ST dominates the effects of the more compact representation of the states.

More Controlled Tests. When the test engineer wants more control over the test there are several options. By using a partial specification one can exclude parts of the behavior from the tests. For instance if the right hand side of the function alternatives of line 7 and 8 are replaced by [] (undefined) no tests for input values outside the range of possible correct numbers will be done. In this example the error is found quicker by inputs that have to yield *too low* or *too high*. These inputs are excluded in the test by the partial specification. Hence it takes about 20% more transitions to find the error.

Another possibility to control the test process is by specifying a function that determines the possible inputs for a given state. This function can be supplied as optional argument to G∀ST. In this way we can force G∀ST to test only guessing by binary search and changing names:

```
iFun (RunningS l h) = [StringTextBox "tester2", IntTextBox ((l+h)/2)]
iFun InitS          = [StringTextBox "tester1", IntTextBox ((low+up)/2)]
```

Using binary search and the original specification form Fig. 2, the error is found in about 20% less transitions. No matter what variant of testing we use the error is always found pretty quickly. The longest test run to the first error observed is 1605 transitions and takes less than 5 seconds. For more complicated examples it might be worthwhile to guide the testing process more precisely. This section just indicates that G∀ST offers the tools to do this easily.

4.2 Example 2: A Web-Shop

Our second example is a highly dynamic web-shop selling CD's. This application contains four main views: **(1)** the initial home-view; **(2)** the shop-view to browse, search and order the CDs in the shop; **(3)** the basket-view to examine and change the CDs the user is ordering; **(4)** the order-view to make the order definitive and pay. The actual contents of the shop-view is determined by the contents of a database. The contents of the basket-view and order-view are determined by the CDs selected by the user.

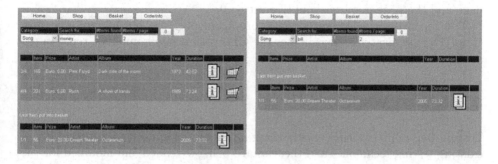

Fig. 3. Screen shots of the web-shop. On the left page 3 of the shop-view, on the right the graphical representation of the error found by G∀ST

The specification does not know the contents of the database, so we cannot check whether the right CDs are displayed. Still, the specification does prescribe consistent behavior during the navigation and searching in the shop-pages, and takes care that ordered items appear in the basket and the final order.

Also in this web-application G∀ST found an error. If the user is not on the first page with CDs and makes a selection (on artist name, album or song), the web application does not go to the first page of CDs. This can cause that an empty page with CDs is shown although there are CDs in the selection.

The complete specification is too large for this paper. Fig. 4 contains a self-contained specification that is just capable of finding the described error. This

```
shopSpec :: ShopState ShopInput → [[Html] → [ShopState]]                          1
shopSpec s=:{view=InitView} input = [λo → [{s&view = HomeView}]]                   2
shopSpec s ShopButton                                                             3
  = [ λ[html] → [{s&view = ShopView, cds = findCdCount html}]]                    4
shopSpec s=:{view = ShopView} (PageButton (PageNum n))                            5
  | n ≠ s.pageNum ∧ n*s.itemsPage < s.cds                                         6
              = [λ[html] → [{s & pageNum = n}]]                                   7
  | otherwise = []                                                                8
shopSpec s=:{view = ShopView} (SearchTextBox str)                                 9
  = [ λ[html] → [{s & pageNum = 0, cds = findCdCount html}]]                     10
shopSpec s i = []        /* default: undefined */                                11
```

Fig. 4. The partial specification of the web-shop

is only part of the complete specification, but it can be used on its own by G∀ST and finds the error quickly. Line 2 covers the standard transition from the initial state to the home page. The lines 3 and 4 states that the shop-button brings you from any state to the shop-view. The number of CDs is retrieved from the HTML code and stored in the cds field of the shop state record of type ShopState. Lines 5 − 8 handle navigation through the various pages in the shop-view. Such a transition is only possible if the target page is different from the current page and exists. Entering a new text in the search box is specified in line 9 − 10. The specification states that the number of CDs in the state must be read from the page and the page number should be set to 0.

The inconsistency is spotted by a predicate over the output and the new state. This predicate checks whether the CDs with desired numbers, represented as string like "3/7" (third of seven CDs), are listed on the current page.

5   Related Work

Testing web applications is experiencing an increased interest. A wide variety of existing testing techniques and theories are being extended and modified for the web. It is beyond the scope of this paper to discuss them all.

In van Beek and Mauw [22] black box conformance testing of thin (no local client based computations) Internet applications is presented. In their approach, Internet applications are modelled with MRRTS-es (*multi request-response transition systems*). In order to create specifications conveniently, they use the process algebraic DiCons [21] specification language. DiCons has been developed specifically for *distributed consensus* applications. These are applications in which several users have a common goal that needs to be reached. In their test system, they run the implementation under test and consider the link-activations and form submissions. Differences with our approach are that we use a functional specification style with rich algebraic data types; the implementation under test is a function that yields HTML code; we test only form submissions.

In Sect. 1 we have argued that interactive applications are modelled naturally with Extended State Machines, which are LTSs over input/output pairs. Conformance of these systems is well studied by Latella and Massink [11]. They prove that a *quiescence* supporting semantics is crucial to obtain substitutivity properties: implementations conforming to a specification can be safely replaced with a testing equivalent implementation without breaking conformance, and implementations conforming to a specification also conform to testing equivalent specifications. Our approach is geared towards practical situations in the sense that we consider states, input and output labels to be values of arbitrarily complex, recursive ADTs. It is an interesting and open question whether the theoretical results also hold for our approach.

Frantzen *et al.*[4] study black box conformance testing with symbolic state. This is related to our work because they address the issue of working with arbitrarily complex data structures. In their approach the data structures are specified by means of first order logic specifications. Their approach is more general than our approach, but this leads to a number of open issues, such as finding the solution to a logical formula (if it exists at all), and the actual computation of concrete input values to the iut. Our approach is based on ADTs, and functional term graph rewriting. Confluence holds for these systems, and our ESMs can rely on arbitrarily complex state transition functions to describe complex systems.

Andrews *et al.*[2] employ FSMs with constraints to model and test web applications. Hierarchical decomposition and constraints are used to control the usual state space explosion problem: with hierarchical decomposition the FSM can be decomposed recursively into subsystems. For each subsystem tests can be generated and assembled into compound tests up to the entire application level. Constraints for sequencing and sets remove the need to tediously specify all different possible input sequences in terms of state transitions. The hierarchical decomposition is done manually by the tester, as well as defining the constraints. The inputs on which the constraints are defined correspond with standard form elements, such as (multi-)lines, URLs, links, (radio) buttons, and so on. As in our approach, they model the web application at the user level.

Wu and Offutt [24] model web applications by identifying the structure of web pages in terms of atomic sections that are composed with process algebraic like operators such as sequential composition, choice, and aggregation. Interactions, such as link transitions, composite transitions, and operational transitions, define the relationship between different pages. From these models, tests can be derived. As with our approach, the authors restrict themselves to monitoring HTML output only. In contrast with our approach, they deliberately ignore state. This is argued by the fact that the HTTP protocol is stateless. However, a standard way to include state is to pass additional information along with the HTML.

Jia and Liu [5] present a general framework to automatically test several key aspects of web applications, such as functionality, page structure (which is what our approach concentrates on), security and performance. XML is chosen to formally specify the test because it also provides access to specify page structure properties using standard utilities such as DOM and XPath. A test specification is a set of test suites. A test suite is a set of test steps. A test case is a tree of test steps. A test sequence is a traversal from root to leaf of a test case. A test step is a (possibly guarded) request-response pair that is executed only if the guard is true. The request is a pattern of HTTP request that need to be matched. The response is an assertion on the HTTP output of the web application. XML is also used by Lee and Offutt [13] as a vehicle for test specifications and data transmissions. In our approach web pages are modelled by means of ADTs, and access to these pages is provided by means of functions. Advantages of our approach are that specifications are type correct, and that the user can specify arbitrarily complex computations on these pages (for instance, extract the complete content of a table and return it as a matrix of values).

Although we have not considered incorporating testing of browser functionality such as window cloning and the use of the back/forward browsing buttons as done e.g. by Di Lucca and Di Penta [3], our framework can be used for these purposes. It is up to the test engineer to model the desired behavior of the application under these circumstances. This is even the case when testing the behavior of web applications in the presence of users who manually edit links or even alter page codes. Usually for these kinds of robustness tests white box testing techniques are used (e.g. Liu et al.[14] and Kung et al.[9]). Our system is independent of the concrete implementation language(s) of the web application.

6   Conclusions

The automatic, model based, testing of web applications is an important topic since the number applications is growing rapidly. Thin-client web applications send a complete new web page in pure HTML to the browser in response to each input. Usually it is undesirable to specify each and every aspect of this HTML code. For most specification techniques this is troublesome since they commonly require to explicitly list the combinations of allowed output and target state. In this paper we introduced a specification technique and the associated, *ioco*-like, conformance relation to tackle this problem. The key step is to replace the combination of allowed outputs and target states by a function from output to allowed target states. This function can check aspects of the output, as well as retrieve information to be stored in the target state.

This technique is implemented as an extension of the on-the-fly test tool G∀ST. In this paper we illustrate with two examples that it is possible to (partially) specify the desired behavior of highly dynamic web applications in this way and to find errors in the concrete implementations of these web applications.

References

1. A. Alimarine and R. Plasmeijer. A Generic Programming Extension for Clean. In T. Arts and M. Mohnen, editors, *The 13th International workshop on the Implementation of Functional Languages, IFL'01, Selected Papers*, volume 2312 of *LNCS*, pages 168–186. Älvsjö, Sweden, Springer, Sept. 2002.
2. A. Andrews, J. Offutt, and R. Alexander. Testing Web Applications by Modelling with FSMs. *Software Systems and Modeling*, 4(3), August 2005.
3. G. Di Lucca and M. Di Penta. Considering Browser Interaction in Web Application Testing. In *Proceedings of the 5th International Workshop on Web Site Evolution*, Amsterdam, The Netherlands, October 2002. IEEE Computer Society, USA.
4. L. Frantzen, J. Tretmans, and T. Willemse. Test Generation Based on Symbolic Specifications. In J. Grabowski and B. Nielsen, editors, *Proceedings 4th International Workshop, FATES 2004, Revised Selected Papers*, volume 3395 of *LNCS*, pages 1–15, Linz, Austria, September 21 2004. Springer-Verlag.
5. X. Jia and H. Liu. Rigorous and Automatic Testing of Web Applications. In *Proceedings of the 6th IASTED International Conference on Software Engineering and Applications (SEA 2002)*, pages 280–285, Cambridge, MA, USA, Nov. 2002.
6. P. Koopman, A. Alimarine, J. Tretmans, and R. Plasmeijer. Gast: Generic automated software testing. In R. Peña and T. Arts, editors, *The 14th International Workshop on the Implementation of Functional Languages, IFL'02, Selected Papers*, volume 2670 of *LNCS*, pages 84–100. Springer, 2003.

7. P. Koopman and R. Plasmeijer. Testing reactive systems with GAST. In S. Gilmore, editor, *Trends in Functional Programming 4*, pages 111–129, 2004.
8. P. Koopman and R. Plasmeijer. Generic Generation of Elements of Types. In *Sixth Symposium on Trends in Functional Programming (TFP2005)*, Tallin, Estonia, Sep 23-24 2005.
9. D. Kung, C. Liu, and P. Hsia. An Object-Oriented Web Test Model for Testing Web Applications. In *IEEE Proceedings of the 24th Annual International Computer Software & Applications Conference (COMPSAC'00)*, pages 537–542, Taipei, Taiwan, Oct. 2000.
10. K. Larsen, M. Mikucionis, and B. Nielsen. Online Testing of Real-Time Systems Using UPPAAL. In J. Grabowski and B. Nielsen, editors, *Formal Approaches to Software Testing, 4th International Workshop, FATES 2004 - Revised Selected Papers*, volume 3395 of *LNCS*, pages 79–94. Springer, September 21 2004.
11. D. Latella and M. Massink. On Testing and Conformance Relations for UML Statechart Diagrams Behaviours. In *Proceedings of the 2002 ACM SIGSOFT International Symposium on Software Testing and Analysis (ISSTA '02)*, pages 144–153, New York, NY, USA, 2002. ACM Press.
12. D. Lee and M. Yannakakis. Principles and methods of testing finite state machines – a survey. In *Proc. IEEE*, volume 84(8), pages 1090–1126, 1996.
13. S. Lee and J. Offutt. Generating Test Cases for XML-based Web Component Interactions Using Mutation Analysis. In *12th International Symposium on Software Reliability Engineering (ISSRE 2001)*, pages 200–209, Hong Kong, November 2001.
14. C. Liu, D. Kung, P. Hsia, and C. Hsu. Object-Based Data Flow Testing of Web Applications. In *Proceedings First Asian Pacific Conference on Quality Software (APAQS 2000)*, pages 7–16, Oct. 2000.
15. T. Margaria, O. Niese, and B. Steffen. Automated Functional Testing of Web-based Applications. In *Proceedings of the 5th International Conference on Software and Internet Quality Week Europe*, pages 157–166, Brussels, March 2002.
16. R. Plasmeijer and P. Achten. The Implementation of iData - A Case Study in Generic Programming. In A. Butterfield, editor, *Proceedings Implementation and Application of Functional Languages, 17th International Workshop, IFL05*, Dublin, Ireland, September 19-21 2005. Technical Report No: TCD-CS-2005-60.
17. R. Plasmeijer and P. Achten. iData For The World Wide Web - Programming Interconnected Web Forms. In *Proceedings Eighth International Symposium on Functional and Logic Programming (FLOPS 2006)*, volume 3945 of *LNCS*, Fuji Susono, Japan, Apr 24-26 2006. Springer Verlag.
18. R. Plasmeijer and M. van Eekelen. *Concurrent CLEAN Language Report (version 2.0)*, December 2001. http://www.cs.ru.nl/~clean/.
19. J. Tretmans. Test generation with inputs, outputs and repetitive quiescence. *Software—Concepts and Tools*, 17(3):103–120, 1996.
20. J. Tretmans. Testing Concurrent Systems: A Formal Approach. In J. Baeten and S. Mauw, editors, *CONCUR'99*, volume 1664 of *LNCS*, pages 46–65. Springer-Verlag, 1999.
21. H. van Beek. *Specification and Analysis of Internet Applications*. PhD thesis, Technical University Eindhoven, The Netherlands, 2005. ISBN 90-386-0564-1.
22. H. van Beek and S. Mauw. Automatic Conformance Testing of Internet Applications. In A. Petrenko and A. Ulrich, editors, *Proceedings Third International Workshop on Formal Approaches to Testing of Software, FATES 2003*, volume 2931 of *LNCS*, pages 205–222, Montreal, Quebec, Canada, October 6 2003. Springer-Verlag.

23. A. van Weelden, M. Oostdijk, L. Frantzen, P. Koopman, and J. Tretmans. On-the-fly formal testing of a smart card applet. In R. Sasaki, S. Qing, E. Okamoto, and H. Yoshiura, editors, *Proceedings of the 20th IFIP TC11 International Information Security Conference SEC 2005*, pages 564–576, Makuhari Messe, Chiba, Japan, May 2005. Springer. Also available as Technical Report NIII-R0428.
24. Y. Wu and J. Offutt. Modeling and Testing Web-based Applications. GMU ISE Technical ISE-TR-02-08, Information and Software Engineering Department, George Mason University, Fairfax, USA, Nov. 2002.

Synthesis of Scenario Based Test Cases
from B Models*

Manoranjan Satpathy, Qaisar A. Malik, and Johan Lilius

Abo Akademi University
Department of Information Technologies
Joukahaisenkatu 3–5
Fin - 20520, Turku, Finland
{mannu.satpathy, qaisar.malik, johan.lilius}@abo.fi

Abstract. When models are formal, model based testing approaches usually construct a coverage graph through symbolic execution and derive test cases in the form of paths in the coverage graph. Thereafter consistency between the model and the implementation is verified in relation to the test cases. Existing approaches, especially when dealing with model oriented languages like B, partition the input space of each operation in the model to create operation instances, and then animate the model in relation to these instances. The paths or the test cases are now a sequence of operation instances. However, in this approach, there is no guarantee that we test the user scenarios. In this paper, we first define scenario based test cases in relation to the initial specification. When this specification passes through a succession of refinements, we derive scenario based test cases for each refinement and show that all these test cases are equivalent to the test cases of the original specification.

Keywords: Model Based Testing; Scenarios; B-Method.

1 Introduction

Software models are usually built to reduce the complexity of the development process and to ensure software quality. A software model is an abstraction in the sense that it captures the most important requirements of the system while omitting unimportant details. A model is usually a specification of the system which is developed from the requirements early in the development cycle [4]. This paper concerns formal models; in particular, we deal with model oriented formal languages like Z [16], VDM [9] , B [1] and Event-B [11]. By model oriented we mean, the system behavior is described using an explicit model of the system state along with operations (or events) on the state.

Model based testing is usually based on the notion of a coverage graph obtained from the symbolic execution of the model. A subset of the paths in

---

* This research was carried out as part of the EU research project IST 511599 RODIN (Rigorous Open Development Environment for Complex Systems) http://rodin.cs. ncl.ac.uk.

K. Havelund et al. (Eds.): FATES/RV 2006, LNCS 4262, pp. 133–147, 2006.

this graph can be treated as a test suite from the viewpoint of test case generation. Even though model based testing is an incomplete activity, the selected behaviors could be enriched to capture interesting properties of the system and hence using those in testing would give us confidence about the correctness of the system.

Existing testing tools or techniques dealing with model oriented languages [2,15] partition the input space of an operation into equivalence classes to create operation instances. Then a Finite State Automaton (FSA) or a coverage graph is constructed in which the initial node corresponds to the initial state of the model, and edges correspond to application of operation instances. Usually a coverage graph is constructed up to a predefined depth or size. Some paths of this graph are selected as test cases. When the implementation is subjected to the same sequence of operations as in a test case, we get an image of the original path in the model execution. Now if the properties of the implementation path matches with the properties of the path in the model, we declare that the implementation has passed the test case; otherwise, a failure.

However, in these approaches, there is no guarantee that the user scenarios are tested. A user scenario is like a usecase scenario in UML [12]; in this article, we use scenarios and usecases interchangeably. The paths that we test as test cases may be unrelated to the usecases. How to know that we are not missing some scenarios? Of course if all possible operation instances do appear in the coverage graph, and we are able to test all of them, we can say that the user scenarios have been tested in an implicit way. But since we fix a predefined bound on the depth of the coverage graph, some operation instances may lie beyond this bound, and then there is no way to locate them. Furthermore, some valid operation instance may not appear in the graph at all. In this paper, we address these issues. Of course, here we assume that the entire development path from the specification to code is not entirely formal, in which case testing may not be necessary; however, in practice, the entire development process is less often formal.

The basic idea behind our paper can be seen from Figure 1. We define an initial usecase-based test case T_0 in terms of a sequence of operations in relation to the initial specification R_0. Thereafter, given any successive refinement pair R_i and R_{i+1}, and T_i as the usecase-based test case for R_i, we derive T_{i+1} such that it is a valid behavior of R_{i+1}, and then show that T_i and T_{i+1} are equivalent to each other. The main contributions of our paper are:

- We relate our test cases to user scenarios; in the process, we also find out if the refinement has missed out on some scenarios.
- Our approach generates a small number of test cases, and in addition, it takes care to keep the lengths of the test cases small. These may have impact on the time to test the test cases.

The organization of the paper is as follows. Section 2 discusses related work and the testing terminology we use. Section 3 describes the problem in a formal manner. In Section 4, we discuss our approach over a running example. Section 5 discusses the strengths and the weaknesses of our approach. Section 6 concludes the paper.

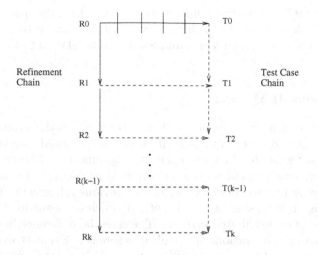

Fig. 1. The Basic Idea

2 Related Work

A *testing criterion* is a set of requirements on test data which reflects a notion of adequacy on the testing of a system [14,18]. An adequacy criterion serves two purposes: (a) it defines a stopping rule which determines whether sufficient testing has already been done; so, testing can now be stopped, and (b) it provides measurements to obtain the degree of adequacy obtained after testing stopped. For our purpose, the testing criterion would be to test the usecases. However, the usecases are usually generic in nature; so the criterion would be to test some instances of the usecases.

The work by Dick and Faivre [3] is a major contribution to the use of formal methods in software testing. A VDM specification has state variables and an invariant (Inv) to restrict the variables. An operation, say OP, is specified by a pre-condition (OP_{pre}) and a post-condition (OP_{post}). The approach partitions the input space of OP by converting the expression ($OP_{pre} \land OP_{post} \land$ Inv) into its Disjunctive Normal Form (DNF), and each disjunct, unless a contradiction, represents an input subdomain of OP. Next as many operation instances are created as the number of non-contradictory disjuncts in the DNF. An attempt is then made to create a FSA in which each node represents a possible machine state and an edge represents an application of an operation instance. A set of test cases is then generated by traversing the FSA, each test case being a sequence of operation instances.

BZ-Testing Tool (BZ-TT) [2] and the ProTest approach [15] both generates functional test cases from B specifications. The partitioning algorithm to obtain operation instances and the generation of test cases from a coverage graph are similar to the methods described in [3].

All approaches usually partition the input space to create operation instances, but when a specification is further refined, the original partitions may have no meaning in relation to the refinements because the data space might have changed. Derrick and Boiten [5] have developed a strategy to transform the operation instances so that they remain meaningful in relation to the appropriate refinement.

2.1   The Event-B Method

The B-method, originally developed by J.-R. Abrial [1], is a theory and methodology for formal development of sequential programs. B is used to cover the whole range of the software development cycle; the specification is used to generate code with a set of refinement steps in between. At each stage, the current refinement needs to be proved consistent with the previous refinement. The Event-B method [11] is an extension of the B method which is meant for the modeling and development of distributed systems. The essential difference between B and Event-B is that in B, operations are invoked, whereas in Event-B, events are executed in response to changes in the environment. This paper focuses on Event-B models.

An Event-B specification has a static part called *context*, and a dynamic part called the *machine*. The context contains the set declarations and constant definitions along with their properties. A machine has access to its context via the SEES relationship. The machine mainly consists of state variables and *events*. The state variables are given their initial values by an INITIALISATION clause and thereafter, the state variables can be modified by the execution of the events. And event is of the form:

$$E \ = \ WHEN \ G(v) \ THEN \ S(v) \ END$$

where G(v) is a guard and S(v) is a generalized substitution, both may involve state variables represented by v. An event becomes enabled only if the guard holds; otherwise, the event is blocked. A generalized substitution can be empty, deterministic or non-deterministic. The empty substitution is skip which does nothing. The deterministic substitution is of the form: $x := E(v)$. A non-deterministic assignment is of the form:

$$ANY \ t \ WHERE \ P(t,v) \ THEN \ x := \ F(t,v) \ END$$

Here t is a local variable which is non-deterministically given a value such that predicate $P(t,v)$ holds. And then the value of t is used to change the machine state through the substitution F.

2.2   Refinement in Event-B

In the Event-B method, the initial specification passes through a succession of refinements and the code can be generated from the final refinement. In practice, the whole refinement sequence is generated less often. One approach could be to produce a few refinement steps and then to generate code from the most concrete refinement; consistency of the implementation is then left to model based testing. Our approach is relevant in this context.

Refining a machine consists of refining its states and events. A machine which is a refinement of another, has a state which is related to the abstract state by a predicate, called the gluing invariant. The gluing predicate usually involves the state variables of both the original machine and its refinement. The refinement machine retains the original abstract events, but may have some new events. Each new event must be proved to refine the event skip which does nothing. In addition, the new events are not allowed to take control collectively for ever. This is ensured by providing a unique variant expression $V(w)$ which is strictly decreased by each new event. If the new event evt with $J(v,w)$ as the gluing predicate is:

$$evt = WHEN\ R(w)\ THEN\ w := G(w)\ END$$

then for termination, one has to prove:

$$I(v) \wedge J(v,w) \Rightarrow V(w) \in N \wedge V(G(w)) < V(w)$$

This means that the variant expression evaluates to a natural number. This also means that once the value of w is known then one can always put an upper bound on the value of $V(w)$. In summary, the number of times that all the new events can be executed is limited by this upper bound.

If an event in the refinement is not a new event, it must have a *forward simulation* relationship [6,10] with its abstract version. Let us consider two successive refinements: R_1 and R_2, the latter being a refinement of the former. Let GI be the gluing invariant between them. Furthermore, let AI and CI represent the abstract and concrete initial states of the two refinements. Let AOP and COP stand for an abstract operation in R_1 and its concrete version in R_2 respectively. Then forward simulation as a relational definition is as shown in Figure 2 [8,10]. In other words:

- Every concrete initial state must be related to some initial abstract state
- If concrete state c and abstract state a are linked by GI, and a concrete operation COP takes c to c', then there must exist an abstract state a' so that the relationship in the diagram holds.

If R_1 and R_2 satisfy these relationships then we can say that R_2 is consistent with R_1. The proof obligations generated by the tools supporting Event-B prove this relationship.

2.3   An Example

We have taken the leader election problem as our running example. The Event-B machine Leader.mch shows the initial specification. The Appendix presents this machine along with its two successive refinements. A finite number of processors are arranged in a ring, each processor has a numeric ID. The processor with

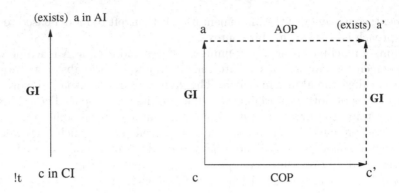

Fig. 2. Relational Definition of Forward Simulation

the highest numeric value is elected as the leader. In machine Leader.mch, after initialization, one execution of the event *elect* finds the leader.

LeaderR.mch is the first refinement of Leader.mch. It has two new events, called *accept and reject* in addition to the single event in the original machine. LeaderRR.mch is a refinement of LeaderR.mch. It has one more new event called *send*. We will refer to the new events in a refinement as τ-operations in relation to its previous refinement (or specification); they are internal operations from the viewpoint of the parent machine.

3   The Problem

In the B-method, partitioning of the input space creates operation instances; similarly, partition of the input space of an event will give rise to event instances. Usually all the operation (or event) instances do not appear in a coverage graph generation. The reasons are as follows:

- If the model invariant is weak then a valid operation instance may not be reachable. For instance, the constraint $10 \le X \le 20$ could be present in a model as $0 \le X \le 100$. If X in a state gets a value of 50, then some valid operations may not be applicable and so would not appear in the coverage graph. Usually the invariants suffer from incompleteness.
- A poor initialization may stop some operation instances to appear. For instance, let an invariant be: num_of_rooms ≥ 1. Now if num_of_rooms gets initialized to 1, then many interesting operation instances would not appear.
- An operation instance may not occur because we make a finite construction of the coverage graph according to some predefined depth; but, had we continued with graph construction, possibly some more instances might have appeared. But the missing operation instances may be related to the usecases.

3.1   Scenario Based Test Cases

A scenario shows a typical interaction between the system and the environment [13]. In other words, it is a possible situation within an usecase. The initial specification that we refer to usually defines a small set of very high level events and they are meaningful from the viewpoint of a user. Note this from the machine Leader.mch which has a single high level event elect. Therefore, in general, the a scenario can easily be expressed as a linear sequence in terms of these high level events, and its length would be small. For the present example, the only possible scenario would be: *elect a leader.* There is only one state variable and only one operation called *elect* besides the initialization clause. This lone usecase can be expressed as the sequence: $< init, elect >$.

However, some usecases may be non-terminating. Consider the use case: send messages; this means any number of messages can be sent. This usecase can be expressed by the regular expression: $send.(send)^*$. In such a case, we only take a finite instance of this as our initial test cases, say the sequence: $< send, send, send, send >$.

Usually the initial specification undergoes a succession of refinements, and one such refinement, say R_i, is referred to while writing the code. Let us call this as the *implementation refinement.* Now our initial test cases in this situation do not hold any ground because the semantic gap between the current refinement and the initial specification could be very high. There is a need to make the test cases we have created for the initial specification meaningful to R_i. This is the problem that we address in this paper.

3.2   The Approach

Refer to Figure 3. Let us assume that refinement R_{i+1} has been obtained from R_i through forward simulation. Further R_i satisfies test case T_i; in other words, T_i is a valid trace of R_i. Under this situation, our intention is to derive a test case T_{i+1} which is satisfied by R_{i+1}, and in addition T_{i+1} is a trace refinement of T_i. The algorithm of Table 1 does exactly this.

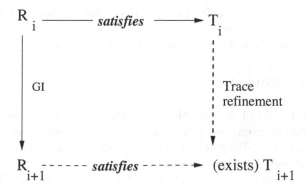

Fig. 3. A step in the synthesis of Test Cases

Table 1. Algorithm for graph creation

Algorithm: GenerateTestCases

Input: (i) Event-B specification (R_0) and its K successive refinements as $R_1, \ldots, R_K$
  with GI_i as the gluing invariant between R_i and R_{i-1}.
  (ii) Test case T_0 as a sequence of events in R_0 (to be a trace needs instantiation).
Output: $K + 1$ test sequences : $T_0, \ldots, T_K$ (all instantiated).
step 1:
  Create $K + 1$ nodes $I_0, \ldots, I_K$ as initial nodes of $T_0, \ldots, T_K$.
  Let I_i have the assignments of the Initialization clause in R_i.
  /* constants and deferred sets in each R_i not yet instantiated */
step 2
  Consider the variant in R_K. Instantiate the deferred sets
  and the constants so that the variant value remains small.
  Based on this, instantiate I_K
step 3:
  Project I_K backwards to give full instantiation to $I_0, \ldots I_{K-1}$.
step 4:
  Instantiate T_0 to make it a valid trace of R_0 in a symbolic execution.
  i = 1;
step 5:
  Looking at T_{i-1}, construct T_i as follows:
  Let T_{i-1} have t states (nodes) as $I_{i-1} = A_1, \ldots, A_t$
  for $(j = 2, \ldots, t)$ **do**
      Construct for T_i, node B_j; Using GI_i, project the instantiated node A_j
      to obtain possible instantiations of variables in B_j.
      Let eve_j be the event of the edge joining A_{j-1} and A_j.
      Construct a path from B_{j-1} to B_j such that the path has a single
      occurrence of eve_j, and the rest are the τ-operations of R_i.
          /*This path length would be limited by the variant in R_i.*/
  endfor
  output: *the current path is* T_i
step 6:
  if $(i = K)$ stop.
  else i = i + 1, Goto step 5.

Refer to the initial specification as R_0. We are given a usecase-based test case
T_0 for R_0. We then can apply the same algorithm repeatedly to obtain test cases
for successive refinements. Figure 1 illustrates exactly this.

4   The Algorithm

The Algorithm in Table 1 assumes that a scenario based test case for the initial
specification (R_0) is given, and then it synthesizes corresponding test cases for
subsequent refinements. We will illustrate our algorithm over the leader election
problem as the running example. The uninstantiated test case here is the sequence
$< init, elect >$. In the first step, the algorithm creates initial nodes for all the
refinements. In Figure 4, this is shown by nodes A0, B0, and C0 respectively.

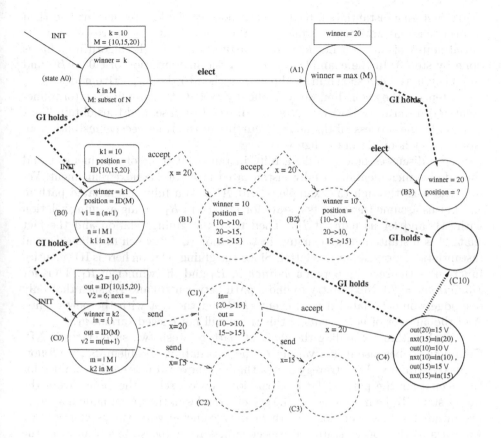

Fig. 4. Steps in generating the Coverage Graphs

Because of the new events, a test case for the current refinement could be larger in size in relation to the test case of the previous refinement; the extent to which it could be larger is strictly dependent on the variant upper-bound defined in the current refinement. As we will soon discuss, the construction algorithm is of exponential complexity. Therefore, we limit this bound by a suitable instantiation of the constants and the deferred sets (and possibly to some state variables). This task is performed by Step 2 in the algorithm.

For the present example, the variant to control the new events in R_1 is $v_1 = n*(n+1)$, where n is the value of constant N. This also means that the combination of the accept and the reject events in a trace is limited by v_1. The variant v_2 for R_2 is also $n*(n+1)$.

Now in order to control the problem size, we give a small to N, say 3; thus $v2$ gets the value of 12. We then can select any values for M, say the set $\{10, 15, 20\}$. And then we give some instantiation to the constant function $next = \{(10, 20), (20, 15), (15, 10)\}$ which shows the directions to treat the subset as a ring. This instantiation has been shown in a box on top of node $C0$.

We first give instantiation to the initial node of the last refinement and then project these instantiations through the gluing invariants backwards so that the initial states of all refinements receive instantiation. In the algorithm, this is done by step 3. In the example, we project the instantiation of $C0$ to $B0$ and $A0$. They have been shown in the boxes attached to the respective nodes.

In step 4 of the algorithm, we symbolically execute the specification (or refinement R_0) in terms of the event sequence in the test case, and thus obtain T_0 as a trace. In the process all the nodes occurring in the trace receive instantiation. Note this at node $A1$ in the figure.

Step 5 discusses how we take a fully instantiated trace of a refinement and then derive incrementally a fully instantiated trace of the next refinement. We illustrate this through the example. $< A0, A1 >$ is a fully instantiated path in R_0. Let us assume there exists a state for a trace in R_1 having a gluing relation with $A1$, and let us name it $B3$. Then from the gluing relation and the fact that $A1$ is instantiated, we can give instantiation to $B3$ which may be a partial instantiation; more about this latter. Since the gluing relation here is ID (identity function) – the relation between $winner$ in R_0 and the winner in R_1. Thus for $B3$, $winner = 20$. Next we try to find a path between $B0$ and $B3$ such that only one edge would be labeled with event $elect$ and the rest with the new events. And the number of new events in this trace will not exceed variant v_1.

The algorithm for finding the shortest path between two such states is NP-Complete [7] because it is a variant of the satisfiability problem. So, we follow a greedy strategy. The strategy states that whenever you need data values for the events for the path under construction, always select the values from the target state. To be more specific, the state variables in the target node may have instantiated values, and some of them may coincide with values of the state variables in the source state. We select values from the state variables in the target state which differ from the assignments in the source state.

For the current example, we have `winner`= 20 in the target state; so we try to use this value as choice options of the events meant for the current path. In the process we create the path $< B0, B1, B2, B3 >$. We could have applied he other τ-event `reject`, but giving it the value of 20 made its guard false.

Thereafter we repeat step 5 to complete the graph construction for all the refinements. For the current example, we need to obtain a trace for refinement R_2. The gluing relation, say GI_1 between R_1 and R_2 is:

$$position(x) = y \Leftrightarrow out(x) = y \vee next(y) = in(x)$$

We now discover a node to be sync with B1 such that the above gluing relation holds. However, we can discover many nodes denoted by X which can be related with $B1$; we go for the most generic one. For the present C4 is the state which is in sync with B1 in terms of the gluing relation. Note in the Figure 4, how assignment of some state variables of C4 have been given in the form of predicates which makes it generic.

As per our greedy strategy, whenever we select choices for events `accept` and `send`, we select 15 or 20; this is because these are the places where C0 and C4 differ. In the process we discover the path $< C0, C1, C4 >$. Next, we discover a node $C10$ in sync with node B2. So, now our task is to find a path between C4 till C10 by use of Step 5 once again. And this continues till we discover test cases for all the refinements.

4.1 Exponential Nature of the Algorithm

While constructing a path as discussed above, it may so happen that we may not succeed in obtaining the complete path. Refer to Figure 5. The graph at the top shows some traces for refinement R_1 and assume that all the traces shown implements the single test case of its previous refinement. If we hide the internal events of some traces of R_1, and then if it reduces to be a trace of R_0, then we say that all the traces of R_1 implement the trace of R_0. The image of a trace of R_0 need not be unique in R_1.

Now as per the rules of refinement, if R_2 implements any of the traces of R_1 then we are done and we can conclude that R_2 implements the original usecase. However, the situation is much more difficult when we have to show that R_2 does not implement the usecase.

Let us see how our algorithm works. Consider the situation when the construction for R_1 is over and we are dealing with R_2. The algorithm first takes the trace $< A, B, E >$ and constructs a path $< X, Y, Z, \ldots >$ to show the correspondence. It may so happen that we fail to find such a trace. If so, we next consider the path $< A, B, F >$ and see if a trace for it exists in R_2. If

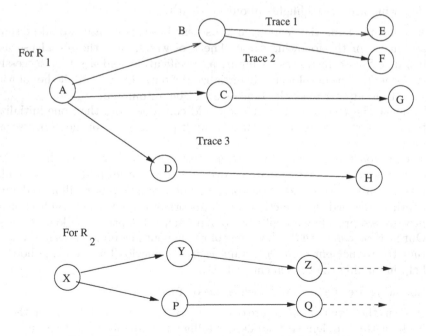

Fig. 5. Showing non-existence of trace implementation

we fail again we try $< A, C, G >$. If we fail for all traces, it may be legal from refinement point of view, but it would also mean that R_2 does not implement the given usecase. And then a warning could be given to the developer to show this deficiency in the refinement process.

Since in the worst case we may have to go for exhaustive enumeration of traces, the algorithm is of exponential nature. However, the length of each trace is limited by the variants of the τ-operations in the refinement. But we always select small values for our variants because of which we do not let the algorithm explode.

Theorem: *The traces obtained by the algorithm in Section 4 conform to the commutative diagram of Figure 3.*

Proof: Refer to Figure 3. The algorithm assumes that R_i, R_{i+1} and T_i are given, and then it computes a trace T_{i+1}. The fact that R_{i+1} satisfies T_{i+1} is obvious, since the trace is one of the behaviors of R_{i+1}. The construction also ensures that T_{i+1} preserves the trace of T_i. More formally, when we treat the new events in R_{i+1} as the internal τ-operations then there exists a *rooted branching bisimulation* [17] between T_i and T_{i+1} with respect to the gluing relation; this simply comes from our construction method. Rooted branching bisimulation preserves trace equivalence under refinement of actions provided actions are atomic [17]. And in B, the operations or actions are atomic.   □

5   Analysis

The following are the highlights of our approach:

- A tool supporting the generation of usecase-based test cases would be semi-automatic in the following sense. The tool would take the initial usecase-based test case instances as input, a specification and a set of successive refinements. The developer may initialize the parameters to limit the solution size. Thereafter, rest of the process could be automated.
- To make the test cases robust one could consider more than one initialization. Furthermore, one could consider multiple instances of the same usecase scenario.
- The approach is capable of generating test cases of shorter length. The current approaches usually create a coverage graph in an ad-hoc manner like: take the initial state and go on applying operation instances till a predefined depth is reached. Our method gives an orientation to the graph creating process; we predefine a depth but our predefined depth has a logical basis.
- Our method can warn the developer of refinement incompleteness in the sense that the refinement omits a certain desired scenario. Thus, our method can help in making the refinements robust.

The following are the low points which needs further research.

- It seems the exponential nature of our algorithm is unavoidable. Even though we limit the problem size, we need intelligent strategies to further cut down the creation of redundant nodes.

– When we show the non-existence of a desired path in a refinement, we need enumeration of all possible paths limited by the variants. Optimization issues in this situation need to be addressed.

6 Conclusion

We have presented a method in which model based test cases are usecase oriented. Whenever, a specification or a refinement is further refined, our usecase-based test cases can be upgraded to remain in sync with the refinement. Our approach also finds incompleteness in refinements which can be corrected much ahead in the development cycle. Most of the steps in our method can be automated.

Our approach also helps in the formal development process. The method can help in making refinements themselves robust in relation to the original specification. It can also help in cutting down the time to prove proof obligations. After creating a refinement and before proving the proof obligations, the refinement can be tested against the specification in relation to the test cases derived from our method. If it shows some inconsistencies, then certainly, we have avoided performing some unnecessary proofs.

Acknowledgment. The authors would like to thank Ralph Back, Linas Laibinis and Marina Walden for valuable comments.

References

1. Abrial J.-R. (1996). *The B–Book: Assigning Programs to Meanings*, Cambridge University Press.
2. Bernard E., Legeard B., Luck X., Peureux F. (2004). Generation of test sequences from formal specifications: GSM 11-11 standard case study, *Software Practice and Experience*, Volume 34 (10) , pp. 915 - 948.
3. Dick, J.; Faivre, A. (1993). Automating the Generation and Sequencing of Test Cases from Model-based Specifications, Proc. of the FME,03: Industrial Strength Formal Methods, LNCS 670, 1993, pp. 268–284.
4. Dalal, S.R., Jain A., Karunanithi, N., Leaton J.M., Lott C.M., Patton G.C., Horowitz B.M. (1999). Model Based Testing in Practice, Proc. of ICSE '99, Los Angeles, pp. 285–294.
5. Derrick, J., Boiten, E. (1999). Testing refinements of state-based formal specifications, *Software Testing, Verification and Reliability*, John Wiley, (9):27-50.
6. Dunne S. (2005). Introducing Backward Refinement into B, Proc. of ZB 2003, LNCS Volume 2651, Springer, pp. 178–196.
7. Garey, M.R., Johnson, D.S. (1979). Computers and Intractability, W. H. Freeman and Company.
8. He, J., Hoare C.A.R., Sanders, J.W. (1986). Data refinement refined, ESOP 1986, LNCS Volume 213, Springer; pp. 187-196.

9. Jones, C.B. (1990). Systematic Software Development using VDM (2nd Edn), Prentice Hall.
10. Leuschel, M., Butler M. (2005). Automatic Refinement Checking for B, Proc. of ICFEM'05, LNCS Volume 3785, Springer, pp. 345–359.
11. Metayer, C., Abrial,J.-R., Voisin, L. (2005). Event-B Language, RODIN deliverable 3.2, http://rodin.cs.cnl.ac.uk
12. OMG . (2005). Unified Modeling Language (UML), Version 2.0, The Object Management Group, website: www.omg.org
13. Plosch, R. (2004). *Contracts, Scenarios and Prototypes*, Springer Verlag.
14. Richardson D.J., Leif Aha A., O'Malley T.O. (1992). Specification-based Test Oracles for Reactive Systems, Proc. of the 14th ICSE, Melbourne, pp. 105–118.
15. Satpathy, M., Leuschel, M., Butler,M. (2005). ProTest: An Automatic Test Environment for B Specifications, ENTCS, 111, pp: 113–136.
16. Spivey, J.M. (1988). *Understanding Z*, Cambridge University Press.
17. Van Glabbeek, R.J., Weijland, W.P. (1996). Branching Time and Abstraction in Bisimulation Semantics, Journal of the ACM, 43(3): 555-600.
18. Zhu, H., Hall P.A.V., May J.H.R. (1997). Software Unit Test Coverage and Adequacy, *ACM Computing Surveys*, 29(4):366–427.

Appendix

Machine Leader.mch
CONSTANTS M
PROPERTIES $M \subset \mathbb{N}$
VARIABLES winner
INITIALISATION $winner :\in M$ /* assign any element of M */
OPERATIONS
elect = BEGIN $winner := max(M)$ END
END

Machine LeaderR.mch
CONSTANTS $next, n$ /* next gives ordering in the ring */
PROPERTIES $next \in M{-}{>} M \wedge next = \{(10, 20, (20, 15), (15, 10)\} \wedge n \in M \wedge n = card(M)$
VARIABLES $position, v1$
INVARIANT $position = M{+}{-}{>} M \ \wedge v1 \in \mathbb{N}$ /*+-> : partial function*/
INITIALISATION
　　　　$winner :\in M \,\|\, position := ID(M) \,\|\, v1 := n * (n + 1)$
accept = ANY x WHERE $x \in dom(position) \wedge next(position(x)) < x$ THEN
　　　　$position(x) := next(position(x)) \,\|\, v1 := v1 - 1$ END;
reject = ANY x WHERE $x \in dom(position) \wedge X < next(position(X))$ THEN
　　　　$position := \{x\} {<}{+} position \,\|\, v1 := v1 - 1$ END;
elect = ANY x WHERE $x \in dom(position) \wedge x = next(position(x))$ THEN
　　　　$winner := x$ END
END

MACHINE LeaderRR.mch
VARIABLES in, out , v2
INVARIANT $in = M{+}{-}{>} M \ \wedge out = M{+}{-}{>} M \ \wedge v2 \in \mathbb{N}$

INITIALISATION

$winner :\in M \parallel in := \emptyset \parallel out := ID(M) \parallel v2 := m(m+1)$

send = ANY x WHERE $x \in dom(out)$ THEN

$in(x) := next(out(X)) \parallel out := \{x\} \lessdot + out \parallel v2 := v2 - 1$ END

accept = ANY x WHERE $x \in dom(in) \wedge in(x) < x$ THEN

$out(x) := in(x) \parallel in := \{x\} \lessdot + in$ END

reject = ANY x WHERE $x \in dom(in) \wedge x < in(x)$ THEN

$in := \{x\} \lessdot + in$ END;

elect = ANY x WHERE $x \in dom(in) \wedge in(x) = x$ THEN

$winner := x$ END

END

State-Identification Problems for Finite-State Transducers

Moez Krichen[1] and Stavros Tripakis[2]

[1] Verimag Laboratory, Centre Equation 2, avenue de Vignate, 38610 Gières, France
[2] Verimag Laboratory and Cadence Berkeley Labs, 1995 University avenue, Berkeley, CA, USA
krichen@imag.fr, tripakis@cadence.com

Abstract. A well-established theory exists for testing finite-state machines, in particular Moore and Mealy machines. A fundamental class of problems handled by this theory is state identification: we are given a machine with known state space and transition relation but unknown initial state, and we are asked to find experiments which permit to identify the initial or final state of the machine, called distinguishing and homing experiments, respectively.

In this paper, we study state-identification for finite-state transducers. The latter are a generalization of Mealy machines where outputs are sequences rather than symbols. Transducers permit to model systems where inputs and outputs are not synchronous, as is the case in Mealy machines. It is well-known that every deterministic and minimal Mealy machine admits a homing experiment. We show that this property fails for transducers, even when the latter are deterministic and minimal. We provide answers to the decidability question, namely, checking whether a given transducer admits a particular type of experiment. First, we show how the standard successor-tree algorithm for Mealy machines can be turned into a semi-algorithm for transducers. Second, we show that the state-identification problems are undecidable for finite-state transducers in general. Finally, we identify a sub-class of transducers for which these problems are decidable. A transducer in this sub-class can be transformed into a Mealy machine, to which existing methods apply.

1 Introduction

Testing is a fundamental step in any development process. It consists in applying a set of experiments to a system, with multiple aims, from obtaining some piece of unknown information to checking correctness or measuring performance. These different aims give rise to different classes of testing problems, for instance, conformance testing or performance testing.

A particularly interesting class of testing problems, pioneered in the seminal 1956 paper of Moore [6], is *state identification*. We are given an input-output machine with known state-transition diagram but unknown initial state. We are asked to perform an experiment in order to, either find the unknown initial state

K. Havelund et al. (Eds.): FATES/RV 2006, LNCS 4262, pp. 148–162, 2006.
© Springer-Verlag Berlin Heidelberg 2006

(*distinguishing* experiment), or verify that the machine is indeed in an assumed-to-be state (*state-verification* experiment), or identify the final state, reached at the end of the experiment (*homing* experiment), or lead the machine to a given state (*synchronizing* experiment), etc.

An extensive theory is available on state identification problems for Moore and Mealy machines. These machines have a common characteristic, namely, that inputs and outputs are *synchronous*: an input is immediately followed by an output. This implies that each output symbol in an output sequence σ corresponds to a unique input symbol in the input sequence that generated σ. Such a machine models a *length-preserving* function from input sequences to output sequences.

Models where inputs and outputs are synchronous are particularly well-suited for a number of applications, for example, synchronous circuits. They are not suitable, however, for other applications such as multi-threaded software, concurrent or real-time systems. In such systems, inputs and outputs are inherently *asynchronous*: an input may not give rise to an output immediately, but only some time latter; an output may require more than one inputs to occur in a certain order (thus, a single input produces no output at all); an input may produce a sequence of outputs rather than a single output; and so on.

Sometimes, with appropriate modeling, such applications can be casted in a synchronous input-output framework. For example, one may model an absence of output by a special output symbol $\perp$ which denotes precisely "no output"; or one may model a sequence of outputs by a special output symbol which denotes precisely this sequence. However, when doing so in a testing context, it is important to realize that one implicitly makes certain assumptions on the capabilities of the tester. For instance, in the case of $\perp$, one implicitly assumes that the absence of output is observable. In the case of a sequence of outputs, one implicitly assumes that this sequence can be distinguished from sequences which are identical but result from more than one inputs (thus, the output symbol o_{ab} modeling the sequence of outputs ab is distinguishable from the output sequence $o_a \cdot o_b$, where o_a models the output a and o_b the output b).

In this paper we study state identification problems in a more general context, namely, for the model of *finite-state transducers*. Each transition of a transducer is labeled by an input symbol and a sequence (possibly empty) of output symbols. Thus, a transducer is a generalization of a Mealy machine where the output of a transition is a sequence rather than a single output symbol.

It is well-known that in the case of deterministic and minimal Mealy machines a homing experiment always exists. We show that this is not the case for finite-state transducers, even when the latter are deterministic and minimal. Consequently, the question arises: is there an algorithm to check, given a finite-state transducer, whether it admits a homing experiment? We generalize this question to consider distinguishing experiments as well. Since existence of any type of experiment is not guaranteed anyway, we make no assumptions on determinism or minimality of the transducers.

In the rest of the paper, we offer answers to the above question. First, we consider a standard algorithm for finding state identification experiments in Mealy machine, namely, the *successor-tree* algorithm [4].[1] There is a simple way to modify this algorithm and obtain a *semi-algorithm* which can handle transducers. It is a semi-algorithm in the sense that termination is not guaranteed. Indeed, the standard termination conditions do not apply in our case.

Second, we prove that the state-identification problems are undecidable for finite-state transducers in general.

Finally, we consider a sub-class of the FST model, called *wait-synchronize* transducers (WS-FSTs). Roughly speaking, a WS-FST is a transducer where (1) the user (tester) can eventually apply a special input wait after which it is allowed to "synchronize" with the outputs (i.e., it can safely observe all remaining outputs) and (2) the number of outputs that can be generated until the synchronization occurs is finite. We show that state identification is decidable for WS-FSTs. The method consists in transforming the transducer to a (possibly non-deterministic) Mealy machine and then applying existing algorithms [1].

The rest of this paper is organized as follows. In Section 2 we present the model of finite-state transducers. In Section 3 we define the various state identification problems. In Section 4 we recall the successor-tree algorithm and show how it can be turned into a semi-algorithm for the transducer model. In section 5 we show the state-identification problems to be undecidable in general. In Section 6 we define the sub-class of WS-FSTs and provide an algorithm for state-identification problems in this class. Section 7 gives directions for future work.

2   Finite-State Transducers

Definition 1. *A finite-state transducer (FST) is a quadruple $T = (Q, \mathsf{In}, \mathsf{Out}, E)$ where:*

- $Q = \{q_1, q_2, ..., q_n\}$ *is a finite set of states;*
- $\mathsf{In} = \{a, b, ...\}$ *is a finite set of input symbols;*
- $\mathsf{Out} = \{0, 1, ...\}$ *is a finite set of output symbols;*
- $E \subseteq Q \times Q \times \mathsf{In} \times \mathsf{Out}^*$ *is a finite set of transitions.*

A transition $(q, q', a, \sigma) \in E$ is denoted as $q \xrightarrow{a/\sigma} q'$. The interpretation is that, when the transducer is at state q and receives input a, it may move to q' and output σ. Notice that σ may be the empty sequence, $\sigma = \epsilon$. Also note that non-determinism is allowed.

For $a_1, ..., a_k \in \mathsf{In}$, $\sigma_1, ..., \sigma_k \in \mathsf{Out}^*$ and $q_0, q_1, ..., q_k \in Q$, we use the notation $q_0 \xrightarrow{\pi/\sigma} q_k$ iff $\forall i \in \{1, ..., k\}.q_{i-1} \xrightarrow{a_i/\sigma_i} q_i$, $\pi = a_1 \cdots a_k$ and $\sigma = \sigma_1 \cdots \sigma_k$. By convention $q \xrightarrow{\epsilon/\epsilon} q$ holds for any $q \in Q$. We also use the notation $q \xrightarrow{\pi/\sigma}$ as a shorthand for $\exists q'.q \xrightarrow{\pi/\sigma} q'$.

---

[1] Although this is not the most efficient algorithm, it is the simplest, thus, serves as a good starting point for studying decidability.

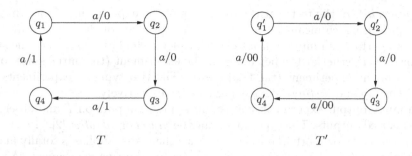

Fig. 1. Two FSTs T and T'

T is called *input-complete* if $\forall q \in Q. \forall a \in \text{In}. \exists \sigma \in \text{Out}^*. q \xrightarrow{a/\sigma}$. It is called *deterministic* if $\forall q, q', q'' \in Q . \forall a \in \text{In} . \forall \sigma', \sigma'' \in \text{Out}^* . (q \xrightarrow{a/\sigma'} q' \wedge q \xrightarrow{a/\sigma''} q'') \Rightarrow (q' = q'' \wedge \sigma' = \sigma'')$.

A FST is a generalization of a Mealy machine. A Mealy machine is a special case of a FST where every output sequence σ consists of a single output symbol.

Two examples of FSTs are given in Figure 1. T is a Mealy machine. It has four states (q_1, q_2, q_3 and q_4), one input (a) and two outputs (0 and 1). T' is obtained from T by substituting the output symbol 1 by the output sequence 00.

Next, we also use the following notation:

- For $a \in \text{In}$: $q \xrightarrow{a} \overset{Def}{=} \exists \sigma. q \xrightarrow{a/\sigma}$;
- For $q \in Q$ and $\pi \in \text{In}^+$: $out_{T,q}(\pi) \overset{Def}{=} \{\sigma \in \text{Out}^* | q \xrightarrow{\pi/\sigma}\}$;
- For $q \in Q$, $\pi \in \text{In}^+$ and $\sigma \in \text{Out}^*$: $succ_{T,q}(\pi, \sigma) \overset{Def}{=} \{q' \in Q | q \xrightarrow{\pi/\sigma} q'\}$;
- For $x \in \text{In}^* \cup \text{Out}^*$: $|x| \overset{Def}{=}$ the length of x;
- For $Q' \subseteq Q$: $|Q'| \overset{Def}{=}$ the cardinality of Q';
- For $X, Y \subseteq \text{Out}^*$: $XY = \{xy \mid x \in X \wedge y \in Y\}$;
- For $T_1 = (Q_1, \text{In}_1, \text{Out}_1, E_1)$ and $T_2 = (Q_2, \text{In}_2, \text{Out}_2, E_2)$:

$$T_1 \cup T_2 = (Q_1 \cup Q_2, \text{In}_1 \cup \text{In}_2, \text{Out}_1 \cup \text{Out}_2, E_1 \cup E_2).$$

A FST T is called *minimal* if for any distinct states $q_1, q_2 \in Q$ there exists $\pi \in \text{In}^*$ such that $out_{T,q_1}(\pi) \neq out_{T,q_2}(\pi)$. The two FSTs T and T' given in Figure 1 are both input-complete, deterministic and minimal.

3   State-Identification Problems for FSTs

We consider a FST T the model of which is known.[2] The current state of T is not known precisely, but known to be in a set of states $Q_0 \subseteq Q$. Q_0 models

---

[2] For the moment, we make no assumption on T (i.e., T may be non-input-complete, non-deterministic or non-minimal).

the *uncertainty* of the tester at the beginning of the experiment. Notice that Q_0 may equal Q, which means the tester has no knowledge of the initial state. The goal is to perform an input/output experiment which allows to deduce the state occupied by T either at the beginning of the experiment (the initial state) or at the end of the experiment (the final state). The two types of experiments are called *homing* and *distinguishing* experiments, respectively.

An input/output experiment consists in applying inputs on T and observing the generated outputs. The experiment may be *preset* or *adaptive* [2].[3] In a preset experiment (PX for short) the input sequence the tester applies is totally known in advance (before the experiment starts). In an adaptive experiment (AX for short) the tester is allowed to decide which inputs to apply depending on the outputs observed so far. Clearly, adaptive experiments are more general.

AXs and PXs are illustrated in Figure 2. An AX is a tree the internal nodes of which are labeled with finite non-empty input sequences $\pi_i \in \mathsf{In}^+$. The edges of the tree are labeled with finite output-sequences $\sigma_i \in \mathsf{Out}^*$. The labels of two edges emanating from the same internal node must be distinct (e.g., in the figure, $\sigma_1 \neq \sigma_2$ and $\sigma_3 \neq \sigma_4$). Each leaf is labeled with state in Q. The AX shown in the figure is to be interpreted as follows:

> Issue the input sequence π_1 and collect the observed output sequence. If the latter equals σ_2 then stop the experiment and declare that the result of the experiment is q_2. Otherwise (i.e., σ_1 is observed), issue the input sequence π_2 and collect the observed output sequence. If the latter equals σ_3 then the result of the experiment is q_2. Otherwise (i.e., σ_4 is observed) the result is q_1.[4]

The definition of AX proposed above is a slight generalization of the standard definition (for instance, found in [5]) in the sense that we allow π_i to contain more than one symbols. As mentioned in the introduction, a definition of an experiment captures a set of *implicit assumptions made on the observational capabilities of the tester*. This is particularly true for adaptive experiments. For instance, the AX shown in Figure 2 implicitly assumes that, having issued input sequence π_1 the tester can "stop and wait", until it observes the entire output sequence produced as a result of π_1. This assumption may not be valid in all situations.

For example, the FST in Figure 3 models a mouse device which produces single and double clicks. Here, the tester cannot stop and wait after issuing the first click, because waiting implicitly means that a "timeout" will occur and the mouse will output a single click. Thus, waiting for the timeout must be considered as an input action of the tester.

The above discussion shows that it is probably a good idea to model explicitly the assumptions on the observational capabilities of the tester. We do this by a subset of *synchronizing* input events, $\mathsf{In}_{sync} \subseteq \mathsf{In}$. The tester is allowed to stop

---

[3] Adaptive experiments are called *branching* experiments in [6].

[4] Depending on whether we are dealing with a distinguishing or a homing experiment, the result will be interpreted differently.

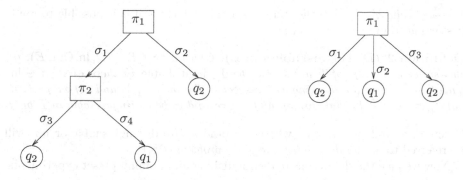

Fig. 2. The general scheme of adaptive experiments (left) and preset experiments (right)

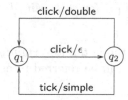

Fig. 3. A mouse device producing single and double clicks

and wait after issuing a iff $a \in \mathsf{In}_{sync}$. Formally, each π_i in an internal (non-leaf) node of the AX must end with a symbol in In_{sync}.

In the special case where $\mathsf{In}_{sync} = \mathsf{In}$, the problem of finding an AX for a FST T can be reduced to an equivalent problem of finding an AX for a Mealy machine M: it suffices to associate, for each output sequence ρ appearing in a transition of T, an output symbol o_ρ in M, such that $o_\rho \neq o'_\rho$ iff $\rho \neq \rho'$. Thus, the problem is interesting only when In_{sync} is a strict subset of In.

The situation is somewhat simpler in the case of PXs. Here, the tester is not allowed to make decisions while executing the test, but only at the end. Thus, there is an implicit "end-of-test" action where the tester is allowed to observe the entire output sequence. Here, we will assume that the tester cannot distinguish which part of the output sequence corresponds to which symbol of the input sequence (otherwise, we can reduce the problem to a problem for Mealy machines, as previously). For example, if the tester issues aa to the FST T' of Figure 1 while T' is initially at state q'_2, then the tester will observe 000. The same will happen if T' is initially at state q'_4.

For sake of simplicity, in the sequel we restrict ourselves to the case of preset experiments.

Next we introduce the notion of *distinguishable states* Before that, we need to introduce the notion of non-blockingness. Given a FST $T = (Q, \mathsf{In}, \mathsf{Out}, E)$, $Q_0 \subseteq Q$ and $\pi \in \mathsf{In}^*$, π is said to be *non-blocking* with respect to T and Q_0 iff for all $q \in Q_0, q' \in Q, \pi' \in \mathsf{In}^*, \sigma' \in \mathsf{Out}^*$ and $a \in \mathsf{In}$: if $\pi'a$ is a prefix of π and

$q \xrightarrow{\pi'/\sigma'} q'$ then $q' \xrightarrow{a}$. In other terms, π is non-blocking if it is possible to apply it starting from any state q in Q_0.

Definition 2 (Distinguishable states). *Given a FST $T = (Q, \mathsf{In}, \mathsf{Out}, E)$, the two states q_i and q_j of T are said to be* distinguishable *iff there exists $\pi \in \mathsf{In}^*$ such that (1) π is non-blocking with respect to T and $\{q_i, q_j\}$, and (2) $out_{T,q_i}(\pi) \cap out_{T,q_j}(\pi) = \emptyset$.* [5] *In that case, q_i and q_j are said to be* distinguishable in T by π.

Given T, q_i and q_j, checking whether q_i and q_j are distinguishable or not will be referred to as the *distinguishable-state problem* ($\mathsf{DS_t P}$).

Now we give the definitions of distinguishing and homing preset experiments.

Definition 3 (Distinguishing preset experiment). *For a given FST $T = (Q, \mathsf{In}, \mathsf{Out}, E)$ and $Q_0 \subseteq Q$, the input sequence $\pi \in \mathsf{In}^*$ is said to be a* distinguishing preset experiment *or* DPX *with respect to T and Q_0 iff (1) π is non-blocking with respect to T and Q_0, and (2) for each pair of states (q_i, q_j) from Q_0 q_i and q_j are distinguishable by π.*

The subset Q_0 corresponds to the *initial uncertainty* about the FST T. Checking whether T has a DPX or not will be referred to as the *distinguishing sequence problem* ($\mathsf{DS_q P}$).

Definition 4 (Homing preset experiment). *Given $T = (Q, \mathsf{In}, \mathsf{Out}, E)$ and $Q_0 \subseteq Q$, the input sequence $\pi \in \mathsf{In}^*$ is said to be a* homing preset experiment *or* HPX *with respect to T and Q_0 iff (1) π is non-blocking with respect to T and Q_0, and (2) for each pair of states (q_i, q_j) from Q_0 q_i and q_j we have*

$$\forall \sigma \in out_{T,q_i}(\pi) \cup out_{T,q_j}(\pi).|succ_{T,q_i}(\pi, \sigma) \cup succ_{T,q_j}(\pi, \sigma)| = 1.$$

Checking whether T has a HPX or not will be referred to as the *homing sequence problem* ($\mathsf{HS_q P}$).

Note that in the definitions above we make no restriction on whether the considered FST T is deterministic, minimal, input-complete or not.

It is well-known that, for deterministic Mealy machines, every distinguishing experiment is also a homing experiment. For example, the sequence aa is both a DPX and a HPX for the machine T shown in Figure 1. This property carries over to deterministic FSTs as well: if T is deterministic then every DPX is a HPX. However, other properties do not carry over. In particular, it is known that every deterministic and minimal Mealy machine possesses a HPX (although it may not possess a DPX). We now show that this is not true for deterministic and minimal FSTs.

Consider the FST T' of Figure 1. We claim that T' has no HPX with respect to $Q_0 = \{q_1', q_2', q_3', q_4'\}$. To show this, we first argue that none of a, aa, or aaa is a HPX. Then we argue that the effect of input sequence a^n, where $n \geq 4$ is equivalent to the effect of input sequence $a^{n \bmod 4}$, where $\bmod$ is the *modulo* operator.

---

[5] Note that $\{\epsilon\} \neq \emptyset$.

a is not a HPX because, on input a and starting from q_1' and q_2', respectively, T' produces the same sequence of outputs, 00, and moves to different final states, q_2' and q_3', respectively. Thus, a cannot resolve the initial uncertainty between q_1' and q_2'. Similarly, aa cannot resolve the initial uncertainty between q_2' and q_4', and aaa cannot resolve the initial uncertainty between q_1' and q_4'.

Longer input sequences do not help: a^4 has the same effect as giving no input at all, since it brings the machine to exactly the state it started from and it produces the output sequence 0^6, no matter what the initial state was. Similarly, a^5 has the same effect as a, a^6 has the same effect as aa, and so on.

4   The Successor-Tree Method

A standard method for solving state-identification problems for a Mealy machine is based on the machine's *successor-tree* [2,4]. Let us briefly recall this method before studying its application to FSTs. For simplicity, we restrict our discussion to homing preset experiments. It can be generalized to other types of experiments as well.

We first recall the notion of *current uncertainty*. Given a FST T and an input sequence π of it, $C(\pi)$ the initial uncertainty of T with respect to Q_0 is defined as the set of subblocks $B_{\sigma_1}, B_{\sigma_2}, ..., B_{\sigma_N}$, where σ_i are all the possible output sequences T may produce starting from any arbitrary state in Q_0. The subblock B_{σ_i} contains all the states q' for which $\exists q \in Q_0$ such that $q \xrightarrow{\pi/\sigma_i} q'$. That is, if on π the FST T produces σ_i then we are sure that the current state of T is in B_{σ_i}. For example for the FST T given in Figure 1, we have $C(a) = \{\{q_2, q_3\}_0, \{q_4, q_1\}_1\}$.

Clearly, a given input sequence π is a HPX for T iff $C(\pi)$ is made up only by singletons. For instance, aa is a HPX for the FST T given in Figure 1 since we have $C(aa) = \{\{q_3\}_{00}, \{q_4\}_{01}, \{q_1\}_{11}, \{q_2\}_{10}\}$.

In the case of Mealy machines, the classical way for checking whether such a HPX exists or not consists in computing the successor tree of the considered Mealy machine T. The successor tree of T is a (possibly infinite) graph S. For each node v of S, the edges emanating from v are labeled with input symbols: one outgoing edge for each input symbol of the machine. Let π_v denote the input sequence obtained by the concatenation of the labels of the edges on the path from the root of S to v. The node v is labeled with $C(\pi_v)$.

The definition of the successor tree of a FST is given in the same manner as above. For instance, a FST and a portion of its successor tree (up to depth 3) are given in Figure 5. Furthermore, the graphs S and S' given in Figure 4 are portions of the successor trees of the FSTs T and T' given in Figure 1, respectively. [6] S and S' are one-branch trees since T and T' have only one input.

The difference between S and S' starts from depth 3. This difference amounts to the fact that the former is able to distinguish between the two output sequences " $0 \cdot 1$ " and " $1 \cdot 0$ ", however, the latter considers " $0 \cdot 00$ " and " $00 \cdot 0$ "

---

[6] In order not to overload the figure, we write 0^2 instead of 00, 0^3 instead of 000 and so on.

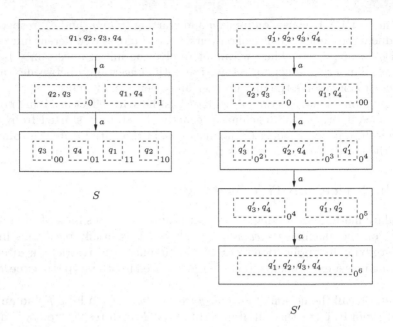

Fig. 4. S and S': portions of the successor trees of the FSTs T and T' given in Figure 1 , respectively

as the same output sequence ("000"). So in S, q_2 and q_4 are splitted into $\{q_2\}_{10}$ and $\{q_4\}_{01}$. However in S', q_2' and q_4' are grouped together in $\{q_2', q_4'\}_{000}$.

In the case of Mealy machines, checking the existence of a HPX is decidable due to the fact that two nodes v and v' of the successor tree of the considered machine labeled with $\{B_{\sigma_1}, .., B_{\sigma_N}\}$ and $\{B_{\sigma_1'}, ..., B_{\sigma_N'}\}$ are considered equivalent if $B_{\sigma_1} = B_{\sigma_1'} \wedge ... \wedge B_{\sigma_N} = B_{\sigma_N'}$. Now, since the number of combinations of the form $\{B_1, .., B_N\}$ is finite then an equivalent finite representation of the successor tree of the machine can be given and therefore the problem turns out to be decidable.

Now for the case of FSTs, v and v' are to be considered equivalent if we have $B_{\sigma_1} = B_{\sigma_1'} \wedge ... \wedge B_{\sigma_N} = B_{\sigma_N'}$ and also $\exists \alpha \in \mathsf{Out}^*$ such that $\sigma_1 = \alpha \cdot \sigma_1' \wedge ... \wedge \sigma_N = \alpha \cdot \sigma_N'$. For example in the successor tree given in Figure 5, the nodes labeled with $\{q_1, q_2, q_3, q_4\}$, $\{q_1, q_2, q_3, q_4\}_0$ and $\{q_1, q_2, q_3, q_4\}_{00}$, respectively, are equivalent. The nodes of the successor tree S' (Figure 4) labeled with $\{q_1, q_2, q_3, q_4\}$ and $\{q_1, q_2, q_3, q_4\}_{0^6}$, respectively, are equivalent. That even allows us to deduce that the corresponding FST has no HPX.

The problem with FSTs is that the number of possible combinations of the form $\{B_{\sigma_1}, .., B_{\sigma_N}\}$ may be infinite, since the equences σ_i may be arbitrarily long. Thus, we are not always guaranteed to have a finite representation of the successor tree of the considered FST. Consequently, we are not sure whether checking the existence of a HPX for a FST is decidable or not.

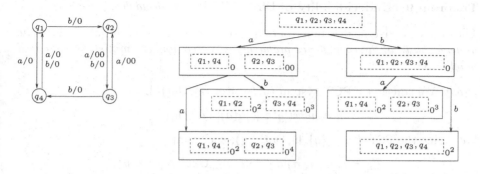

Fig. 5. A FST (left) and a portion of its successor tree (right)

5   Undecidability of the State-Identification Problems for FSTs

In this section we prove that $\mathsf{DS_tP}$, $\mathsf{DS_qP}$ and $\mathsf{HS_qP}$ are all undecidable. For that we reduce the famous *Post's correspondence problem*. So, we first give a brief recall about this problem [7].

Definition 5 (Post's correspondence problem). *An instance of the Post's correspondence problem* (PCP) *is an ordered quadruple* (V, n, α, β) *where* V *is an alphabet,* $n \geq 1$ *and*

$$\alpha = (\alpha_1, \cdots, \alpha_n) \text{ and } \beta = (\beta_1, \cdots, \beta_n)$$

are ordered n-tuples of nonempty words over V. *A solution to* PCP *is a nonempty sequence of indices* $i_1, \cdots, i_k$ *such that*

$$\alpha_{i_1} \cdots \alpha_{i_k} = \beta_{i_1} \cdots \beta_{i_k}.$$

Theorem 6 (Undecidability of PCP **[7]).** *There is no algorithm for deciding whether or not an arbitrary Post's correspondence problem possesses a solution.*

More precisely, we reduce the variant of PCP introduced in [3].

Definition 7 (Variant of PCP **[3]).** PCP′ *is a variant of* PCP. *A* PCP′ *system over* (In, Out) *is a pair of maps* (g, h) *from* In *to* $\mathsf{Out}^+ - \mathsf{Out}$. *Maps* g *and* h *are extended to* In^+ *as follows. If* $\pi, \varpi \in \mathsf{In}^+$,

$$g(\pi\varpi) = g(\pi)g(\varpi) \text{ and } h(\pi\varpi) = h(\pi)h(\varpi).$$

The associated problem is to tell whether there is a string $\pi \in \mathsf{In}^+$ *such that* $g(\pi) = h(\pi)$.

Theorem 8 (Undecidability of PCP′ **[3]).** PCP′ *is undecidable.*

We first prove that $\mathsf{DS_tP}$ is undecidable.

Theorem 9 (Undecidability of DS_tP). DS_tP *is undecidable.*

The proof we give next is quite parallel to the one proposed in [3] to show *the undecidability of the equivalence problem for Λ-free nondeterministic generalized machines.*

Proof. We consider a PCP' system (g, h) over (In, Out). Let

$$n = max(|g(a)|, |h(a)| : a \in In). \;^7$$

We define the FST $T_n = (\{q\}, In, Out, E_n)$, such that

$$E_n = \{(q, q, a, \sigma) | a \in In \wedge \sigma \in Out^+ \wedge |\sigma| \leq n\}.$$

Then

$$out_{T_n, q}(\pi) = \{\sigma \in Out^+ | \; |\pi| \leq |\sigma| \leq n|\pi|\}, \forall \pi \in In^+.$$

Let $T' = (Q', In, Out, E')$ a new FST such that

$$\exists r \in Q'. \forall \pi \in In^+. out_{T', r}(\pi) = out_{T_n, q}(\pi) - \{g(\pi)\}. \tag{1}$$

A possible way for constructing T' is given in [3]. Furthermore, T' is guaranteed to be input-complete. Let s be a new state and $T'' = (\{s\}, In, Out, E'')$ a new FST such that

$$E'' = \{(s, s, a, h(a)) | a \in In\}.$$

Clearly T'' is input-complete and

$$out_{T'', s}(\pi) = \{h(\pi)\}, \; \forall \pi \in In^+. \tag{2}$$

Finally, let us consider the FST $\tilde{T} = T' \cup T''$. Since T' and T'' are input-complete then $\tilde{T}$ is so too and all $\pi \in In^*$ are non-blocking with respect to $\tilde{T}$ and $\{r, s\}$. By (1) and (2), we deduce that for $\pi \in In^+$:

$$out_{\tilde{T}, r}(\pi) \cap out_{\tilde{T}, s}(\pi) = \emptyset \text{ iff } g(\pi) = h(\pi).$$

Thus we conclude that

r and s are distinguishable in $\tilde{T}$ iff the PCP' system (g, h) has a solution.

$\square$

Now, we prove that DS_qP is undecidable.

Theorem 10 (Undecidability of DS_qP). DS_qP *is undecidable.*

Proof. It is not difficult to see that each instance of DS_tP is a particular instance of DS_qP. That is "$DS_tP \subseteq DS_qP$". So, since DS_tP is undecidable (Theorem 9) then DS_qP is so too. $\square$

Finally, we prove that HS_qP is undecidable too.

---

[7] Since we deal with a PCP' system then n is guaranteed to be ≥ 2. That will help for the construction of T' mentioned later on.

Theorem 11 (Undecidability of HS_qP). HS_qP *is undecidable.*

Proof. Once again we reduce from PCP'. We consider a PCP' system (g, h) over $(\mathsf{In}, \mathsf{Out})$. We construct the FST $\tilde{T} = (\tilde{Q}, \mathsf{In}, \mathsf{Out}, \tilde{E})$ in the same manner we did in proof of Theorem 9. Let $\hat{T} = (\tilde{Q}, \mathsf{In} \cup \{\diamond\}, \mathsf{Out}, \hat{E})$ be a new FST such that $\diamond \notin \mathsf{In}$ and

$$\hat{E} = \tilde{E} \cup \{(t, r, \diamond, \epsilon) \mid t \in Q'\} \cup \{(s, s, \diamond, \epsilon)\}.$$

Since $\hat{T}$ is input-complete then $\hat{T}$ is so too. Next we prove the following

The PCP' (g, h) has a solution $\Leftrightarrow \hat{T}$ has a homing sequence with respect to $\hat{Q}$.

($\Rightarrow$) We assume that there exists $\pi \in \mathsf{In}^+$ such that $g(\pi) = h(\pi)$. Let $\pi' = \diamond\pi\diamond$. Since $\hat{T}$ is input-complete then π' is clearly non-blocking with respect to $\hat{T}$ and $\hat{Q}$. Furthermore, it is not difficult to see that π' is homing sequence for $\hat{T}$. That is, if we apply π' and then observe $\sigma = g(\pi) = h(\pi)$ then we know that $\hat{T}$ has just moved to s. Otherwise, if we observe $\sigma \neq g(\pi)$ then $\hat{T}$ has just moved to r.

($\Leftarrow$) Now, we assume that $\hat{T}$ has a homing sequence $\pi' \in (\mathsf{In} \cup \{\diamond\})^+$. Let $\pi_1, \cdots, \pi_k$ the elements of In^* such that

$$\pi' = \pi_1 \diamond \pi_2 \diamond \cdots \diamond \pi_k .$$

Since π' is homing sequence for $\hat{T}$ with respect to $\hat{Q}$ and that there is no common reachable state starting from s and r then we necessarily have

$$out_{\hat{T},r}(\pi') \cap out_{\hat{T},s}(\pi') = \emptyset . \tag{3}$$

Next we prove by contradiction that there exists at least one π_i such that $out_{\hat{T},s}(\pi_i) \cap out_{\hat{T},r}(\pi_i) = \emptyset$. For that, let us assume that $\forall i \in \{1, \cdots, k\}$

$$out_{\hat{T},r}(\pi_i) \cap out_{\hat{T},s}(\pi_i) \neq \emptyset . \tag{4}$$

We know that $out_{\hat{T},r}(\pi') = out_{\hat{T},r}(\pi_1 \diamond \pi_2 \diamond \cdots \diamond \pi_k)$. Moreover, it not difficult to see that all the possible transitions labeled by $\diamond$ appearing on this path are of the form $t \xrightarrow{\diamond/\epsilon} r$. That is, they all produce the empty sequence ϵ and move back to state r. Thus, it can be deduced that

$$out_{\hat{T},r}(\pi') = out_{\hat{T},r}(\pi_1) \cdots out_{\hat{T},r}(\pi_k) .$$

By the same reasoning we deduce that

$$out_{\hat{T},s}(\pi') = out_{\hat{T},s}(\pi_1) \cdots out_{\hat{T},s}(\pi_k) .$$

By assumption (4), it turns out that $out_{\hat{T},r}(\pi') \cap out_{\hat{T},s}(\pi') \neq \emptyset$ which is in contradiction with (3). Consequently, assumption (4) is false. That is, there exists at least one π_i such that $out_{\hat{T},r}(\pi_i) \cap out_{\hat{T},s}(\pi_i) = \emptyset$. For that to be true, we must clearly have $g(\pi_i) = h(\pi_i)$. Thus the PCP' system (g, h) has a solution.

$\square$

6   Decidability for a Sub-class of FSTs

We first consider a sub-class of FSTs called *wait-synchronize* FSTs, or WS-FSTs. A WS-FST is a FST which has a special input action wait $\in$ In and a special output action sync $\in$ Out satisfying the following properties:

P1. wait and sync appear only in transitions of the form $q \xrightarrow{\text{wait}/\sigma \cdot \text{sync}} q'$ where $\sigma \in (\text{Out} \setminus \{\text{sync}\})^*$.

P2. From any state q and any infinite sequence of transitions starting at q, wait eventually appears on this sequence.

Property P1 says that the output symbol sync is generated iff the input symbol wait is applied. It also says that once wait is applied the considered FST T generates an output sequence which ends with sync and contains no other sync. Property P2 says that from any state q, wait is eventually possible.[8]

Intuitively, wait and sync are to be interpreted as follows: wait models explicitly the waiting of the user of the machine; sync models the "timeout" after which the user can safely assume that all remaining outputs have been generated.

An input sequence $\pi \in (\text{In} \setminus \{\text{wait}\})^* \cdot \text{wait}$ is called an *input-vertebra*. Similarly, an output sequence $\sigma \in (\text{Out} \setminus \{\text{sync}\})^* \cdot \text{sync}$ is called an *output-vertebra*. The sets of input- and output-vertebrae are denoted Vert_{in} and Vert_{out}, respectively. In view of the discussion in Section 3, we set $\text{In}_{sync} = \{\text{wait}\}$. Thus, the internal nodes of the AX tree are labeled with input-vertebrae and its edges are labeled with output-vertebrae.

A FST T is said to be *output-bounded* iff all the possible output-vertebrae that T may produce are of bounded length. Formally:

P3. $\exists n_{max} . \forall q \in Q . \forall \pi \in \text{Vert}_{\text{in}} . \forall \sigma \in \text{Vert}_{\text{out}} . q \xrightarrow{\pi/\sigma} \Rightarrow |\sigma| \leq n_{max}.$

It is not difficult to see that each WS-FST is output-bounded.

We now propose a method which permits to solve state-identification problems for a given WS-FST T. The method is based on transforming T into a (possibly non-deterministic) Mealy machine M and then applying existing algorithms for state-identification problems on non-deterministic Mealy machines [1].

M has the same set of states as T. The transformation consists of the following steps:

Step 1. We identify the states of T with an incoming edge the input-label of which is wait. These states are called wait-*states*. The latter are these states which can be reached by an input-vertebra.

Step 2. For every state q and every wait-state q_{wait} of T, we compute the language $L^O_{q,q_{\text{wait}}}$ containing all $\sigma \in \text{Vert}_{\text{out}}$ such that $q \xrightarrow{\pi/\sigma} q_{\text{wait}}$, for some $\pi \in \text{Vert}_{\text{in}}$. $L^O_{q,q_{\text{wait}}}$ is a finite set of output-vertebrae since T is output-bounded.

---

[8] Notice that Mealy machines are essentially a special case of WS-FSTs: we can "split" every transition $q \xrightarrow{a/x} q'$ of a Mealy machine into two transitions $q \xrightarrow{a/x} q'' \xrightarrow{\text{wait}/\text{sync}} q'$ and obtain an equivalent, for the purposes of testing, WS-FST.

Step 3. For each $\sigma \in L^O_{q,q_{\text{wait}}}$, we compute $L^I_{q,q_{\text{wait}},\sigma} = \{\pi \mid \pi \in \text{Vert}_{\text{in}} \text{ and } q \overset{\pi/\sigma}{\rightarrow} q_{\text{wait}}\}$, the set of input-vertebrae the execution of which may generate σ. $L^I_{q,q_{\text{wait}},\sigma}$ is a regular language since it is induced by a subgraph of T. After computing $L^I_{q,q_{\text{tick}},\text{wait}}$, we add, in M, a new edge from q to q_{wait} labeled with $L^I_{q,q_{\text{wait}},\sigma}/\sigma$. $L^I_{q,q_{\text{wait}},\sigma}$ is called the *language-symbol* of the edge.

Step 4. We collect the language-symbols that appear on the edges of the machine M so far constructed. Let $L_1, ..., L_N$ be the list of these language-symbols. For being able to solve the identification problems, the latter must be disjoint. Only if this holds we have the right to consider two different language-symbols as different input symbols in M. For this purpose, we compute $L'_1, ..., L'_{N'}$, the coarsest partition of $L_1 \cup L_2 \cup ... \cup L_N$ which respects each L_i. Thus, L'_k are pairwise disjoint and each L_i is "split" into a number of L'_k, namely:

$$L_i = L'_{j_1} \cup \cdots \cup L'_{j_i}.$$

Then, we replace each edge $q \overset{L_i/\sigma}{\rightarrow} q'$ by the edges $q \overset{L'_{j_1}/\sigma}{\rightarrow} q', ..., q \overset{L'_{j_i}/\sigma}{\rightarrow} q'$.

Checking whether M has a given type of experiment can be done using the algorithms of [1]. These algorithms permit not only to check existence but also to construct an experiment in case it exists. The algorithms are based on the synthesis of *strategies* in *games with incomplete information*. The game is played between the tester who provides the inputs and the system under test who provides the outputs. The strategy of the system corresponds to resolving non-deterministic choices (when such choices exist). The strategy of the tester corresponds to choosing the inputs. The tester has incomplete information because it only observes the outputs, not the current state of the game. Finding preset experiments corresponds to finding a *blindfold* strategy for the tester, that is, a strategy which is totally defined in advance. Finding preset and adaptive experiments is shown in the above paper to be PSPACE-complete and EXPTIME-complete problems, respectively.

It is not difficult to show that T has a DPX (resp., HPX) iff M has a DPX (resp., HPX). Moreover, the way for constructing an experiment for T given an experiment for M is straightforward.

7   Perspectives

We have presented a framework for state-identification problems for finite-state transducers. A number of open questions remain: decidability in the case of deterministic finite-state transducers, complexity, properties on the worst-case size of experiments, when the latter exist, and so on. We are currently studying these questions. We are also experimenting with the modeling possibilities of the sub-class identified in this paper, in particular in the context of testing with timing constraints.

References

1. R. Alur, C. Courcoubetis, and M. Yannakakis. Distinguishing tests for nondeterministic and probabilistic machines. In *27th ACM Symposium on Theory of Computing (STOC'95)*, pages 363–372, 1995.
2. A. Gill. State-identification experiments in finite automata. *Information and Control*, 4:132–154, 1961.
3. T. V. Griffiths. The unsolvability of the equivalence problem for Λ-free nondeterministic generalized machines. *J. ACM*, 15(3):409–413, 1968.
4. Z. Kohavi. *Switching and finite automata theory, 2nd ed.* McGraw-Hill, 1978.
5. D. Lee and M. Yannakakis. Principles and methods of testing finite state machines - A survey. *Proceedings of the IEEE*, 84:1090–1126, 1996.
6. E.F. Moore. Gedanken-experiments on sequential machines. In *Automata Studies*, number 34. Princeton University Press, 1956.
7. Arto Salomaa. *Formal languages*. Academic Press Professional, Inc., San Diego, CA, USA, 1987.

Deterministic Dynamic Monitors for Linear-Time Assertions

Roy Armoni, Dmitry Korchemny[1], Andreas Tiemeyer[1],
Moshe Y. Vardi[2],[*], and Yael Zbar[1]

[1] Intel
[2] Rice University and Microsoft Research

Abstract. We describe a framework for dynamic verification of temporal assertions based on assertion compilation into deterministic automata. The novelty of our approach is that it allows efficient dynamic verification of general linear temporal formulas written in formal property specification languages such as LTL, ForSpec, PSL, and SVA, while the existing approaches are applicable to limited subsets only. We also show an advantage of the described framework over industrial simulators, which typically use transaction-based verification. Another advantage of our approach is its ability to use deterministic checkers directly for hardware emulation. Finally, we compare the deterministic compilation with the OBDD-based on-the-fly simulation of deterministic automata. We show that although the OBDD-based simulation method is much slower, the two methods may be efficiently combined for hybrid simulation, when the RTL signals in assertions are mixed with symbolic variables.

1 Introduction

One of the most significant results in the area of formal methods over the last two decades has been the development of algorithmic methods for verifying temporal specifications of *finite-state* programs, cf. [17]. By now, these methods have had important industrial impact, cf. [11,19]. Nevertheless, even in design projects with significant application of formal methods, such methods rarely account for more than 10% of the verification effort [9]. It seems that, in the near future at least, traditional, simulation-based, dynamic verification techniques will continue to constitute the basic approach to design verification. This calls for exploration of techniques that combine the dynamic and formal approaches to verification, cf. [30].

An important aspect of verification consists of expressing assertions that capture the intended behavior of the design. Using the same formal verification languages based on linear temporal logic (LTL)[36] such as ForSpec [5], Sugar [7], PSL [18] or SVA[1]

---

[*] Supported in part by NSF grants CCR-9988322, CCR-0124077, CCR-0311326, and ANI-0216467, by BSF grant 9800096, and by Texas ATP grant 003604-0058-2003. Part of this work was done while the author was visiting the Isaac Newton Institute for Mathematical Sciences, as part of a Special Programme on Logic and Algorithms.
[1] SVA is not, strictly speaking, a language based on LTL; nevertheless, the ideas described in this work apply to SVA as well.

K. Havelund et al. (Eds.): FATES/RV 2006, LNCS 4262, pp. 163–177, 2006.
© Springer-Verlag Berlin Heidelberg 2006

[41] for both formal and dynamic verification leads to increased productivity in the verification effort.

Even if the same assertions are used in formal and dynamic verification, their treatment in the two contexts is different. In the formal context, temporal assertions are usually compiled into nondeterministic automata [39] (cf. [4], however), while in the dynamic context the compilation is into deterministic automata, also referred to as *monitors* or *checkers* [1,12,28]. This is because in formal verification we search through the transition graph of the product of the design and the automaton, while in dynamic verification we simulate the monitor along executions of the design. Indeed, the work in [1] reports on a compilation of a *fragment* of Sugar into deterministic monitors. In the same spirit, the PSL Reference Manual [2] defines a fragment called *Simple PSL*, which is suitable for compilation into deterministic monitors (cf. also [26]). Such an approach, however, poses two difficulties. First, it is possible that an assertion written for formal verification is not compilable for dynamic verification, making it difficult to use the same specification base for both formal and dynamic verification. Second, the existence of two compilers, one for formal verification and one for dynamic verification, raises the risk that the two compilers may actually differ in their semantics, as they might compile the same assertion into inequivalent automata. For example, in [29,30], LTL semantics is defined over infinite traces for formal verification, but over finite traces for dynamic verification, creating a potential mismatch. The focus on assertion compilation for both formal and dynamic verification distinguishes our approach to dynamic temporal monitors from that of many published works in this area, cf. [6,20,35].

We describe in this paper a framework for dynamic verification, which uses assertions expressed in ForSpec. (We express the ideas in terms of LTL, but they are applicable also to other linear-temporal languages extended with regular events, such as PSL, without the Optional Branching Extension, and SVA). The key goals underlying the framework are: (1) the semantics of assertions in dynamic verification should be consistent with the semantics of assertions in formal verification; (2) all assertions in the underlying assertion language should be accepted, rather than just a fragment of the language; and (3) the compilation into deterministic monitors should be as close as possible to the compilation into nondeterministic automata.

To accomplish semantic consistency, we adopt a three-valued semantics for finite traces. When a formula is reported to hold in a finite trace, the formula holds in all extensions of the trace; this is a *pass*. When a formula is reported to fall in a finite traces, the formula fails in all extensions of the trace; this is a *fail*. When a formula is reported to be *ongoing*, it means that the finite trace does not provide enough information to decide the truth value of the formula. Our notion of success and failure over finite traces is that defined for ForSpec [3,5], and elucidated further in [22]. We define it here in automata-theoretic terms (see below). This approach allows us to accomplish our second goal. *Every* assertion in the language can be compiled for dynamic verification; there is no need to define a "simple" fragment. (Of course, for some assertions this approach is not useful. For example, it is not useful to test the assertion always eventually p over finite traces. We generate a trivial monitor for this assertion.)

We describe two approaches to accomplish the third goal, which is to keep formal compilation and dynamic compilation as close as possible. The first approach attempts to eliminate the deterministic compilation completely. The ForSpec compiler compiles temporal assertions into alternating Büchi automata on infinite traces [38], where every state is responsible for checking one subformula. The fairness condition guarantees that all eventualities are satisfied rather than postponed forever. As suggested in [32], by considering this automaton as an automaton on finite words, we get an automaton that accepts finite traces on which the formula is guaranteed to succeed. The ForSpec compiler translates the alternating automaton to an implicit representation of a nondeterministic automaton. Instead of compiling this nondeterministic automaton into a deterministic monitor using the subset construction, we generate the states of the monitor on the fly during dynamic verification. Since the nondeterministic automaton is represented implicitly, states of the monitor are sets of truth assignments, represented using Ordered Binary Decision Diagrams (OBDDs) [13] over the variables of the implicit representation. While this approach offers the smallest "distance" between the compilations for formal and dynamic verification, it proves empirically to be, in general, too slow in comparison to our second approach.

The second approach addresses the performance issue by direct conversion of the alternating automaton into an explicitly represented nondeterministic automaton. This step involves an exponential blowup in the worst case, but our experience with LTL compilation has shown that this translation is quite amenable to optimization, cf. [21,24,37]. Once the nondeterministic automaton is represented explicitly, we do not explicitly generate a deterministic automaton, as, for example, in [29]. Rather, we synthesize an implicitly represented, equivalent deterministic monitor represented in a register transfer level (RTL). Every state of the nondeterministic automaton gives rise to a sequential element, and the combinational logic describes the subset construction. Thus, the size of the RTL description is *linear* in the size of the explicitly represented nondeterministic automaton, while an explicit determinization may incur an exponential blowup. The advantage of using RTL representation is that it matches the representation used in dynamic verification, as both design and assertion are now represented in RTL. We show that this approach yields dramatic improvement in performance. (Another advantage of this approach is that the monitors can also be used in hardware emulation, and not only in software simulation, of the design under verification.)

The two compilation methods may be combined to implement an efficient hybrid simulation engine: the deterministic part of the assertion can be compiled into a deterministic monitor, while the nondeterministic part can be simulate by means of OBDDs.

Example 1. Nondeterministic model.[2]

```
rigid bit [64] data; // unknown constant
assert always /start & data = /datain ->
    eventually [2,5] /end & data = /dataout &
        /z[64] = /x[64] * /y[64];
```

The above assertion is nondeterministic, since the variable data is symbolic and its value is unknown. On the other hand the product is deterministic and can be very

---

[2] rigid declares property variables that are assigned a nondeterministic value at time 0, which then does not change. Names that are prefixed with "/" refer to design variables.

efficiently computed by an RTL simulator. The assumption and the rest of the assertion are simulated as OBDD. Attempting to simulate everything as OBDD would result in a blowup, since the OBDD for the product is known to be exponential in the length of the arguments.

A key feature of our deterministic approach is its scalability with respect to simulation length. Since we generate a deterministic finite-state monitor, monitoring overhead is independent of simulation run length. A common approach in the semiconductor industry (e.g., Synopsys' VCS®) is transaction-based monitoring, which in effect constructs the monitor dynamically [16]. For example, in monitoring the property always (p → eventually q), the simulator spawns a new thread waiting for q each time it observes $p \land \neg q$. Such a thread is called a *transaction*. With this approach the number of active transactions is potentially unbounded, resulting in degraded performance for long simulation runs. (The conventional methodology [10] advises users to prevent this problem by bounding the number of active transactions.)

The outline of the paper is as follows. In Section 2 we describe the theory underlying our approach. Section 3 describes experimental results for both OBDD-based and RTL-based monitors. Section 4 describes the framework. We conclude with a discussion in Section 5.

2   Underlying Theory

LTL formulas are constructed from a set AP of atomic proposition using the usual Boolean operators and the temporal operators X ("next time"), U ("until"), and V ("release"). Formally, given a set AP, an LTL formula in *positive normal form* (PNF) is defined as follows: (1) **true**, **false**, p, or $\neg p$, for $p \in AP$, (2) $\psi_1 \lor \psi_2$, $\psi_1 \land \psi_2$, $X\psi_1$, $\psi_1 U \psi_2$, or $\psi_1 V \psi_2$, where ψ_1 and ψ_2 are LTL formulas. The semantics of LTL is defined over infinite traces, which are elements of $(2^{AP})^\omega$; see details in [23]. For an LTL formula ψ over a set AP of atomic propositions, let $\|\psi\|$ denote the set of traces in that satisfy ψ.

For a given set X, let $\mathcal{B}^+(X)$ be the set of positive Boolean formulas over X, where we also allow the formulas **true** and **false**. For $Y \subseteq X$, we say that Y *satisfies* a formula $\theta \in \mathcal{B}^+(X)$ iff the truth assignment that assigns *true* to the members of Y and assigns *false* to the members of $X \setminus Y$ satisfies θ. The transition function $\rho : Q \times \Sigma \to 2^Q$ of a nondeterministic automaton with state space Q and alphabet Σ can be represented using $\mathcal{B}^+(Q)$. For example, a transition $\rho(q, \sigma) = \{q_1, q_2, q_3\}$ can be written as $\rho(q, \sigma) = q_1 \lor q_2 \lor q_3$. While transitions of nondeterministic automata correspond to disjunctions, transitions of *alternating automata* can be arbitrary formulas in $\mathcal{B}^+(Q)$. We can have, for instance, a transition $\delta(q, \sigma) = (q_1 \land q_2) \lor (q_3 \land q_4)$, meaning that the automaton accepts from state q a suffix w^l, starting by σ, of w, if it accepts w^{l+1} from both q_1 and q_2 or from both q_3 and q_4. For a formal definition of runs of alternating automata on finite or infinite words, see [38]. A word (either finite or infinite) is accepted by $\mathcal{A}$ iff there exists an accepting run on it. The language of $\mathcal{A}$, denoted $\mathcal{L}(\mathcal{A})$, is the set of words that $\mathcal{A}$ accepts.

Given an LTL formula ψ in PNF, one can build a nondeterministic Büchi automaton $\mathcal{A}_\psi$ such that $\mathcal{L}(\mathcal{A}_\psi) = \|\psi\|$ [40]. The size of $\mathcal{A}_\psi$ is exponential in $|\psi|$ in the worst case. It is shown in [38] that when alternating automata are used, the translation of ψ to $\mathcal{A}_\psi$ is inductive and it involves only a linear blow up in the number of states.

Theorem 1. [38] *Given an LTL formula ψ, we can construct an alternating Büchi automaton $\mathcal{A}_\psi = \langle 2^{AP}, cl(\psi), \delta, \{\psi\}, F \rangle$, such that $\mathcal{L}(\mathcal{A}_\psi) = \|\psi\|$.*

See [14] for an extension of this construction to LTL extended with a regular layer (which is essentially common to ForSpec, PSL, and SVA).

Using the (potentially exponential) translation described in [34] from alternating Büchi automata to nondeterministic Büchi automata, we get:

Corollary 1. [40] *Given an LTL formula ψ, we can construct a nondeterministic Büchi automaton $\mathcal{N}_\psi$ such that $\mathcal{L}(\mathcal{N}_\psi) = \|\psi\|$.*

Consider a language $L \subseteq \Sigma^\omega$ of infinite words over the alphabet Σ. A finite word $x \in \Sigma^*$ is a *bad prefix* for L iff for all $y \in \Sigma^\omega$, we have $x \cdot y \notin L$. Thus, a bad prefix is a finite word that cannot be extended to an infinite word in L. It is shown in [32] that a nondeterministic automaton that accepts all bad prefixes of ψ is, in general, of size that is doubly exponential in the length of ψ. Thus, instead of trying to detect *all* bad prefixes, we focus on detecting *informative* prefixes.

For an LTL formula ψ in PNF and a finite trace $\pi = \sigma_1 \cdot \sigma_2 \cdots \sigma_n$, with $\sigma_i \in 2^{AP}$, we say that π is an *informative prefix for* ψ iff there exists a mapping $L : \{1, \ldots, n+1\} \to 2^{cl(\neg\psi)}$ such that the following holds:

(1) $\neg\psi \in L(1)$.
(2) $L(n + 1)$ is empty.
(3) For all $1 \le i \le n$ and $\varphi \in L(i)$, the following hold.
  - If φ is a propositional assertion, it is satisfied by σ_i.
  - If $\varphi = \varphi_1 \vee \varphi_2$ then $\varphi_1 \in L(i)$ or $\varphi_2 \in L(i)$.
  - If $\varphi = \varphi_1 \wedge \varphi_2$ then $\varphi_1 \in L(i)$ and $\varphi_2 \in L(i)$.
  - If $\varphi = X\varphi_1$, then $\varphi_1 \in L(i + 1)$.
  - If $\varphi = \varphi_1 U \varphi_2$, then $\varphi_2 \in L(i)$ or $[\varphi_1 \in L(i)$ and $\varphi_1 U \varphi_2 \in L(i+1)]$.
  - If $\varphi = \varphi_1 V \varphi_2$, then $\varphi_2 \in L(i)$ and $[\varphi_1 \in L(i)$ or $\varphi_1 V \varphi_2 \in L(i+1)]$.

Note that the emptiness of $L(n+1)$ guarantees that all the requirements imposed by $\neg\psi$ are fulfilled along π. For example, while the finite computation $\{p\} \cdot \emptyset$ is informative for Gp (e.g., with a mapping L for which $L(1) = \{F\neg p\}, L(2) = \{F\neg p, \neg p\}$, and $L(3) = \emptyset$), it is not informative for $\psi = G(p \vee (Xq \wedge X\neg q))$. Indeed, as $\neg\psi = F(\neg p \wedge (X\neg q \vee Xq))$, an informative prefix for ψ must contain at least one state after the first state in which $\neg p$ holds.

An informative prefix for ψ is also a bad prefix for ψ. Thus, if π is an informative prefix for ψ, we say that ψ *fails* on π, and if π is an informative prefix for $\neg\psi$, we say that ψ *passes* on π. It is possible for π to be informative neither for ψ nor for $\neg\psi$. In this case ψ is *ongoing* on π. The vast majority of the assertions used in practice have `always` as the outmost temporal operator. Such assertions cannot pass, but only fail or remain ongoing. Dynamic verification engineers are typically interested in assertion failure, and do not distinguish between passed and ongoing assertions.

Given an LTL formula ψ and a finite trace π of length n, the problem of deciding whether π is an informative prefix for ψ can be solved in time $O(n \cdot |\psi|)$. [32]. However, this algorithm requires offline access to the finite trace π and, therefore is not appropriate for dynamic monitoring. For that we need a deterministic automaton that accepts the informative prefixes of ψ.

As described earlier, given a PNF formula ψ, one can build an alternating Büchi automaton $\mathcal{A}_\psi = \langle 2^{AP}, 2^{cl(\psi)}, \delta, \psi, F \rangle$ such that $\mathcal{L}(\mathcal{A}_\psi) = \|\psi\|$. Essentially, each state of $\mathcal{L}(\mathcal{A}_\psi)$ corresponds to a subformula of ψ, and its transitions follow the semantics of LTL. We define the alternating Büchi automaton $\mathcal{A}_\psi^{true} = \langle 2^{AP}, 2^{cl(\psi)}, \delta, \psi, \emptyset \rangle$ by redefining the set of accepting states to be the empty set. So, while in $\mathcal{A}_\psi$ a copy of the automaton may accept by either reaching a state from which it proceeds to **true** or visiting states of the form $\varphi_1 V \varphi_2$ infinitely often, in $\mathcal{A}_\psi^{true}$ all copies must reach a state from which they proceed to **true**. Accordingly, $\mathcal{A}_\psi^{true}$ accepts exactly these computations that have a finite prefix that is informative for ψ. To see this, note that such computations can be accepted by a run of $\mathcal{A}_\psi$ in which all the copies eventually reach a state that is associated with propositional assertions that are satisfied. Now, let $fin(\mathcal{A}_\psi^{true})$ be $\mathcal{A}_\psi^{true}$ when regarded as an automaton on finite words; we claim that we have constructed an automaton for informative prefixes [32] (see also [25,27,33]).

Theorem 2. *For every formula ψ, the automaton $fin(\mathcal{A}_{\neg\psi}^{true})$ accepts exactly the prefixes that are informative for ψ.*

We note that searching for informative prefixes rather than for bad prefixes is the basic idea underlying finite failure of temporal formulas in [3,22]. Thus, the construction of $fin(\mathcal{A}_{\neg\psi}^{true})$ essentially extracts from ψ its "informative safety" part (a safety property is a property whose failure is always witnessed by a bad prefix).

The automaton $fin(\mathcal{A}_{\neg\psi}^{true})$ is an alternating automaton, and it is compiled into a non-deterministic automaton. All that remains now is to apply a determinization construction and we get a monitor automaton for informative prefixes. We have thus accomplished the three goals we set out: (1) Informative prefixes provide an approximation to bad prefixes, using the *standard* semantics of LTL; (2) The construction applies to the *full* assertion language, with no need to define special fragments; (3) the compilation into deterministic monitors is very close to the compilation into nondeterministic automata, as it requires just a final determinization construction. Of course, automata determinization is exponential in the worst case, so the final step is far from trivial and is discussed further below. (Note, however, that directly constructing of deterministic monitors from LTL formulas, by induction on the structure of the formula, as in [12,28], can yield monitors of nonelementary size [3], unless care is taken to minimize the monitor after each step of the induction.)

A nondeterministic automaton over finite words is a tuple $\mathcal{A} = \langle \Sigma, Q, \rho, Q_0, F \rangle$, where $\rho : Q \times \Sigma \to 2^Q$ is the transition function. To determinize, one applies the subset construction and obtains $\mathcal{A}^d = \langle \Sigma, 2^Q, \{Q_0\}, \rho^d, F^d \rangle$, where $F^d = \{P : P \cap F \neq \emptyset\}$,

---

[3] That is, the blow-up may not be bounded by any finite tower of exponentials.

and $\rho^d(P, a) = \cup_{s \in P} \rho(s, a)$. Note that in our case the nondeterministic automaton is obtained via a potentially exponential translation from an alternating automaton [15]. Thus, the translation from an alternating automaton to a deterministic automaton is potentially doubly exponential [15].

One way to avoid this blow-up is to avoid constructing $\mathcal{A}^d$. Instead, we can simulate $\mathcal{A}^d$ *on the fly*. Given a finite trace $a_0, \ldots, a_{n-1}$, we construct a run $P_0, \ldots, P_n$ of $\mathcal{A}^d$ as follows: $P_0 = \{Q_0\}$, and $P_{i+1} = \rho^d(P_i, a_i)$. Note that each state of $\mathcal{A}^d$ in this run is of size linear in the size of $\mathcal{A}$. Thus, we have avoided the exponential blowup of the determinization construction, with the price of having to compute transitions on the fly. To implement this the nondeterministic automaton is represented implicitly. Recall that informative prefixes are accepted by the alternating automaton $fin(\mathcal{A}_\psi^{true}) = \langle 2^{AP}, S, \delta, \{s_0\}, \emptyset \rangle$, where $S = 2^{cl(\psi)}$ and $s_0 = \psi$. We can represent a nondeterministic automaton that is equivalent to $fin(\mathcal{A}_\psi^{true})$ as a *nondeterministic sequential circuit*, where we consider AP as the set of input variables and S as the set of state variables. (That is, the state set of the nondeterministic automaton is $Q = 2^S$.) Finally, the transition relation of the circuit is represented as a Boolean function f with domain $2^{AP} \times 2^S \times 2^S$: $f(a, P, P') = 1$ precisely when P' satisfies $\delta(p, a)$ for all $p \in P$. We can describe this function as the conjunction of constraints of the form $p \wedge a \rightarrow next(\delta(p, a))$, where *next* replaces each variable s by its primed version s', referring to the value of s in the next cycle. The initial and final state of the nondeterministic automaton can be expressed as Boolean functions over 2^S; the representation has size that is linear in the size of the input formula. Note that since a state of the nondeterministic automaton is an element of 2^S, a state of $\mathcal{A}^d$ is a subset of 2^S. Thus, a state of $\mathcal{A}^d$ can be represented via OBDD over the variables in S, and the next state function of ρ^d can be computed using an OBDD-based image operation.

It may seem surprising to consider using OBDD operations that are known to be quite "heavy" in formal-verification applications. There is a fundamental difference, however, between the symbolic operations used here and the symbolic operations used in the model checking. In the model checking, we conduct a breadth-first search over the state space of the design. In essence, we simulate $\mathcal{A}^d$ across *all* possible traces. Here, we simulate $\mathcal{A}^d$ over a *single* trace, so one would expect the OBDDs to be significantly smaller. In practice, however, we discovered that OBDDs operations did slow the simulator significantly, and symbolic simulation did not prove to be a viable approach.

A more successful approach is to construct the nondeterministic automaton *explicitly*. This translation can be exponential in the worst case, but a lot of research has been reported on optimizing this translation (cf. [21,24,37]) and an unacceptable blow-up is rarely seen in practice. Once the nondeterministic automaton $\mathcal{A}$ is represented explicitly, the deterministic automaton $\mathcal{A}^d$ can be represented *implicitly*, as a *deterministic sequential circuit*. That is, every proposition in AP is viewed as an input signal and every element of Q is viewed as a sequential element. The initial state of A^d is the one in which precisely the elements in Q_0 are assigned 1 and the accepting states are the one in which some element in F is assigned 1. Finally, with each element $q \in Q$ we associate a Boolean transition function $f_q : 2^Q \times 2^{AP} \rightarrow \{0, 1\}$ defined as follows: $f_q(P, a) = 1$ if $q \in \rho^d(P, a)$.

By viewing A^d as a *deterministic* sequential circuit, we can synthesize an RTL representation of A^d from A with *no* blowup. The advantage of using RTL representation is that it matches the representation used in dynamic verification, as both design and assertion are now represented in RTL. We show in Section 4 that this approach yields significant improvement in performance over the symbolic-simulation approach.

However, as was mentioned in the introduction, the symbolic and the deterministic approaches may be successfully combined when some of the variables used in the assertion are symbolic.

Example 2. Consider the following safety property: `next a wuntil next b`. The property is first negated and then the negation is propagated:

`next !b until ((next !a) & (next !b))`. The negated property is then translated into an alternating automaton on finite words; see Fig. 1.

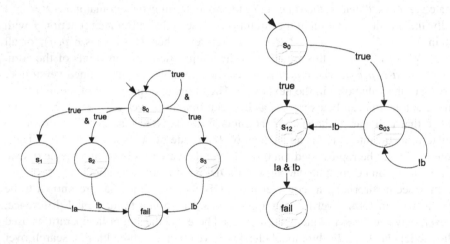

Fig. 1. Alternating automaton   **Fig. 2.** Nondeterministic automaton

For the non-deterministic compilation the alternating automaton can be converted to an implicitly represented nondeterministic automaton:

$$s_0 \rightarrow (s_1' \wedge s_2') \vee (s_0' \wedge s_3')$$
$$s_1 \wedge \neg a \rightarrow fail$$
$$s_2 \wedge \neg b \rightarrow fail$$
$$s_3 \wedge \neg b \rightarrow fail$$

Alternatively, for the deterministic compilation we can convert the nondeterministic automaton to an explicit representation [4]; see Fig. 2. Finally, the explicitly represented nondeterministic automaton can be converted to an implicitly represented deterministic automaton, using an RTL; we use here Verilog. (In the following code `sysclk` is an auxiliary signal corresponding to the reference clock):

```
reg s0, s12, s03;
wire fail, sysclk;
assign fail = s12 && !a & !b;
initial begin
    s0 = 1'b1; s12 = 1'b0; s03 = 1'b0;
end
always @(posedge sysclk) begin
    s0    <= 1'b0;
    s12   <= s0 || !b && s03;
    s03 <= s0 || s03 && !b;
end
```

3 Dynamic-Verification Framework

ARCHITECTURE: This framework was developed for dynamic verification of ForSpec assertions. It can easily be adapted to other LTL-based property specification languages, such as PSL or SVA, by changing the compiler front-end.

The framework consists of two parts: a compiler and a run-time system. The compiler first checks whether the assertion is deterministic. If not, it generates an implicit representation of a nondeterministic automaton. For such assertions, the compiler produces a persistent OBDD representation of the nondeterministic automaton.

Otherwise, is generates an explicit representation of the nondeterministic automaton, cf. [4]. Although this stage theoretically involves an exponential blowup [38], it has always been feasible in practice. Then an RTL-represented deterministic monitor is generated from this automaton.

Explicitly compiled monitors are directly simulated by the run-time system. For implicitly compiled monitors the run-time system generates OBDD-represented states on the fly by means of OBDD operations. The run-time system runs in parallel to the DUT (Design Under Test) simulation environment and reads signal values from it. These signals are used to exercise the monitor. The run-time system queries the DUT model for checker signal changes and reports checker violation or success. The compilation flow overview is shown in Fig. 3; the simulation paradigm is shown in Fig. 4.

COMPILER OPTIMIZATIONS: The compiler applies several optimizations. Some optimizations result in a more efficient synthesis, while others are necessary to avoid the blowup, and to make the compilation feasible. In this section we sketch the following optimizations: reachability analysis, automata minimization, *next* normalization, explicit conjunction, permanent state elimination, and state counting:

Reachability analysis for nondeterministic automata. To analyze a property failure, only states that are backward reachable from the accepting state need to be kept. Other states can be pruned away.

Automata minimization. Automata minimization may be used to synthesize a more efficient code and sometimes to avoid an exponential blowup. The minimization may be held at different stages - at the stage of an alternating, non-deterministic and

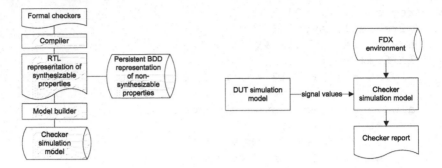

Fig. 3. Compilation flow   **Fig. 4.** Simulation flow

deterministic automaton. (It should be emphasized that the goal is not necessarily to minimize the *number* of the automaton states.)

next normalization. In many cases it pays off to "pull out" *next* operators. For example, consider the property a until next[10] b. It is preferable to rewrite it first as next[10] past(a,10) until b.

Explicit conjunction. If the complemented assertion in PNF has a form of a conjunction $\varphi_1 \wedge \varphi_2$, then it is preferable to construct separate monitors for φ_1 and $\varphi2$ rather than a monitor for $\varphi_1 \wedge \varphi_2$. This is a rather common case, since when we start with an assumption φ and assertion ψ, the complemented assertion is $\phi \wedge \neg\psi$.

Permanent state elimination. The vast majority of the assertions in practice have the form always φ. The standard monitor construction generate an RTL variable that is always on. Such a variable can be eliminated.

State counting. There are cases when the assertion check is delayed by several cycles. i.e., the assertion has a form next[n] A, where n is a positive integer number, and A is an arbitrary assertion. Then instead of synthesizing a thread of n states for next[n], an appropriate counter may be synthesized using $\log n$ variables.

4   Experimental Results

We ran two sets of experiments: the first one was to compare the OBDD-based and the RTL-based implementations of dynamic monitors for ForSpec assertions; the second one was to compare the RTL-based and the transaction-based monitoring for SVA assertions. (Our experiments were run on Intel®Xeon™CPU 3.06GHz with 4GB RAM, using the Linux operating system.)

RTL-BASED VERSUS BDD-BASED MONITORS: The first experiment was to compare the run time of the two implementations for simple assertions, where we scale up a time window. We ran the assertion always a triggers always[0,n] b for different values of n (we refer to the interval $[0, n]$ as the *time window*) for a simulation run of 25,000 clock cycles. The results are shown i n Table 1. The time reported is the *additional* time required to complete the simulation, compared to an assertion-free simulation run (the latter time is less than one second). We used a big industrial design and the VCS simulation engine. Note that while the number of OBDD variables grows logarithmically in n, the number of RTL variables grows linearly in n. The run time of both implementations of the monitors grows linearly with the size of the time, but the slope is quite steeper for the OBDD implementation.

Table 1. Time Window Scaling

Window size	# BDD vars	#RTL variables	Time BDD (sec)	Time RTL (sec)
1	1	1	4.2	0.22
500	9	500	5.82	0.85
1,000	10	1,000	7.81	1.43
1,500	11	1,500	10.85	1.95
2,000	11	2,000	14.6	2.46

The second experiment was to check the effect of the number of assertions on the run time. We execute n assertions of the form `always` a_i `triggers next` b_i, for different design signals a_i and b_i, for a simulation run of 25,000 clock cycles. The results are shown in Table 2. Again, we report on incremental running time. We can see that the number of assertions has a significant impact for the OBDD implementation, whereas the impact is marginal for the RTL implementation. Therefore the RTL implementation can handle large amount of assertions, while the OBDD implementation is capable of handling only a few tens of assertions. The RTL implementation proved to be efficient in handling thousands of real-life assertions; e.g., 10,000 assertions cause only a 10% overhead for the full-chip simulation of a CPU design.

Table 2. Assertion Scaling

n	# BDD vars	#RTL states	Time BDD (sec)	Time RTL (sec)
1	1	1	3.78	0.22
5	5	5	10.38	0.24
10	10	10	18.24	0.25
15	15	15	28.69	0.26
20	20	20	40.21	0.27
25	25	25	57.4	0.30

The third experiment was to compare between the two implementations for real-life assertions. Only very few real-life monitors, covering a small number of assertions, can be run using pure OBDD implementation without a significant slow-down. The results are shown in Table 3. Again, we can see that the RTL implementation runs in more than one order of magnitude faster than the OBDD implementation.

RTL-BASED VERSUS TRANSACTION-BASED MONITORING: As discussed in the introduction, many industrial assertion monitors use a transaction-based approach [16]. This approach is problematic in two aspects: 1) It is suitable mostly to assertions of the form r_1 `triggers` r_2, where r_1 and r_2 are regular events; it is difficult to adapt

Table 3. Real-life Monitors

Test number	#cycles	#assertions	Time BDD (sec)	Time RTL (sec)
1	4630	8	3.97	0.49
2	4630	9	5.2	0.52
3	4630	27	48.69	0.91
4	4630	25	9.41	0.55
5	1724	4	0.78	0.26
6	1724	8	1.38	0.17
7	1724	23	4.79	0.16

to general temporal assertions. 2) The performance of transaction-based monitors is very sensitive to the number of outstanding transactions. Consequently, the standard methodology recommends to limit the number of the outstanding transactions using time windows [10], which may be inefficient for formal-verification tools. This results in different assertions written for formal and dynamic verification.

We compared the performance of VCS, which implements transaction-based monitoring, with automata-based monitors. We measured only the run time overhead introduced by assertion monitoring for a simulation run of 100,000 cycles.

The following simple Verilog model has been used:

```
module test;
logic clk, a, b, c;
initial begin
    a = 1'b1; b = 1'b0; c = 1'b1; clk = 1'b0;
    #1000000 b = 1'b1;
    #1000000 $finish;
end
always #10 clk = !clk;
// assertion goes here
endmodule
```

with the following SVA assertions:

```
1. @(posedge clk) a ##[0:$] b |=> c
2. @(posedge clk) a[*0:1000] ##1 b |=> c
3. @(posedge clk) a |=> c[*1000]
```

The results are shown in Table 4.

Table 4. RTL monitors vs. VCS

	Assertion 1	Assertion 2	Assertion 3
RTL-based monitors	1.46	3.58	3.58
VCS	525.13	26.71	7.70

Our results clearly show the advantage of the RTL-based approach when the number of active transactions is not bounded by a small constant. The RTL-based approach is insensitive to the number of active transactions since the assertion has been compiled into a finite-state monitor.

5 Discussion

We described here a framework for dynamic verification of temporal assertions. We showed how to obtain deterministic compilation for dynamic verification that is as close as possible to the nondeterministic compilation of temporal assertions for formal verification. Further research is called for, in view of our results. A general issue is how to optimize the construction of monitors. For example, it is known that deterministic automata can be minimized canonically [31]. We do not know, however, whether it would beneficial to minimize monitors using automata-minimization techniques . On one hand, minimization would reduce the number of state variables in the RTL representation of the monitor; on the other hand, the logic of the transition function may get significantly more complex. More generally, the results here and in [4] show the advantage of using deterministic compilation in various settings of functional design verification. We believe that this issue ought to be investigated also in other settings.

References

1. Y. Abarbanel, I. Beer, L. Gluhovsky, S. Keidar, and Y. Wolfstal. FoCs - automatic generation of simulation checkers from formal specifications. In *Computer Aided Verification, Proc. 12th International Conference*, volume 1855 of *Lecture Notes in Computer Science*, pages 538–542. Springer-Verlag, 2000.
2. K. Albin et al. Property specification language reference manual. Technical Report Version 1.1, Accellera, 2004.
3. R. Armoni, D. Bustan, O. Kupferman, and M.Y. Vardi. Resets vs. aborts in linear temporal logic. In *Proc. 9th International Conference on Tools and algorithms for the construction and analysis of systems*, number 2619 in Lecture Notes in Computer Science, pages 65 – 80. Springer-Verlag, 2003.
4. R. Armoni, S. Egorov, R. Fraer, D. Korchemny, and M.Y. Vardi. Efficient LTL compilation for SAT-based model checking. In *Proc. Int'l Conf. on Computer-Aided Design*, pages 877–884, 2005.
5. R. Armoni, L. Fix, A. Flaisher, R. Gerth, B. Ginsburg, T. Kanza, A. Landver, S. Mador-Haim, E. Singerman, A. Tiemeyer, M.Y. Vardi, and Y. Zbar. The ForSpec temporal logic: A new temporal property-specification logic. In *Proc. 8th International Conference on Tools and Algorithms for the Construction and Analysis of Systems*, volume 2280 of *Lecture Notes in Computer Science*, pages 296–211, Grenoble, France, April 2002. Springer-Verlag.
6. H. Barringer, A. Goldberg, K. Havelund, and K. Sen. Program monitoring with LTL in EAGLE. In *Proc. 18th Int'l Parallel and Distributed Processing Symp.* IEEE Computer Society, 2004.
7. I. Beer, S. Ben-David, C. Eisner, D. Fisman, A. Gringauze, and Y. Rodeh. The temporal logic Sugar. In *Proc. 13th International Conference on Computer Aided Verification*, volume 2102 of *Lecture Notes in Computer Science*, pages 363–367, Paris, France, July 2001. Springer-Verlag.

8. L. Bening and H. Foster. *Principles of verifiable RTL design – a functional coding style supporting verification processes.* Springer, 2001.
9. B. Bentley. High level validation of next-generation microprocessors. In *Proc. IEEE Int'l Workshop on High Level Design Validation and Test*, pages 31–35, 2002.
10. J. Bergeron, E. Cerny, A. Hunter, and A. Nightingale. *Verification Methodology Manual for SystemVerilog.* Springer, 2005.
11. P. Biesse, T. Leonard, and A. Mokkedem. Finding bugs in an alpha microprocessor using satisfiability solvers. In *Computer Aided Verification, Proc. 13th International Conference*, volume 2102 of *Lecture Notes in Computer Science*, pages 454–464. Springer-Verlag, 2001.
12. M. Boule and Z. Zilic. Incorporating efficient assertion checkers into hardware emulation. In *Proc. 23rd Int'l Conf. on Computer Design*, pages 221–228. IEEE Computer Society, 2005.
13. R.E. Bryant. Graph-based algorithms for boolean-function manipulation. *IEEE Trans. on Computers*, C-35(8), 1986.
14. D. Bustan, A. Flaisher, O. Grumberg, O. Kupferman, and M.Y. Vardi. Regular vacuity. In *Proc. 13th Advanced Research Working Conference on Correct Hardware Design and Verification Methods*, volume 3725 of *Lecture Notes in Computer Science*, pages 191–206. Springer-Verlag, 2005.
15. A.K. Chandra, D.C. Kozen, and L.J. Stockmeyer. Alternation. *Journal of the Association for Computing Machinery*, 28(1):114–133, January 1981.
16. K.H. Chang, W.T. Tu, Y.J. Yeh, and Kuo S.Y. A simulation-based temporal assertion checker for PSL. In *Proc. 46th IEEE Int'l Midwest Stmp. on Circuits and Systems*, pages 1528–1531. IEEE Computer Society, 2003.
17. E.M. Clarke, O. Grumberg, and D. Peled. *Model Checking.* MIT Press, 1999.
18. B. Cohen. *Using PSL/Sugar with Verilog and VHDL, Guide to Property Specification Language for ABV.* Addison-Wesley, 2003.
19. F. Copty, L. Fix, R. Fraer, E. Giunchiglia, G. Kamhi, A. Tacchella, and M.Y. Vardi. Benefits of bounded model checking at an industrial setting. In *Computer Aided Verification, Proc. 13th International Conference*, volume 2102 of *Lecture Notes in Computer Science*, pages 436–453. Springer-Verlag, 2001.
20. M. d'Amorim and G. Rosu. Efficient monitoring of omega-languages. In *Proc. 17th Int'l Conf. on Computer Aided Verification*, volume 3576 of *Lecture Notes in Computer Science*, pages 364–378. Springer, 2005.
21. N. Daniele, F. Guinchiglia, and M.Y. Vardi. Improved automata generation for linear temporal logic. In *Computer Aided Verification, Proc. 11th International Conference*, volume 1633 of *Lecture Notes in Computer Science*, pages 249–260. Springer-Verlag, 1999.
22. C. Eisner, D. Fisman, J. Havlicek, Y. Lustig, A. McIsaac, and D. Van Campenhout. Reasoning with temporal logic on truncated paths. In *Proc. 15th Int'l Conf. on Computer Aided Verification*, volume 2725 of *Lecture Notes in Computer Science*, pages 27–39. Springer, 2003.
23. E.A. Emerson. Temporal and modal logic. In J. Van Leeuwen, editor, *Handbook of Theoretical Computer Science*, volume B, chapter 16, pages 997–1072. Elsevier, MIT Press, 1990.
24. K. Etessami and G.J. Holzmann. Optimizing Büchi automata. In *Proc. 11th Int'l Conf. on Concurrency Theory*, Lecture Notes in Computer Science 1877, pages 153–167. Springer-Verlag, 2000.
25. B. Finkbeiner and H. Sipma. Checking finite traces using alternating automata. *Electr. Notes Theor. Comput. Sci.*, 55(2), 2001.
26. D. Fisman. The Subset of Linear Violation. *The Weizmann Institute of Science, IBM Haifa Research Lab*, 2005.
27. M. Geilen. On the construction of monitors for temporal logic properties. *Electr. Notes Theor. Comput. Sci.*, 55(2), 2001.

28. S.V. Gheorghita and R. Grigore. Constructing checkers from PSL properties. In *Proc. 15th Int'l Conf. on Control Systems and Computer Science* , *Vol. 2*, pages 757–762, 2005.

29. D. Giannakopoulou and K. Havelund. Automata-based verification of temporal properties on running programs. In *Proc. 16th International Conference on Automated Software Engineering*, pages 412–416. IEEE Computer Society, 2001.

30. D.W. Hoffmann, J. Ruf, T. Kropf, and W. Rosenstiel. Simulation meets verification: Checking temporal properties in SystemC. In *Proc. 26th EUROMICRO 2000 Conference*, page 1435. IEEE Computer Society, 2000.

31. J.E. Hopcroft and J.D. Ullman. *Introduction to Automata Theory, Languages, and Computation*. Addison-Wesley, 1979.

32. O. Kupferman and M.Y. Vardi. Model checking of safety properties. *Formal methods in System Design*, 19(3):291–314, November 2001.

33. T. Latvala. Efficient model checking of safety properties. In *Proc. 10th SPIN Workshop on Model Checking of Software*, volume 2648 of *Lecture Notes in Computer Science*, pages 74–88, 2003.

34. S. Miyano and T. Hayashi. Alternating finite automata on ω-words. *Theoretical Computer Science*, 32:321–330, 1984.

35. D. Pidan, S. Keider-Barner, M. Moulin, and D. Fisman. Optimized algorithms for dynamic verification. Technical Report FP6-IST-507219, PROSYD, 2005.

36. A. Pnueli. The temporal logic of programs. In *Proc. 18th IEEE Symp. on Foundation of Computer Science*, pages 46–57, 1977.

37. F. Somenzi and R. Bloem. Efficient Büchi automata from LTL formulae. In *Computer Aided Verification, Proc. 12th International Conference*, volume 1855 of *Lecture Notes in Computer Science*, pages 248–263. Springer-Verlag, 2000.

38. M.Y. Vardi. An automata-theoretic approach to linear temporal logic. In F. Moller and G. Birtwistle, editors, *Logics for Concurrency: Structure versus Automata*, volume 1043 of *Lecture Notes in Computer Science*, pages 238–266. Springer-Verlag, Berlin, 1996.

39. M.Y. Vardi and P. Wolper. An automata-theoretic approach to automatic program verification. In *Proc. 1st Symp. on Logic in Computer Science*, pages 332–344, Cambridge, June 1986.

40. M.Y. Vardi and P. Wolper. Reasoning about infinite computations. *Information and Computation*, 115(1):1–37, November 1994.

41. S. Vijayaraghavan and M. Ramanathan. *A Practical Guide for SystemVerilog Assertions*. Springer, 2005.

Robustness of Temporal Logic Specifications

Georgios E. Fainekos[1] and George J. Pappas[2]

[1] Department of Computer and Information Science, Univ. of Pennsylvania
`fainekos@cis.upenn.edu`
[2] Department of Electrical and Systems Engineering, Univ. of Pennsylvania
`pappasg@ee.upenn.edu`

Abstract. In this paper, we consider the robust interpretation of metric temporal logic (MTL) formulas over timed sequences of states. For systems whose states are equipped with nontrivial metrics, such as continuous, hybrid, or general metric transition systems, robustness is not only natural, but also a critical measure of system performance. In this paper, we define robust, multi-valued semantics for MTL formulas, which capture not only the usual Boolean satisfiability of the formula, but also topological information regarding the distance, ε, from unsatisfiability. We prove that any other timed trace which remains ε-close to the initial one also satisfies the same MTL specification with the usual Boolean semantics. We derive a computational procedure for determining an under-approximation to the robustness degree ε of the specification with respect to a given finite timed state sequence. Our approach can be used for robust system simulation and testing, as well as form the basis for simulation-based verification.

Keywords: Robustness, Metric spaces, Monitoring, Timed State Sequences, Metric and Linear Temporal Logic.

1 Introduction

Model checking [1] has been proven to be a very useful tool for the verification of the properties of software and hardware systems. The tools and methodologies developed for such systems do not naturally extend to systems whose state space is some general metric space, for example linear, nonlinear and hybrid systems. In this case, the model checking problem becomes harder and in most of the cases is undecidable [2]. Therefore, the verification of such systems still relies heavily on methods that involve monitoring and testing [3,4,5,6]. Furthermore, general metric transition systems either model physical processes or the interaction between some software and/or hardware system and the continuous physical world. Up to now no formal model exists that can capture accurately the behaviour of such a system – especially if it also exhibits a chaotic behaviour. Moreover, these types of systems have a certain degree of sensitivity with respect to initial conditions or to system parameters. This has one major implication. Deciding the Boolean truth value of a temporal logic specification with respect to a system's trajectory - in some of the cases - does not allow us to draw any

K. Havelund et al. (Eds.): FATES/RV 2006, LNCS 4262, pp. 178–192, 2006.
© Springer-Verlag Berlin Heidelberg 2006

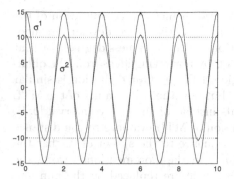 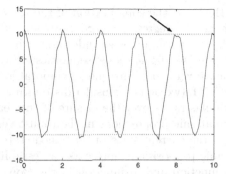

Fig. 1. Two trajectories σ^1 and σ^2 which satisfy the specification: $\Box(\pi_1 \rightarrow \Diamond_{\leq 2}\pi_2)$. Here, $\mathcal{O}(\pi_1) = \mathbb{R}_{\leq -10}$ and $\mathcal{O}(\pi_1) = \mathbb{R}_{\geq 10}$.

Fig. 2. The trajectory σ^2 modified by random noise. The arrow points to the point in time where the property fails.

conclusions about the real system. A small perturbation of the trajectory or the parameters of the system can lead to a different truth value for the formula.

For example, consider the trajectories σ^1 and σ^2 in Fig. 1. Both of them satisfy the same specification "if the value of the state drops below -10, then it should also raise above 10 within 2 time units". Nevertheless, a visual inspection of Fig. 1 indicates that there exists a qualitative difference between σ^1 and σ^2. The later "barely" satisfies the specification. Indeed as we can see in Fig. 2, adding a bounded noise on σ^2 renders the property unsatisfiable on σ^2.

In order to differentiate between such trajectories of a system, we introduce the concept of robustness degree. Informally, we define the robustness degree to be the bound on the perturbation that the trajectory[1] can tolerate without changing the truth value of a specification expressed in the Linear [7] or Metric Temporal Logic [8]. To formally define the robustness degree, we take a topological perspective. We consider finite timed state sequences which take values in some space X equipped with a metric d. If these trajectories are of length n, then each sequence of states is isomorphic to a point in X^n, which is the space of all possible trajectories of length n. In order to quantify how close are two different state sequences in X^n, we define the notion of distance using a metric ρ on the space X^n. Given an LTL or MTL formula ϕ, we can partition the space X^n into two sets: the set P^ϕ of state sequences that satisfy ϕ and the set N^ϕ of state sequences that do not satisfy ϕ. Then, the formal definition of robustness comes naturally, it is just the distance of a state sequence σ from the set P^ϕ or its complement N^ϕ. Using the degree of robustness and the metric ρ, we can define an open ball (tube) around σ and, therefore, we can be sure that any state sequence σ' that remains within the open ball also stays either in P^ϕ or in N^ϕ.

---

[1] We should bring to notice that we are not interested in the properties of the (possibly) continuous trajectory, but in the properties of its finite representation. Here, we model the finite representation of a continuous trajectory using timed state sequences. Under certain assumptions about the structure of the system, the results in this paper could be mapped back to the continuous case.

However, the computation of the set P^ϕ and, hence, the computation of the robustness degree are hard problems. To address them, we develop an algorithm that computes an under-approximation of the robustness degree. For that purpose, we define robust semantics for MTL by borrowing ideas from the quantitative version of the linear temporal logic QLTL [9]. Our definition is similar to QLTL (we do not consider discounting), but now the truth values of the MTL formulas range over the closure of the reals instead of the closed interval $[0, 1]$. The atomic propositions in the robust version of MTL evaluate to the distance from the current state in the timed state sequence to the subset of X that the atomic proposition represents. As established in the aforementioned work, the conjunction and disjunction in the Boolean logic are replaced by the min and max operations. Here, the logical negation is replaced by the usual negation of the reals. We prove that when an MTL formula is evaluated with robust semantics over a timed state sequence $\mathcal{T}_1$, then it returns an under-approximation ε of the robustness degree and, therefore, any other timed state sequence $\mathcal{T}_2$ that remains ε-close to $\mathcal{T}_1$ satisfies the same specification. We conclude the paper by presenting a monitoring algorithm (similar to [10,11]) that is based on the robust semantics of MTL and computes the under-approximation of the robustness degree.

Application-wise the importance of the main contribution of this paper is straightforward: if a system has the property that under bounded disturbances its trajectories remain δ close to the nominal one and, also, its robustness degree with respect to an MTL formula ϕ is $\varepsilon > \delta$, then we know that all the system's trajectories also satisfy the same specification. The timing bounds on the temporal operators, that is the use of MTL instead of LTL, can be justified if one considers that the applications of such a framework are within the systems area. For example, signal processing and simulations of physical systems most of the times do require such constraints. The methodology that we present in this paper can be readily used in several applications such as Qualitative Simulation [12], verification using simulation [13], mobile robot path planning [14] and in behavioral robotics [15].

2 Metric Temporal Logic over Timed State Sequences

2.1 Metric Spaces

Let $\mathbb{R}$ be the set of the real numbers, $\mathbb{Q}$ the set of the rational numbers and $\mathbb{N}$ the set of the natural numbers. We denote the extended real number line by $\overline{\mathbb{R}} = \mathbb{R} \cup \{\pm\infty\}$. Furthermore, we let $\mathbb{B} = \{\top, \bot\}$, where $\top$ and $\bot$ are the symbols for the boolean constants *true* and *false* respectively. If $(X, \leq)$ is a totally ordered set with an ordering relation $\leq$, then an interval of X is denoted by $[a, b]_X = \{x \in X \mid a \leq x \leq b\}$. When $X = \mathbb{R}$, we drop the subscript $\mathbb{R}$. In addition, we use pseudo-arithmetic expressions to represent certain subsets of the aforementioned sets. For example, $\mathbb{R}_{\geq 0}$ denotes the subset of the reals whose elements are greater or equal to zero. If C is a set, then $cl(C)$ denotes the *closure* of the set C. Let (X, d) be a metric space, i.e. a set X whose topology is induced by the metric d.

Definition 1 (Metric). *A metric on a set X is a positive function $d : X \times X \to \mathbb{R}_{\geq 0}$, such that the three following properties hold*

1. $\forall x_1, x_2, x_3 \in X . d(x_1, x_3) \leq d(x_1, x_2) + d(x_2, x_3)$
2. $\forall x_1, x_2 \in X . d(x_1, x_2) = 0 \Leftrightarrow x_1 = x_2$
3. $\forall x_1, x_2 \in X . d(x_1, x_2) = d(x_2, x_1)$

Using a metric d, we can define the distance of a point $x \in X$ from a set $C \subseteq X$. Intuitively, this distance is the shortest distance from x to all the points in C. In a similar way, the depth of a point x in a set C is defined to be the shortest distance of x from the boundary of C. Both the notions of distance and depth (Fig. 3) will play a fundamental role in the definition of the robustness degree (see Sect. 3).

Definition 2 (Distance, Depth, Signed Distance [16] §8). *Let $x \in X$ be a point, $C \subseteq X$ be a set and d be a metric. Then, we define the*

- Distance *from x to C to be* $\mathbf{dist}_d(x, C) := \inf\{d(x, y) \mid y \in cl(C)\}$
- Depth *of x in C to be* $\mathbf{depth}_d(x, C) := \mathbf{dist}_d(x, X \backslash C)$
- Signed Distance *from x to C to be*

$$\mathbf{Dist}_d(x, C) := \begin{cases} -\mathbf{dist}_d(x, C) & \textit{if } x \notin C \\ \mathbf{depth}_d(x, C) & \textit{if } x \in C \end{cases}$$

We should point out that we use the extended definition of supremum and infimum, where $\sup \emptyset = -\infty$ and $\inf \emptyset = +\infty$. Also of importance is the notion of an open ball of radius ε centered at a point $x \in X$.

Definition 3 (ε-Ball). *Given a metric d, a radius $\varepsilon \in \overline{\mathbb{R}}_{>0}$ and a point $x \in X$, the open ε-ball centered at x is defined as $B_d(x, \varepsilon) = \{y \in X \mid d(x, y) < \varepsilon\}$.*

It is easy to verify that if the distance ($\mathbf{dist}_d$) of a point x from a set C is $\varepsilon > 0$, then $B_d(x, \varepsilon) \cap C = \emptyset$. And similarly, if $\mathbf{depth}_d(x, C) = \varepsilon > 0$, then $B_d(x, \varepsilon) \subseteq C$.

2.2 Timed State Sequences in Metric Spaces

In this paper, we use *timed state sequences* (TSS) to describe the behavior of a real-time system. Typical models of real time systems are the formalisms of hybrid automata, timed automata, linear and non-linear systems. A *state* of such a system is a point x in a metric space $\mathcal{X} = (X, d)$. With each state of the system x we associate a *time period* Δt, which represents the duration between the occurrence of the current and the previous system states.

Let AP be a finite set of atomic propositions, then the *predicate mapping* $\mathcal{O} : AP \to 2^X$ is a set valued function that assigns to each atomic proposition $\pi \in AP$

a set of states $\mathcal{O}(\pi) \subseteq X$. Furthermore, if the collection of sets $\{\mathcal{O}(\pi)\}_{\pi \in AP}$ is not a cover of X, i.e. $\cup_{\pi \in AP} \mathcal{O}(\pi) \neq X$, then we add to AP a special proposition π_c that maps to the set $\mathcal{O}(\pi_c) = X \setminus \cup_{\pi \in AP} \mathcal{O}(\pi)$. Therefore, we can now define the "inverse" map of $\mathcal{O}$ as $\mathcal{O}^{-1}(x) = \{\pi \in AP \mid x \in \mathcal{O}(\pi)\}$ for $x \in X$. If $x \in \mathcal{O}(\pi)$, then we say that x is a π state. Notice that using the notion of distance, we can quantify how close is a state x to becoming a π state.

The execution of a system can result in an infinite or finite sequence of states. In this paper, we focus on finite sequences of states, which can model the finite representation of a real valued signal or the result of the numerical integration of differential equations.

Definition 4 (TSS). *A timed state sequence $\mathcal{T}$ is a tuple $(\sigma, \tau, \mathcal{O})$ where: $\sigma = x_0, x_1, \ldots, x_n$ is a sequence of states, $\tau = \Delta t_0, \Delta t_1, \ldots, \Delta t_n$ is a sequence of time periods and $\mathcal{O} : AP \to 2^X$ is a predicate mapping; such that $n \in \mathbb{N}$, $x_i \in X$ and $\Delta t_i \in \mathbb{R}_{\geq 0}$ for all $i \in \{0, 1, \ldots, n\}$ and $\Delta t_0, \Delta t_0 + \Delta t_1, \ldots, \sum_{i=0}^{n} \Delta t_i$ is a strictly monotonically increasing sequence.*

We let σ_i and τ_i denote x_i and Δt_i respectively. By convention, we set $\Delta t_0 = 0$. We define $\sigma \downarrow_i$ to be the prefix of the state sequence σ, i.e. $\sigma \downarrow_i = x_0, x_1, \ldots, x_i$, while $\sigma \uparrow_i$ is the suffix, i.e. $\sigma \uparrow_i = x_i, x_{i+1}, \ldots, x_n$. The length of $\sigma = x_0, x_1, \ldots, x_n$ is defined to be $|\sigma| = n + 1$. For convenience, we let $|\mathcal{T}| = |\tau| = |\sigma|$ and $\mathcal{T} \uparrow_i = (\sigma \uparrow_i, \tau \uparrow_i, \mathcal{O})$ (similarly for $\downarrow$).

In the following, we use the convention that $\mathcal{T}$ and $\mathcal{S}$ denote the timed state sequences $\mathcal{T} = (\sigma, \tau, \mathcal{O})$ and $\mathcal{S} = (\sigma', \tau, \mathcal{O})$ (and similarly for their superscripted versions). We define Σ_X to be the set of all possible timed state sequences in the space $\mathcal{X} = (X, d)$ and $\Sigma(\mathcal{T})$ to be the set of all possible timed state sequences with the same predicate mapping $\mathcal{O}$ and the same sequence of time periods as $\mathcal{T}$. That is $\Sigma(\mathcal{T}) = \{(\sigma', \tau, \mathcal{O}) \mid \sigma' \in X^{|\mathcal{T}|}\}$. Notice that the sequence σ is isomorphic to a point in the product space $X^{|\sigma|}$.

2.3   Metric Temporal Logic over Finite Timed State Sequences

The Metric Temporal Logic (MTL) [8] is an extension of the Linear Temporal Logic (LTL) [7]. In MTL, the syntax of the logic is extended to include timing constraints on the usual temporal operators of LTL. Using LTL specifications we can check qualitative timing properties, while with MTL specifications quantitative timing properties. Recently, it was shown by Ouaknine and Worrell [17] that MTL is decidable over finite timed state sequences. In this section, we review the basics of MTL with point-based semantics (as opposed to interval based semantics [18]) over finite timed state sequences.

Definition 5 (Syntax of MTL). *Let AP be the set of atomic propositions, D the set of truth degree constants and $\mathcal{I}$ an interval of $\mathbb{R}_{\geq 0}$ with rational endpoints. The set Φ_D of all well-formed formulas (wff) is the smallest set such that*

- *it contains all the members of D and AP, i.e. $D, AP \subseteq \Phi_D$*
- *if $\phi_1, \phi_2 \in \Phi_D$, then $\neg\phi_1, \phi_1 \vee \phi_2, \bigcirc_{\mathcal{I}}\phi_1, \phi_1 \mathcal{U}_{\mathcal{I}}\phi_2$ belong to Φ_D*

In the following, we fix the set AP, while the set D varies. As usual, $\phi_1 \wedge \phi_2 = \neg(\neg\phi_1 \vee \neg\phi_2)$ and $\phi_1 \to \phi_2 = \neg\phi_1 \vee \phi_2$. Here, $\bigcirc_{\mathcal{I}}$ is the *next* time operator and $\mathcal{U}_{\mathcal{I}}$ the *until* operator. We can also define the common temporal operators *eventually* $\Diamond_{\mathcal{I}}\phi = \top \mathcal{U}_{\mathcal{I}}\phi$ and *always* $\Box_{\mathcal{I}}\phi = \neg\Diamond_{\mathcal{I}}\neg\phi$. In the case where $\mathcal{I} = [0, +\infty)$, we remove the subscript $\mathcal{I}$ from the temporal operators, i.e. we just write $\mathcal{U}$, $\bigcirc$, $\Diamond$ and $\Box$. When all the subscripts of the temporal operators are of the form $[0, +\infty)$, then the MTL formula ϕ reduces to an LTL formula and we can ignore the time periods.

The subscript $\mathcal{I}$ imposes timing constraints on the temporal operators. The interval $\mathcal{I}$ can be open, half-open or closed, bounded or unbounded. The function lb returns the lower (or left) bound of the interval $\mathcal{I}$ whereas the function ub returns the upper (or right) bound. Note that $lb(\mathcal{I}), ub(\mathcal{I}) \in \mathbb{Q}_{\geq 0}$ and that it could be the case that $ub(\mathcal{I}) = lb(\mathcal{I})$, i.e. $\mathcal{I}$ is a singleton. For any $t \in \mathbb{Q}$, we define $\mathcal{I} + t = \{t' + t \mid t' \in \mathcal{I}\}$. Also, we do not consider relative [10] and absolute congruences [19] and we have not included the *since* and *last* temporal operators (the past fragment) in the syntax of MTL.

Metric Temporal Logic (MTL) formulas are interpreted over timed state sequences $\mathcal{T}$ with $|\mathcal{T}| > 0$. The constraint $|\mathcal{T}| > 0$ implies that the sequence has at least one state, that is we ignore the pathological cases of empty state sequences. In this paper, we denote formula satisfiability using a membership function $\langle\!\langle \phi \rangle\!\rangle : \Sigma_X \to \mathbb{B}$ instead of the usual notation $\mathcal{T} \models \phi$. The functional approach enables us to maintain a uniform presentation throughout this paper. We say that a timed state sequence $\mathcal{T}$ satisfies the formula ϕ when $\langle\!\langle \phi \rangle\!\rangle(\mathcal{T}) = \top$. In this case, we refer to $\mathcal{T}$ as a *model* of ϕ. The set of all models of ϕ is denoted by $\mathcal{L}(\phi)$, i.e. $\mathcal{L}(\phi) = \{\mathcal{T} \in \Sigma_X \mid \langle\!\langle \phi \rangle\!\rangle(\mathcal{T}) = \top\}$.

Definition 6 (Semantics of MTL). *Let* $\mathcal{T} = (\sigma, \tau, \mathcal{O}) \in \Sigma_X$, $v \in \mathbb{B}$, $\pi \in AP$, $i, j \in \mathbb{N}$ *and* $K_{\mathcal{I}}^{\mathcal{T}} = \{i \in [0, |\mathcal{T}| - 1]_{\mathbb{N}} \mid \sum_{j=0}^{i} \tau_j \in \mathcal{I}\}$, *then the semantics*[2] *of any formula* $\phi \in \Phi_{\mathbb{B}}$ *are inductively defined by*

$$\langle\!\langle v \rangle\!\rangle(\mathcal{T}) := v$$

$$\langle\!\langle \pi \rangle\!\rangle(\mathcal{T}) := \sigma_0 \in \mathcal{O}(\pi)$$

$$\langle\!\langle \neg\psi \rangle\!\rangle(\mathcal{T}) := \neg\langle\!\langle \psi \rangle\!\rangle(\mathcal{T})$$

$$\langle\!\langle \phi_1 \vee \phi_2 \rangle\!\rangle(\mathcal{T}) := \langle\!\langle \phi_1 \rangle\!\rangle(\mathcal{T}) \vee \langle\!\langle \phi_2 \rangle\!\rangle(\mathcal{T})$$

$$\langle\!\langle \bigcirc_{\mathcal{I}}\psi \rangle\!\rangle(\mathcal{T}) := \begin{cases} (\tau_1 \in \mathcal{I}) \wedge \langle\!\langle \psi \rangle\!\rangle(\mathcal{T}\!\uparrow_1) & \text{if } |\mathcal{T}| > 1 \\ \bot & \text{otherwise} \end{cases}$$

$$\langle\!\langle \phi_1 \mathcal{U}_{\mathcal{I}}\phi_2 \rangle\!\rangle(\mathcal{T}) := \bigvee_{i=0}^{|\mathcal{T}|-1} \left((i \in K_{\mathcal{I}}^{\mathcal{T}}) \wedge \langle\!\langle \phi_2 \rangle\!\rangle(\mathcal{T}\!\uparrow_i) \wedge \bigwedge_{j=0}^{i-1} \langle\!\langle \phi_1 \rangle\!\rangle(\mathcal{T}\!\uparrow_j) \right)$$

Informally, the path formula $\phi_1 \mathcal{U}_{[a,b]}\phi_2$ expresses the property that over the timed state sequence $\mathcal{T}$ and in the time interval $[a, b]$, ϕ_2 becomes true and for all previous time ϕ_1 holds.

---

[2] Note that here we overload the symbols and we use the same notation for both the logical connectives in the MTL formulas and their respective Boolean truth degree functions.

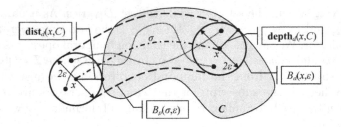

Fig. 3. A tube (*dashed lines*) around a nominal state sequence σ (*dash-dotted line*). The tube encloses a set of state sequences (*dotted lines*). Also, the definition of distance and depth and the associated neighborhoods.

3   Robust Satisfaction of MTL Specifications

3.1   Toward a Notion of Robust Satisfaction

In this section, we define what it means for a timed state sequence (taking values in some metric space) to satisfy a Metric Temporal Logic specification *robustly*. In the case of the timed state sequences that we consider in this paper, we can quantify how close are two different state sequences by using the metric d. Let $\mathcal{T} = (\sigma, \tau, \mathcal{O})$ be a timed state sequence and $(\sigma', \tau, \mathcal{O}) \in \Sigma(\mathcal{T})$, then

$$\rho(\sigma, \sigma') = \max\{d(\sigma_i, \sigma_i') \mid i \in [0, |\sigma| - 1]_{\mathbb{N}}\} \tag{1}$$

is a metric on the set $X^{|\mathcal{T}|}$, which is well defined since $|\mathcal{T}|$ is finite. Now that the space of state sequences is equipped with a metric, we can define a tube around a timed state sequence $\mathcal{T}$. Given an $\varepsilon > 0$, we let

$$\Sigma_\varepsilon(\mathcal{T}) = \{(\sigma', \tau, \mathcal{O}) \in \Sigma(\mathcal{T}) \mid \sigma' \in B_\rho(\sigma, \varepsilon)\}$$

to be the set of all timed state sequences that remain ε-close to $\mathcal{T}$.

Informally, we define the degree of robustness that a timed state sequence $\mathcal{T}$ satisfies an MTL formula ϕ to be a number $\varepsilon \in \mathbb{R}$. Intuitively, a positive ε means that the formula ϕ is satisfiable and, moreover, that all the other timed state sequences that remain ε-close to the nominal one also satisfy ϕ. Accordingly, if ε is negative, then $\mathcal{T}$ does not satisfy ϕ and all the other timed state sequences that remain within the open tube of radius $|\varepsilon|$ also do not satisfy ϕ.

Definition 7 (Robustness Degree). *Let* $\phi \in \Phi_\mathbb{B}$, $\mathcal{T} = (\sigma, \tau, \mathcal{O}) \in \Sigma_X$ *and* ρ *be the metric (1). Define* $P_\mathcal{T}^\phi := \{\sigma' \mid (\sigma', \tau, \mathcal{O}) \in \Sigma(\mathcal{T}) \cap \mathcal{L}(\phi)\}$, *then the robustness degree* $\varepsilon \in \mathbb{R}$ *of* $\mathcal{T}$ *with respect to* ϕ *is defined as* $\varepsilon := \mathbf{Dist}_\rho(\sigma, P_\mathcal{T}^\phi)$.

Remark 1. $P_\mathcal{T}^\phi$ is the set of all models with a sequence of time periods τ that satisfy ϕ. If we define $N_\mathcal{T}^\phi := \{\sigma' \mid (\sigma', \tau, \mathcal{O}) \in \Sigma(\mathcal{T}) \cap \Sigma_X \backslash \mathcal{L}(\phi)\}$, then the set $\{P_\mathcal{T}^\phi, N_\mathcal{T}^\phi\}$ forms a partition of the set $X^{|\mathcal{T}|}$. Therefore, we have duality $P_\mathcal{T}^\phi = X^{|\mathcal{T}|} \backslash N_\mathcal{T}^\phi$ and $N_\mathcal{T}^\phi = X^{|\mathcal{T}|} \backslash P_\mathcal{T}^\phi$.

The following proposition is derived directly from the definitions. It states that all the timed state sequences $\mathcal{S}$, which have distance from $\mathcal{T}$ less than the robustness degree of $\mathcal{T}$ with respect to ϕ, satisfy the same specification ϕ as $\mathcal{T}$.

Proposition 1. *Let $\phi \in \Phi_\mathbb{B}$, $\mathcal{T} = (\sigma, \tau, \mathcal{O}) \in \Sigma_X$ and $\varepsilon = \mathbf{Dist}_\rho(\sigma, P_\mathcal{T}^\phi)$. If $|\varepsilon| > 0$, then for all $\mathcal{S} \in \Sigma_{|\varepsilon|}(\mathcal{T})$ it is $\langle\!\langle\phi\rangle\!\rangle(\mathcal{S}) = \langle\!\langle\phi\rangle\!\rangle(\mathcal{T})$.*

Remark 2. If $\varepsilon = 0$, then the truth value of ϕ with respect to $\mathcal{T}$ is not robust, i.e. any small perturbation of a critical state in the timed state sequence can change the satisfiability of the formula with respect to $\mathcal{T}$.

Theoretically, the set $P_\mathcal{T}^\phi$ (or $N_\mathcal{T}^\phi$) can be computed. A naive, but straightforward, way to construct the set $P_\mathcal{T}^\phi$ is as follows. Instead of timed state sequences in a metric space X, let us consider finite timed state sequences where each state is a set of atomic propositions. We will refer to the later as timed words for clarity. In more detail, consider the timed word $\mathcal{T}_w = (\xi, \tau)$ where for all $i = 0, 1, \ldots, |\mathcal{T}_w| - 1$ it is $\xi_i \in \overline{AP} = 2^{AP}\backslash\emptyset$. In [17], it was proven the one can construct an acceptor $\mathcal{A}_\phi$ (in the form of a timed alternating automaton with one clock) for the finite models $\mathcal{T}_w$ of any formula ϕ in the logic MTL with the standard semantics (that is $\langle\!\langle\pi\rangle\!\rangle(\mathcal{T}_w) := \pi \in \xi_0$). Assume now that we are given an MTL formula ϕ, a sequence of time periods τ and a predicate mapping $\mathcal{O}$. For that particular τ, we can find the set $\mathcal{L}_\tau(\mathcal{A}_\phi)$ of timed words (ξ, τ) that are accepted by $\mathcal{A}_\phi$. One way to do so is to construct the set UW_τ of all possible untimed words ξ of length $|\tau|$, that is $UW_\tau = \overline{AP}^{|\tau|}$, and, then, for each $\xi \in UW_\tau$ verify whether (ξ, τ) is accepted by $\mathcal{A}_\phi$, i.e. whether $(\xi, \tau) \in \mathcal{L}(\mathcal{A}_\phi)$ and, thus, $(\xi, \tau) \in \mathcal{L}_\tau(\mathcal{A}_\phi)$. This can be done in time $O(|\tau||\overline{AP}|^{|\tau|})$ since given the automaton $\mathcal{A}_\phi$ it takes linear time in the length of the timed word to decide whether the word is in the language or not. From the set $\mathcal{L}_\tau(\mathcal{A}_\phi)$, we can easily derive the set $P_\mathcal{T}^\phi = \bigcup_{(\xi,\tau)\in\mathcal{L}_\tau(\mathcal{A}_\phi)}\left((\cap_{\pi\in\xi_0}\mathcal{O}(\pi)) \times \ldots \times (\cap_{\pi\in\xi_{|\tau|-1}}\mathcal{O}(\pi))\right)$.

The following toy example illustrates the concept of robustness for temporal logic formulas interpreted over finite (timed) state sequences.

Example 1. Assume that we are given the LTL specification $\phi = \pi_1 \mathcal{U} \pi_2$ such that $\mathcal{O}(\pi_1) = [1, 2] \subseteq \mathbb{R}$ and $\mathcal{O}(\pi_2) = [0, 1) \subseteq \mathbb{R}$. Moreover, we have $\mathcal{O}(\pi_c) =$

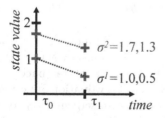
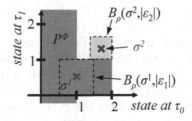

Fig. 4. On the left appears the time-domain representation of the timed state sequences $\mathcal{T}_1$ (*blue crosses*) and $\mathcal{T}_2$ (*green crosses*) of Example 1. On the right appears the space of the state sequences of length 2. Each x represents a state sequence as a point in $\mathbb{R}^2$.

$\mathbb{R}\backslash(\mathcal{O}(\pi_1) \cup \mathcal{O}(\pi_2)) = (-\infty, 0) \cup (2, +\infty)$. Note that the sets $\mathcal{O}(\pi_1)$, $\mathcal{O}(\pi_2)$ and $\mathcal{O}(\pi_c)$ are mutually disjoint. Consider now two timed state sequences $\mathcal{T}_1 = (\sigma^1, \tau, \mathcal{O})$ and $\mathcal{T}_2 = (\sigma^2, \tau, \mathcal{O})$ taking values in $\mathbb{R}$ such that $\sigma^1 = 1, 0.5$ and $\sigma^2 = 1.7, 1.3$. Since ϕ is an LTL formula, we can ignore the sequence of time periods τ. In this simple case, we can compute the set P^Φ with the procedure described above. The four untimed words that satisfy the specification ϕ and generate non-empty sets are $\xi^1 = \{\pi_2\}, \{\pi_1\}$, $\xi^2 = \{\pi_2\}, \{\pi_2\}$, $\xi^3 = \{\pi_2\}, \{\pi_c\}$ and $\xi^4 = \{\pi_1\}, \{\pi_2\}$. Therefore, we get $P^\phi = P^\phi_{\mathcal{T}_1} = P^\phi_{\mathcal{T}_2} = \mathcal{O}(\pi_2) \times \mathcal{O}(\pi_1) \cup \mathcal{O}(\pi_2) \times \mathcal{O}(\pi_2) \cup \mathcal{O}(\pi_2) \times \mathcal{O}(\pi_c) \cup \mathcal{O}(\pi_1) \times \mathcal{O}(\pi_2) = [0, 1) \times \mathbb{R} \cup [1, 2] \times [0, 1)$ (see Fig. 4). Therefore, $\varepsilon_1 = \mathbf{Dist}_\rho(\sigma^1, P^\phi) = 0.5$ and $\varepsilon_2 = \mathbf{Dist}_\rho(\sigma^2, P^\phi) = -0.3$.

3.2   Computing an Under-Approximation of the Robustness Degree

The aforementioned theoretical construction of the set $P^\phi_{\mathcal{T}}$ cannot be of any practical interest. Moreover, the definition of robustness degree involves a number of set operations (union, intersection and complementation) in the possibly high dimensional spaces X and $X^{|\mathcal{T}|}$, which can be computationally expensive in practice. Therefore in this section, we develop an algorithm that computes an under-approximation of the robustness degree ε by directly operating on the timed state sequence while avoiding set operations. In the following, we refer to the approximation of the robustness degree as the *robustness estimate*. As it is usually the case in trade-offs, we gain computational efficiency at the expense of accuracy.

In order to compute the robustness estimate, we define robust semantics for MTL. For this purpose, we extend the classical notion of formula satisfiability to the multi-valued case. In this framework, each formula takes truth values over a finite or infinite set of values that have an associated partial or total order relation. In this paper, we differentiate from previous works [9] by providing the definition of multi-valued semantics for MTL based on robustness considerations.

Let $\mathfrak{R} = (\overline{\mathbb{R}}, \leq)$ be the closure of the reals with the usual ordering relation. We define the binary operators $\sqcup : \overline{\mathbb{R}} \times \overline{\mathbb{R}} \rightarrow \overline{\mathbb{R}}$ and $\sqcap : \overline{\mathbb{R}} \times \overline{\mathbb{R}} \rightarrow \overline{\mathbb{R}}$ using the maximum and minimum functions as $x \sqcup y := \max\{x, y\}$ and $x \sqcap y := \min\{x, y\}$. Also, for some $R \subseteq \overline{\mathbb{R}}$ we extend the above definitions as follows $\bigsqcup R := \sup R$ and $\bigsqcap R := \inf R$. Recall that $\bigsqcup \overline{\mathbb{R}} = +\infty$ and $\bigsqcap \overline{\mathbb{R}} = -\infty$ and that any subset of $\overline{\mathbb{R}}$ has a supremum and infimum. Finally, because $\mathfrak{R}$ is a totally ordered set, it is *distributive*, i.e. for all $a, b, c \in \overline{\mathbb{R}}$ it is $a \sqcap (b \sqcup c) = (a \sqcap b) \sqcup (a \sqcap c)$ and $a \sqcup (b \sqcap c) = (a \sqcup b) \sqcap (a \sqcup c)$.

We propose multi-valued semantics for the Metric Temporal Logic where the valuation function on the atomic propositions takes values over the totally ordered set $\mathfrak{R}$ according to the metric d operating on the state space X of the timed state sequence $\mathcal{T}$. For this purpose, we let the valuation function to be the signed distance from the current point in the state sequence σ_0 to a set C labeled by the atomic proposition. Intuitively, this distance represents how robustly is the point σ_0 within a set C. If this metric is zero, then even the smallest perturbation of the point can drive it inside or outside the set C, dramatically affecting membership.

For the purposes of the following discussion, we use the notation $[\![\phi]\!](\mathcal{T})$ to denote the robustness estimate with which the structure $\mathcal{T}$ satisfies the specification ϕ (formally $[\![\phi]\!] : \Sigma_X \to \overline{\mathbb{R}}$).

Definition 8 (Robust Semantics of MTL). Let $\mathcal{T} = (\sigma, \tau, \mathcal{O}) \in \Sigma_X$, $v \in \overline{\mathbb{R}}$, $\pi \in AP$, $i, j \in \mathbb{N}$ and $K_{\mathcal{I}}^{\mathcal{T}} = \{i \in [0, |\mathcal{T}| - 1]_{\mathbb{N}} \mid \sum_{j=0}^{i} \tau_j \in \mathcal{I}\}$, then the robust semantics of a formula $\phi \in \Phi_{\overline{\mathbb{R}}}$ with respect to $\mathcal{T}$ are inductively defined by

$$[\![v]\!](\mathcal{T}) := v$$
$$[\![\pi]\!](\mathcal{T}) := \mathbf{Dist}_d(\sigma_0, \mathcal{O}(\pi))$$
$$[\![\neg\psi]\!](\mathcal{T}) := -[\![\psi]\!](\mathcal{T})$$
$$[\![\phi_1 \vee \phi_2]\!](\mathcal{T}) := [\![\phi_1]\!](\mathcal{T}) \sqcup [\![\phi_2]\!](\mathcal{T})$$
$$[\![\bigcirc_{\mathcal{I}}\psi]\!](\mathcal{T}) := \begin{cases} \mathbf{mv}(\tau_1 \in \mathcal{I}) \sqcap [\![\psi]\!](\mathcal{T}{\uparrow}_1) & \text{if } |\mathcal{T}| > 1 \\ -\infty & \text{otherwise} \end{cases}$$
$$[\![\phi_1 \, \mathcal{U}_{\mathcal{I}} \phi_2]\!](\mathcal{T}) := \bigsqcup_{i=0}^{|\mathcal{T}|-1} \left(\mathbf{mv}(i \in K_{\mathcal{I}}^{\mathcal{T}}) \sqcap [\![\phi_2]\!](\mathcal{T}{\uparrow}_i) \sqcap \bigsqcap_{j=0}^{i-1} [\![\phi_1]\!](\mathcal{T}{\uparrow}_j) \right)$$

where the unary operator $(-)$ is defined to be the negation over the reals.

Remark 3. It is easy to verify that the semantics of the negation operator give us all the usual nice properties such as the *De Morgan laws:* $a \sqcup b = -(-a \sqcap -b)$ and $a \sqcap b = -(-a \sqcup -b)$, *involution:* $-(-a) = a$ and *antisymmetry:* $a \leq b$ iff $-a \geq -b$ for $a, b \in \overline{\mathbb{R}}$.

Since the truth degree constants of the formulas in $\Phi_{\mathbb{B}}$ differ from those of the formulas in $\Phi_{\overline{\mathbb{R}}}$, we define a translation function $\mathbf{mv} : \Phi_{\mathbb{B}} \to \Phi_{\overline{\mathbb{R}}}$ which takes as input a formula $\phi \in \Phi_{\mathbb{B}}$ and replaces the occurrences of $\bot$ and $\top$ by $-\infty$ and $+\infty$ respectively. All the other symbols in ϕ are left the same. The following proposition states the relationship between the usual and the robust semantics of MTL (the proof uses induction on the structure of ϕ).

Proposition 2 (proof in [20]). Let $\phi \in \Phi_{\mathbb{B}}$, $\psi = \mathbf{mv}(\phi)$ and $\mathcal{T} \in \Sigma_X$, then

(1) $[\![\psi]\!](\mathcal{T}) > 0 \Rightarrow \langle\!\langle\phi\rangle\!\rangle(\mathcal{T}) = \top$ (2) $\langle\!\langle\phi\rangle\!\rangle(\mathcal{T}) = \top \Rightarrow [\![\psi]\!](\mathcal{T}) \geq 0$

(3) $[\![\psi]\!](\mathcal{T}) < 0 \Rightarrow \langle\!\langle\phi\rangle\!\rangle(\mathcal{T}) = \bot$ (4) $\langle\!\langle\phi\rangle\!\rangle(\mathcal{T}) = \bot \Rightarrow [\![\psi]\!](\mathcal{T}) \leq 0$

Note that the equivalence in the above proposition fails because, if a point is on the boundary of the set, its distance to the set or its depth in the set is by definition zero. Therefore, the point is classified to belong to that set even if the set is open in the topology.

The following theorem identifies the robustness estimate as an underapproximation of the robustness degree (proof by induction on the structure of ϕ).

Theorem 1 (proof in [20]). Given $\phi \in \Phi_{\mathbb{B}}$ and $\mathcal{T} = (\sigma, \tau, \mathcal{O}) \in \Sigma_X$, then

$$|[\![\mathbf{mv}(\phi)]\!](\mathcal{T})| \leq |\mathbf{Dist}_\rho(\sigma, P_{\mathcal{T}}^\phi)| \tag{2}$$

In more detail, $-\mathbf{depth}_\rho(\sigma, N_{\mathcal{T}}^\phi) \leq [\![\phi]\!](\mathcal{T}) \leq \mathbf{depth}_\rho(\sigma, P_{\mathcal{T}}^\phi)$.

In the above theorem, the equality in equation (2) fails due to the robust interpretation of the disjunction connective. The inequality manifests itself in four distinct ways: (i) at the level of the atomic propositions, i.e. $\pi_1 \vee \pi_2$, (ii) due to the existence of tautologies in the formula, i.e. $\pi \vee \neg\pi$, (iii) when we consider disjuncts of MTL subformulas, i.e. $\phi_1 \vee \phi_2$, and more importantly, (iv) due to the disjunctions in the semantics of the until temporal operator.

The first case can be remedied by introducing a new symbol for each Boolean combination of atomic propositions. The second and third conditions require the attention of the user of the algorithm. Even though the above cases can be fixed by introducing syntactic restrictions, the last case (iv) captures a fundamental shortcoming of the robust semantics. The timed state sequences that have state sequences in $B_\rho(\sigma, |\mathbf{Dist}_\rho(\sigma, P_{\mathcal{T}}^\phi)|)$ can satisfy or falsify the specification ϕ at different time instants than $\mathcal{T}$. On the other hand, the robustness estimate returns the "radius" of the neighborhood of traces that satisfy the specification at the same point in time.

Example 2. Going back to Example 1, we have seen that $\varepsilon_1 = \mathbf{Dist}_\rho(\sigma^1, P^\phi) = 0.5$. Nevertheless, $[\![\phi]\!](\mathcal{T}_1) = [\![\pi_2]\!](\mathcal{T}_1) \sqcup ([\![\pi_1]\!](\mathcal{T}_1) \sqcap [\![\pi_2]\!](\mathcal{T}_1{\uparrow}1)) = 0 \sqcup (0 \sqcap 0.5) = 0 \neq \varepsilon_1$. Consider now a timed state sequence $\mathcal{T}' = (\sigma', \tau, \mathcal{O})$ such that $\sigma' = 1.1, 0.5$. It is immediate to see that $\langle\!\langle \phi \rangle\!\rangle(\mathcal{T}') = \top$ and that $\mathcal{T}' \in \Sigma_{\varepsilon_1}(\mathcal{T}_1)$. Note that $\mathcal{T}_1$ satisfies the specification at time τ_1, while $\mathcal{T}'$ satisfies ϕ at time τ_0. The robust semantics of MTL cannot capture this.

From Proposition 1 and Theorem 1 we derive the next theorem as a corollary.

Theorem 2. *Given $\phi \in \Phi_{\mathbb{B}}$ and $\mathcal{T} \in \Sigma_X$, if $[\![\mathbf{mv}(\phi)]\!](\mathcal{T}) = \varepsilon$ and $|\varepsilon| > 0$, then for all $\mathcal{S} \in \Sigma_{|\varepsilon|}(\mathcal{T})$ it is $\langle\!\langle \phi \rangle\!\rangle(\mathcal{S}) = \langle\!\langle \phi \rangle\!\rangle(\mathcal{T})$.*

Theorem 2 has several implications. First, in the simplest case where we just simulate the response of a system, we can derive bounds for the magnitude of the disturbances that the system can tolerate while still satisfying the same MTL specification. Second, we can use approximation metrics [21] in order to verify a system using simulations [22].

4   Monitoring the Robustness of Temporal Properties

In this section, we present a procedure that computes the robustness estimate of a timed state sequence $\mathcal{T}$ with respect to a specification ϕ stated in the Metric Temporal Logic. For this purpose, we design a monitoring algorithm based on the classical and robust semantics of MTL.

Starting from the definition of the Boolean semantics of the until operator and using the distributive law, we can derive an equivalent recursive formulation (see also [10]):

$$\langle\!\langle \phi_1 \, \mathcal{U}_{\mathcal{I}} \phi_2 \rangle\!\rangle(\mathcal{T}) = \begin{cases} ((0 \in \mathcal{I}) \wedge \langle\!\langle \phi_2 \rangle\!\rangle(\mathcal{T})) \vee \\ \vee(\langle\!\langle \phi_1 \rangle\!\rangle(\mathcal{T}) \wedge \langle\!\langle \phi_1 \, \mathcal{U}_{\mathcal{I}-\tau_1} \phi_2 \rangle\!\rangle(\mathcal{T}{\uparrow}1)) & \text{if } |\mathcal{T}| > 1 \\ (0 \in \mathcal{I}) \wedge \langle\!\langle \phi_2 \rangle\!\rangle(\mathcal{T}) & \text{otherwise} \end{cases}$$

Algorithm 1. Monitoring the Robustness of Timed State Sequences

---

Input: The MTL formula ϕ and the timed state sequence $\mathcal{T} = (\sigma, \tau, \mathcal{O})$
Output: The formula's Boolean truth value and the robustness parameter
1: **procedure** MONITOR(ϕ,$\mathcal{T}$)
2:      **if** $|\mathcal{T}| > 1$ **then return** $\phi \leftarrow$ PROGRESS($\phi, \sigma_0, \tau_1, \bot, \mathcal{O}$)
3:      **else return** $\phi \leftarrow$ PROGRESS($\phi, \sigma_0, 0, \top, \mathcal{O}$)
4:      **end if**
5:      **if** $\phi = (v, \varepsilon)$ **then return** (v, ε) $\triangleright\ v \in \{\top, \bot\}$ and $\varepsilon \in \overline{\mathbb{R}}$
6:      **else return** MONITOR($\phi, \mathcal{T}{\uparrow}_1$)
7:      **end if**
8: **end procedure**

A similar recursive formulation holds for the robust MTL semantics (see [20]). Using the recursive definitions, it is easy to derive an algorithm that returns the Boolean truth value[3] of the formula and its robustness degree. The main observation is that each value node in the parse tree of the MTL formula should also contain its robustness degree. Therefore, the only operations that we need to modify are the negation and disjunction which must perform, respectively, a negation and a maximum operation on the robustness values of their operants. Then, the new semantics for the conjunction operator can be easily derived from these two.

Definition 9 (Hybrid Semantics for Negation and Disjunction). *Let* $(v_1, \varepsilon_1), (v_2, \varepsilon_2) \in \mathbb{B} \times \overline{\mathbb{R}}$, *then we define*

- *Negation:* $\neg(v, \varepsilon) := (\neg v, -\varepsilon)$
- *Disjunction:* $(v_1, \varepsilon_1) \vee (v_2, \varepsilon_2) := (v_1 \vee v_2, \max\{\varepsilon_1, \varepsilon_2\})$

Given a timed state sequence $\mathcal{T}$ and an MTL formula ϕ, we can construct a monitoring algorithm (Algorithm 1) that can decide both the satisfaction of the formula and the robustness parameter ε on-the-fly. Algorithm 2 is the core of the monitoring procedure. It takes as input the temporal logic formula ϕ, the current state s and the time period before the next state occurs, it evaluates the part of the formula that must hold on the current state and returns the formula that it has to hold at the next state of the timed trace. In Algorithm 2, $\overleftarrow{\mathcal{I}}$ is defined as follows

$$\overleftarrow{\mathcal{I}} = \begin{cases} [0, lb(\mathcal{I})] \cup \mathcal{I} & \text{if } 0 < lb(\mathcal{I}) \\ \mathcal{I} & \text{otherwise} \end{cases}$$

The constraint $0 \in \overleftarrow{\mathcal{I}}$ is added in order to terminate the propagation of the subformula $\phi_1 \mathcal{U}_{\mathcal{I}-\tau_1} \phi_2$, when the timing constraints for the occurrence of ϕ_2 have already been violated. Note that this timing constraint is meaningful only if we also perform the following simplifications at each recursive call of the algorithm PROGRESS: (i) $\phi \wedge (\top, +\infty) \equiv \phi$, (ii) $\phi \vee (\bot, -\infty) \equiv \phi$, (iii) $\phi \vee (\top, +\infty) \equiv (\top, +\infty)$ and (iv) $\phi \wedge (\bot, -\infty) \equiv (\bot, -\infty)$.

---

[3] Note that the Boolean truth valued is required in the cases where the robustness degree is zero (see Proposition 2).

Algorithm 2. Formula Progression Algorithm

Input: The MTL formula ϕ, the current state s, the time period Δt for the next state, a variable *last* indicating whether the next state is the last and the mapping $\mathcal{O}$

Output: The MTL formula ϕ that has to hold at the next state

1: **procedure** PROGRESS($\phi, s, \Delta t, last, \mathcal{O}$)
2:     **if** $\phi = (v, \varepsilon) \in \{\perp, \top\} \times \overline{\mathbb{R}}$ **then return** (v, ε)
3:     **else if** $\phi = \pi$ **then return** $(s \in \mathcal{O}(\pi), \mathbf{Dist}_d(s, \mathcal{O}(\pi)))$
4:     **else if** $\phi = \neg\psi$ **then return** $\neg$PROGRESS($\psi, s, \Delta t, last, \mathcal{O}$)
5:     **else if** $\phi = \phi_1 \vee \phi_2$ **then**
6:         **return** PROGRESS($\phi_1, s, \Delta t, last, \mathcal{O}$)$\vee$ PROGRESS($\phi_2, s, \Delta t, last, \mathcal{O}$)
7:     **else if** $\phi = \bigcirc_\mathcal{I}\psi$ **then return** HYBRID($\neg last \wedge (\Delta t \in \mathcal{I})$) $\wedge \psi$
8:     **else if** $\phi = \phi_1\mathcal{U}_\mathcal{I}\phi_2$ **then**
9:         $\alpha \leftarrow$ HYBRID($0 \in \mathcal{I}$)$\wedge$ PROGRESS($\phi_2, s, \Delta t, last, \mathcal{O}$)
10:        $\beta \leftarrow$ HYBRID($\neg last \wedge (0 \in \overleftarrow{\mathcal{I}})$)$\wedge$ PROGRESS($\phi_1, s, \Delta t, last, \mathcal{O}$) $\wedge \phi_1\mathcal{U}_{\mathcal{I}-\Delta t}\phi_2$
11:        **return** $\alpha \vee \beta$
12:    **end if**
13: **end procedure**
1: **function** HYBRID(*Bool*)
2:     **if** *Bool* $= \top$ **return** $(\top, +\infty)$ **else return** $(\perp, -\infty)$ **end if**
3: **end function**

When we check how robustly a timed state sequence $\mathcal{T}$ satisfies a specification ϕ, we cannot stop the monitoring process as soon as we can determine that the MTL formula holds on $\mathcal{T}$. This is because a future state in the timed state sequence may satisfy the specification more robustly. Therefore, it is preferable to execute the procedure MONITOR for the whole length of the timed state sequence $\mathcal{T}$.

The proof of the following theorem is standard and uses induction on the structure of ϕ based on the classical and robust semantics of MTL.

Theorem 3 (proof in [20]). *Given an MTL formula $\phi \in \Phi_\mathbb{B}$ and a timed state sequence $\mathcal{T} \in \Sigma_X$, the procedure* MONITOR($\phi, \mathcal{T}$) *returns*

- $(\top, \varepsilon)$ *if and only if* $\langle\langle\phi\rangle\rangle(\mathcal{T}) = \top$ *and* $[\![\mathbf{mv}(\phi)]\!](\mathcal{T}) = \varepsilon \geq 0$
- $(\perp, \varepsilon)$ *if and only if* $\langle\langle\phi\rangle\rangle(\mathcal{T}) = \perp$ *and* $[\![\mathbf{mv}(\phi)]\!](\mathcal{T}) = \varepsilon \leq 0$.

The theoretical complexity of the monitoring algorithms has been studied in the past for both the Linear [23] and the Metric Temporal Logic [10]. Practical algorithms for monitoring using rewriting have been developed by several authors [11,24]. The new part in Algorithm 2 is the evaluation of the atomic propositions. How easy is to compute the signed distance? When the set X is just $\mathbb{R}$, the set C is an interval and the metric d is the function $d(x, y) = |x - y|$, then the problem reduces to finding the minimum of two values. For example, if $C = [a, b] \subseteq \mathbb{R}$ and $x \in C$, then $\mathbf{Dist}_d(x, C) = \min\{|x - a|, |x - b|\}$. When the set X is $\mathbb{R}^n$, $C \subseteq \mathbb{R}^n$ is a closed and convex set and the metric d is the euclidean distance, i.e. $d(x, y) = ||x - y||_2$, then we can calculate the distance ($\mathbf{dist}_d$) by solving a convex optimization problem. If in addition the set C is a hyperplane $C = \{x \mid a^T x = b\}$

or a halfspace $C = \{x \mid a^T x \leq b\}$, then there exist analytical solutions. For further details see [16].

5 Conclusions and Future Work

The main contribution of this work is the definition of a notion of robust satisfaction of a Linear or Metric Temporal Logic formula which is interpreted over finite timed state sequences that reside in some metric space. We have also presented an algorithmic procedure that can monitor such a timed state sequence and determine an under-approximation of its robustness degree. As mentioned in the introduction, the applications of this framework can extend to several areas. We are currently exploring several new directions such as the extension of the definitions of the robustness degree and the robust MTL semantics so they can handle infinite timed state sequences. Also of interest to us is the addition of a metric on the time bounds as it is advocated in [25] and [26]. Finally, the methodology that we have presented in this paper comprises the basis for the extension of recent results on the safety verification of discrete time systems [13] to a more general verification framework using the metric temporal logic as a specification language [22].

Acknowledgments. The authors would like to thank Oleg Sokolsky, Rajeev Alur, Antoine Girard and Nader Motee for the fruitful discussions and one of the reviewers for the many useful remarks. This work has been partially supported by NSF EHS 0311123, NSF ITR 0324977 and ARO MURI DAAD 19-02-01-0383.

References

1. Clarke, E.M., Grumberg, O., Peled, D.A.: Model Checking. MIT Press, Cambridge, Massachusetts (1999)
2. Alur, R., Courcoubetis, C., Halbwachs, N., Henzinger, T.A., Ho, P.H., Nicollin, X., Olivero, A., Sifakis, J., Yovine, S.: The algorithmic analysis of hybrid systems. Theoretical Computer Science **138** (1995) 3–34
3. Tan, L., Kim, J., Sokolsky, O., Lee, I.: Model-based testing and monitoring for hybrid embedded systems. In: Proceedings of the 2004 IEEE International Conference on Information Reuse and Integration. (2004) 487–492
4. Maler, O., Nickovic, D.: Monitoring temporal properties of continuous signals. In: Proceedings of FORMATS-FTRTFT. Volume 3253 of LNCS. (2004) 152–166
5. Kapinski, J., Krogh, B.H., Maler, O., Stursberg, O.: On systematic simulation of open continuous systems. In: Hybrid Systems: Computation and Control. Volume 2623 of LNCS., Springer (2003) 283–297
6. Esposito, J.M., Kim, J., Kumar, V.: Adaptive RRTs for validating hybrid robotic control systems. In: Proceedings of the International Workshop on the Algorithmic Foundations of Robotics. (2004)
7. Emerson, E.A.: Temporal and modal logic. In van Leeuwen, J., ed.: Handbook of Theoretical Computer Science: Formal Models and Semantics. Volume B., North-Holland Pub. Co./MIT Press (1990) 995–1072

8. Koymans, R.: Specifying real-time properties with metric temporal logic. Real-Time Systems **2** (1990) 255–299
9. de Alfaro, L., Faella, M., Stoelinga, M.: Linear and branching metrics for quantitative transition systems. In: Proceedings of the 31st ICALP. Volume 3142 of LNCS., Springer (2004) 97–109
10. Thati, P., Rosu, G.: Monitoring algorithms for metric temporal logic specifications. In: Runtime Verification. Volume 113 of ENTCS., Elsevier (2005) 145–162
11. Havelund, K., Rosu, G.: Monitoring programs using rewriting. In: Proceedings of the 16th IEEE international conference on Automated software engineering. (2001)
12. Shults, B., Kuipers, B.: Qualitative simulation and temporal logic: proving properties of continuous systems. Technical Report TR AI96-244, Dept. of Computer Sciences, University of Texas at Austin (1996)
13. Girard, A., Pappas, G.J.: Verification using simulation. In: Hybrid Systems: Computation and Control (HSCC). Volume 3927 of LNCS., Springer (2006) 272 – 286
14. Fainekos, G.E., Kress-Gazit, H., Pappas, G.J.: Hybrid controllers for path planning: A temporal logic approach. In: Proceedings of the 44th IEEE Conference on Decision and Control. (2005) 4885 – 4890
15. Lamine, K.B., Kabanza, F.: Reasoning about robot actions: A model checking approach. In: Advances in Plan-Based Control of Robotic Agents. Volume 2466 of LNCS., Springer (2002) 123–139
16. Boyd, S., Vandenberghe, L.: Convex Optimization. Cambridge University Press (2004)
17. Ouaknine, J., Worrell, J.: On the decidability of metric temporal logic. In: 20th IEEE Symposium on Logic in Computer Science (LICS). (2005) 188–197
18. Alur, R., Feder, T., Henzinger, T.A.: The benefits of relaxing punctuality. In: Symposium on Principles of Distributed Computing. (1991) 139–152
19. Alur, R., Henzinger, T.A.: Real-Time Logics: Complexity and Expressiveness. In: Fifth Annual IEEE Symposium on Logic in Computer Science, Washington, D.C., IEEE Computer Society Press (1990) 390–401
20. Fainekos, G.E., Pappas, G.J.: Robustness of temporal logic specifications for finite state sequences in metric spaces. Technical Report MS-CIS-06-05, Dept. of CIS, Univ. of Pennsylvania (2006)
21. Girard, A., Pappas, G.J.: Approximation metrics for discrete and continuous systems. Technical Report MS-CIS-05-10, Dept. of CIS, Univ. of Pennsylvania (2005)
22. Fainekos, G.E., Girard, A., Pappas, G.J.: Temporal logic verification using simulation. In: FORMATS 2006. Volume 4202 of LNCS., Springer (2006) 171–186
23. Markey, N., Schnoebelen, Ph.: Model checking a path (preliminary report). In: Proceedings of the 14th International Conference on Concurrency Theory. Volume 2761 of LNCS. (2003) 251–265
24. Kristoffersen, K.J., Pedersen, C., Andersen, H.R.: Runtime verification of timed LTL using disjunctive normalized equation systems. In: Proceedings of the 3rd Workshop on Run-time Verification. Volume 89 of ENTCS. (2003) 1–16
25. Huang, J., Voeten, J., Geilen, M.: Real-time property preservation in approximations of timed systems. In: Proceedings of the 1st ACM & IEEE International Conference on Formal Methods and Models for Co-Design. (2003) 163–171
26. Henzinger, T.A., Majumdar, R., Prabhu, V.S.: Quantifying similarities between timed systems. In: FORMATS. Volume 3829 of LNCS., Springer (2005) 226–241

Goldilocks: Efficiently Computing the Happens-Before Relation Using Locksets

Tayfun Elmas[1], Shaz Qadeer[2], and Serdar Tasiran[1]

[1] Koç University
[2] Microsoft Research

Abstract. We present a new lockset-based algorithm, Goldilocks, for precisely computing the happens-before relation and thereby detecting data-races at runtime. Dynamic race detection algorithms in the literature are based on vector clocks or locksets. Vector-clock-based algorithms precisely compute the happens-before relation but have significantly more overhead. Previous lockset-based race detection algorithms, on the other hand, are imprecise. They check adherence to a particular synchronization discipline, i.e., a sufficient condition for race freedom and may generate false race warnings. Our algorithm, like vector clocks, is precise, yet it is efficient since it is purely lockset based.

We have implemented our algorithm inside the Kaffe Java Virtual Machine. Our implementation incorporates lazy evaluation of locksets and certain "short-circuit checks" which contribute significantly to its efficiency. Experimental results indicate that our algorithm's overhead is much less than that of the vector-clock algorithm and is very close to our implementation of the Eraser lockset algorithm.

1 Introduction

Race conditions on shared data are often symptomatic of a bug and their detection is a central issue in the functional verification of concurrent software. Numerous techniques and tools have been developed to analyze races and to guard against them [15,19,7,1]. These techniques can be broadly classified as static and dynamic. Some state-of-the-art tools combine techniques from both categories. This paper is about a dynamic race detection algorithm.

Algorithms for runtime race detection make use of two key techniques: locksets and vector clocks. Roughly speaking, lockset-based algorithms compute at each point during an execution for each shared variable q a set $LS(q)$. The lockset $LS(q)$ consists of the locks and other synchronization primitives that, according to the algorithm, protect accesses to q at that point. Typically, $LS(q)$ is a small set and can be updated relatively efficiently during an execution. The key weakness of lockset-based algorithms in the literature is that they are specific to a particular locking discipline which they try to capture directly in $LS(q)$. For instance, the classic lockset algorithm popularized by the Eraser tool [15], is based on the assumption that each potentially shared variable must be protected by a single lock throughout the whole computation. Other similar algorithms can

K. Havelund et al. (Eds.): FATES/RV 2006, LNCS 4262, pp. 193–208, 2006.

handle more sophisticated locking mechanisms [1] by incorporating knowledge of these mechanisms into the lockset inference rules. Still, lockset-based algorithms based on a particular synchronization discipline have the fundamental shortcoming that they may report false races when this discipline is not obeyed. Vector-clock [11] based race detection algorithms, on the other hand, are precise, i.e., declare a race exactly when an execution contains two accesses to a shared variable that are not ordered by the happens-before relation. However, they are significantly more expensive computationally than lockset-based algorithms as argued and demonstrated experimentally in this work.

In this paper we provide, for the first time, a lockset-based algorithm, Goldilocks, that precisely captures the happens-before relation. In other words, we provide a set of lockset update rules and formulate a *necessary and sufficient* condition for race-freedom based solely on locksets computed using these rules. Goldilocks combines the precision of vector clocks with the computational efficiency of locksets. We can uniformly handle a variety of synchronization idioms such as thread-local data that later becomes shared, shared data protected by different locks at different points in time, and data protected indirectly by locks on container objects.

For dynamic race detection tools used for stress-testing concurrent programs, precision may not be desired or necessary. One might prefer an algorithm to signal a warning about not only about races in the execution being checked, but also about "feasible" races in similar executions [12]. It is possible to incorporate this kind of capability into our algorithm by slightly modifying the lockset update rules or the race condition check. However, the target applications for our race detection algorithm are continuous monitoring for actual races during early development and deployment, and for partial-order reduction during model checking as is done in [8]. False alarms and reports of feasible rather than actual races unnecessarily interrupt execution and take up developers' time in the first application and cause computational inefficiency in the latter. For these reasons, for the targeted applications, the precision of our algorithm is a strength and not a weakness.

We present an implementation of our algorithm that incorporates lazy computation of locksets and "short circuit checks": constant time sufficient checks for race freedom. These implementation improvements contribute significantly to the computational efficiency of our technique and they appear not to be applicable to vector clocks. We implemented our race-detection algorithm in C, integrated with the Kaffe Java Virtual Machine [18]. An important contribution of this paper is an experimental comparison of the Goldilocks algorithm with the vector-clock algorithm and our implementation of the Eraser algorithm. We demonstrate that our algorithm is much more efficient than vector clocks and about as efficient as Eraser.

This paper is organized as follows. Section 2 describes the Goldilocks algorithm and presents an example which contrasts our algorithm with existing locksets algorithms. Section 3 explains the implementation of our algorithm in the

Kaffe JVM. Experimental evaluation of our algorithm is presented in Section 4. Related work is discussed in Section 5.

2   The Goldilocks Algorithm

In this section, we describe our algorithm for checking whether a given execution σ has a data-race. We use the standard characterization of data-races based on the happens-before relation, i.e., there is a data race between two accesses to a shared variable if they are not ordered by the happens-before relation. The happens-before relation for an execution is defined by the memory model. We use a memory model similar to the Java memory model [10] in this paper. Our algorithm is sound and precise, that is, it reports a data-race on an execution iff there is a data-race in that execution.

2.1   Preliminaries

A state of a concurrent program consists of a set of local variables for each thread and a set of global objects shared among all threads. Let Tid be the set of thread identifiers and $Addr$ be the set of object identifiers. Each object has a finite collection of fields. $Field$ represents the set of all fields. and is a union of two disjoint sets, the set $Data$ of $data$ fields and the set $Volatile$ of $volatile$ fields. A $data\ variable$ is a pair (o, d) of an object o and a data field d. A $synchronization$ $variable$ is a pair (o, v) of an object o and a volatile field v. A concurrent execution σ is represented by a finite sequence $s_1 \xrightarrow{\alpha_1}_{t_1} s_2 \xrightarrow{\alpha_2}_{t_2} \ldots \xrightarrow{\alpha_n}_{t_n} s_{n+1}$, where s_i is a program state for all $i \in [1 \ldots n+1]$ and α_i is one of the following actions for all $i \in [1 \ldots n]$: $acq(o)$, $rel(o)$, $read(o, d)$, $write(o, d)$, $read(o, v)$, $write(o, v)$, $fork(u)$, $join(u)$, and $alloc(o)$. We use a linearly-ordered sequence of actions and states to represent an execution for ease of expressing the lockset-update rules and the correctness of the algorithm. This sequence can be any linearization of the union of the following partial orders defined in [10]: (i) the program order for each thread and (ii) the synchronizes-with order for each synchronization variable. The particular choice of the linearization is immaterial for our algorithm. In our implementation (Section 3) each thread separately checks races on a (linearly-ordered) execution that represents its view of the evolution of program state.

The actions $acq(o)$ and $rel(o)$ respectively acquire and release a lock on object o. There is a special field $l \in Volatile$ containing values from $Tid \cup \{null\}$ to model the semantics of an object lock. The action $acq(o)$ being performed by thread t blocks until $o.l = null$ and then atomically sets $o.l$ to t. The action $rel(o)$ being performed by thread t fails if $o.l \neq t$, otherwise it atomically sets $o.l$ to $null$. Although we assume non-reentrant locks for ease of exposition in this paper, our algorithm is easily extended to reentrant locks. The actions $read(o, d)$ and $write(o, d)$ respectively read and write the data field d of an object o. A thread $accesses$ a variable (o, d) if it executes either $read(o, d)$ or $write(o, d)$. Similarly, the actions $read(o, v)$ and $write(o, v)$ respectively read and write the volatile field v of an object o. The action $fork(u)$ creates a new thread with identifier u. The action $join(u)$ blocks until the thread with identifier u terminates. The action $alloc(o)$ allocates a new object o. Of course, other actions (such as arithmetic computation, function calls, etc.) also occur in a real execution but these actions are irrelevant for our exposition and have consequently been elided.

Following the Java Memory Model [10], we define the happens-before relation for a given execution as follows.

Definition 1. *Let* $\sigma = s_1 \xrightarrow{\alpha_1}_{t_1} s_2 \xrightarrow{\alpha_2}_{t_2} \ldots \xrightarrow{\alpha_n}_{t_n} s_{n+1}$ *be an execution of the program. The happens-before relation* $\xrightarrow{hb}$ *for* σ *is the smallest transitively-closed relation on the set* $\{1, 2, \ldots, n\}$ *such that for any* k *and* l, *we have* $k \xrightarrow{hb} l$ *if* $1 \leq k \leq l \leq n$ *and one of the following holds:*

1. $t_k = t_l$.
2. $\alpha_k = rel(o)$ *and* $\alpha_l = acq(o)$.
3. $\alpha_k = write(o, v)$ *and* $\alpha_l = read(o, v)$.
4. $\alpha_k = fork(t_l)$.
5. $\alpha_l = join(t_k)$.

We use the happens-before relation to define data-race free executions as follows. Consider a data variable (o, d) in the execution σ. The execution σ is *race-free* on (o, d) if for all $k, l \in [1, n]$ such that $\alpha_k, \alpha_l \in \{read(o, d), write(o, d)\}$, we have $k \xrightarrow{hb} l$ or $l \xrightarrow{hb} k$. For now, our definition does not distinguish between read and write accesses. We are currently refining our algorithm to make this distinction in order to support concurrent-read/exclusive-write schemes.

2.2   The Algorithm

Our algorithm for detecting data races in an execution σ uses an auxiliary partial map LS from $(Addr \times Data)$ to $Powerset((Addr \times Volatile) \cup Tid)$. This map provides for each data variable (o, d) its lockset $LS(o, d)$ which contains volatile variables, some of which represent locks and thread identifiers. The algorithm updates LS with the execution of each transition in σ. The set of rules for these updates are shown in Figure 1. Initially, the partial map LS is empty. When an action α happens, the map LS is updated according to the rules in the figure.

Goldilocks maintains for each lockset $LS(o, d)$ the following invariants: 1) If $(o', l) \in LS(o, d)$ then the last access to (o, d) happens-before a subsequent $acq(o')$. 2) If $(o', v) \in LS(o, d)$ then the last access to (o, d) happens-before a subsequent $read(o', v)$. 3) If $t \in LS(o, d)$ then the last access to (o, d) happens-before any subsequent action by thread t. The first two invariants indicate that $LS(o, d)$ contains the locks and volatile variables whose acquisitions and reads, respectively, create a happens-before edge from the last access of (o, d) to any subsequent access of (o, d), thereby preventing a race. As a result of the last invariant, if $t \in LS(o, d)$ at an access to a data variable (o, d) by thread t, then the previous access to (o, d) is related to this access by the happens-before relation. A race on (o, d) is reported in Rule 1, if $LS(o, d) \neq \emptyset$ and $t \notin LS(o, d)$ just before the update.

1. $\alpha = read(o,d)$ or $\alpha = write(o,d)$:
   if $LS(o,d) \neq \emptyset$ and $t \notin LS(o,d)$, report data race on (o,d); $LS(o,d) := \{t\}$
2. $\alpha = read(o,v)$:
   for each $(o,d) \in dom(LS)$: if $(o,v) \in LS(o,d)$ add t to $LS(o,d)$
3. $\alpha = write(o,v)$:
   for each $(o,d) \in dom(LS)$: if $t \in LS(o,d)$ add (o,v) to $LS(o,d)$
4. $\alpha = acq(o)$:
   for each $(o,d) \in dom(LS)$: if $(o,l) \in LS(o,d)$ add t to $LS(o,d)$
5. $\alpha = rel(o)$:
   for each $(o,d) \in dom(LS)$: if $t \in LS(o,d)$ add (o,l) to $LS(o,d)$
6. $\alpha = fork(u)$:
   for each $(o,d) \in dom(LS)$: if $t \in LS(o,d)$ add u to $LS(o,d)$
7. $\alpha = join(u)$:
   for each $(o,d) \in dom(LS)$: if $u \in LS(o,d)$ add t to $LS(o,d)$
8. $\alpha = alloc(x)$:
   for each $d \in Data$: $LS(x,d) := \emptyset$

Fig. 1. The lockset update rules for the Goldilocks algorithm

We now present the intuition behind our algorithm. Let (o,d) be a data variable, α be the last access to it by a thread a, and β be the current access to it by thread b. Then α happens-before β if there is a sequence of happens-before edges connecting α to β. The rules in Figure 1 are designed to compute the transitive closure of such edges. When α is executed, the lockset $LS(o,d)$ is set to the singleton set $\{a\}$. This lockset grows as synchronizing actions happen after the access. The algorithm maintains the invariant that a thread identifier t is in $LS(o,d)$ iff there is a sequence of happens-before edges between α and the next action performed by thread t. The algorithm adds a thread identifier to $LS(o,d)$ as soon as such a sequence of happens-before edges is established.

Note that each of the rules 2–7 requires updating the lockset of each data variable. A naive implementation of this algorithm would be too expensive for programs that manipulate large heaps. In Section 3, we present a scheme to implement our algorithm by applying these updates lazily.

The following theorem expresses the fact that our algorithm is both sound and precise.

Theorem 1 (Correctness). *Consider an execution* $\sigma = s_1 \xrightarrow{\alpha_1}_{t_1} s_2 \cdots s_n \xrightarrow{\alpha_n}_{t_n}$ s_{n+1} *and let* LS_i *be the value of the lockset map* LS *as computed by the Goldilocks algorithm when* σ *reaches state* s_i. *Let* (o,d) *be a data variable and* $i \in [1, n-1]$ *be such that* α_i *and* α_n *access* (o,d) *but* α_j *does not access* (o,d) *for all* $j \in [i+1, n-1]$. *Then* $t_n \in LS_n(o,d)$ *iff* $i \xrightarrow{hb} n$.

The proof appears in the appendix of the full version of our paper [6].

Our algorithm has the ability to track happens-before edges from a write to a subsequent read of a volatile variable. Therefore, our algorithm can handle any synchronization primitive, such as semaphores and barriers in the `java.util.-concurrent` package of the Java standard library, whose underlying implementation can be described using a collection of volatile variables.

Goldilocks can also handle the happens-before edges induced by the wait-notify mechanism of Java without needing to add new rules. The following restrictions of Java ensure that, for an execution the happens-before relation computed by our lockset algorithm projected onto data variable accesses remains unchanged even if the wait/notify synchronization adds new happens-before edges: 1) Each call to `o.wait()` and `o.notify()` be performed while holding the lock on object o. 2) The lock of o released when `o.wait()` is entered and it is again acquired before returning from `o.wait()`.

2.3   Example

In this section, we present an example of a concurrent program execution in which lockset algorithms from the literature declare a false race while our algorithm does not. The lockset algorithms that we compare ours with are based on the Eraser algorithm [15], which is sound but not precise.

The pseudocode for the example is given below. The code executed by each thread `Ti` is listed next to `Ti:`.

```
Class IntBox { Int x; }

IntBox a = new IntBox();   // IntBox object o1 created
IntBox b = new IntBox();   // IntBox object o2 created

  T1:   acq(L1); a.x++; rel(L1);
  T2:   acq(L1); acq(L2);   tmp = a; a = b; b = tmp;   rel(L1); rel(L2);
  T3:   acq(L2); b.x++; rel(L2);
```

In this example, two `IntBox` objects o1 and o2 are created and locks L1 and L2 are used for synchronization. The program follows the convention that L1 protects accesses to a and a.x, similarly, L2 protects accesses to b and b.x. At all times, each `IntBox` object and its integer field x are protected by the same lock. T2 swaps the objects referred to by the variables a and b.

Consider the interleaving in which all actions of T1 are completed, followed by those of T2 and then T3. T2 swaps the objects referred to by variables a and b so that during T3's actions b refers to o1. o1.x is initially protected by L1 but is protected by L2 after T2's actions are completed.

The most straightforward lockset algorithm is based on the assumption that each shared variable is protected by a fixed set of locks throughout the execution. Let $LH(t)$ represent the set of locks held by thread t at a given point in an execution. This algorithm attempts to infer this set by updating $LS(o, d)$ to be the intersection $LH(t) \cap LS(o, d)$ at each access to (o, d) by a thread t. If this intersection becomes empty, a race is reported. This approach is too conservative since it reports a false race if the lock protecting a variable changes over time. In the example above, when T3 accesses b.x, the standard lockset algorithm

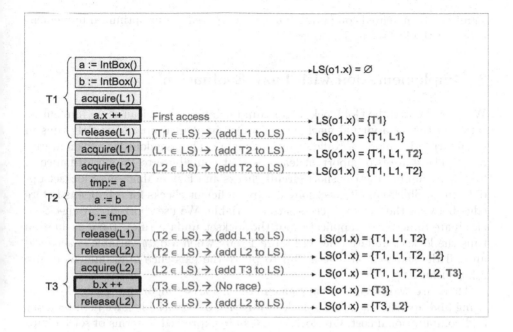

Fig. 2. Evaluation of $LS(\text{o1.x})$ by Goldilocks

declares a race since $LS(\text{o1.x}) = \{\text{L1}\}$ (b points to o1) before this access and T3 does not hold L1.

A less conservative alternative is to update $LS(o,d)$ to $LH(t)$ rather than $LH(t) \cap LS(o,d)$ after a race-free access to (o,d) by a thread t. For any given execution, this strategy, just like the previous strategy, will report a data-race if there is one but is still imprecise and might report false races. In the example above, this approach is unable to infer the correct new lockset for o1.x after T2's actions are completed. This is because T2 does not directly access o1.x and, as a result, $LS(\text{o1.x})$ is not modified by T2's actions.

Variants of lockset algorithms in the literature use additional mechanisms such as a state machine per shared variable in order to handle special cases such as thread locality, object initialization and escape. However these variants are neither sound nor precise, and they all report false alarms in scenarios similar to the one in the example above.

Our algorithm's lockset update rules allow a variable's locksets to grow and change during the execution. The lockset of a variable may be modified even without the variable being accessed. In this way, we are able to handle dynamically changing locksets and ownership transfers and avoid false alarms. In the example above, the lockset of o1.x evolves with our update rules during the execution as illustrated in Figure 2.

The vector-clock algorithm does not declare a false race in this example and similar scenarios. However, as discussed in Section 3, it accomplishes this at significantly increased computational cost compared to our optimized implementation of the lockset update rules.

3   Implementation with Lazy Evaluation

We implemented the Goldilocks algorithm in Kaffe [18], a clean room implementation of the Java virtual machine in C. Our implementation currently runs in the interpreting mode of Kaffe's runtime engine. The pseudocode is given in Figure 3. There are two important features that contribute to the performance of the algorithm in practice: short-circuit checks and lazy evaluation of lockset update rules. Short-circuit checks are cheap, sufficient checks for a happens-before edge between the last two accesses to a variable. We use short-circuit checks to eliminate unnecessary application of the lockset update rules. Lazy evaluation runs the lockset update rules in Figure 1 only when a data variable is accessed and all the short-circuit checks fail to prove the existence of a happens-before relationship.

There are two reasons we implemented our lockset algorithm lazily: 1) Managing and updating a separate lockset for each data variable have high memory and computational cost. Our lockset rules are expressed in terms of set lookups and insertions, and making the lockset a singleton set with the current thread id after an access. These simple update rules make possible a very easy and efficient form of computing locksets lazily only at an access. 2) For thread-local and well-synchronized variables, there may be no need to run (all of) the lockset update rules, because a short-circuit check or a subset of synchronization actions may be sufficient to show race freedom.

In our way of performing lazy evaluation, we do not explicitly associate a separate lockset $LS(o, d)$ for each data variable (o, d). Instead, $LS(o, d)$ is created temporarily, when (o, d) is accessed and the algorithm, after all short-circuit checks fail, finds it necessary to compute happens-before for that access using locksets. In addition, the lockset update rule for a synchronization action in Figure 1 is not applied to $LS(o, d)$ when the action is performed. We defer the application of these rules until (o, d) is accessed and the lockset update rules are applied for that access. We store the necessary information about a synchronization action in a *cell*, consisting of the current thread and the action. During the execution, cells are kept in a list that we call *update list*, which is represented by its *head* and *tail* pointers in the pseudocode. When a thread performs a synchronization action, it atomically appends its corresponding cell to the update list .

Each variable (o, d) is associated with an instance of *Info*. *info* maps variables to *Info* instances. $info(o, d)$ keeps track of three pieces of information necessary to check an access to (o, d): 1) *pos* is a pointer to a cell in the update list ($ref(Cell)$ is the reference type for *Cell*). 2) *owner* is the identifier of the thread that last accessed (o, d). After each access to (o, d) by thread t, $info(o, d)$ is updated so that *pos* is assigned to the reference of the cell at the tail of the update list and *owner* is assigned to t. 3) *alock* is used in a short-circuit check as explained

```
record Cell {                      record Info {
    thread: Tid;                       pos: ref(Cell);
    action: Action;                    owner: Tid;
    next: ref(Cell);}                  alock: Addr; }


head, tail: ref(Cell);             info: (Addr × Data) ⟶ Info;


Initially head := new Cell; tail := head; info := EmptyMap;


    Handle-Action (t, α):
1   if (α ∈ {acq(o), rel(o), fork(u), join(u), read(o,v), write(o,v),
                finalize(x), terminate(t)}) {
2       tail→thread := t;
3       tail→action := α;
4       tail→next := new Cell;
5       tail := tail→next;
6   }
7   else if (α ∈ {read(o,d), write(o,d)}) {
8       if (info(o,d) is not defined) { //initialize info(o,d) for the first access to (o,d)
9           info(o,d) := new Info;
10          info(o,d).alock := (choose randomly a lock held by t, if any exists);
11      } else {
12          if ((info(o,d).owner ≠ t) ∧ (info(o,d).alock is not held by t)) {
13              Apply-Lockset-Rules (t, (o,d)); // run the lockset algorithm
14              // because short circuits failed, reassign the random lock for (o,d)
15              info(o,d).alock := (choose randomly a lock held by t, if any exists);
16          }
17      }
18      // reset info(o,d) after each access to (o,d)
19      info(o,d).owner := t;
20      info(o,d).pos := tail;
21      Garbage-Collect-Cells (head, tail);
22  }
```

Fig. 3. Implementation of the Goldilocks algorithm

below. Notice that because locksets are created temporarily only when the full checking for the lockset rules is to be done, there is no field of $info(o,d)$ that points to a lockset.

We instrumented the JVM code by inserting calls to *Handle-Action*. The procedure *Handle-Action* is invoked each time a thread performs an action relevant to our algorithm. We performed the instrumentation so that the synchronizes-with order and the order of corresponding cells in the update list are kept consistent throughout the execution. Similarly, the order of cells respects the program order of the threads in the execution. We needed only for volatile reads/writes to insert explicit locks to make atomic the volatile access and appending the cell for that action to the update list.

Handle-Action takes as input a thread t and an action α performed by t. If α is a synchronization action, *Handle-Action* appends a cell referring to α to the end of the update list (lines 1-6). If α reads from or writes to a data variable (o, d) and it is the first access to (o, d) it creates a new *Info* for (o, d) and sets its *alock* to one of the locks held by t (lines 8-11). Otherwise, it first runs two short-circuit checks (line 12). If both of the short-circuit checks fail, the procedure *Apply-Lockset-Rules* is called. Before exiting *Handle-Action*, *info*(o,d) is updated to reflect the last access to (o, d) (lines 19-20). *Handle-Action* also garbage collects the cells in the update list that are no longer referenced, by calling *Garbage-Collect-Cells* (line 21).

Apply-Lockset-Rules applies the lockset update rules in Figure 1 but uses a local, temporarily-created lockset $LS(o, d)$. $LS(o, d)$ is initialized to contain *info*(o,d).*owner*, the identifier of the thread that last accessed (o, d), to reflect the effect of Rule 1 for variable accesses. Then the rules for the synchronization actions performed after the last access to (o, d) are applied to $LS(o, d)$ in turn. The cells in the update list between the cell pointed by *info*(o,d).*pos* and the cell pointed by *tail* are used in this computation. The access causes no warning if the current thread t is added to $LS(o, d)$ by some rule. This check is performed after handling each cell and is also used to terminate the lockset computation before reaching the tail of the update list. If t is not found in $LS(o, d)$, a race condition on (o, d) is reported.

Short-circuit checks: Our current implementation contains two constant time, sufficient checks for the happens-before relation between the last two accesses to a variable (see line 12 of *Handle-Action*). 1) We first check whether the currently accessing thread is the same as the last thread accessed the variable by comparing t and *info*(o,d).*owner*. This helps us to handle checking thread local variables in constant time without needing the lockset rules. 2) The second check handles variables that are protected by the same lock for a long time. We keep track of a lock *alock* for each variable (o, d). *info*(o, d).*alock* represents an element of $LS(o, d)$ chosen randomly. At the first access to (o, d) *info*(o, d).*alock* is assigned one of the locks held by the current thread randomly, or *null* if there is no such lock (line 10). After the next access to (o, d) we check if the lock *info*(o, d).*alock* is held by the current thread. If this check fails, *info*(o, d).*alock* is reassigned by choosing a new lock (line 15).

Comparison with the vector-clock algorithm: The vector-clock algorithm is as precise as our algorithm. However, the precision of the vector-clock algorithm may come at a significantly higher computational cost than Goldilocks because lazy evaluation and the short circuit checks make our approach very efficient. This fact is highlighted by the following example. Consider a program with a large number of threads $t_1, ..., t_n$ all accessing the same shared variable (o, d), where all accesses to (o, d) are protected by a single lock l. At each synchronization operation, $acq(l)$ or $rel(l)$, Goldilocks performs a constant-time operation to add the synchronization operation to the update list. Moreover, once *info*(o, d).*alock* $= l$, then at each access to (o, d) Goldilocks performs a

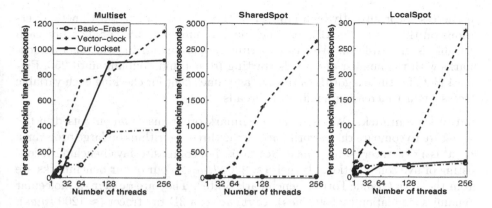

Fig. 4. Per access race checking time against the increasing number of threads

constant-time look-up to determine the absence of a race. The vector-clock algorithm, on the other hand, maintains a vector of size n for each thread and for each variable. At each synchronization operation, two such vectors are compared element-wise and updated. At each access to (o, d), the vector-clock algorithm performs constant-time work just like Goldilocks. While the vector-clock algorithm does $\Theta(n)$ work for each synchronization operation and $\Theta(1)$ for each data variable access, Goldilocks does $\Theta(1)$ work for every operation. As this example highlights and our experimental results demonstrate, the Goldilocks algorithm is more efficient than the vector-clock algorithm. The `SharedSpot` microbenchmark in Section 4 is based on the example described above and the experiments confirm the preceding analysis.

4 Evaluation

In order to evaluate the performance our algorithm, we ran the instrumented version of the Kaffe JVM on a set of benchmarks. In order to concentrate on the races in the applications, we disabled checks for fields of the standard library classes. Arrays were checked by treating each array element as a separate variable. We first present our experiments and discuss their results in Section 4.1.

In order to compare our algorithm with traditional lockset and vector-clock algorithms, we implemented a basic version of the Eraser algorithm that we call Basic-Eraser and a vector-clock based algorithm similar to the one used by Trade [5]. Where possible, we used the same data structure implementations while implementing the three algorithms. For Basic-Eraser, we used the same code for keeping and manipulating locksets that we developed for Goldilocks.

Microbenchmarks: The `Multiset` microbenchmark consists of a number of threads accessing a multiset of integers concurrently by inserting, deleting and querying elements to/from it. The `SharedSpot` benchmark illustrates the case in which a number of integers, each of which is protected by a separate unique lock, are accessed concurrently by a number of threads for applying arithmetic operations on them. The `LocalSpot` benchmark is similar to `SharedSpot` but each variable is thread-local. We ran experiments parameterizing the microbenchmarks with the number of threads starting from 1 and doubling until 256. Figure 4 plots for three algorithms the average time spent for checking each variable access against increasing number of threads.

Large benchmarks: We used six benchmark programs commonly used in the literature to compare the performance of the three algorithms on large programs: `Raja`[1] is a ray tracer ($\approx 6K\ lines$). `SciMark`[2] is a composite Java benchmark consisting of five computational kernels ($\approx 2300\ lines$). Four of our benchmarks are from the Java Grande Forum Benchmark Suite[3]. They are `moldyn`, a molecular dynamics simulation ($\approx 650\ lines$), `raytracer`, a 3D ray tracer ($\approx 1200\ lines$), `montecarlo`, a Monte Carlo simulation ($\approx 3K\ lines$) and `sor`, a successive over-relaxation program ($\approx 220\ lines$).

Table 1 presents the performance statistics of the three algorithms on the benchmark programs. The purpose of this batch of experiments is to contrast the overhead that each of the three approaches incur while checking for races. In this batch of experiments, race checking for a variable was *not* turned off after detecting a race on it, as would be the case in normal usage of a race detection tool. The purpose of this was to enable a fair comparison between algorithms. On this set of benchmarks, Basic-Eraser conservatively declared false races on many variables early in the execution. If race checking on these variables were turned off after Basic-Eraser detects a race on them, Basic-Eraser would have ended up doing a lot less work and checking a lot fewer accesses than the other two approaches, especially since these variables are typically very likely to have races on them later in the execution as well. This would have made the overhead numbers difficult to compare. In Table 1, we give the number of threads created in each program below the name of the benchmark. The column titled "Uninstrumented" reports the total runtime of the program in the uninstrumented JVM, and the total number of variable accesses (fields+array indices) performed at runtime. Each column for an algorithm presents, for each benchmark, the total execution time and the slowdown ratio of the program with instrumentation. The time values are given in seconds. The slowdown ratio is the ratio of the difference between the instrumented runtime and the uninstrumented runtime to the uninstrumented runtime. The number of variable accesses checked for races is important for assessing the amount of work carried out by the algorithm during execution and average checking time for each variable access.

Table 2 lists the results of our experiments with Goldilocks where checks for fields on which a race is detected are disabled. This is a more realistic setting to judge the overhead of our algorithm in absolute terms. The measurements reported in the first three rows are the same as the ones in Table 1, taken

---

[1] `Raja` can be obtained at *http://raja.sourceforge.net/*.

[2] `Scimark` can be obtained at *http://math.nist.gov/scimark2/*.

[3] `Java Grande Forum Benchmark Suite` can be obtained at
http://www.epcc.ed.ac.uk/computing/research_activities/java_grande/threads.html.

Table 1. Runtime statistics of the benchmark programs

	Uninstrumented	Vector-clock	Basic-Eraser	Goldilocks
Benchmark	Runtime (sec.)	Runtime (sec.)	Runtime (sec.)	Runtime (sec.)
# threads	# accesses	Slowdown	Slowdown	Slowdown
Raja	8.6	145.1	105.9	70.2
3	5979629	15.7	11.1	7
SciMark	28.2	51.3	46.1	33.1
7	3647012	0.8	0.6	0.1
moldyn	11.2	195	138.9	92.8
7	8610585	16.3	11.3	7.2
raytracer	1.9	122.8	79.8	50
7	5299350	63.1	40.6	25.1
montecarlo	5.7	243.8	160	117.5
7	10491747	41.4	26.8	19.4
sor	27.2	145.9	157.5	107
7	7696597	4.3	4.7	2.9

Table 2. Runtime statistics when fields with races detected on them are disabled

Algorithm	Raja	SciMark	moldyn	raytracer	montecarlo	sor
Runtime	70.2	33.1	92.8	50	117.6	107
Slowdown	7	0.1	7.2	25.1	19.4	2.9
# checks	5979629	3647012	8610585	5299350	10491747	7696597
Runtime*	65.8	35.5	57.0	17.6	111.2	63.8
Slowdown*	6.5	0.2	4	8.2	18.3	1.3
# checks*	5979629	4104754	5268021	1884836	10484544	3416928

* Results after disabling checks to the fields.

without disabling any checks. The second three rows give the runtime statistics when we followed the approach described above.

4.1 Discussion

The plots in Figure 4 show per access checking times of the three algorithms. The very low acceleration in the per access runtime overhead of our algorithm and Eraser in the SharedSpot and LocalSpot examples is noteworthy. Short circuit checks in our algorithm allow constant time overhead for thread-local variables and variables protected by a unique lock. This makes our algorithm asymptotically better than the vector-clock algorithm.

The runtime statistics in Table 1 indicate that Goldilocks performs better than the vector-clock algorithm for large-scale programs. As the number of checks done for variable accesses are the same, we can conclude that per variable access checking time of our lockset algorithm on average is less than the vector-clock algorithm.

SciMark, moldyn and sor are well-synchronized programs with few races and a simple locking discipline. Thus the short circuit checks mostly succeed and the overhead of the lockset algorithm is low. However, more elaborate synchronization policies in Raja, raytracer and montecarlo caused long runs of the lockset algorithm, thus the slowdown ratio increases. These programs have a relatively high number of races.

The results indicate that our algorithm works as efficiently as Basic-Eraser while Basic-Eraser can not handle all the synchronization policies used in the benchmarks. The main reason for our algorithm performing slightly better in our experiments is the fact that Basic-Eraser does lockset intersections while checking the accesses. Intersection is fundamentally an expensive operation. Our algorithm, on the other hand, requires insertions and lookups, which can be implemented in constant amortized time. Clearly, a more optimized implementation of Eraser would have performed better. The goal of the comparison with Basic-Eraser was to demonstrate that our algorithm does not have significantly more cost than other lockset algorithms.

Disabling checking accesses to fields on which races were detected dramatically decreases the number of accesses to be checked against races, thus the total runtime of the instrumented program. This can be seen from Table 1. For the benchmarks `moldyn`, `raytracer` and `sor`, the differences in the number of accesses point to this effect.

5   Related Work

Dynamic race-detection methods do not suffer from false positives as much as static methods do but are not exhaustive. Eraser [15] is a well-known tool for detecting race conditions dynamically by enforcing the locking discipline that every shared variable is protected by a unique lock. It handles object initialization patterns using a state-based approach but can not handle dynamically changing locksets since it only allows a lockset to get smaller. There is much work that refines the Eraser algorithm by improving the state machine it uses and the transitions to reduce the number of false positives. One such refinement is extending the state-based handling of object initialization and making use of object-oriented concepts [17]. Harrow used thread segments to identify the portions of the execution in which objects are accessed concurrently among threads [9]. Another approach is using a basic vector-clock algorithm to capture thread-local accesses to objects and thus eliminates unnecessary and imprecise applications of the Eraser algorithm [19]. Precise lockset algorithms exist for Cilk programs but their use for real programs is still under question [2]. The general algorithm in [2] is quite inefficient while the efficient version of this algorithm requires programs to obey the umbrella locking discipline, which can be violated by race-free programs.

The approaches that check a happens-before relation [5,14,16] are based on vector clocks [11], which create a partial order on program statements. Trade [5] uses a precise vector-clock algorithm. Trade is implemented at the Java byte code level and in interpreter mode of JVM as is our algorithm. To reduce the overhead of the vector clocks for programs with a large number of threads, they use reachability information through the threads, which makes Trade more efficient than other similar tools. Schonberg computes for each thread shared variable sets and concurrency lists to capture the set of shared variables between synchronization points of an execution [16]. His algorithm is imprecise for synchronization disciplines that use locks and needs to be extended for asynchronous coordination to get precision for these disciplines.

Hybrid techniques [13,19] combine lockset and happens-before analysis. For example, RaceTrack's happens-before computation is based on both vector clocks and locksets. but is not sound as its lockset part of the algorithm is based on Eraser algorithm. Our technique, for the first time, computes a precise happens-before relation using an implementation that makes use of only locksets. Choi et.al. present an unsound runtime algorithm [4] for race detection. They used a static method [3] to eliminate unnecessary checks for well-protected variables. This is a capability we intend to integrate into Goldilocks in the future.

6 Conclusions

In this paper, we present a new sound and precise race-detection algorithm. Goldilocks is based solely on the concept of locksets and is able to capture all mutual-exclusion synchronization idioms uniformly with one mechanism. The algorithm can be used, both in the static or the dynamic context, to develop analyses for concurrent programs, particularly those for detecting data-races, atomicity violations, and failures of safety specifications. In our future work, we plan to develop and integrate into Goldilocks a static analysis technique to reduce the cost of runtime checking.

Acknowledgements

We thank Madan Musuvathi for many interesting discussions that contributed to the implementation technique described in Section 3.

References

1. C. Boyapati, R. Lee, and M. Rinard. A type system for preventing data races and deadlocks in Java programs. In *OOPSLA 02: Object-Oriented Programming, Systems, Languages and Applications*, pages 211–230. ACM, 2002.
2. Guang-Ien Cheng, Mingdong Feng, Charles E. Leiserson, Keith H. Randall, and Andrew F. Stark. Detecting data races in cilk programs that use locks. In *Proceedings of the ACM Symposium on Parallel Algorithms and Architectures (SPAA '98)*, pages 298–309, Puerto Vallarta, Mexico, June 28–July 2 1998.
3. J.-D. Choi, A. Loginov, and V. Sarkar. Static datarace analysis for multithreaded object-oriented programs. Technical Report RC22146, IBM Research, 2001.
4. Jong-Deok Choi, Keunwoo Lee, Alexey Loginov, Robert O'Callahan, Vivek Sarkar, and Manu Sridharan. Efficient and precise datarace detection for multithreaded object-oriented programs. In *PLDI 02: Programming Language Design and Implementation*, pages 258–269. ACM, 2002.
5. Mark Christiaens and Koen De Bosschere. Trade, a topological approach to on-the-fly race detection in Java programs. In *JVM 01: Java Virtual Machine Research and Technology Symposium*, pages 105–116. USENIX, 2001.

6. Tayfun Elmas, Shaz Qadeer, and Serdar Tasiran. Goldilocks: Efficiently Computing the Happens-Before Relation Using Locksets, 2006. Full version available at http://www.research.microsoft.com/~qadeer/fatesrv06-fullversion.ps.
7. C. Flanagan and S. N. Freund. Type-based race detection for Java. In *PLDI 00: Programming Language Design and Implementation*, pages 219–232. ACM, 2000.
8. C. Flanagan and P. Godefroid. Dynamic partial-order reduction for model checking software. In *POPL 05: Principles of Programming Languages*, pages 110–121. ACM Press, 2005.
9. J. J. Harrow. Runtime checking of multithreaded applications with visual threads. In *SPIN 00: Workshop on Model Checking and Software Verification*, pages 331–342. Springer-Verlag, 2000.
10. Jeremy Manson, William Pugh, and Sarita Adve. The Java memory model. In *POPL 05: Principles of Programming Languages*, pages 378–391. ACM Press, 2005.
11. Friedemann Mattern. Virtual time and global states of distributed systems. In *International Workshop on Parallel and Distributed Algorithms*, pages 215–226. North-Holland, 1989.
12. Robert H. B. Netzer and Barton P. Miller. What are race conditions?: Some issues and formalizations. *ACM Lett. Program. Lang. Syst.*, 1(1):74–88, 1992.
13. E. Pozniansky and A. Schuster. Efficient on-the-fly race detection in multithreaded c++ programs. In *PPoPP 03: Principles and Practice of Parallel Programming*, pages 179–190. ACM, 2003.
14. M. Ronsse and K. De Bosschere. Recplay: A fully integrated practical record/replay system. *ACM Transactions on Computer Systems*, 17(2):133–152, 1999.
15. Stefan Savage, Michael Burrows, Greg Nelson, Patrick Sobalvarro, and Thomas Anderson. Eraser: A dynamic data race detector for multithreaded programs. *ACM Transactions on Computer Systems*, 15(4):391–411, 1997.
16. Edith Schonberg. On-the-fly detection of access anomalies. In *PLDI 89: Programming Language Design and Implementation*, pages 313–327, 1989.
17. Christoph von Praun and Thomas R. Gross. Object race detection. In *OOPSLA 01: Object-Oriented Programming, Systems, Languages and Applications*, pages 70–82. ACM, 2001.
18. T. Wilkinson. Kaffe: A JIT and interpreting virtual machine to run Java code. http://www.transvirtual.com/, 1998.
19. Yuan Yu, Tom Rodeheffer, and Wei Chen. Racetrack: efficient detection of data race conditions via adaptive tracking. In *SOSP 05: Symposium on Operating Systems Principles*, pages 221–234. ACM, 2005.

Dynamic Architecture Extraction

Cormac Flanagan[1] and Stephen N. Freund[2]

[1] Dept. of Computer Science, University of California at Santa Cruz,
Santa Cruz, CA 95064
[2] Dept. of Computer Science, Williams College, Williamstown, MA 01267

Abstract. Object models capture key properties of object-oriented architectures, and they can highlight relationships between types, occurrences of sharing, and object encapsulation. We present a dynamic analysis to extract object models from legacy code bases. Our analysis reconstructs each intermediate heap from a log of object allocations and field writes, applies a sequence of abstraction-based operations to each heap, and combines the results into a single object model that conservatively approximates all observed heaps from the program's execution. The resulting object models reflect many interesting and useful architectural properties.

1 Introduction

Object models capture the essence of object-oriented designs. However, many systems are developed without documented object models or evolve in ways that deviate from the original model. Tools to reconstruct object models are a valuable aid for understanding and reasoning about such systems. This paper presents a dynamic analysis to extract object models from existing code bases. We have found that these inferred object models explicate key structural invariants of object-oriented designs.

As an illustrative example, Figure 1 shows the inferred object model for parts of the abstract syntax tree (AST) data structure related to class declarations from the ESC/Java code base [15]. This object model is drawn as a UML class diagram [7], in which nodes represent classes and edges represent indicate both association and generalization relationships between classes. The graph reveals a number of important (and occasionally surprising) properties of ASTs:

- Each `ClassDecl` (at the top of the graph) has a `superClass` field with the somewhat unexpected multiplicity label '?', indicating that this field may be null. Inspection of the code revealed that the `superClass` field can in fact be null in one special case, namely when the `ClassDecl` is for `java.lang.Object`, the root of the class hierarchy.
- Each `ClassDecl` has a field `elems` containing one or more `TypeDeclElem` objects, as indicated by the multiplicity '+'. Again, this label was somewhat unexpected, since empty class declarations are valid in Java. However, further investigation revealed that the parser automatically adds an implicit nullary constructor to such classes.

K. Havelund et al. (Eds.): FATES/RV 2006, LNCS 4262, pp. 209–224, 2006.

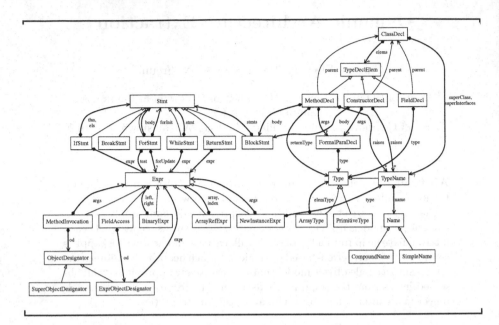

Fig. 1. Object Model for the AST Package from ESC/Java's Front-End

- Each `TypeDeclElem` may be a `MethodDecl`, `ConstructorDecl`, or `FieldDecl`, as indicated by the hollow-tipped generalization arrows from the subtypes to the supertype.
- Each `MethodDecl` contains zero or more `FormalParaDecls`, as shown via the multiplicity '*'.
- The bold, diamond-tailed edges indicate unique references. All edges in this object model are unique, except for the **parent** pointers from each `TypeDeclElem`, which point back to the containing `ClassDecl`. Thus, the overall structure is mostly a tree, but documenting the non-unique **parent** pointers is crucial since any tree traversal algorithm must include special treatment for these pointers.
- Although not present in Figure 1, we also infer *ownership* and *containment* properties, which we found necessary to express encapsulation properties in complex situations where unique references are not sufficient, and we have enriched UML class diagrams to express these additional properties.

Object models could be reconstructed statically, by analyzing the program source code [5,25,23,26]. However, precise static alias analysis is a notoriously difficult problem, and so static analyses have some difficulties inferring precise invariants regarding heap structure and sharing (although progress continues to be made on this topic).

In contrast, dynamic alias analysis reduces to a simple pointer comparison, and so dynamic analyses can provide very precise information regarding structural properties of heaps, such as: which portions of the heap follow a tree structure,

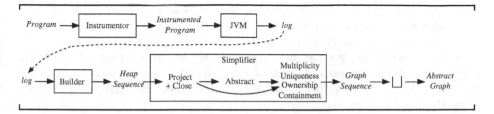

Fig. 2. Schematic

which pointers are unique, and which objects are encapsulated within other objects. Of course, any dynamic analysis is limited by test coverage and may infer false invariants. In our experience, such anomalies, once discovered, are straightforward to rectify by appropriately extending the test inputs.

Figure 2 presents a schematic of our analysis tool, AARDVARK, which is based on *offline heap reconstruction*. It first executes an instrumented version of the target program that records a log of all object allocations and field writes. The *Builder* phase then uses this log to reconstruct a snapshot of the heap at each intermediate stage in the program's execution. The primary focus of this paper is on how to infer object models from these reconstructed heaps.

For each heap snapshot, AARDVARK isolates the relevant fragment of that heap via the *projection* and *closure* operations described in Section 2. It then uses *abstraction* (or object merging) to generate an initial object model for that heap, as described in Section 3. That object model is extended with additional information regarding multiplicities, unique pointers, ownership, and containment (see Section 4). Thus, the sequence of heap snapshots is abstracted into a corresponding sequence of object models.

We formalize the space of object models as labeled graphs, which form an abstract domain [12] with abstraction and concretization functions. Section 5 defines the upper bound operation ⊔ on this domain, which we use to compute a single object model that conservatively approximates all of the heap snapshots from the program's execution.

The implementation of AARDVARK is described in Section 6. Preliminary experiments indicate that the inferred object models are quite precise and useful, and that they explicate important architectural details. In many cases, we can produce sufficiently accurate results by analyzing only a small sample of heap snapshots. Section 8 discusses some important topics for future work, including developing incremental versions of our abstraction algorithms.

2   Heap Projection and Closure

We begin by formalizing the notion of an object heap. We ignore primitive data (such as integers) and focus only on the structure of the heap. Let A be the set of object addresses (or simply objects) and let F be the set of field names in the program. We use $a, b, c, \ldots$ as meta-variables ranging over object addresses, and use f to range over field names. A *heap* H is a relation[1] $H \subseteq A \times F \times A$ describing how fields of some objects point to other objects.[1] Each edge in H is written as $(a \rightarrow_f b)$, meaning that field f of object a points to object b.

In many situations, we may be interested only in certain parts of the heap, such as the objects corresponding to a particular package or data structure. If the object set $J \subseteq A$ describes these objects of interest, then the *projection* of a heap H onto J isolates them:

$$proj_J(H) = \{(a \rightarrow_f b) \mid (a \rightarrow_f b) \in H \wedge a, b \in J\}$$

Figure 3(a) shows a heap projection that focuses on the AST data structure of the ESC/Java front-end. The diagram shows that each class declaration contains a set of method, constructor, and field declarations.

This diagram also includes nodes that describe *how* class declarations are represented, via a `TypeDeclElemVec` object that contains an array. We often want to abstract away such low-level representation details, which is accomplished via the following *closure* operation that elides these intermediate objects (or *representation nodes*. For any set of low-level representation nodes $J \subseteq A$, the closure of a heap H with respect to J is defined by

$$close_J(H) = \left\{ (a \rightarrow_f b) \;\middle|\; \begin{array}{l} a, b \notin J \text{ and } \exists \text{ a path in } H \text{ from } a \text{ to } b \text{ whose first} \\ \text{field is } f \text{ and whose intermediate nodes are in } J \end{array} \right\}$$

The closure of Figure 3(a) with respect to representation nodes yields the diagram of Figure 3(b), which more directly shows the relationship between class declarations and their elements.

3   Abstraction

After projection and closure, the next step is to *abstract* from each program heap H (with perhaps millions of objects) a concise graphical representation G of the object model. Here, G is simply a graph over a collection of abstract nodes and edges, as defined precisely in Section 3.1. We consider a sequence of increasingly-precise abstractions. For clarity, we formalize the semantics of each representation with a *concretization function* γ that defines the meaning of a graph G as the set of heaps $\gamma(G)$ matching that description. Conversely, the *abstraction function* α maps a given concrete heap H to a corresponding graph $G = \alpha(H)$. For soundness, we require that the meaning of G includes the original graph H, i.e., $H \in \gamma(\alpha(H))$.

A graph G_1 is *more precise* than G_2, denoted $G_1 \sqsubseteq G_2$, if $\gamma(G_1) \subseteq \gamma(G_2)$. Unlike in static analyses where the primary purpose of abstraction is to facilitate convergence, the purpose of abstraction in our setting is to ignore low-level details and isolate architectural invariants. For this reason, we do not require $\alpha(H)$ to be a most precise element of $\{G \mid H \in \gamma(G)\}$.

---

[1] We formalize the heap as a relation instead of a partial function $A \times F \rightarrow_p A$ to facilitate our subsequent development.

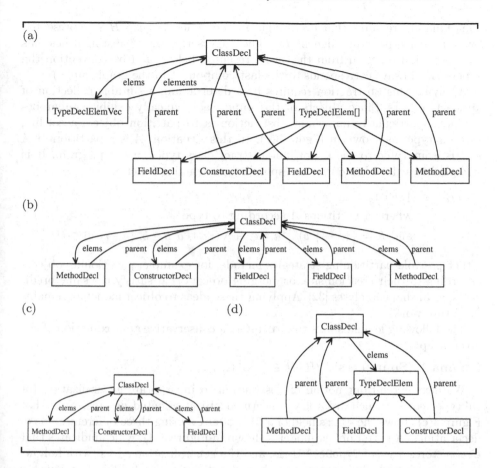

Fig. 3. Closure, Abstraction, and Generalization

3.1 Heap Abstraction

The first class of abstractions we consider simply merges concrete objects into summary, or *abstract*, objects. Each abstract object $\hat{a}$ is a set of corresponding concrete objects (*i.e.*, $\hat{a} \subseteq A$), and we use $\hat{A}$ to denote the set of abstract objects. Thus $\hat{A} \subseteq 2^A$. An *(abstract) graph* G is a pair $(\hat{A}, \hat{E})$, where $\hat{E} \subseteq \hat{A} \times F \times \hat{A}$ is a set of field-labeled edges between abstract objects. Each abstract edge $(\hat{a} \to_f \hat{b})$ describes a set of possible concrete edges according to the *edge concretization function* γ:

$$\gamma(\hat{a} \to_f \hat{b}) = \{(a \to_f b) \mid a \in \hat{a}, b \in \hat{b}\}$$

Each abstract graph $(\hat{A}, \hat{E})$ represents a set of concrete heaps according to the concretization function γ^e:

$$\gamma^e(\hat{A}, \hat{E}) = \{H \mid \forall e \in H. \exists \hat{e} \in \hat{E}. e \in \gamma(\hat{e})\}$$

This function requires that every edge in the concrete heap H is represented by some corresponding edge in $\hat{E}$. (The superscript on γ^e distinguishes this concretization function from the ones presented below, and by convention the superscript always corresponds to the last component in the graph tuple.)

Applying this abstraction requires first determining a suitable collection of abstract objects. Since objects of the same class typically exhibit similar behavior, a particularly important abstraction is to partition objects according to their type, as shown in Figure 3(c). In this situation, $\hat{A}$ is a partition of A and is isomorphic to the set of non-abstract class types in the program. It is straightforward to define the corresponding abstraction function α^e:

$$\alpha^e(H) = (\hat{A}, \hat{E})$$
$$\text{where } \hat{A} \text{ partitions } A \text{ according to type}$$
$$\text{and } \hat{E} = \left\{ (\hat{a} \rightarrow_f \hat{b}) \mid \hat{a}, \hat{b} \in \hat{A} \wedge (\exists a \in \hat{a}, b \in \hat{b}. \ (a \rightarrow_f b) \in H) \right\}$$

Other possible partitioning strategies include, for example, partitioning objects according to their creation site, or merging objects that satisfy the same predicates, as in shape analyses [32]. Applying these ideas to object modeling remains for future work.

The following lemma states that α^e infers a conservative approximation of the given heap.

Lemma 1 (Soundness). $\forall H. \ H \in \gamma^e(\alpha^e(H))$.

We next extend our notion of abstraction to incorporate generalization (or subtype) edges, which are a key concern in object-oriented designs. Note that Figure 3(c) shows the `elems` field of a `ClassDecl` storing three different kinds of declarations. A better object model is shown in Figure 3(d), which indicates that `elems` stores a set of `TypeDeclElems`, and the generalization edges (with hollow-tipped arrowheads) indicate that method, constructor, and field declarations are all subtypes of `TypeDeclElem`.

To illustrate how we perform generalization, suppose a class A extends B. We create corresponding abstract objects $\hat{a}$ and $\hat{b}$ as before, except that $\hat{b}$ now contains all concrete objects whose type is B or any subtype of B, including A. Thus $\hat{a} \subseteq \hat{b}$, and we indicate this containment relationship by drawing a generalization edge from $\hat{a}$ to $\hat{b}$.

The presence of generalization edges complicates the abstraction mapping. In general, a set of classes to which a field (such as `elems`) points could be generalized to any common supertype, but the best choice is the most-specific common supertype. Due to Java's multiple interface inheritance, this most-specific common supertype may not be unique, in which case AARDVARK employs simple heuristics to choose the most appropriate generalization.

4   Multiplicities and Structural Attributes

The abstractions of the previous section can produce precise summaries of large heaps, but they can also lose key information. This section enriches those abstract

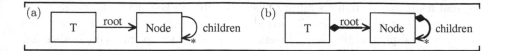

Fig. 4. Uniqueness

graphs with additional attributes describing the multiplicity of abstract edges, as well as sharing and structural properties of the heap.

4.1 Multiplicities

The object model in Figure 1 labels each abstract edge with a multiplicity that describes how many objects it points to: "?" for at most one, "ϵ" for exactly one, "*" for zero or more, and "+" for one or more. Here ϵ indicates the absence of a multiplicity label. These multiplicity labels reveal that class declarations contain at least one element, method declarations contain zero or more formal parameters, and method declarations contain exactly one statement.

To compute this information, we annotate each abstract edge $(\hat{a} \to_f \hat{b})$ with a *multiplicity set* that describes, for each concrete object $a \in \hat{a}$, how many $\hat{b}$-objects the object a points to. Specifically, the multiplicity set $m((\hat{a} \to_f \hat{b}), H)$ of an abstract edge $(\hat{a} \to_f \hat{b})$ in a heap H is the set of natural numbers given by:

$$m((\hat{a} \to_f \hat{b}), H) = \{t_1, \ldots t_n\} \quad \text{where } \hat{a} = \{a_1, \ldots, a_n\}$$
$$\text{and } t_i = \left| \{b \mid b \in \hat{b} \wedge (a_i \to_f b) \in H\} \right|$$

We extend the abstract graph $(\hat{A}, \hat{E})$ with an additional component $M : \hat{E} \to 2^{\text{Nat}}$ describing the multiplicity sets of each abstract edge. The concretization function enforces this intended meaning, and the abstraction function computes the appropriate multiplicities from the concrete graph:

$$\gamma^m(\hat{A}, \hat{E}, M) = \left\{ H \in \gamma^e(\hat{A}, \hat{E}) \mid \forall \hat{e} \in \hat{E}.\ m(\hat{e}, H) \subseteq M(\hat{e}) \right\}$$
$$\alpha^m(H) = (\hat{A}, \hat{E}, M) \quad \text{where } (\hat{A}, \hat{E}) = \alpha^e(H) \text{ and } M = \lambda \hat{e} \in \hat{E}.\ m(\hat{e}, H)$$

Lemma 2 (Soundness Of Multiplicities). $\forall H.\ H \in \gamma^m(\alpha^m(H))$.

Since multiplicity sets are rather dependent on the specific program execution, when drawing diagrams we generalize them to the more abstract multiplicity labels "?", "ϵ", "*", and "+", described above.

4.2 Uniqueness

The process of abstracting or object merging loses information about cycles or sharing in the underlying concrete heap. This limitation is illustrated by the abstract graph of Figure 4(a). From this graph, it is unclear whether the original heap was actually a binary tree, a doubly-linked list, a DAG, or some more general graph structure. To avoid this limitation, we next describe three increasingly sophisticated ways to enrich the abstract graph with additional information describing the degree to which sharing can occur in the underlying heap.

We begin by introducing the notion of unique edges. A concrete edge $(a \rightarrow_f b) \in H$ is *unique* if it points to an unshared object, that is, if H does not contain any other edge $(c \rightarrow_g b)$ that also points to b. This notion of uniqueness naturally extends to abstract edges: an abstract edge is unique if it only corresponds to unique concrete edges. In Figure 4(b), these unique edges (drawn in bold with a solid diamond on the tail) clarify that no sharing occurs, and thus this object model is more precise than Figure 4(a) since it describes only trees, and not other DAG or graph structures.

To formalize this notion of uniqueness, we extend the abstract graph $(\hat{A}, \hat{E}, M)$ of the previous section with an additional component $U \subseteq \hat{E}$ that describes which abstract edges are unique. The concretization and abstraction functions become:

$$\gamma^u(\hat{A}, \hat{E}, M, U) =$$
$$\left\{ H \in \gamma^m(\hat{A}, \hat{E}, M) \mid \forall \hat{e} \in U. \; \forall e \in \gamma(\hat{e}) \cap H. \; e \text{ is unique in } H \right\}$$
$$\alpha^u(H) = (\hat{A}, \hat{E}, M, U) \quad \text{where } (\hat{A}, \hat{E}, M) = \alpha^m(H) \text{ and}$$
$$U = \{\hat{e} \in \hat{E} \mid \forall e \in \gamma(\hat{e}) \cap H. \; e \text{ is unique in } H\}$$

Lemma 3 (Soundness Of Uniqueness). $\forall H. \; H \in \gamma^u(\alpha^u(H))$.

4.3   Ownership

Unique pointers provide precise information in the ideal case where there is *no* sharing but cannot describe controlled or encapsulated sharing. For example, the concrete heap of Figure 5(a) includes two `java.util.LinkedLists`, each of which is represented by a doubly-linked list of `LinkedList$Entrys`. Each `LinkedList$Entry` contains a `Point`, except for the dummy node at the head of the list.

Even though `LinkedList$Entrys` are encapsulated by their owning list, pointers to `LinkedList$Entrys` are not unique. Thus, the abstract graph of Figure 5(b) loses this key encapsulation information and instead suggests that `LinkedList$Entrys` could be shared between `LinkedLists`.

To remedy this limitation, we incorporate the notion of object *ownership* based on *dominators* [11]. An object a dominates object b if every path from a root of the heap to b must pass through a. Thus, the *dominates* relation $dom_H \subseteq A \times A$ for a heap H is the greatest fixpoint of the equations:

$$dom_H(b) = \{b\} \qquad \qquad \text{if } b \text{ is a root of } H$$
$$dom_H(b) = \{b\} \cup \left(\bigcap_{(a \rightarrow_f b) \in H} dom_H(a) \right) \qquad \text{otherwise}$$

Roots could be, for example, all static fields in a program, or perhaps a more specific collection of objects, depending on the particular domain.

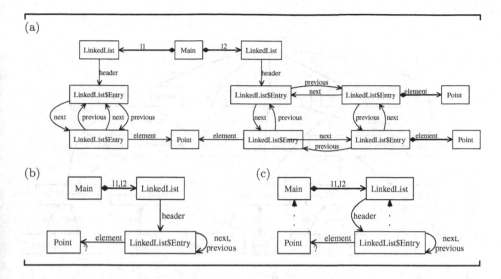

Fig. 5. Ownership

We extend this dominator relation to abstract graphs, and say that $\hat{a}$ *dominates* $\hat{b}$ *in* H (written $\hat{a} \rhd_H \hat{b}$) if every $\hat{b}$-object is dominated by some $\hat{a}$-object, i.e., if $\forall b \in \hat{b}. \exists a \in \hat{a}. a \in dom_H(b)$. When drawing abstract graphs, we indicate the closest, most precise dominator of each abstract object as an *ownership edge*, drawn as a dashed arrow. In Figure 5(c), these ownership edges show that each `LinkedList$Entry` object is owned by some `LinkedList`, which means that `LinkedList$Entrys` are never shared between `LinkedLists`. As expected, `Points` are owned by the object `Main` and not the lists, since a `Point` is shared between both lists. For `LinkedList`, which is the target of a unique pointer, an ownership edge would be a redundant inverse of that unique pointer, and so is omitted.

We include this abstract domination relation $\rhd_H \subseteq \hat{A} \times \hat{A}$ as an additional component in the abstract graph, whose concretization and abstraction functions become:

$$\gamma^{\rhd}(\hat{A}, \hat{E}, M, U, \rhd) = \left\{ H \in \gamma^u(\hat{A}, \hat{E}, M, U) \mid \rhd \subseteq \rhd_H \right\}$$
$$\alpha^{\rhd}(H) = (\hat{A}, \hat{E}, M, U, \rhd_H) \quad \text{where } (\hat{A}, \hat{E}, M, U) = \alpha^u(H)$$

Lemma 4 (Soundness Of Ownership). $\forall H. H \in \gamma^{\rhd}(\alpha^{\rhd}(H))$.

4.4 Containment

Our final refinement captures encapsulation in complex situations for which neither uniqueness nor ownership suffices. Consider the concrete heap of Figure 6(a), which shows two `java.util.HashMap` objects, each of which has an array of `HashMap$Entry` objects and some iterators that also point to the `HashMap$Entry`

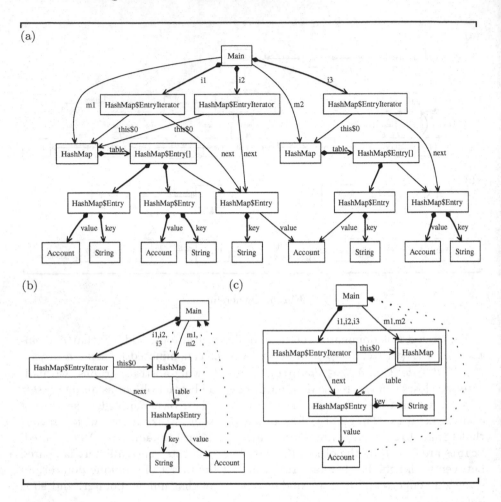

Fig. 6. Containment

objects. Each `HashMap$Entry` object is encapsulated in its `HashMap` and corresponding iterators. Thus, the `HashMap` representations can be partitioned into two connected components or *containers*.

However, in the abstract graph of Figure 6(b), neither uniqueness nor ownership is sufficient to explicate this partitioning. In particular, the only owner for the `HashMap$Entry`s is the object `Main`, since `HashMap$Entry`s are not dominated by either `HashMap`s or the iterator. Thus, the graph suggests that `HashMap$Entry` objects could be shared between `HashMap`s, in which case updating one `HashMap` could then change the state of other `HashMap`s.

To remedy this limitation, we introduce the notion of *containment* and *singletons*. A container *C* is a set of abstract objects that represents an encapsulated data structure. For example, Figure 6(c) includes a container (drawn as a large box) encompassing the `HashMap` and related objects. Each concrete heap contains some number of *container instances* $c_1, \ldots, c_n$, where each container instance c_i is a set of concrete objects. The key concept of containment is that there can be no concrete edges between container instances.

Figure 6(c) also shows that `HashMap` is a *singleton* (drawn as a double box), indicating that each container instance contains exactly one `HashMap` object. Thus, each container instance includes a single `HashMap` and its associated iterators, entries, and `Strings`, which means that `HashMap$Entrys` are never shared between `HashMaps`. To formalize these notions, we extend abstract graphs and the concretization function with two additional components, the container C and the set of singleton objects S:

$$\gamma^s(\hat{A}, \hat{E}, M, U, \rhd, C, S) =$$
$$\left\{ H \in \gamma^\rhd(\hat{A}, \hat{E}, M, U, \rhd) \; \middle| \; \begin{array}{l} \exists n, c_1, \ldots, c_n. \\ \forall \hat{a}, \hat{b} \in C, a \in \hat{a}, b \in \hat{b}. \\ \quad ((a \to_f b) \in H \Rightarrow \exists i. \, a, b \in c_i) \\ \wedge \, \forall \hat{a} \in S. \, \forall i \in 1..n. \, |\hat{a} \cap c_i| = 1 \end{array} \right\}$$

The corresponding abstraction function assumes we are given a fixed container C by the programmer[2]. This function infers the set of container instances by computing (using a union-find algorithm) the maximal partition P of the container objects into valid container instances, and it then computes the set S of singleton objects with respect to these containers:

$\alpha^s(H) = (\hat{A}, \hat{E}, M, U, \rhd, C, S)$
  where $(\hat{A}, \hat{E}, M, U, \rhd) = \alpha^\rhd(H)$
  and P is the maximal partitioning of the container objects $\cup C$ such that
  $\forall \hat{a}, \hat{b} \in C, a \in \hat{a}, b \in \hat{b}$, if $(a \to_f b) \in H$ then a and b are in the same partition
  and $S = \{\hat{a} \in C \mid \forall c \in P. \, |\hat{a} \cap c| = 1\}$

Lemma 5 (Soundness Of Containment). $\forall H. \, H \in \gamma^s(\alpha^s(H))$.

5   From Heaps to Traces

The previous two sections show how to extract an abstract graph from each concrete heap. Applying this abstraction process to each observed heap $H_1, \ldots, H_n$ in the instrumented execution yields a sequence of graphs $G_1, \ldots, G_n$, where $G_i = \alpha(H_i)$. The final step is to merge these graphs into a single graph.

For this purpose, we introduce the following upper bound operation on abstract graphs $(\hat{A}, \hat{E}, M, U, \rhd, C, S)$. We assume that the graphs are defined over the same collection of abstract objects $\hat{A}$, heap roots, and container C. The upper bound operation then combines the remaining components by taking the union of the abstract edge sets; the point-wise union (denoted $\cup^m$) of the multiplicity maps; and the intersection of the unique edge sets, the domination relations, and the singleton sets:

---

[2] This technique generalizes to multiple different containers, and we are currently exploring ways to algorithmically or heuristically identify likely containers.

$$(\hat{A}, \hat{E}_1, M_1, U_1, \triangleright_1, C, S_1) \ \sqcup \ (\hat{A}, \hat{E}_2, M_2, U_2, \triangleright_2, C, S_2) \ = $$
$$(\hat{A}, \hat{E}_1 \cup \hat{E}_2, M_1 \cup^m M_2, U_1 \cap U_2, \triangleright_1 \cap \triangleright_2, C, S_1 \cap S_2)$$

The point-wise union of two multiplicity maps is defined as:

$$(M_1 \cup^m M_2)(\hat{e}) = \begin{cases} M_1(\hat{e}) \cup M_2(\hat{e}) & \text{if } \hat{e} \in domain(M_1), \hat{e} \in domain(M_2) \\ M_1(\hat{e}) \cup \{0\} & \text{if } \hat{e} \in domain(M_1), \hat{e} \notin domain(M_2) \\ \{0\} \cup M_2(\hat{e}) & \text{if } \hat{e} \notin domain(M_1), \hat{e} \in domain(M_2) \end{cases}$$

The next lemma states that operation $\sqcup$ is an upper bound operation on abstract graphs.

Lemma 6 (Upper Bound). *For any graphs G_1 and G_2:*

$$G_i \sqsubseteq G_1 \sqcup G_2 \quad \text{for all } i \in 1..2$$

We use this upper bound operation to combine the sequence of abstract graphs $G_1, \ldots, G_n$ into a single graphical summary $G = G_1 \sqcup \cdots \sqcup G_n$. The following lemma states that the final graph G is a conservative approximation for each observed heap in the program's execution.

Theorem 1 (Soundness for Traces). *Suppose $G_i = \alpha^s(H_i)$ for $i \in 1..n$ and that $G = G_1 \sqcup \cdots \sqcup G_n$. Then $H_i \in \gamma^s(G)$ for all $i \in 1..n$.*

6   Implementation

We have implemented our analysis in the AARDVARK tool. AARDVARK uses the BCEL binary instrumentor [6] to modify Java class files to record each object allocation and field write in a log file. The instrumentation overhead is roughly 10x–50x, depending on how memory-intensive the target program is. Currently, only single-threaded programs are supported, and analyzing concurrent programs remains for future work.

The off-line analysis then reconstructs a sequence of heaps from this log and applies the abstractions of the previous sections to each heap before finally merging the results into a single object model. The visual output is then generated by the dot utility [16].

A key characteristic of architectural diagrams is that they highlight concepts by eliding, or abstracting away, extraneous details, such as the representation nodes discussed in Section 2. Since which details are considered extraneous is domain-dependent, we intend our tool to be used in an interactive setting in which the software architect iteratively converges on an abstraction highlighting the desired architectural features. To support this methodology, AARDVARK is extensible and driven by a script that configures and composes various pre-defined, or user-defined, abstractions. Figure 7 shows an example script.

Our prototype is capable of handling fairly large graphs. For example, the concrete heap used to construct Figure 1 contains 380,000 nodes and 435,000 edges. AARDVARK reconstructs this concrete heap in 15 seconds and computes

```
// g starts as the graph for the concrete heap.
// First, filter out nodes not reachable from ClassDecls:
g = proj(g, reachable(g, "ClassDecl"));
// Close over arrays and program-specific collections:
g = close(g, match(g, ".*\[\]|.*Vec|.*Set"));
g = abstractTypes(g);
g = generalizeTypes(g);
uniqueness(g); multiplicity(g);
ownership(g, match(g, "ClassDecl")); // ClassDecls are the roots
```

Fig. 7. AARDVARK Script for ESC/Java AST Package

the abstract graph in another 15 seconds on a 3.06GHz Pentium Xeon worksta-tion. While the concrete heaps for a trace are built incrementally, we currently do not use incremental abstraction algorithms, meaning that the tool cannot ef-ficiently examine the several million intermediate heaps reconstructed from that log file. Instead, AARDVARK samples these heaps in a configurable manner, which in most cases is sufficient to yield precise object models. Figure 1 was produced by sampling only the last heap from the log; all other graphs were produced by abstracting and merging all intermediate heaps, which required only a couple of seconds.

Further experimentation is needed to determine the best sampling technique for AARDVARK, both in terms of performance and precision. Specifically, chang-ing the granularity of logging from individual heap updates to, for example, method call boundaries, may lead to more precise models. The current low-level logging can reveal a method call's intermediate states in which structural in-variants have been temporarily violated, resulting in imprecisions in the overall abstraction. We are currently designing incremental algorithms, which we expect to substantially improve scalability.

7   Related Work

Our tool produces graph representations similar in spirit, and based on, UML class diagrams [7]. Other tools extract some pieces of UML class diagrams from source code statically [5,25,23,26], but they do not compute, or use unsound or imprecise heuristics to compute, the structural attributes we have discussed. Of these static tools, only SuperWomble [34] supports a limited form of user-defined abstraction. PTIDEJ [18] uses a dynamic analysis similar to AARDVARK to refine statically-computed class diagrams. That tool does not explore the richer notions of ownership and containment or support user-defined abstractions.

Several studies have explored how to compute and visually present ownership information [21,30,28] from a program's heap. However, since no abstraction is performed, even small heaps can be too large to view effectively. More recently, Mitchell [27] shows how to compute ownership information for very large heaps in order to identify inefficiencies in a program's memory footprint. That approach uses a similar technique of repeatedly refining an initial heap configuration into an abstract summary, but it deals primarily with allocation and storage patterns and not other architectural issues. A number of other heap visualization tools also focus on memory or garbage collector profiling, *i.e.* [29,22].

Several projects have dynamically inferred likely program invariants, including pre- and post- conditions [13], algebraic class specifications [20], and API usage requirements [35,4]. Ernst *et al.* [14] have developed a technique to infer a class of common, but lower-level, data invariants for collection classes. We plan to generalize AARDVARK to dynamically infer high-level, architectural specifications, such as usage patterns [19] and communication integrity constraints [1], which describe how components in a system may interact.

Shape analysis computes a set of abstract memory locations reachable from a pointer [24,9,17,31,32]. The goal of our work is similar to shape analysis in that we infer the relationships between objects in an abstract heap. One interesting avenue for future work is to extend AARDVARK with additional notions of abstraction that compute shape information for use in subsequent dynamic or static analyses.

There are many static analyses for ownership and confinement, such as [11,10,3,2,8] and [33], respectively. For confinement, static analysis can ensure that specified containment relationships are not violated by leaking references to contained objects outside of a protection domain. While we capture similar containment relationships between objects, we have not focused on enforcing them. A dynamic enforcement mechanism may be an interesting, and perhaps more precise, alternative in some situations.

8   Conclusions and Future Directions

Tools for inferring architecture-level models can be very valuable for reasoning about legacy systems. This paper proposes that dynamic analysis is a promising approach that can identify not only relationships between types, but also interesting structural properties such as uniqueness, ownership, and containment. We see a number of interesting extensions and applications for this work, including:

- inferring (and enforcing) architecture-level specifications and invariants, including data dependent and temporal properties;
- seeding subsequent static, or dynamic, analyses with the shape information computed by our tool;
- exploring how object models evolve in large systems;
- inferring object models for lower-level languages such as C or C++; and
- supporting concurrency.

To support the studies of large systems, we are also currently developing incremental abstraction algorithms to improve scalability.

Acknowledgments. This work was supported in part by the National Science Foundation under Grants CCR-0341179 and CCR-0341387 and by a Fellowship from the Alfred P. Sloan Foundation.

References

1. J. Aldrich. Using types to enforce architectural structure, 2006. Available at http://www.cs.cmu.edu/~aldrich/papers/.
2. J. Aldrich and C. Chambers. Ownership domains: Separating aliasing policy from mechanism. In *European Conference on Object-Oriented Programming*, pages 1–25, 2004.
3. J. Aldrich, V. Kostadinov, and C. Chambers. Alias annotations for program understanding. In *ACM Conference Object-Oriented Programming, Systems, Languages and Applications*, pages 311–330, 2002.
4. G. Ammons, R. Bodik, and J. R. Larus. Mining specifications. In *ACM Symposium on the Principles of Programming Languages*, pages 4–16, 2002.
5. ArgoUML. http://argouml.tigris.org/, 2006.
6. Byte Code Engineering Library. http://jakarta.apache.org/bcel/, 2006.
7. G. Booch, J. Rumbaugh, and I. Jacobson. *The Unified Modeling Language User Guide (2nd edition)*. Addison-Wesley, 2005.
8. C. Boyapati, B. Liskov, and L. Shrira. Ownership types for object encapsulation. In *ACM Symposium on the Principles of Programming Languages*, pages 213–223, 2003.
9. D. R. Chase, M. N. Wegman, and F. K. Zadeck. Analysis of pointers and structures. In *ACM Conference on Programming Language Design and Implementation*, pages 296–310, 1990.
10. D. G. Clarke, J. Noble, and J. Potter. Simple ownership types for object containment. In *European Conference on Object-Oriented Programming*, pages 53–76, 2001.
11. D. G. Clarke, J. Potter, and J. Noble. Ownership types for flexible alias protection. In *ACM Conference Object-Oriented Programming, Systems, Languages and Applications*, pages 48–64, 1998.
12. P. Cousot and R. Cousot. Abstract interpretation: A unified lattice model for static analysis of programs by construction or approximation of fixpoints. In *ACM Symposium on the Principles of Programming Languages*, pages 238–252, 1977.
13. M. D. Ernst, J. Cockrell, W. G. Griswold, and D. Notkin. Dynamically discovering likely program invariants to support program evolution. *IEEE Transactions on Software Engineering*, 27(2):99–123, 2001.
14. M. D. Ernst, W. G. Griswold, Y. Kataoka, and D. Notkin. Dynamically discovering pointer-based program invariants. Technical Report UW-CSE-99-11-02, University of Washington Department of Computer Science and Engineering, Seattle, WA, 1999.
15. C. Flanagan, K. R. M. Leino, M. Lillibridge, G. Nelson, J. B. Saxe, and R. Stata. Extended static checking for Java. In *ACM Conference on Programming Language Design and Implementation*, pages 234–245, 2002.
16. E. R. Gansner and S. C. North. An open graph visualization system and its applications to software engineering. *Software Practice Experience*, 30(11):1203–1233, 2000.
17. R. Ghiya and L. J. Hendren. Is it a tree, a dag, or a cyclic graph? A shape analysis for heap-directed pointers in C. In *ACM Symposium on the Principles of Programming Languages*, pages 1–15, 1996.
18. Y.-G. Guéhéneuc. A reverse engineering tool for precise class diagrams. In *Conference of the Centre for Advanced Studies on Collaborative Research*, pages 28–41, 2004.

19. B. Hackett and A. Aiken. How is aliasing used in systems software?, 2006. Available at http://glide.stanford.edu/saturn/.

20. J. Henkel and A. Diwan. Discovering algebraic specifications from Java classes. In *European Conference on Object-Oriented Programming*, pages 431–456, 2003.

21. T. Hill, J. Noble, and J. Potter. Scalable visualizations of object-oriented systems with ownership trees. *J. Vis. Lang. Comput.*, 13(3):319–339, 2002.

22. M. Hirzel, J. Henkel, A. Diwan, and M. Hind. Understanding the connectivity of heap objects. In *MSP/ISMM*, pages 143–156, 2002.

23. D. Jackson and A. Waingold. Lightweight extraction of object models from bytecode. In *International Conference on Software Engineering*, pages 194–202, 1999.

24. N. D. Jones and S. S. Muchnick. A flexible approach to interprocedural data flow analysis and programs with recursive data structures. In *ACM Symposium on the Principles of Programming Languages*, pages 66–74, 1982.

25. B. A. Malloy and J. F. Power. Exploiting UML dynamic object modeling for the visualization of C++ programs. In *ACM Symposium on Software Visualization*, pages 105–114, 2005.

26. A. Milanova. Precise identification of composition relationships for UML class diagrams. In *Automated Software Engineering*, pages 76–85, 2005.

27. N. Mitchell. The runtime structure of object ownership. In *European Conference on Object-Oriented Programming*, 2006.

28. J. Noble. Visualising objects: Abstraction, encapsulation, aliasing, and ownership. In S. Diehl, editor, *Software Visualization: International Seminar*, pages 58–72.

29. T. Printezis and R. Jones. GCspy: An adaptable heap visualisation framework. In *ACM Conference Object-Oriented Programming, Systems, Languages and Applications*, pages 343–358, 2002.

30. D. Rayside, L. Mendel, and D. Jackson. A dynamic analysis for revealing object ownership and sharing. In *Workshop on Dynamic Analysis*, 2006.

31. S. Sagiv, T. W. Reps, and R. Wilhelm. Solving shape-analysis problems in languages with destructive updating. *ACM Transactions on Programming Languages and Systems*, 20(1):1–50, 1998.

32. S. Sagiv, T. W. Reps, and R. Wilhelm. Parametric shape analysis via 3-valued logic. In *ACM Symposium on the Principles of Programming Languages*, pages 105–118, 1999.

33. J. Vitek and B. Bokowski. Confined types in Java. *Software– Practice and Experience*, 31(6):507–532, 2001.

34. A. Waingold. Automatic extraction of abstract object models. Masters thesis, Department of Electrical Engineering and Computer Science, MIT, 2001.

35. J. Whaley, M. C. Martin, and M. S. Lam. Automatic extraction of object-oriented component interfaces. In *ACM International Symposium on Software Testing and Analysis*, pages 218–228, 2002.

Safety Property Driven Test Generation from JML Specifications

Fabrice Bouquet, Frédéric Dadeau, Julien Groslambert, and Jacques Julliand

Université de Franche-Comté - LIFC - CNRS - INRIA
16 route de Gray - 25030 Besançon cedex France
Tel.: (+33)(0)381 666 664
{bouquet, dadeau, groslambert, julliand}@lifc.univ-fcomte.fr

Abstract. This paper describes the automated generation of test sequences derived from a JML specification and a safety property written in an ad hoc language, named JTPL. The functional JML model is animated to build the test sequences w.r.t. the safety properties, which represent the test targets. From these properties, we derive strategies that are used to guide the symbolic animation. Moreover, additional JML annotations reinforce the oracle in order to guarantee that the safety properties are not violated during the execution of the test suite. Finally, we illustrate this approach on an industrial JavaCard case study.

Keywords: automated testing, safety properties, black-box testing, Java Modeling Language, JavaCard.

1 Motivations

Annotation languages provide an interesting approach for the verification and validation of programs, allowing to describe, using annotations, the expected behavior of a class. Their advantage is to share a common level of abstraction with the considered programming language, which is useful in program verification/validation activities such as testing [11]. In this latter category, the Java Modeling Language [12] (JML) makes it possible to use lightweight annotations as well as heavyweight annotations to specify the behaviors of the methods. JML is well tool-supported and has shown its usefulness in industrial case studies, especially in the domain of JavaCard verification [6].

We propose an automated model-based testing approach for the validation of safety properties on a JavaCard application. A previous work [3], introducing JML-TESTING-TOOLS[1] (JML-TT), has presented our ability to generate functional test sequences from a JML model, by performing the symbolic animation of the JML specification in order to reach a pertinent test target. We present in this paper the extension of this technology destined to the generation of test sequences that cover a user-defined safety property. This latter is expressed using the Java Temporal Pattern Language (JTPL) [19]. The JAG tool[2] [9] has been

---

[1] http://lifc.univ-fcomte.fr/~jmltt/
[2] http://lifc.univ-fcomte.fr/~groslambert/JAG/

K. Havelund et al. (Eds.): FATES/RV 2006, LNCS 4262, pp. 225–239, 2006.
© Springer-Verlag Berlin Heidelberg 2006

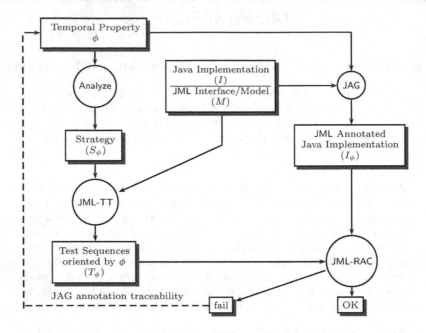

Fig. 1. General Approach

designed to use the JTPL in order to express and to check safety properties on a model or on an implementation, by generating extra JML annotations ensuring the satisfaction of the JTPL property. Our proposal is to combine JAG and JML-TT in order to generate test cases that are complementary of the functional ones and relevant w.r.t. the safety property.

For example, suppose that after the invocation of a method m, a property P must be established in all the states of the program. This property can be written with a JTPL pattern as follows:

$$\textbf{after } m \textbf{ called always } P \tag{1}$$

Then, only executions where the method m is invoked are relevant for this property. Therefore, we would like to generate only these kinds of executions.

Our approach is summarized in Fig. 1. Firstly, we analyze the safety property ϕ and generate a strategy of test sequences generation S_ϕ. This strategy is built by combining test patterns according to the safety property schema. Secondly, from the JML interface M and S_ϕ, JML-TT computes a test suite, relevant w.r.t. ϕ and covering the functional behavior of the application. Then, these test sequences are executed on the annotated implementation I_ϕ generated by the JAG tool from the annotated implementation I enriched by annotations specifying the temporal property ϕ. These JML annotations provides the oracle that concludes on the verdict of the test. In addition, the extra annotations provide an oracle that concludes on the satisfaction of the property ϕ. If the annotations derived from this latter fail to be checked at run-time, and thanks to the JAG traceability, we are able to retrieve the original temporal property that is not satisfied on the implementation, and furthermore, to retrieve the requirements of the security policies that have not been correctly implemented.

This paper is organized as follows. Section 2 presents the Java Modeling Language and its on-the-fly verification capacities, using the JML Runtime Assertion Checker (RAC). Section 3 presents the JTPL temporal logic language, used to express the requirements of an application in terms of a temporal property. The generation of annotations for these properties is also described. Section 4 explains how the JML-TT framework computes test sequences driven by a safety property. Section 5 presents the result of an experiment made on a case study, and draws a comparison between our approach and a combinatorial test generation tool. Section 6 compares our approach with related works and discusses its originality. Finally, Section 7 concludes and presents the future work.

2   JML and Runtime Assertion Checking

The Java Modeling Language [12] is a behavioral interface specification language for Java programs, designed by G.T. Leavens et al. The specification consists in decorating a Java code or an interface in a comment-like syntax (//@ for single-line annotations, /*@ ...@*/ for multiple-line annotations). JML is based on the *Design By Contract* principles, stating that the system has to fulfill the methods requirements (i.e., their preconditions) to invoke them. As a counterpart, the methods establish their postconditions.

JML considers different *clauses* to express the specifications. They involve the use of predicates in a Java-based syntax, enriched with specific JML keywords. Figure 2 presents an example of a JML specification. This specification describes a simplified electronic purse, specified by a balance (**bal**), to which money can be credited or withdrawn, using methods **init(byte,short)** and **complete()** to respectively initialize and complete the transaction. This specification illustrates the different clauses that can be used to design the JML model. The **invariant** clause describes the class invariant that applies on the class attributes. The method specifications are described using by specifying the precondition (**requires** clause), the normal postcondition (**ensures** clause) which gives the postcondition established when the method terminates normally, the exceptional postcondition (**signals** clause) which gives the postcondition that is established when the method throws an exception, and the list of the attributes which are modified by the invocation of the method (**assignable** clause). An expression enclosed by the keyword \old must be evaluated with the value of the variables in the preceding state.

The Runtime Assertion Checker is a compiler that enriches the Java byte-code with the checking of the different JML clauses. The execution of the RAC-compiled Java classes makes it possible to automatically check the specification predicates when running the program. If an execution violates one of the JML assertions, a specific exception is raised indicating which assertion has not been

```
class Purse {
                                              private short transVal;
    //@ invariant max >= 0;
    protected short max;                      final static byte CREDIT_MODE = 0;
                                              final static byte DEBIT_MODE = 1;
    /*@ invariant bal >= 0 && bal <= max; */
    protected short bal;                      /*@ behavior
                                                @   requires a > 0 && transVal == 0;
    /*@ public normal_behavior                  @   {|
      @   assignable bal, max, transVal;        @     requires   P1 == CREDIT_MODE &&
      @   ensures                               @                  bal + a <= max;
      @           (m > 0  ==> max == m) &&      @     assignable transVal;
      @           (m <= 0 ==> max == 1) &&      @     ensures     transVal == a;
      @           bal == 0 && transVal == 0;    @   also
      @*/                                       @     requires   P1 == DEBIT_MODE &&
    public Purse(short m) {...}                 @                  bal - a >= 0;
                                                @     assignable transVal;
    /*@ behavior                                @     ensures     transVal == (short)(- a);
      @   requires   transVal != 0;             @   |}
      @   assignable bal, transVal;             @   also
      @   ensures     bal ==                     @     requires   (P1 != CREDIT_MODE &&
      @           (short) (\old(bal)+transVal); @                   P1 != DEBIT_MODE) ||
      @   ensures     transVal == 0;            @                   a <= 0 || transVal != 0;
      @ also                                    @     assignable \nothing;
      @   requires   transVal == 0;             @     signals (IllegalUseException) true;
      @   assignable \nothing;                  @*/
      @   signals (IllegalUseException) true;   public void init(byte P1, short a)
      @*/                                               throws IllegalUseException {...}
    public void complete()
            throws IllegalUseException { ... }  ... }
```

Fig. 2. Example of a JML specification

satisfied. Therefore, this feature is used as an oracle. JML can be used to reinforce the code or to help the proof of the code (e.g. using JACK [7]). For model-based testing, the user must provide a complete model of its application. If the hypothesis may seem strong for all Java programs, we believe that it is worth doing the effort of writing a complete JML specification, with strong pre- and postconditions, in the domain of embedded programs, such as JavaCard [17]. In our approach, we use JML as a source for test target definition and model-based test case computation. A recent evolution has been proposed to express temporal properties in JML, involving the use of the RAC. It is now described.

3   A Temporal Logic Extension for JML-Like Language

We present an extension of JML with temporal specifications, first defined in [19]. This language, called *Java Temporal Pattern Language* (JTLP), is inspired by Dwyer's *specification patterns* [8]. Dwyer shows through a study of 500 specification examples, that 80% of the temporal specification requirements can be covered by a finite number of formulae. This high-level temporal logic language for Java follows this philosophy, providing to the user structures to express common temporal requirements on Java classes. Moreover, the language can deal with both normal and exceptional terminations of methods. This language can be used to express safety or liveness properties. In this paper, we only focus

```
      <Event> ::= <Method> called [ with <JMLProp>]
               |  <Method> normal [ with <JMLProp>]
               |  <Method> exceptional [ with <JMLProp>]
               |  <Method> terminates [with <JMLProp> ]
    <Events> ::= <Event>,<Events>
  <StateProp> ::= <JMLProp>
               |  <Method> enabled [ with <JMLProp>]
               |  <Method> not enabled[ with <JMLProp>]
  <TraceProp> ::= always <StateProp>
               |  never <StateProp>
               |  <TraceProp> and <TraceProp>
               |  <TraceProp> or <TraceProp>
       <Temp> ::= after <Events> <Temp>
               |  before <Events> <TraceProp>
               |  <TraceProp> unless <Events>
               |  <TraceProp>
```

Fig. 3. Syntax of the safety patterns

on safety properties, for which we give the corresponding syntax and semantics. Readers can refer to [19] for a formal definition of the whole language semantics.

3.1   Syntax and Semantics of the Language

The syntax of the subset of the JTPL language expressing safety properties is displayed given in Fig. 3. This language is based on the notions of *events* and *state properties*.

Events can be either: (i) m **called**, meaning that the method m has been called, without considering the method termination; (ii) m **normal**, meaning that the method m has terminated normally; (iii) m **exceptional**, meaning that the method m has terminated exceptionally (by throwing an exception); (iv) m **terminates**, meaning that the method m has terminated (either normally or by throwing an exception). The events can be enriched with a predicate P introduced by the keyword **with**. Thus, m **called with** P means that m has been called within a state satisfying P and m **terminates** (resp. **normal** and **exceptional**) **with** P means that m terminates (resp. terminates normally and terminates by throwing an exception) in a state satisfying the predicate P.

A state property P can be either: (i) a JML predicate; (ii) m **enabled**, meaning that if the method m is called and if the method m terminates, then it terminates normally; (iii) m **not enabled**, meaning that if the method m is called and if the method m terminates, then it terminates exceptionally, i.e., by throwing an exception.

The state properties m **enabled** and m **not enabled** are especially designed to express properties on JavaCard applets, since JavaCard commands can be called from any state. Thus, once a method is called, either the call is licit w.r.t. the expected state variable values and the parameters values and thus the method terminates normally, or the call is illicit and the method terminates exceptionally. Notice that these two state properties are true if the method is not called or if the method is called but does not terminate (i.e., the method diverges). This clause can also be enriched with a predicate P introduced by the keyword **with**.

```
class Purse {                                 /*@ behavior
                                               @   ...
  //@ ghost boolean inProgress = false;        @    ensures inProgress == true;
  ...                                           @    ensures \old(inProgress) ==> false;
                                               @ also
  /*@ behavior                                  @   ...
   @   ...                                      @*/
   @    ensures   inProgress == false;        public void init(byte P1, short a)
   @ also                                                       throws IllegalUseException {
   @   ...                                        ...
   @*/                                          }
  public void complete()                       finally {
             throws IllegalUseException {        //@ set inProgress = true;
    //@ set inProgress = false;                 }
    ...                                       }
  }                                         }
}
```

Fig. 4. Example of annotations produced by the JAG tool

Finally, events and state properties can be combined with the keywords of the language: (i) **always** P, which is true on an execution σ if the state properties P holds on every state of σ; (ii) **never** P, which is true on an execution σ if the state properties P never holds on any state of σ. It is equivalent to **always** $\neg P$; (iii) C **unless** E, which is true on an execution σ if the trace property C is satisfied on the segment of σ ending with an event in E, or if the trace property C is satisfied on the whole of σ and no event in E happens; (iv) **before** E C, which is true on an execution σ if any occurrences of an event in E is preceded by a prefix of σ satisfying the trace property C; or (v) **after** E T, which is true on an execution σ if the suffix of σ starting with any event in E satisfies the temporal formula T. Notice that conjunctions and disjunctions, respectively denoted by **and** and **or**, have a standard meaning. Notice also that the language expresses a property of a class like a class invariant, state properties inside JTPL can refer to the instances of the other classes included in the fields of the class. This language is an input of the JAG tool, presented in the next subsection.

3.2   Translation of JTPL into JML with JAG

The JAG tool [9] generates JML annotations ensuring a given temporal property. As an illustration, we present a safety property that has to hold on the example of Fig. 2, specifying that after a successful `init`, one can invoke `init` once again only if the transaction has been validated by invoking `complete`:

$$\begin{array}{l} \textbf{after init normal} \\ \qquad \textbf{always init not enabled unless complete called} \end{array} \qquad (S_0)$$

The additional annotations, automatically generated and related to this property, are given in Fig. 4. This property is expressed by:

- a *ghost* boolean variable `inProgress`, initialized to `false`. This variable is set to `true` when the event `init` **normal** occurs and set to `false` again when `complete` **called** occurs.

– a postcondition ensuring that `init` cannot terminate normally when variable `inProgress` is equal to `true`. This predicate reinforces the normal postcondition by preventing it from being evaluated to true if `inProgress` is true, stating, as a consequence, that the method can not terminate normally in this particular case.

The interested reader will find in [19] the details of the translation, for all structures of the language. Notice that JAG keeps a trace of the generation: given a generated annotation, JAG is able to find the original temporal property.

4 Test Generation from Temporal Properties

We describe in this section the definition of the principles which consist in animating the specification according to a given temporal logic property. Then, we present the coverage criteria that we apply on the specification. Finally, we explain the test sequences computation.

4.1 Principles

Our approach is an extension of the previous work about functional test generation that is presented in [4] on the symbolic animation of JML specifications. The principle of our approach is to associate a test suite to each safety property we consider. Thus, we perform the symbolic animation of the specification in order to build a test sequence that exercises the property, by activating the behaviors of the JML specification.

A *behavior* is described as a before-after predicate extracted from the JML method specification. It represents a transition between states. Informally, the execution of the transition represents the resolution of a constraint satisfaction problem (CSP) between the constraints representing the state before and the constraints given by the behavior. The satisfiability of this constraint system gives the activability of the behavior. (More details can be found in [4]).

The computation of the test sequences is driven by a strategy derived from the temporal formula, to guide the animation of the specification. A strategy is composed of a sequence of steps in which our aim is to activate a particular behavior of the specification or to cover all the behaviors. When the last step is done, the test generation stops. In addition, we consider a bound that limits the test sequences length, and guarantees the termination for each step of the research. In addition, we rely on the JML annotations describing the safety property, and produced by the JAG tool, to complete the oracle. Thus, if one of these annotations fails to be checked at run-time, we are able to provide to the user an indication concerning the original temporal property and the original requirement that have been violated.

4.2 Coverage Criteria

Our approach considers the classical coverage of the specification, at three levels: the specification coverage, the decision coverage, and the data coverage.

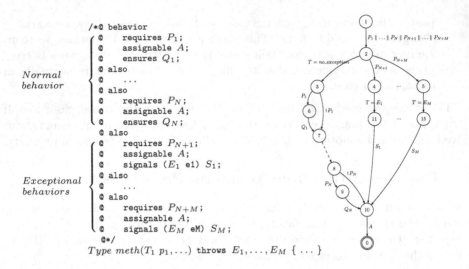

```
    /*@ behavior
    @       requires P₁;
    @       assignable A;
    @       ensures Q₁;
    @ also
    @   ...
    @ also
    @       requires P_N;
    @       assignable A;
    @       ensures Q_N;
    @ also
    @       requires P_{N+1};
    @       assignable A;
    @       signals (E₁ e1) S₁;
    @ also
    @   ...
    @ also
    @       requires P_{N+M};
    @       assignable A;
    @       signals (E_M eM) S_M;
    @*/
    Type meth(T₁ p₁,...) throws E₁,...,E_M { ... }
```

Normal behavior

Exceptional behaviors

Fig. 5. Extraction of the behaviors from a JML method specification

Specification coverage The specification coverage is achieved by activating the different behaviors that we extract from the JML method specifications. Figure 5 describes the extraction of behaviors from a JML method specification. A behavior is represented by a path leading from node 1 to node 0. According to this figure, we assume that the method may deterministically terminate (expressed by T) either normally ($T = $ no_exception) or by throwing one of its M specified exceptions ($T = E_i$ for $1 \leq i \leq M$). We also assume that the exceptional behaviors are deterministic, which means that their guards are mutually exclusive. *De facto*, the behaviors of the methods only depend on the current state variables values, and the parameter values.

Decision coverage. We achieve the decision coverage by rewriting the disjunctions within the preconditions of the JML specifications. We consider four classical rewritings of the disjunctions, described by $a \vee b$. Rewriting 1 consists in leaving the disjunction unmodified. Rewriting 2 consists in creating a choice between the two predicates ($a \; [] \; b$). Thus, the first branch and the second branch independently have to succeed when being evaluated. Rewriting 3 consists in creating an exclusive choice between the two predicates ($a \wedge \neg b \; [] \; \neg a \wedge b$). Only one of the sub-predicates of the disjunction is checked at one time. Rewriting 4 consists in testing all the possible values for the two sub-predicates to satisfy the disjunction ($a \wedge \neg b \; [] \; \neg a \wedge b \; [] \; a \wedge b$). Each one of these rewritings guarantees at least one decision coverage.

Data coverage. When performing the symbolic animation of the specification, the input parameters of the methods that are invoked are left unspecified, and their symbolic values are managed by constraint solvers. When the symbolic sequence computation is over, we select the boundary values for the unspecified parameters. More details about the application of this work to JML can be found in [3].

Strategy(**after** Events Temp) = Research(Events); Strategy(Temp)

Strategy(**before** Events TraceProp) = Cover; Strategy(TraceProp); Research(Event)

Strategy(TraceProp **unless** Events) = CoverStop(Events); Strategy(TraceProp)

Strategy(**always** StateProp) = Cover;Strategy(StateProp)

Strategy(StateProp$_1$ **and** StateProp$_2$) = Strategy(StateProp$_1$) [] Strategy(StateProp$_2$)

Strategy(StateProp$_1$ **or** StateProp$_2$) = Strategy(StateProp$_1$) [] Strategy(StateProp$_2$)

Strategy(<JMLProp>) = ϵ

Strategy(m **enabled** [**with** <JMLProp>]) = Active(m **exceptional** [**with** <JMLProp>])

Strategy(m **not enabled** [**with** <JMLProp>]) = Active(m **normal** [**with** <JMLProp>])

Fig. 6. Strategies for the JTPL language

In addition to these classical coverage criteria, we are especially interested in exercising the temporal property. This is achieved by defining different strategies that are in charge of activating the JML method behaviors w.r.t. the temporal property. We now describe these strategies, which represent the main contribution of the paper.

4.3 Test Sequence Computation

The test sequence computation strategy depends on the safety property that has been defined. According to the pattern that matches the temporal property, a specific strategy is employed.

The translation from JTPL into JML-TT strategies is described by the function **Strategy** given in Fig. 6, in which ϵ denotes that no strategy is applied. A strategy consist of sequences (denoted by ";") or choices (denoted by "[]") of steps among the four following patterns:

- **Research of** E (Research(E)). This strategy performs a *best-first* algorithm that aims at activating an event in E. This principle has been already described in [3].
- **Coverage of behaviors** (Cover). This strategy performs the symbolic animation of the specification in order to cover all the behaviors. This is done by a *depth-first* algorithm that activates the normal behaviors of the model. The main advantage of using the specification is that it delays the combinatorial explosion occurring during the exploration of the reachability graph by filtering the sequence of methods, so as to comply with the methods contracts. When a behavior is newly activated, the current execution sequence is returned to provide a test case. A "backtracking" mechanism makes it possible to resume the depth-first research.
- **Coverage of behaviors with stop on** E (CoverStop(E)). This strategy is similar to the previous one, but the depth-first algorithm stops when an event in E is activated. As in the previous case, a backtracking occurs to resume the computation.
- **Activation of** E (Active(E)). This consists in a systematic activation of the events in E. This step is crucial since it will be used to activate the expected or unexpected events, expressed in the property. For example, if the state

property is of type m [not] **enabled**, the method m is tried to be activated. This step is also performed using a depth-first algorithm. (Un)Expected behaviors are detected by considering the specification and performed in a try-catch mecanism that is in charge of either catching a unexpected exception, or throwing a specific exception when the expected exceptional behavior has not been thrown.

Notice that the sequences Cover;CoverStop(E) and CoverStop(E);Cover are reduced to CoverStop(E).

Example 1 (Strategy for S_0). The strategy associated to S_0, given by the function **Strategy** of Fig. 6 is the following:

Research(init **normal**); CoverStop(complete **called**); Active(init **normal**)

It corresponds to the following steps: (i) we research a sequence that ends with the activation of the normal behavior of init; (ii) we cover all the behaviors of the class, the research is stopped when the event complete **called** occurs; (iii) we try to activate the normal behavior of method init to test if init is effectively **not enabled**.

This automatic test generation approach, using the strategies explained above, has been applied to a case study. The results of this experiment are exposed in the next Section.

5   Experiment of a Case Study

We now present an experiment that we have done on a case study. We start by describing the specification, before expressing the temporal properties from which we want to generate test cases, and finally we compare our approach with a similar tool.

5.1   Presentation of the Demoney Specification

Demoney is an electronic purse developed by Trusted Logic [15]. This JavaCard application makes it possible to pay a purchase in a store using a terminal and can be credited from cash or from a bank account in an ATM. Demoney is not an industrial application but is complex enough to handle typical features and security problems related to banking systems.

Similarly to the other JavaCard applications, the life cycle of the card starts with a personalization phase, where particular variables, such as the maximum balance amount, are fixed using the PUT_DATA command. Then, a STORE_DATA command stores the personalization variables. The application can only be personalized once. There are four access levels (public, debit, credit and admin), which restrict the activation of the commands. For example, the STORE_DATA command can only be invoked with the admin access level. Access levels can be selected using the INITIALIZE_UPDATE and EXTERNAL_AUTHENTICATE commands. For a successful change, the methods have to be atomically invoked, e.g. INITIALIZE_UPDATE must immediately be followed by EXTERNAL_AUTHENTI-CATE. INITIALIZE_TRANSACTION and COMPLETE_TRANSACTION are used to perform transactions, whose types (debit or credit from cash or from bank) are expressed using parameter P1 of the first command. These two commands also have to be atomically invoked for a successful transaction. For a credit from a bank account, the PIN code of the card must have been checked using the VERIFY_PIN command. The number of tries is limited and chosen at the personalization time. Finally, when the pin is blocked after unsuccessful VERIFY_PIN invocations, it is possible to unblock the card using the PIN_CHANGE_UNBLOCK command.

For the test generation, we use a JML model of Demoney designed from the informal public specification. This model represents over 500 lines of JML and has been validated with the JML-TT Symbolic Animator [4].

5.2   Temporal Properties

We illustrate the test generation on two safety properties. In addition, in order to pilot the test generation and to have interesting test sequences, we add some requirements on the state in which the considered commands terminate. These requirements are used to force the first part of the test cases to configure the card with interesting values for the maximal balance on the card (maxBalance), the maximal debit amount (maxDebit) and the pin code (pin.code). These requirements are expressed using the **with** clause of the JTPL expressions, by a context predicate C:

$$maxBalance == 10000 \ \& \ maxDebit == 5000 \ \& \ pin.code == 1234$$

We address the verification of the two following safety properties.

1. The personalization is unique:

after STORE_DATA normal with C always STORE_DATA not enabled (S_1)

2. When the pin is blocked, it is impossible to credit the card from a bank unless a successful call to the PIN_CHANGE_UNBLOCK method in the unblocking mode (expressed by value UNBLOCK for parameter P1).

after VERIFY_PIN terminates with pin.tries $== 0$ & C
  always INITIALIZE_TRANSACTION not enabled
      with P1 $==$ CREDIT_FROM_BANK (S_2)
  unless PIN_CHANGE_UNBLOCK normal with P1 $==$ UNBLOCK;

Using the JAG tool, we generate the JML annotations that ensures the satisfaction of these properties. The challenge is to validate the implementation w.r.t. these temporal properties. According to Sect. 4.3, the JAG tool computes the following strategies for S_1 and S_2:

Research(**STORE_DATA normal with** C); Cover; Active(**STORE_DATA normal**) (S_1)

Research(VERIFY_PIN **terminates with** pin.tries $==$ 0 & C);
CoverStop(PIN_CHANGE_UNBLOCK **normal with** p1 $==$ UNBLOCK); (S_2)
Active(INITIALIZE_TRANSACTION **with** P1 $==$ CREDIT_FROM_BANK)

These strategies are used in JML-TT to drive the automated test generation previously explained. Results of the generation for these two properties are now presented, and a comparison with a combinatorial test generation tool is exposed.

5.3   Results, Comparison, and Discussion

Tests have been generated for different values n of the depth search. An example of test generated for the property S_1 is displayed in Fig. 7. The test is composed as follows: (a) a *prelude* reaches a state where STORE_DATA is activated under the C condition; (b) we try to cover a particular behavior (here COMPLETE_TRANSACTION); (c) the method STORE_DATA is activated once again; (d) a try...catch statement observes if a exception has been thrown by the execution of STORE_DATA. Table 2 displays the general results of the test generation. We remark that the number of test cases is twice the number of behaviors covered. This is explained by the boundary values selection which both minimizes and maximizes data values. For each property we cover all the reachable behaviors (13 for S_1, 8 for S_2) for a reasonable depth, with a minimal number of test cases.

The test suites driven by temporal properties complement the test suites we obtained using the functional techniques presented in [3], as it was expected. Moreover, these two approaches do not generate the same test cases, since the functional test cases try to activate each behavior by reaching the shortest path leading to a state that makes it possible to activate it. For example, the test case, displayed in Fig. 7, is not produced in the functional approach. Since these two approaches can not be compared, i.e., they do not aim at the same purpose, we wanted to draw a comparison with a tool that has a similar approach to ours: Tobias [13].

Tobias is a combinatorial test generation tool that uses user-defined regular expressions to build test sequences consisting of Java method calls. This approach

Table 2. Results of experiments with JML-TT

Safety Property	n	# of tests	# of behaviors covered
S_1	1	10	4/17
S_1	2	12	5/17
S_1	3	18	9/17
S_1	4, 5, 6	22	11/17
S_1	7	24	12/17
S_1	≥ 8	26	13/17
S_2	1	8	4/17
S_2	2	12	6/17
S_2	3, 4	14	7/17
S_2	≥ 5	16	8/17

then relies on the JML-RAC to provide an oracle that gives the test verdict. Since this approach does not consider the JML specification for the generation, it may produce *inconclusive* tests, when the precondition of a method is not satisfied. Both Tobias and our approach consist in semi-automatic testing, since a user is asked to respectively provide a test schema or a safety property. We tried to cover the property S_1 using the following Tobias test schema:

$$\texttt{prelude; STORE\_DATA; (other\_methods)}^{0..n}\texttt{; STORE\_DATA}$$

This test schema's automaton recognizes the test cases that we have produced. With $n = 4$, this schema produces roughly 45436 test cases, of which 10% are relevant, and covering 11 behaviors, as we also do. The `prelude` part consists in configuring the card before the personalization. This part had to be manually generated.

The second property gave similar results, asking much more effort to manually define the `prelude` and describe the remainder of the test schema.

This experiment has shown the advantages of our approach, since: (*i*) we achieved a higher level of automation in the test case generation; (*ii*) we mastered the combinatorial explosion and created less test cases which are all relevant (since they are based on the symbolic animation of the model), and which cover all the reachable behaviors for a given depth; (*iii*) the effort asked to the user is minimal and requires less expertise from the validation engineer, since he only has to describe a temporal property (and its optional context) instead of providing subsets of the test sequences; (*iv*) the expressiveness of our approach, and especially the possibility of expressing an optional context, allows to subtly drive the test generation.

```
Demoney v = new Demoney();
v.INITIALIZE_UPDATE((byte) 3,(byte) 1);
v.EXTERNAL_AUTHENTICATE((byte) 11,(byte) 0);
v.PUT_DATA((byte) 3,(byte) 15,(short) 1234);      a
v.PUT_DATA((byte) 2,(byte) 0,(short) 5000);
v.PUT_DATA((byte) 1,(byte) 0,(short) 20000);
v.STORE_DATA((byte) 80,(byte) 0);
v.INITIALIZE_UPDATE((byte) 2,(byte) 1);
v.EXTERNAL_AUTHENTICATE((byte) 1,(byte) 0);
v.INITIALIZE_TRANSACTION((byte) 1,(byte) 0,       b
                         (short) 20000);
v.COMPLETE_TRANSACTION((byte) 0,(byte) 0);
v.INITIALIZE_UPDATE((byte) 3,(byte) 1);
v.EXTERNAL_AUTHENTICATE((byte) 1,(byte) 0);       c
try {
  v.STORE_DATA((byte) 80,(byte) 0);
  throw new JMLTTUnraisedException
      ("IllegalUseException");
}
catch (IllegalUseException e) {                   d
  // Nothing to do in this case.
}
```

Fig. 7. A test case generated by JML-TT

6 Related Work

Testing Java programs using JML annotations has already been well studied and other tools are available. Korat [5] aims at providing an exhaustive set of structures satisfying a Java predicate, using SAT solving technologies. This approach has been adapted to JML, and relies on the method preconditions to build satisfying test data. Whereas Korat only considers an object creation and a method invocation, our approach proposes to build complex test sequences of method invocations. Jartege [16] produces stochastic test cases based on a

Java program. The Runtime Assertion Checker is used when the test sequence is being built, in order to filter the irrelevant method invocations. The major advantage of Jartege is its full automation, but its main problem is the absence of strategy in the test generation which prevents it from being used in the domain of JavaCard.

Most of LTL based testing approaches use model checkers such as Spin [10] to generate test cases. By fully exploring the state space of a model of the application, a model checker verifies that every configuration of the model satisfies a given property. When the property is not satisfied, the model checker exhibits a counter-example, i.e., a run of the model that does not satisfy the property. Approaches based on model checking use this counter-example mechanism to produce traces that can be transformed in test sequences. Sokolsky and al. [18], for a given LTL formula ϕ, compute a set of $\exists$LTL formulae that covers every subformulae of ϕ. In [2], Ammann and al. propose the mutation of the model or of the property to generate the counter-examples and then, the test suite. Both approaches need to use a finite abstraction of the model to generate the tests.

Our approach, based on symbolic animation and constraint solving that reduces the state place explosion, can handle potentially huge or infinite models. Although the JML-TT framework does not provide a complete exploration of the state space, it shows its effectiveness in practice.

The coverage metrics of the temporal property is an important and well-studied criteria for selecting relevant test cases. The approach of Sokolsky in [18], relies on the concept of *non-vacuity* in model checking, capturing traces of the model that satisfy a property non-trivially. Implicitly, we have used this notion on our approach, since for each pattern of the language, we only generate tests that are relevant for the property.

7   Conclusion and Future Work

In this paper, we proposed an extension of the JML-TT framework, for the generation of test suites driven by safety properties. Based on the experimentation on a case study, this approach has shown its complementarity with the existing techniques of test for Java/JML and has led to effective results.

Our next task is to establish the coverage of the test suites in terms of coverage criteria of the safety property. Intuitively, it requires to consider the Büchi automaton extracted from the property and to define coverage in terms of states, transitions, or paths.

Our approach can be easily adapted to other specification languages such as SPEC♯ [14] or B [1]. One of the future challenge is to generalize the methodology presented in this paper to other temporal specification languages supported by the JAG tool. In particular, we are interested in LTL. Model checking techniques, such as presented in Sect. 6, based on mutation of the formula or the model, can also be adapted to our automatic test generation framework, since our approach is close to bounded model checking.

Another interesting future work is using property-driven generation for a collaboration between proof and test techniques. Using the JAG tools, one can generate the JML annotations on the implementation of an application and trying to prove it with a proof obligation generator such as Jack [7]. If the proof of a generated annotation fails, and using the JAG traceability, we are able to retrieve the temporal annotations and generate, via JML-TT, intensive test sets related to this particular property.

References

1. J.-R. Abrial. *The B Book*. Cambridge University Press, 1996.
2. P. Ammann, P. E. Black, and W. Majurski. Using model checking to generate tests from specifications. In *ICFEM'98*, pages 46–55. IEEE Comp. Soc. Press, 1998.
3. F. Bouquet, F. Dadeau, and B. Legeard. Automated Boundary Test Generation from JML Specifications. In *FM'06*, LNCS 4085, pages 428–443. Springer, 2006.
4. F. Bouquet, F. Dadeau, B. Legeard, and M. Utting. Symbolic Animation of JML Specifications. In *FM'05*, LNCS 3582, pages 75–90. Springer-Verlag, 2005.
5. C. Boyapati, S. Khurshid, and D. Marinov. Korat: automated testing based on java predicates. In *ISSTA'02*, pages 123–133. ACM Press, 2002.
6. C-B. Breunesse, N. Cataño, M. Huisman, and B. Jacobs. Formal methods for smart cards: an experience report. *Sci. Comput. Program.*, 55(1-3):53–80, 2005.
7. L. Burdy, A. Requet, and J.-L. Lanet. Java Applet Correctness: a Developer-Oriented Approach. In *FME'03*, lncs 2805, pages 422–439. Springer, 2003.
8. M. B. Dwyer, G. S. Avrunin, and J. C. Corbett. Patterns in property specifications for finite-state verification. In *ICSE*, pages 411–420, 1999.
9. A. Giorgetti and J. Groslambert. Jag: Jml annotation generation for verifying temporal properties. In *FASE*, LNCS 3922, pages 373–376. Springer, 2006.
10. G.J. Holzmann. The model checker SPIN. In *IEEE Trans. on Software Engineering*, volume 23-5, pages 279–295, 1997.
11. G. T. Leavens, Y. Cheon, C. Clifton, C. Ruby, and D. R. Cok. How the Design of JML Accomodates Both Runtime Assertion Checking and Formal Verification. In *FMCO*, volume 2852 of *LNCS*, pages 262–284. Springer, 2002.
12. G.T. Leavens, A.L. Baker, and C Ruby. JML: A notation for detailed design. In H. Kilov, B. Rumpe, and I. Simmonds, editors, *Behavioral Specifications of Businesses and Systems*, pages 175–188. Kluwer Academic Publishers, Boston, 1999.
13. Y. Ledru, L. du Bousquet, O. Maury, and P. Bontron. Filtering tobias combinatorial test suites. In *FASE*, LNCS 2984, pages 281–294. Springer, 2004.
14. K.R.M. Leino M. Barnett and W. Schulte. The Spec# Programming System: An Overview. In *CASSIS'04*, LNCS 3362, pages 49–69. Springer-Verlag, 2004.
15. R. Marlet and C. Mesnil. Demoney: A demonstrative electronic purse - card specification. Technical report, Trusted Logic, 2002.
16. C. Oriat. Jartege: A tool for random generation of unit tests for java classes. In *SOQUA 2005*, volume 3712 of *LNCS*, pages 242–256. Springer-Verlag, 2005.
17. Sun microsystems. *Java Card 2.1.1 Virtual Machine Specification*, May 2000. http://java.sun.com/products/javacard/javacard21.html#specification.
18. L. Tan, O. Sokolsky, and I. Lee. Specification-based testing with linear temporal logic. In *IRI*, pages 493–498. IEEE Systems, Man, and Cybernetics Society, 2004.
19. K. Trentelman and M. Huisman. Extending JML Specifications with Temporal Logic. In *AMAST'02*, number 2422 in LNCS, pages 334–348. Springer, 2002.

Online Testing with Reinforcement Learning

Margus Veanes[1], Pritam Roy[2,*], and Colin Campbell[1]

[1] Microsoft Research, Redmond, WA, USA
{margus, colin}@microsoft.com
[2] University of California, Santa Cruz, USA
pritam@soe.ucsc.edu

Abstract. Online testing is a practical technique where test derivation and test execution are combined into a single algorithm. In this paper we describe a new online testing algorithm that optimizes the choice of test actions using Reinforcement Learning (RL) techniques. This provides an advantage in covering system behaviors in less time than with a purely random choice of test actions. Online testing with conformance checking is modeled as a $1\frac{1}{2}$-player game, or Markov Decision Process (MDP), between the tester as one player and the implementation under test (IUT) as the opponent. Our approach has been implemented in C#, and benchmark results are presented in the paper. The specifications that generate the tests are written as model programs in any .NET language such as C# or VB.

1 Introduction

Many software systems are reactive. The behavior of a reactive system, especially when distributed or multithreaded, can be nondeterministic. For example, systems may produce spontaneous outputs like asynchronous events. Factors such as thread scheduling are not entirely under the control of the tester but may still affect the behavior observed. In these cases, a test suite generated offline may be infeasible, since all of the observable behaviors would have to be encoded a priori as a decision tree, and the size of such a decision tree can be very large.

Online testing (also called on-the-fly testing) can be more appropriate than offline tests for reactive systems. The reason is that with online testing the tests may be dynamically adapted at runtime, effectively pruning the search space to include only those behaviors actually observed instead of all possible behaviors. The interaction between tester and implementation under test (IUT) is seen as a game [1] where the tester chooses moves based on the observed behavior of the implementation under test. Only the tester is assumed to have a goal; the other player (the IUT) is unaware that it is playing. This kind of game is known in the literature as a $1\frac{1}{2}$-player game [6].

Online testing is a form of *model-based testing (MBT)*, where the tester uses a specification (or *model*) of the system's behavior to guide the testing and to detect the discrepancies between the IUT and the model. It is an established technique, supported in tools like TorX [18] and Spec Explorer [20]. For the purposes of this paper, we express the model as a set of guarded update rules that operate on an abstract state. This formulation

---

* Part of this work was done during the author's summer internship at Microsoft Research.

K. Havelund et al. (Eds.): FATES/RV 2006, LNCS 4262, pp. 240–253, 2006.
© Springer-Verlag Berlin Heidelberg 2006

is called a *model program*. Both the IUT and the model are viewed as *interface automata* [8] in order to establish a a formal conformance relation between them.

We distinguish between moves of the tester and moves of the IUT. The actions available to the tester are called *controllable* actions. The IUT's responses are *observable* actions. A *conformance failure* occurs when the IUT rejects a controllable action produced by the model or when the model rejects an observable action produced by the IUT.

A principal concern of online testing is the *strategy* used to choose test actions. A poor strategy may fail to provoke behaviors of interest or may take an infeasible amount to time to achieve good coverage. One can think of strategy in economic terms. The cost of testing increases with the number of test runs and the number of steps per run. We want to minimize the number of steps taken to achieve a given level of coverage for the possible behaviors. Exhaustive coverage is often infeasible. Instead, we strive for the best coverage possible within fixed resource constraints. The main challenge is to choose actions that minimize backtracking, since resetting the IUT to its initial state can be an expensive operation.

A purely random strategy for selecting test actions can be wasteful in this regard, since the tester may repeat actions that have already been tested or fail to systematically explore the reachable model states. A random strategy cannot benefit from remembering actions chosen in previous runs.

In this paper we propose an algorithm for online testing, using the ideas from *Reinforcement Learning (RL)* [16,12]. RL techniques address some of the drawbacks of random action selection. Our algorithm is related to the anti-ant algorithm introduced in [13], which avoids the generation of redundant test cases from UML diagrams.

RL refers to a collection of techniques in which an *agent* makes moves (called *actions*) with respect to the *state* of an environment. Actions are associated with *rewards* or *costs* in each state. The agent's goal is to choose a sequence of actions to maximize expected reward or, equivalently, to minimize expected cost.

The history needed to compute the strategy is encoded in a data structure called a "Test-Trace Graph (TTG)". We compare several such strategies below. The results show that a greedy strategy (*LeastCost*) has a suboptimal solution. The probability of reaching a failure state does not change with a purely randomized strategy (*Random*), though the probability reduces monotonically in a randomized greedy strategy (*RandomizedLeastCost*). This is because the probability in the latter case is negatively reinforced by the number of times a failure state has been visited, whereas it remains same in the former case.

The contributions of this paper are the following:

– We transform the online testing problem into a special case of reinforcement learning where the frequencies of various abstract behaviors are recorded. This allows us to better choose controllable actions.
– We show with benchmarks that an RL-based approach can significantly outperform random action selection.

The rest of the paper is organized as follows. In Section 2 we provide definitions for model programs, interface automata and a conformance relation. In Section 3 we give a detailed description of the algorithm. In Section 4 we give the experimental results from our benchmarks. We discuss related work in Section 5 and open problems and future work in Section 6.

2   Testing Theory

In model-based testing a tester uses a specification for two purposes. One is *conformance checking*: to decide if the IUT behaves as expected or specified. The other is *scenario control*: which actions should be taken in which order and pattern. Model-based testing is currently a growing practice in industry. In many respects the second purpose is the main use of models to drive tests and relates closely to test scenarios is traditional testing. However, with a growing complexity and need for protocol level testing and interaction testing, the first purpose is gaining importance.

Formally, model programs are mapped (unwound) to interface automata in order to do conformance checking. The conformance relation that is used can be defined as a form of alternating refinement. This form of testing is provided by the Spec Explorer tool, see e.g. [20].

2.1   Model Programs as Specifications

States are *memories* that are finite mappings from (memory) locations to a fixed universe of values. By an update rule we mean here a finite representation of a function that given a memory (state) produces an updated memory (state). An update rule p may be parameterized with respect to a sequence of *formal input parameters* $\bar{x}$, denoted by $p[\bar{x}]$. The instantiation of $p[\bar{x}]$ with input values $\bar{v}$ of appropriate type, is denoted by $p[\bar{v}]$. In general, an update rule may be *nondeterministic*, in which case it may yield several states from a given state and given inputs. Thus, an *update rule* $p[x_1, \ldots, x_n]$ denotes a relation $[\![p]\!] \subseteq States \times Values^n \times States$. When p is deterministic, we consider $[\![p]\!]$ as a function $[\![p]\!] : States \times Values^n \to States$ and we say that the *invocation* (or *execution*) of $p[\bar{v}]$ from state s yields the state $[\![p]\!](s, \bar{v})$.

A *guard* φ is a state dependent formula that may contain free logic variables $\bar{x} = x_1, \ldots, x_n$, denoted by $\varphi[\bar{x}]$; φ is *closed* if it contains no free variables. Given values $\bar{v} = v_1 \ldots, v_n$ we write $\varphi[\bar{v}]$ for the replacement of x_i in φ by v_i for $1 \leq i \leq n$. A closed formula φ has the standard truth interpretation $s \models \varphi$ in a state s. A *guarded update rule* is a pair (φ, p) containing a guard $\varphi[\bar{x}]$ and an update rule $p[\bar{x}]$; intuitively (φ, p) limits the execution of p to those states and arguments $\bar{v}$ where $\varphi[\bar{v}]$ holds.

Definition 1. A *model program* P has the following components.

- A state space *States*.
- A value space *Values*.
- An *initial state* $s_0 \in States$,
- A finite vocabulary Σ of *action symbols* partitioned into two disjoint sets
    - Σ^c of *controllable* action symbols, and
    - Σ^o of *observable* action symbols.
- A *reset* action symbol *Reset* $\in \Sigma^c$.
- A family $(\varphi_f, p_f)_{f \in \Sigma}$ of guarded update rules.

- The *arity* of f is the number of input parameters of p_f.
- The arity of *Reset* is 0 and $[\![p_{Reset}]\!](s) = s_0$ for all $s \models \varphi_{Reset}$.

P is *deterministic* if, for all action symbols $f \in \Sigma$, p_f is deterministic.

An n-ary action symbol has logically the term interpretation, i.e. two ground terms whose function symbols are action symbols are equal if and only if the action symbols are identical and their corresponding arguments are equal. An *action* has the form $f(v_1, \ldots, v_n)$ where f is an n-ary action symbol and each v_i is a value that matches the required type of the corresponding input parameter of p_f. We say that an action $f(\bar{v})$ is *enabled* in a state s if $s \models \varphi(\bar{v})$. Notice the two special cases regarding reset: one when reset is always disabled ($\varphi_{Reset} = false$), in which case the definition of p_{Reset} is irrelevant, and the other one when reset is always enabled ($\varphi_{Reset} = true$), in which case p_{Reset} must be able to reestablish the initial state from any other program state.

We sometimes use *action* to mean an action symbol, when this is clear from the context or when the action symbol is nullary in which case there is no distinction between the two.

2.2 Example: *Recycling Robot*

We show a model program of a collection of *recycling robots* written in C# in Figure 1. A robot is a movable recycle-bin, it can either

1. move and *search* for a can if its power level (measured in percentage) is above the given threshold 30%, or
2. remain stationary and *wait* for people to dispose of a can if its power level is below the given threshold 50%.

Notice that both cases are possible when the power level is between 30% and 50%. A robot gets a reward by collecting cans. The reward is bigger when searching than while waiting, but each search reduces the power level of the robot by 30%. A robot can be *recharged* when it is not fully charged, i.e when the power level is less than 100%. New robots can be *started* dynamically provided that the total number of robots does not exceed a limit (if such a limit is given).

Actions. In this example, the action symbols are Start, Search, Wait and Recharge, where the first three symbols are classified as being controllable and the last one is classified as being observable. All of the symbols are unary (i.e., they take one input). All actions have the form $f(i)$ where f is one of the four action symbols and i is a non-negative integer representing the id of a robot. The reset action is in this example implicit, and is assumed to be enabled in all states.

States. The state signature has three state variables, a map Robot.Instances from object ids (natural numbers) to robots (objects of type Robot), and two field value maps power and reward that map robots to their corresponding power and reward values. The initial state is the state where all those maps are empty.

```
class Robot : EnumeratedInstance // The base class keeps track of created robot instances
{
    int power  = 0;
    int reward = 0;
}

class RobotModel
{
    static int maxNoOfRobots = ...;

    [Action]
    static void Start(int robotId)
    {
        Assume.IsTrue(Robot.Instances.Count < maxNoOfRobots &&
                    ¬ Robot.Instances.Count == robotId));
        new Robot(robotId);
    }

    [Action]
    static void Search(int robotId)
    {
        Assume.IsTrue(robotId ∈ Robot.Instances);
        Robot robot = Robot.Instances[robotId];
        Assume.IsTrue(robot.power > 30);

        robot.power  = robot.power - 30;
        robot.reward = robot.reward + 2;
    }

    [Action]
    static void Wait(int robotId)
    {
        Assume.IsTrue(robotId ∈ Robot.Instances);
        Robot robot = Robot.Instances[robotId];
        Assume.IsTrue(robot.power <= 50);

        robot.reward = robot.reward + 1;
    }

    [Action(Kind = Observable)]
    static void Recharge(int robotId)
    {
        Assume.IsTrue(robotId ∈ Robot.Instances);
        Robot robot = Robot.Instances[robotId];
        Assume.IsTrue(robot.power < 100);

        robot.power = 100;
    }
}
```

Fig. 1. Model Program of the *Recycling Robot* example

Guarded update rules. For each of the four actions f the guarded update rule (φ_f, p_f) is defined by the corresponding static method f of the RobotModel class. Given a robot id i and a state s, the guard $\varphi_f(i)$ is true in s, if all the Assume.IsTrue statements evaluate to *true* in s. Execution of $p_f[i]$ corresponds to the method invocation of $f(i)$. For example, in the initial state, say s_0, of the robot model, the single enabled action is Start(0). In the resulting state $[\![p_{Start}]\!](s_0, 0)$ a new robot with id 0 has been created whose reward and power are 0.

2.3 Deterministic Model Programs as Interface Automata

We use the notion of interface automata [8,7] following the exposition in [7]. The view of a model program as an interface automaton is important for formalizing the conformance relation. To be consistent with the rest of the paper, we use the terms "controllable" and "observable" here instead of the terms "input" and "output" used in [7].

Definition 2. An *interface automaton* M has the following components:

- A set S of *states*.
- A nonempty subset S^{init} of S called the *initial states*.
- Mutually disjoint sets of *controllable actions* A^c and *observable actions* A^o.
- *Enabling functions* Γ^c and Γ^o from S to subsets of A^c and A^o, respectively.
- A *transition function* δ that maps a source state and an action enabled in the source state to a target state.

In order to identify a component of an interface automaton M, we index that component by M, unless M is clear from the context. Let P be a deterministic model program $(States, Values, s_0, \Sigma, \Sigma^c, \Sigma^o, Reset, (\varphi_f, p_f)_{f \in \Sigma})$. P has the following straightforward denotation $[\![P]\!]$ as an interface automaton:

$$S_{[\![P]\!]} = States$$
$$S_{[\![P]\!]}^{init} = \{s_0\}$$
$$A_{[\![P]\!]}^c = \{f(\bar{v}) \mid f \in \Sigma^c, \bar{v} \subseteq Values\}$$
$$A_{[\![P]\!]}^o = \{f(\bar{v}) \mid f \in \Sigma^o, \bar{v} \subseteq Values\}$$
$$\Gamma_{[\![P]\!]}^c(s) = \{f(\bar{v}) \in A_{[\![P]\!]}^c \mid s \models \varphi_f(\bar{v})\}$$
$$\Gamma_{[\![P]\!]}^o(s) = \{f(\bar{v}) \in A_{[\![P]\!]}^o \mid s \models \varphi_f(\bar{v})\}$$
$$\delta_{[\![P]\!]}(s, f(\bar{v})) = [\![P_f]\!](s, \bar{v}) \quad (\text{for } f \in \Sigma, \ s \in States, \ s \models \varphi_f(\bar{v}))$$

Note that $\delta_{[\![P]\!]}$ is well-defined, since P is deterministic. In light of the above definition we occasionally drop the distinction between P and the interface automaton $[\![P]\!]$ it denotes.

2.4   Implementing a Model Program as an Interface Automaton

A model program P exposes itself as an interface automaton through a *stepper* that provides a particular "walk" through the interface automaton one transition at a time. A stepper of P is implemented through the Istepper interface defined below. A stepper has an implicit *current state* that is initially the initial state of P. In the current state s of a stepper, the enabled actions are given by $\Gamma_{[\![P]\!]}(s)$. Doing a step in the current state s of the stepper according to a given action a corresponds to setting the current state of the stepper to $\delta_{[\![P]\!]}(s, a)$. The *Reset* action is handled separately and is not included in the set of currently enabled actions EnabledControllables.

```
interface IStepper
{
    Sequence<Action> EnabledControllables { get; }
    Sequence<Action> EnabledObservables { get; }
    void DoStep(Action action);

    void Reset();
    bool ResetEnabled { get; }
}
```

For conformance testing, an implementation is also assumed to be an interface automaton that is exposed through a stepper. If both the model and the IUT are interface automata with a common action signature, we test the conformance of the two automata using the refinement relation between interface automata as defined in [7].

3   Online Testing Algorithm

In this section we describe an algorithm that uses reinforcement learning to choose controllable actions during conformance testing of an implementation I against a model (specification) M. Both M and I are assumed to be given as model programs that expose an IStepper interface to the algorithm. In addition, the model exposes an interface that provides an abstract value of the current state of the model and an abstract value of any action enabled in a given state. It is convenient to view this interface as an extension IModelStepper of the IStepper interface:

```
interface IModelStepper : IStepper
{
    IComparable GetAbstractState(Action action);
    IComparable GetAbstractAction(Action action);
}
```

The main motivation for these functions is to divide the state space and the action space into equivalence classes that reflect "interesting" groups of states and actions for the purposes of coverage.

Example 1. Consider the Robot model. We could define the abstract states and abstract actions to be the concrete states and the concrete actions as follows. In other words, there is no grouping of either states or actions in this case.

```
class RobotModel : IModelStepper
{
    Sequence<Pair<int,int>> GetAbstractState(Action action)
    {
        return [(r.power, r.reward) | r in Robot.Instances]
    }
    Action GetAbstractAction(Action action);
    {
        return action;
    }
}
```

Example 2. A more interesting case is if we abstract away the id of the robot and project the state to the state of the robot doing the action, or a default value if the robot has not been started yet. This is reasonable because the robots do not interact with each other.

```
class RobotModel : IModelStepper
{
    Pair<int,int> GetAbstractState(Action action)
    {
        if (action.Name == "Start") return (-1, -1);
        Robot r = Robot.Instances[action.Argument(0)];
        return (r.power, r.reward);
    }
    string GetAbstractAction(Action action);
    {
        return action.Name;
    }
}
```

We use pseudo code that is similar to the original implementation code written in C# to describe the algorithm. We consider two controllable action selection *strategies* Lct and Rlc that are explained below, in addition to a memoryless purely randomized strategy Rnd.

```
enum Strategy {Rnd, Lct, Rlc}
```

The algorithm uses also an "oracle" to ask advice about whether to observe an observable action from the implementation, to call a controllable action, or to end a particular test run, during a single step of the algorithm. The oracle makes a random choice between controlling an observing when an observable action is enabled in the implementation at the same time as a controllable action is enabled in the model. If there are no observable actions enabled in the implementation and no controllable actions enabled in the model then the only meaningful advice the oracle can give is to end the current test run.

```
enum Advice {Control, Observe, End}

class Oracle
{
   IStepper M;
   IStepper I;

   Advice Advise()
   {
      bool noCtlrs = M.EnabledControllables.IsEmpty;
      bool noObs = I.EnabledObservables.IsEmpty;

      if (noCtlrs ∧ noObs) return Advice.End;
      if (noCtlrs) return Advice.Observe;
      if (noObs) return Advice.Control;
      return new Choose(Advice.Control, Advice.Observe);
   }
}
```

3.1   Top Level Loop

The top level loop of the algorithm is described by the following pseudo code.

```
class OnlineTesting
{
   IModelStepper M;
   IStepper I;
   int maxRun;
   int maxStep;
   Strategy h;
   Oracle oracle;

   bool ResetEnabled {get return M.ResetEnabled ∧ I.ResetEnabled;}

   void Run()
   {
      int run = 0;
      while (run < maxRun)
      {
         RunTestCase();          // The core algorithm
         if (¬ResetEnabled) return; // Cannot continue, must abort
         Reset();
         run += 1;
      }
   }
}
```

The inputs to the algorithm are a model program M that provides the IModelStepper interface and is the specification, a model program I that provides the IStepper interface an is the implementation under test, an upper bound maxRun on the total number of runs, an upper bound maxStep on the total number of steps (state transitions) per one run, a strategy h, and an oracle oracle as explained above.

3.2   The Core Algorithm

The algorithm keeps track of the *weights* of *abstract transitions* that have occurred during the test runs. An abstract transition is a pair (s, a) where s is an abstract state and

a is an abstract action. The weight of an abstract transition is total number of times it has occurred plus one, since the algorithm was started. The abstract state and action values are calculated using the `IModelStepper` interface introduced above. This weight information is stored in a *test trace graph* that is updated dynamically and is initially empty.

```
class TestTraceGraph
{
    Map<AbstractTransition, int> F = ∅;   // Frequencies of explored abstract transitions
    IModelStepper M;

    int W(Action a)                        // Weights are positive
    {
        AbstractState s = M.GetAbstractState(a);
        AbstractAction b = M.GetAbstractAction(a);
        if ((s,b) ∈ F) return F[(s,b)]; else return 1;
    }

    void Update(Action a, int w)
    {
        AbstractState s = M.GetAbstractState(a);
        AbstractAction b = M.GetAbstractAction(a);
        F[(s,b)] = W(a) + w;
    }
}
```

The next controllable action is chosen by the algorithm from a nonempty set of controllable actions that are currently enabled, using the given strategy.

```
class TestTraceGraph
{
    Action ChooseAction(Sequence<Action> acts, Strategy h)
    {
        switch (h)
        {
            case Strategy.Lct:
                Action a = acts.Head;
                Pair<Set<Action>,int> lct =
                    acts.Tail.Reduce(Reducer, ({acts.Head},W(acts.Head)));
                return lct.First.Choose();

            case Strategy.Rlc:
                Sequence<int> costs = [W(a) | a ∈ acts];
                int prod = ...;  // Compute an approximate common multiple of costs
                Sequence<int> occurs = [prod/x | x ∈ costs];
                Bag<Action> bg = {|(acts[i], occurs[i]) | i < acts.Count|};
                return bg.Choose();

            default:
                return acts.Choose();
        }
    }
    Pair<Set<Action>,int> Reducer(Action a, Pair<Set<Action>,int> lct)
    {
        if (W(a) < lct.Second) return ({a}, w);
        else if (W(a) == lct.Second) return (lct.First ∪ {a}, w);
        else return lct;
    }
}
```

Lct: Choose an action that has the "least cost". Here *cost* of an action a is measured as the current weight of the abstract transition (s, b), where s is the abstract state computed in the current model state with respect to a, and b is the abstract action corresponding to a, computed in the current model state. If several actions have the same least cost, one is chosen randomly from among those.

Rlc: Choose an action with a likelihood that is inversely proportional to its current cost, with cost having the same meaning as above. Intuitively this means that the least frequent actions are the most favored ones. In other words, if the candidate actions are $(a_i)_{i<k}$ for some k, having costs $(c_i)_{i<k}$, then the probability of selecting the action a_i is $c_i^{-1} / \sum_{j \neq i} c_j^{-1}$. The implementation uses a built-in bag construct to make such a choice.

Rnd: Make a random choice.

The algorithm runs one test case until, either a conformance failure occurs (in form of a violation of the refinement relation between $[\![M]\!]$ and $[\![I]\!]$), or until the given maximum number of steps has been reached.

```
class OnlineTesting
{
    TestTraceGraph ttg = new TestTraceGraph(M);

    bool RunTestCase()
    {
        int step = 0;
        while (step < maxStep)
        {
            Advice advice = oracle.Advise();

            if (advice == Advice.Control)
            {
                Sequence<Action> cs = M.EnabledControllables;
                Action c = ttg.ChooseAction(cs, h);
                ttg.Update(c, 1);          // Increase the weight by 1
                M.DoStep(c);               // Do the step in M

                if (c ∈ I.EnabledControllables)
                    I.DoStep(c);           // Do the corresponding step in I
                else
                    return false;          // Conformance failure occurred
            }
            else if (advice == Advice.Observe)
            {
                Sequence<Action> os = I.EnabledObservables;
                // This is an abstract view of the execution of the implementation, in reality
                // the implementation performs the choice itself and notifies the test harness
                Action o = os.Choose();
                I.DoStep(o);

                if (o ∈ M.EnabledObservables)
                {
                    ttg.Update(o, 1);      // Increase the weight by 1
                    M.DoStep(o);           // Do the corresponding step in M
                }
                else
                    return false;          // Conformance failure occurred

                #endregion
            }
            else
                return true;               // No more steps can be performed
            step += 1;
        }
        return true;                       // The test case succeeds
    }
}
```

The *Lct* strategy is a greedy approach; it is very simple and relatively cheap to compute. However, it favors actions that have been used less frequently, and thus may systematically avoid long sequences of the same action, as is illustrated next.

Example 3. Consider a bounded stack of size n. The stack has two controllable actions, *top* and *push*, enabled in every state. The greedy strategy will alternate between these two actions until the stack is full. If we want to test the behavior of *push* when the stack is full, we need to continue testing for at least $2n$ steps (so that *push* is executed n times).

In the given algorithm, the weight increase is always 1. This value can be made domain specific and can vary depending both on the action and the current state, for example by extending the `IModelStepper` interface with a function that provides the wait increase for the given action in the current state and using that function instead of 1.

By using `Rlc`, the probability of selecting an action is inversely proportional to its frequency. Thus, the more an action has been selected the less likely it is that it will be selected again. So the potential problem shown in Example 3 is still there but ameliorated, since no enabled action is excluded from the choice.

4   Experiments

We used the Robot model to conduct a few experiments with the algorithm in order to evaluate and compare the different strategies. The main purpose was to see if the two proposed strategies `Lct` or `Rlc` are useful by providing better or at least as good coverage of the state space as the purely random approach. Since we are interested in state and transition coverage only, we ran the algorithm against a correct implementation. We ran the algorithm with a different maximum number of robots, different abstraction functions introduced in the examples above, and different limits on the total number of runs and the total number of steps per run. The experiments are summarized in Tables 1 and 2. We ran each case independently 50 times, the entries in the tables are shown on the form $m \pm \sigma$ where m is the mean of the obtained results and σ is the standard deviation. The absolute running times are shown only for comparison, the concrete machine was a 3GHz Pentium 4.

If states and actions are not grouped at all, by assuming the definitions given in Example 1, the majority of abstract transitions will occur only a single time and the strategies perform more or less as the random case, which is shown in Table 1. One can see that `Lct` performs marginally better than `Rnd` when the number of robots and the number of runs increases.

Table 1. Execution of the online algorithm on the Robot model without grouping

Parameters			Lct		Rlc		Rnd	
Robots	Runs	Steps	#States	t(ms)	#States	t(ms)	#States	t(ms)
1	1	100	100 ± 0	3	100 ± 0	1	100 ± 0	1
1	10	100	420 ± 11	20	415 ± 8	19	414 ± 9	15
1	100	100	503 ± 3	275	503 ± 3	241	502 ± 2	172
1	100	500	2485 ± 5	1303	2485 ± 5	1292	2485 ± 6	968
2	1	100	100 ± 0	3	100 ± 0	1	100 ± 0	2
2	10	100	951 ± 8	24	941 ± 10	22	938 ± 12	14
2	100	100	7449 ± 83	286	7085 ± 110	284	7055 ± 114	201
2	100	500	44119 ± 225	1548	42437 ± 339	1479	42364 ± 289	1040
5	1	100	100 ± 0	5	100 ± 0	3	100 ± 0	1
5	10	100	972 ± 3	42	971 ± 3	37	969 ± 4	18
5	100	100	9368 ± 17	516	9328 ± 22	468	9322 ± 24	297
5	100	500	49364 ± 19	2794	49330 ± 25	2541	49320 ± 19	1587

When the states and the actions are mapped to abstract values, as defined in Example 2, then `Lct` starts finding many more abstract states than `Rnd` as the number of robots grows. The robot id is ignored by the abstraction and thus concrete transitions of different robots that differ only by the id are mapped to the same abstract transition. Overall this will have

Table 2. Execution of the online algorithm on the Robot model with state grouping and action grouping

Parameters			Lct		Rlc		Rnd	
Robots	Runs	Steps	#States	$t(ms)$	#States	$t(ms)$	#States	$t(ms)$
1	1	100	100 ± 0	3	100 ± 0	<1	100 ± 0	<1
1	10	100	417 ± 9	9	413 ± 8	7	416 ± 8	4
1	100	100	502 ± 2	100	503 ± 3	88	502 ± 2	44
1	100	500	2486 ± 5	508	2486 ± 6	417	2484 ± 6	234
2	1	100	100 ± 0	1	90 ± 3	<1	93 ± 5	<1
2	10	100	419 ± 7	10	284 ± 21	9	237 ± 8	4
2	100	100	502 ± 3	106	437 ± 12	96	293 ± 6	46
2	100	500	2485 ± 5	561	1602 ± 33	506	1324 ± 15	241
5	1	100	100 ± 0	<1	66 ± 4	1	61 ± 2	<1
5	10	100	418 ± 10	10	279 ± 30	11	117 ± 5	5
5	100	100	503 ± 3	115	472 ± 7	116	155 ± 7	50
5	100	500	2484 ± 5	561	1696 ± 96	657	582 ± 10	247
5	100	1000	4949 ± 8	1200	2467 ± 95	1388	1088 ± 13	540
10	10	100	418 ± 9	10	293 ± 25	12	91 ± 6	5
10	100	100	502 ± 3	103	473 ± 6	137	128 ± 6	59
10	100	1000	4951 ± 11	1131	3541 ± 198	1718	602 ± 10	578
10	1000	1000	4985 ± 8	12521	4352 ± 66	18043	654 ± 9	5953

the effect that the Lct approach will favor actions that transition to new abstract states. The same is true for the Rlc case but the increase in coverage is smaller.

The Robot case study is representative for models that deal with multiple agents at the same time, which is a typical case in testing of multi-threaded software [20]. Often the threads are mostly independent, an abstraction technique that can be used in this context is to look at the part of the state that belongs to the agent doing the action. This is an instance of so-called multiple state-grouping approach that is also used as an exploration technique for FSM generation [4]. This is exactly what is done in Example 2. It seems that Lct is a promising heuristic for online testing of these kinds of models. One can note that, the coverage provided by the random approach degrades almost by half as the number of robots is doubled (for example from 5 to 10).

5   Related Work

The basic idea of online testing has been introduced in the context of labeled transition systems using ioco theory [3,17,19] and implemented in the TorX tool [18]. TGV [11] is another tool frequently used for online or on-the-fly test generation that uses ioco. Ioco theory is a formal testing theory based on labeled transition systems with input actions and output actions. Interface automata [7] are suitable for the game view [5] of online testing and provide the foundation for the conformance relation that we use. Online testing with model programs in the SpecExplorer tool is discussed in in [20]. The algorithm in [20] does not use learning, and as far as we know learning algorithms have not been considered in the context of model based testing. The relation between ioco and refinement of interface automata is briefly discussed in [20]. Specifications given by a guarded command language are used also in [15].

In Black-box testing, some work [14] has been done which uses supervised learning procedures. As far as we know, no previous work has addressed online testing with learning in the context of Model Based Testing. The main intuition behind our algorithm is similar to an anti-ant approach [13] used for test case generation form UML diagrams. From the game point of view, the online testing problem is a $1\frac{1}{2}$-player game. It is known that $1\frac{1}{2}$-player games are Markov Decision Processes [6]. The view of finite explorations of model programs for offline test case generation as negative total reward Markov decision problems with infinite horizon are studied in [2].

6   Open Problems and Future Work

One of the interesting areas that is also practically very relevant is to gain better understating of approaches for online testing that learn from model-coverage that uses abstractions. The experiments reported in Section 4 exploited that idea to a certain extent by using state and action abstraction through the IModelStepper interface, but the general technique and theory need to be developed further. Such abstraction functions can either be user-provided [9,4] or automatically generated from program text similar to iterative refinement [15].

Currently we have an implementation of the presented algorithm using a modeling library developed in C#. As a short-term goal, we are working on a more detailed report where we are considering larger case studies.

The algorithm can also be adapted to run without a model, just as a semi-random (stress) testing tool of implementations. In that case the history of used actions is kept solely based on the test runs of the implementation. In this case, erroneous behaviors would for example manifest themselves through unexpected exceptions thrown by the implementation, rather than trough conformance violations.

Acknowledgment

We thank Nikolai Tillmann and Wolfgang Grieskamp for many valuable discussions and for help in using the underlying exploration framework XRT [10] during the initial implementation of the ideas. We thank Luca de Alfaro and Wolfram Schulte for valuable comments on earlier drafts of this paper.

References

1. R. Alur, C. Courcoubetis, and M. Yannakakis. Distinguishing tests for nondeterministic and probabilistic machines. In *Proc. 27th Ann. ACM Symp. Theory of Computing*, pages 363–372, 1995.
2. A. Blass, Y. Gurevich, L. Nachmanson, and M. Veanes. Play to test. Technical Report MSR-TR-2005-04, Microsoft Research, January 2005. Short version of this report was presented at FATES 2005.
3. E. Brinksma and J. Tretmans. Testing Transition Systems: An Annotated Bibliography. In *Summer School MOVEP'2k – Modelling and Verification of Parallel Processes*, volume 2067 of *LNCS*, pages 187–193. Springer, 2001.

4. C. Campbell and M. Veanes. State exploration with multiple state groupings. In D. Beauquier, E. Börger, and A. Slissenko, editors, *12th International Workshop on Abstract State Machines, ASM'05, March 8–11, 2005, Laboratory of Algorithms, Complexity and Logic, University Paris 12 – Val de Marne, Créteil, France,* pages 119–130, 2005.

5. A. Chakrabarti, L. de Alfaro, T. A. Henzinger, and F. Y. C. Mang. Synchronous and bidirectional component interfaces. In *CAV*, pages 414–427, 2002.

6. K. Chatterjee, L. de Alfaro, and T. A. Henzinger. Trading memory for randomness. In *QEST*, pages 206–217, 2004.

7. L. de Alfaro. Game models for open systems. In N. Dershowitz, editor, *Verification: Theory and Practice: Essays Dedicated to Zohar Manna on the Occasion of His 64th Birthday,* volume 2772 of *LNCS,* pages 269 – 289. Springer, 2004.

8. L. de Alfaro and T. A. Henzinger. Interface automata. In *Proceedings of the 8th European Software Engineering Conference and the 9th ACM SIGSOFT Symposium on the Foundations of Software Engineering (ESEC/FSE),* pages 109–120. ACM, 2001.

9. W. Grieskamp, Y. Gurevich, W. Schulte, and M. Veanes. Generating finite state machines from abstract state machines. In *ISSTA'02,* volume 27 of *Software Engineering Notes,* pages 112–122. ACM, 2002.

10. W. Grieskamp, N. Tillmann, and W. Schulte. Xrt – exploring runtime for .NET architecture and applications. Technical Report MSR-TR-2005-63, Microsoft Research, June 2005. Presented at SoftMC 2005.

11. C. Jard and T. Jéron. TGV: theory, principles and algorithms. In *The Sixth World Conference on Integrated Design and Process Technology, IDPT'02,* Pasadena, California, June 2002.

12. L. Kaelbling, M. Littman, and A. Moore. Reinforcement learning: A survey, 1996.

13. H. Li and C. Lam. Using anti-ant-like agents to generate test threads from the uml diagrams. In *Proc. Testcom 2005,* LNCS. Springer, 2005.

14. D. Peled, M. Y. Vardi, and M. Yannakakis. Black box checking. In *FORTE,* pages 225–240, 1999.

15. C. S. Păsăreanu, R. Pelánek, and W. Visser. Concrete model checking with abstract matching and refinement. In *Computer Aided Verification (CAV 2005),* volume 3576 of *LNCS,* pages 52–66. Springer, 2005.

16. R. S. Sutton and A. G. Barto. *Reinforcement Learning: An Introduction.* MIT, 1998. URL: http://www.cs.ualberta.ca/ sutton/book/ebook/the-book.html.

17. J. Tretmans and A. Belinfante. Automatic testing with formal methods. In *EuroSTAR'99: 7th European Int. Conference on Software Testing, Analysis & Review,* Barcelona, Spain, November 8–12, 1999. EuroStar Conferences, Galway, Ireland.

18. J. Tretmans and E. Brinksma. TorX: Automated model based testing. In *1st European Conference on Model Driven Software Engineering,* pages 31–43, Nuremberg, Germany, December 2003.

19. M. van der Bij, A. Rensink, and J. Tretmans. Compositional testing with ioco. In A. Petrenko and A. Ulrich, editors, *Formal Approaches to Software Testing: Third International Workshop, FATES 2003,* volume 2931 of *LNCS,* pages 86–100. Springer, 2004.

20. M. Veanes, C. Campbell, W. Schulte, and N. Tillmann. Online testing with model programs. In *ESEC/FSE-13: Proceedings of the 10th European software engineering conference held jointly with 13th ACM SIGSOFT international symposium on Foundations of software engineering,* pages 273–282. ACM, 2005.

Author Index

Lecture Notes in Computer Science

For information about Vols. 1–4237

please contact your bookseller or Springer

Vol. 4278: R. Meersman, Z. Tari, P. Herrero (Eds.), On the Move to Meaningful Internet Systems 2006: OTM 2006 Workshops, Part II. XLV, 1004 pages. 2006.

Vol. 4277: R. Meersman, Z. Tari, P. Herrero (Eds.), On the Move to Meaningful Internet Systems 2006: OTM 2006 Workshops, Part I. XLV, 1009 pages. 2006.

Vol. 4276: R. Meersman, Z. Tari (Eds.), On the Move to Meaningful Internet Systems 2006: CoopIS, DOA, GADA, and ODBASE, Part II. XXXII, 752 pages. 2006.

Vol. 4275: R. Meersman, Z. Tari (Eds.), On the Move to Meaningful Internet Systems 2006: CoopIS, DOA, GADA, and ODBASE, Part I. XXXI, 1115 pages. 2006.

Vol. 4274: Q. Huo, B. Ma, E.-S. Chng, H. Li (Eds.), Chinese Spoken Language Processing. XXIV, 805 pages. 2006. (Sublibrary LNAI).

Vol. 4273: I. Cruz, S. Decker, D. Allemang, C. Preist, D. Schwabe, P. Mika, M. Uschold, L. Aroyo (Eds.), The Semantic Web - ISWC 2006. XXIV, 1001 pages. 2006.

Vol. 4272: P. Havinga, M. Lijding, N. Meratnia, M. Wegdam (Eds.), Smart Sensing and Context. XI, 267 pages. 2006.

Vol. 4271: F.V. Fomin (Ed.), Graph-Theoretic Concepts in Computer Science. XIII, 358 pages. 2006.

Vol. 4270: H. Zha, Z. Pan, H. Thwaites, A.C. Addison, M. Forte (Eds.), Interactive Technologies and Sociotechnical Systems. XVI, 547 pages. 2006.

Vol. 4269: R. State, S. van der Meer, D. O'Sullivan, T. Pfeifer (Eds.), Large Scale Management of Distributed Systems. XIII, 282 pages. 2006.

Vol. 4268: G. Parr, D. Malone, M. Ó Foghlú (Eds.), Autonomic Principles of IP Operations and Management. XIII, 237 pages. 2006.

Vol. 4267: A. Helmy, B. Jennings, L. Murphy, T. Pfeifer (Eds.), Autonomic Management of Mobile Multimedia Services. XIII, 257 pages. 2006.

Vol. 4266: H. Yoshiura, K. Sakurai, K. Rannenberg, Y. Murayama, S. Kawamura (Eds.), Advances in Information and Computer Security. XIII, 438 pages. 2006.

Vol. 4265: L. Todorovski, N. Lavrač, K.P. Jantke (Eds.), Discovery Science. XIV, 384 pages. 2006. (Sublibrary LNAI).

Vol. 4264: J.L. Balcázar, P.M. Long, F. Stephan (Eds.), Algorithmic Learning Theory. XIII, 393 pages. 2006. (Sublibrary LNAI).

Vol. 4263: A. Levi, E. Savaş, H. Yenigün, S. Balcısoy, Y. Saygın (Eds.), Computer and Information Sciences – ISCIS 2006. XXIII, 1084 pages. 2006.

Vol. 4262: K. Havelund, M. Núñez, G. Roşu, B. Wolff (Eds.), Formal Approaches to Software Testing and Runtime Verification. VIII, 255 pages. 2006.

Vol. 4261: Y. Zhuang, S. Yang, Y. Rui, Q. He (Eds.), Advances in Multimedia Information Processing - PCM 2006. XXII, 1040 pages. 2006.

Vol. 4260: Z. Liu, J. He (Eds.), Formal Methods and Software Engineering. XII, 778 pages. 2006.

Vol. 4259: S. Greco, Y. Hata, S. Hirano, M. Inuiguchi, S. Miyamoto, H.S. Nguyen, R. Słowiński (Eds.), Rough Sets and Current Trends in Computing. XXII, 951 pages. 2006. (Sublibrary LNAI).

Vol. 4257: I. Richardson, P. Runeson, R. Messnarz (Eds.), Software Process Improvement. XI, 219 pages. 2006.

Vol. 4256: L. Feng, G. Wang, C. Zeng, R. Huang (Eds.), Web Information Systems – WISE 2006 Workshops. XIV, 320 pages. 2006.

Vol. 4255: K. Aberer, Z. Peng, E.A. Rundensteiner, Y. Zhang, X. Li (Eds.), Web Information Systems – WISE 2006. XIV, 563 pages. 2006.

Vol. 4254: T. Grust, H. Höpfner, A. Illarramendi, S. Jablonski, M. Mesiti, S. Müller, P.-L. Patranjan, K.-U. Sattler, M. Spiliopoulou, J. Wijsen (Eds.), Current Trends in Database Technology – EDBT 2006. XXXI, 932 pages. 2006.

Vol. 4253: B. Gabrys, R.J. Howlett, L.C. Jain (Eds.), Knowledge-Based Intelligent Information and Engineering Systems, Part III. XXXII, 1301 pages. 2006. (Sublibrary LNAI).

Vol. 4252: B. Gabrys, R.J. Howlett, L.C. Jain (Eds.), Knowledge-Based Intelligent Information and Engineering Systems, Part II. XXXIII, 1335 pages. 2006. (Sublibrary LNAI).

Vol. 4251: B. Gabrys, R.J. Howlett, L.C. Jain (Eds.), Knowledge-Based Intelligent Information and Engineering Systems, Part I. LXVI, 1297 pages. 2006. (Sublibrary LNAI).

Vol. 4250: H.J. van den Herik, S.-C. Hsu, T.-s. Hsu, H.H.L.M. Donkers (Eds.), Advances in Computer Games. XIV, 273 pages. 2006.

Vol. 4249: L. Goubin, M. Matsui (Eds.), Cryptographic Hardware and Embedded Systems - CHES 2006. XII, 462 pages. 2006.

Vol. 4248: S. Staab, V. Svátek (Eds.), Managing Knowledge in a World of Networks. XIV, 400 pages. 2006. (Sublibrary LNAI).

Vol. 4247: T.-D. Wang, X. Li, S.-H. Chen, X. Wang, H. Abbass, H. Iba, G. Chen, X. Yao (Eds.), Simulated Evolution and Learning. XXI, 940 pages. 2006.

Vol. 4246: M. Hermann, A. Voronkov (Eds.), Logic for Programming, Artificial Intelligence, and Reasoning. XIII, 588 pages. 2006. (Sublibrary LNAI).

Vol. 4245: A. Kuba, L.G. Nyúl, K. Palágyi (Eds.), Discrete Geometry for Computer Imagery. XIII, 688 pages. 2006.

Vol. 4244: S. Spaccapietra (Ed.), Journal on Data Semantics VII. XI, 267 pages. 2006.

Vol. 4243: T. Yakhno, E.J. Neuhold (Eds.), Advances in Information Systems. XIII, 420 pages. 2006.

Vol. 4242: A. Rashid, M. Aksit (Eds.), Transactions on Aspect-Oriented Software Development II. IX, 289 pages. 2006.

Vol. 4241: R.R. Beichel, M. Sonka (Eds.), Computer Vision Approaches to Medical Image Analysis. XI, 262 pages. 2006.

Vol. 4239: H.Y. Youn, M. Kim, H. Morikawa (Eds.), Ubiquitous Computing Systems. XVI, 548 pages. 2006.

Vol. 4238: Y.-T. Kim, M. Takano (Eds.), Management of Convergence Networks and Services. XVIII, 605 pages. 2006.